PUBLIKATIONEN
DER BAYERISCHEN AMERIKA-AKADEMIE
Band 21

PUBLICATIONS
OF THE BAVARIAN AMERICAN ACADEMY
Volume 21

SERIES EDITOR
Bavarian American Academy

NOTE ON THE EDITORS

Heike Paul is professor of American Studies
at Friedrich-Alexander-University Erlangen-Nürnberg
and director of the Bavarian American Academy.

Ursula Prutsch is professor of history of the USA and Latin America
at the Ludwig-Maximilians-Universität München.

Jürgen Gebhardt is professor emeritus of political science
at Friedrich-Alexander-University Erlangen-Nürnberg.

The Comeback of Populism

Transatlantic Perspectives

Edited by
HEIKE PAUL
URSULA PRUTSCH
JÜRGEN GEBHARDT

Universitätsverlag
WINTER
Heidelberg

Bibliografische Information der Deutschen Nationalbibliothek
Die Deutsche Nationalbibliothek verzeichnet diese Publikation
in der Deutschen Nationalbibliografie;
detaillierte bibliografische Daten sind im Internet
über *http://dnb.d-nb.de* abrufbar.

Gedruckt mit freundlicher Unterstützung
der Deutschen Forschungsgemeinschaft (DFG)

Cover picture
© shutterstock

ISBN 978-3-8253-4635-5

Dieses Werk einschließlich aller seiner Teile ist urheberrechtlich geschützt. Jede
Verwertung außerhalb der engen Grenzen des Urheberrechtsgesetzes ist ohne
Zustimmung des Verlages unzulässig und strafbar. Das gilt insbesondere für
Vervielfältigungen, Übersetzungen, Mikroverfilmungen und die Einspeicherung
und Verarbeitung in elektronischen Systemen.

© 2019 Universitätsverlag Winter GmbH Heidelberg
Imprimé en Allemagne · Printed in Germany
Umschlaggestaltung: Klaus Brecht GmbH, Heidelberg
Gesamtherstellung: Memminger MedienCentrum, 87700 Memmingen

Gedruckt auf umweltfreundlichem, chlorfrei gebleichtem
und alterungsbeständigem Papier

Den Verlag erreichen Sie im Internet unter:
www.winter-verlag.de

Table of Contents

Heike Paul
  Introduction 1

Hans Vorländer
  Populism and Modern Democracy – An Outline 13

Frank Decker
  Populism in Germany and Abroad 29

Jürgen Gebhardt
  "We the People": Popular Sovereignty, National Identity, and the
  Democratic Principle 45

Michael Hochgeschwender
  US-Populism in the Late Nineteenth Century 55

Jack Zhou, D. Sunshine Hillygus, John Aldrich
  Understanding the Trump Win: Populism, Partisanship, and Polarization
  in the 2016 Election 65

Laura Vorberg
  #BasketofDeplorables: Digital Imagined Communities, *Twitter*-Populism,
  and the Cross-Media Effects of Popular Political Social Media
  Communication in the 2016 US Presidential Election 89

Michael Oswald
  Jobs, Free Trade, and a Conspiracy: Trump's Use of Producerism 109

Heike Paul
  Authoritarian Populism, White Supremacy, and *Volkskörper*-
  Sentimentalism 127

Simon Strick
  Right-Wing World-Building: Affect and Sexuality in the 'Alternative
  Right' 157

Akwugo Emejulu
Feminism for the 99%: Towards a Populist Feminism?....................... 183

Nicole Anna Schneider
Redefining "We, the People": Black Lives Matter and the
Democratization of Political Culture... 189

Sascha Pöhlmann
Missing the People: Populist Aesthetics and Unpopular Resistance.... 215

Donatella Izzo
Pop(e)ulism: Populist Miracles and Neoliberal Theologies 235

Carlos de la Torre
What Can We Learn from Latin America to Understand Trump's
Populism?.. 253

Ursula Prutsch
Populism in Brazil: Getúlio Vargas and Jair Bolsonaro 275

Notes on Contributors 293

Introduction

Heike Paul

The very day that Donald Trump was inaugurated as US president, the trailer for the fifth season of *House of Cards* was released.[1] It was a trailer that depicted the American flag in a windy breeze against a darkened sky, while children's voices recited the pledge of allegiance. However, the American flag in the trailer is flying upside-down in front of the capitol in Washington, D.C. as the patriotic oath is recited. As such it is "a signal of dire distress in instances of extreme danger to life and property," to quote the United States flag code.[2] The combination of a somewhat gothic lighting and the children's voices (along with doomful foreshadowing instrumentation) is reminiscent of strategies of anticipation in horror films and thus foreshadows uncanny moments, if not an uncanny future. The children's voices synchronized into a choral-like performance evoke processes of disciplining and the production of conformity and unison in the name of the state, a state just turned totalitarian, we may assume, even as the chant appears to be a normal, quotidian cultural practice. In the more recent archive of American television series, this sinister teaser trailer and its mise-en-scène possibly not only reference the new episodes starring Frank Underwood and his wife (who are by now history) craving power but also allude to a possible analogy with Trump's new America (that began on the very day of its release and that is not yet history).[3]

The mood that this trailer conjures up accentuates a sense of impending threat that is attributed to greedy, corrupt, incompetent authoritarian politicians, who disrupt political culture and democratic habitus and who endanger the system of checks and balances, i.e. politicians who prioritize 'being the boss' over 'serving the people,' even as the latter is what they proclaim to do. Any resemblance to actual persons may not be purely incidental here. In that sense, it addresses one appalling aspect of the specter of populism. Momentary shock mixed with deep concern characterized the atmosphere in many academic-activist circles in the wake of the 2016 US presidential elections. Immediate reactions were hands-on and somewhat therapeutic. Publications in the self-help vein joined and counter-balanced the largely dystopian scenarios and tried to advise the citizenry on their best bet in

---

[1] See: <https://www.youtube.com/watch?v=b_NcYIfcVTA>. Last accessed on 1 April 2019. Thanks to Katharina Gerund for pointing out this clip to me.
[2] See: United States Flag Code: Title 4 of the United States Code, Chapter 1, §8a.
[3] Kevin Spacey himself has suggested this analogy in the *Late Show* with Stephen Colbert on 16 September 2015. <https://www.youtube.com/watch?v=qXBIBtXTVNg>. Last accessed on 1 April 2019.

'surviving Trump.' Gene Stone's *The Trump Survival Guide: Everything You Need to Know about Living through What You Hoped Would Never Happen* (2017) is just one exemplary text.[4] *Cultural Anthropology* quickly devoted a special issue on "The Rise of Trumpism" with an introduction by Lucas Bessire and David Bond and with posts by Judith Butler, Michael Taussig, Susan Harding, and Ann Laura Stoler. As the membership in the American Civil Liberties Union sky-rocketed,[5] a whole new (younger) generation became deeply politicized through their opposition to Trump (see, for instance, Miner).

It was in the context of these initial responses (somewhere between red alert and attempts at cold-eyed analysis) that this volume was first conceived. The annual conference of the Bavarian American Academy in July of 2017 in Munich took "The Comeback of Populism: Transatlantic Perspectives" as its theme and initiated a discussion among political scientists, historians, and cultural studies-scholars from both sides of the Atlantic. Ever since then, the conversations have deepened and have been enriched by colleagues in other fields, such as sociology, media studies, and literary studies. In the meantime, the cross-disciplinary scholarship on populism has on the whole become even more voluminous and diverse, yet it has not entirely moved away from alarmism and a sense of urgency. Clearly, the symptoms of crisis are multi-layered, point to quite a number of diverse factors facilitating populism's success, and thus need to be addressed from various angles: political, social, cultural, and economic. This volume hopefully adds some fresh perspectives by younger scholars and renowned experts in their fields to the growing archive on populism's return as an inter- and transnational phenomenon. It seeks to engage this much-debated development with regard to its three key title terms: **populism**, **comeback**, and **transatlantic perspectives**.

Populism has been called many things and remains a fuzzy concept: it has been dubbed "a style" of political communication (Moffitt), a "language" (Kazin), a "logic" (Laclau), a "syndrome" (Wodak 47), a "thin ideology" (Mudde), a "Kampfbegriff" (Manow), and a political strategy that uses "polarization" as a "political method" (Priester 47).[6] Jan-Werner Müller and others have dissected a

---

[4] The notion of survival and survivorship (in the context of self-help and trauma studies/posttraumatic stress) is also addressed in chapter 9, 10, and 12 of *Trumpism: The Politics of Gender in a Post-Propitious America* (2018). One of the more pronounced titles in the proto-therapeutic vein is *One Nation after Trump: A Guide for the Perplexed, the Disillusioned, the Desperate, and the Not-Yet-Deported* (2017) by E.J. Dionne, Jr., et al. For a broader contextualization of events, see Timothy Snyder's *On Tyranny: Twenty Lessons from the Twentieth Century* (2017).

[5] "In the 15 months that followed the election, the A.C.L.U.'s membership went from 400,000 to 1.84 million. Online donations in the years before averaged between $3 and $5 million annually. Since then, it has raised just shy of $120 million" (Lovell).

[6] For an introductory overview, see also *The Oxford Handbook of Populism* (2017) and *Political Populism: A Handbook* (2017).

"populist imaginary" (98) and identified a peculiar construction of 'authenticity' and an illusion of the immediate transposition of the people's will (*Volksnähe*, see also Weale) that satisfies an alleged longing for simplicity among the populace, i.e. it reduces and counters any complex understanding of the world and operates in sharp dichotomies. These attempts at defining populism agree on the insight that the defining criterion is form, not content, and they all ring true with regard to the contemporary political scene. "[F]amily resemblances" (Judis 14) exist between populisms in Europe and the Americas, between left and right, and hence we are not talking about a specific political program but rather about a set of assumptions about the political sphere and the (ab)uses of political language. Populist politics not only thrive on us vs. them-oppositions, they also interpolate the electorate in a direct relation to a leadership figure, often at the expense of those intermediary institutions that co-constitute the democratic system and guard the separation of powers. Populist movements "are very much part of the American political fabric" (Judis 19), and they also have their history in Europe. Often, populism is discussed in conjunction with fascist movements – in his film about the 2016 presidential election, *Fahrenheit 11/9*, Michael Moore does so – however, both are clearly not to be confounded (see Albright 228-9). Recently created subcategories such as "neo-populism" (or "neoliberal populism" [Betz et al.]), "pluto-populism" (Wolf; Pierson) or "authoritarian capitalism" (Bloom), and, last but not least, "Trumpocracy" (Frum) try to programmatically capture the cultural, political, and economic specificities of the current faces of populism in the West.[7] Of particular relevance for an ordering of the often fuzzy discourse on populism is Philip Manow's analysis focusing on the political economy as symptom of crisis in Western Democracies. According to Manow, we cannot talk about populism without talking about capitalism and anti-globalization (8-9). Whereas the essays in this volume define populism in different ways for their arguments and concerns, the elasticity of the label appears to be productive and problematic at the same time: Without a specific cultural and political context to moor it to, it is of little analytical use. Hence, such in-depth contextualization appears to be important even as we are addressing a broader, transnational phenomenon.

The **comeback** of populism has been widely discussed and has been dated variably: some scholars see the rise of populism in Europe dating back to the success of protest movements in Scandinavian countries against tax raises and too much government intervention. In this timeline, the first populist party in Northern Europe is the Danish Progress Party (*Fremskridtspartiet*), which was founded in 1972 by Mogens Glistrup. Those, who focus on political style, see the career of Silvio Berlusconi as reflective of populism's comeback roughly a decade after the end of

---

[7] Martin Wolf calls this policy a mixture of "tax reform, with the familiar combination of unfunded giveaways and magical thinking on deficits" (Wolf).

the cold war. On May 8, 2001, Berlusconi announced in a television talk show his contract with the Italian people, actually holding up a piece of paper to emphasize his supposedly genuine intentions. Italy has often been considered a "laboratory" of populism.[8] This speaking "for the people" or even posing as "the voice of the people" is a topos Donald Trump – among others – has picked up for his campaign and uses it continuously in his statements. This illusion of a direct relation between the leader and the people implies a dramatic erosion of logics of abstraction and is to be found in similar ways in the populist anti-European backlash in Eastern Europe (Poland and Hungary) even as the sense of abstract representation is foundational for the idea of political representation in democratic systems. On the other hand, a left-wing populism with an anti-capitalist agenda (Greece, Spain) also needs to be taken into the equation. With the election of Donald Trump in 2016, the tide of populist movements seems to have reached a new crescendo that upended many predictions about election results in particular and the future of liberal democracies in general.

Yet, the comeback-thesis that this volume largely subscribes to is also partially controversial. Some scholars suggest that politics in liberal democracies have always and continuously had a populist element. Following these observations, Trump's predecessor Barack Obama is characterized as employing populist strategies (he was the first US presidential candidate to make full use of social media in his campaign) and so is Emmanuel Macron, who has been labelled a "populist of the center" ("Populist der Mitte," Merkel quoted in Köppchen). Populism, it is implied here, does not *per se* have to be viewed as a political anomaly or pathology but may also be considered as invigorating politics and increasing participation in all political spheres. And yet, populism and the charisma of populist candidates seem to interpellate the supposedly rationally inclined voter as a primarily affectively invested fan. Performances like those of Trump cater to a fan-base and a "fan-based citizenship" (Hinck's term) rather than to an electorate, and this may not only have the effect of simply mobilizing a constituency but also of producing excessive agitation. In the wake of Max Weber's study on "charismatic authority," sociologists have discussed the compatibility of democracy and charismatic leadership long before election and campaign paraphernalia became fetishes of democratic fandom. Much has been written, for instance, on white women's fandom for Donald Trump (see, for instance, Chira).[9]

---

[8] Lutz Klinkhammer in a panel discussion on "Populism Today and Yesterday" at the Berlin-Brandenburgische Akademie der Wissenschaften on 20 June 2017. Klinkhammer also reminds us of Berlusconi's talkshow-appearance as a kind of "Ur-scene" of European populism.

[9] The popularity of right-wing populists on both sides of the Atlantic with a female constituency (somewhat counterintuitive to their party's anti-feminist agenda) shows the ongoing relevance of classic feminist scholarship on female complicity in patriarchal structures (*Mittäterschaft*, see Türmer-Rohr) and points to the need for a rigorous feminist critique of the phenomenon of populism.

A **transatlantic perspective** is offered in various contributions to this book. It returns us to the conundrum of hyper-nationalist politics in transnational contexts. It points to various top-down and bottom-up attempts at populist stimulation that happen within the nation-state and that are amplified in transnational comparison. Recent scholarship has begun to offer comparative perspectives on populist movements across Europe and beyond. With the recent publication *Populism, Populists, and the Crisis of Political Parties* (Pallaver et al.) our book shares the comparative angle – even as we have above all a transatlantic perspective rather than a focus on comparison in a European context. Clearly, both sides of the Atlantic exhibit a cultural backlash of sorts. Ronald Inglehart and Pippa Norris – examining Trump and Brexit – use this "backlash"-concept in order to analyze the growing appeal of populism. Their argument reconfirms and reinforces the longstanding diagnosis that populism produces a kind of culturalization of predominantly socio-economic conflicts and disparities. In other words: it recasts conflicts about distribution and precarity as conflicts about identity and recognition, i.e. different lifestyles and values. Accordingly, those negatively impacted by the consequences of globalization and the doings of finance capitalism can be recruited by authoritarian politicians via populist promises of (cultural) recognition (of the kind that cannot and will not be kept). This can be rendered in the logic of a backlash because it ultimately aims at the abolishing of pluralism and promotes the return to a symbolic and social order prior to the pluralization of society, the recognition of minority rights, and affirmative action. In such a world, old privileges would be reinstated that mainly favor white men – mostly at the expense of women and non-whites (Brownstein). As a poll conducted on behalf of Associated Press in 2016 has shown, many Americans still harbor the idea that a "typical" American is white and Christian. Republicans, in particular, cherish this notion (57%), among the Democrats only 29% hang on to this image of Americanness. In Europe a 2018-poll by the Bertelsmann foundation indicated that a majority of Europeans share a sense that things were better in the past (de Vries et al.). Drawn together, both polls indicate somewhat of a pull against cultural pluralism, economic globalization, and, yes, gender and race equality. As there will be no return to state-based capitalism (Nancy Fraser), the challenges that populisms present are most likely here to stay.

The following contributions offer multi-disciplinary insights into the phenomenon of populism's returns.

In his opening essay, "Populism and Modern Democracy – An Outline," **Hans Vorländer** puns on the title of a Hollywood classic to look at "the good, the bad, and the ugly" versions of populism in the present-day political landscape. Symptomatically, the resurgence of populism may point to a deficit in representation in modern democracies and hence may infuse new dynamic energies into rather static democratic structures and force fields; yet, the recent "populisms of indignation" in Britain, the United States, and elsewhere cannot easily and simply be considered forces of democratic renewal, Vorländer argues, and often have to be seen as rather "illiberal" in outlook and effect. Still, populism harbors transformative power for liberal democracies across the political spectrum, a power which is currently unfolding in rather complex ways. Following upon this state-of-the-art reappraisal of scholarship on populism, **Frank Decker** examines right-wing populism in Germany and abroad and offers a rationale for its emergence that covers social, economic, and cultural aspects and shows how these aspects have to be re-prioritized depending on the specific country and the political agendas of populist parties. Decker points to the varieties of populism and offers a typology to distinguish different kinds of populist parties. He also suggests crucial root causes for the (belated) rise of right-wing populism in Germany.

Historicizing current debates about populist returns, **Jürgen Gebhardt**'s essay also avoids the recourse to a generic concept of populism that constructs a more or less irreconcilable difference between populism's democratic claim for direct civic participation and a representative system of democracy. Rather, he offers a genealogy of the concept of 'popular sovereignty' as it emerged in the great revolutions and was bound up with the communitarian order of the sovereign nation state. Therefore, Gebhardt suggests, democratic orders reveal an inherent tendency toward self-referential populism and nationalism. At critical junctures, past and present, these moments have characterized the political culture and institutional make-up of constitutional polities in the modern political world. In a similar vein, **Michael Hochgeschwender** provides an overview of American populist movements in the late nineteenth century, where he partly sees the origin for the current return of US populism. He delineates the historical development of populist parties and movements such as the Grangers, the Greenback Labor Party, and Evangelical Protestants and extends this history to the present moment and its political and cultural climate, offering an interpretation of the motivations and goals – mainly of an economic nature – that these movements and their supporters share.

In their contribution to this volume, **Jack Zhou**, **D. Sunshine Hillygus**, and **John Aldrich** address the question whether the outcome of the 2016 presidential elections in the United States can actually be attributed solely to populist sentiments. Using post-election survey data and statistical modeling, they observe, somewhat counterintuitively, that so-called standard predictors, such as party identification, political ideology, and the recent economic conditions, played a more prominent role in the elections than the often foregrounded three dimensions of populism (socio-economic, political, and cultural). In their analysis, voter behavior in 2016 in the United States did not dramatically differ from previous elections, and hence they question that Trump's election in itself can be looked upon as evidence of a return of populism.

Somewhat contrary to these findings in voter motivation, several contributors to this collection do see a shift, at times even fundamental changes in political communication and political style. Donald Trump's particular style is addressed in several contributions: **Laura Vorberg** examines his campaign from the perspective of media studies and systems theory. Her contribution, "*#BasketofDeplorables*: Digital Imagined Communities, *Twitter*-Populism, and the Cross-Media Effects of Popular Political Social Media Communication in the 2016 US Presidential Election," proposes to examine one instance of Donald Trump's campaign – his response to Hillary Clinton's labelling of Trump-supporters as "basket of deplorables." Clinton's phrase allowed him to self-fashion as the "leader of the deplorables" in a most effective way and to capitalize on this across various media. Trump's success as a populist, Vorberg suggests, is very much connected to the specific kind of "twitter-populism" he has introduced to political campaigning. **Michael Oswald** focuses on one particular aspect of Trump's populist formula, that of a rhetoric of producerism. In simplistic binary oppositions, Oswald argues in his analysis of Trump's strategy, Trump pits producers (of value, money, goods) against parasites and successful businessmen (like himself), who are thriving in a low-tax, anti-regulation environment, against a corrupt government with a bureaucratic apparatus that takes money out of the system (and everybody else's pockets) and 'kills' jobs. Trump has told this narrative excessively and in doing so has catered to an important part of the American voters.

Heike Paul's contribution on "Authoritarian Populism, White Supremacy, and *Volkskörper*-Sentimentalism" analyzes the return of a *Volkskörper*-logic in right-wing populism that is thoroughly racialized and gendered in disturbing ways. This *Volkskörper*-sentimentalism (discernible in the rhetoric of Trump as well as among right-wing anti-feminist groups in Europe) is part of a "white Atlantic"-imaginary; it insists on an organicist model of society that is conceived as homogenous, even 'pure,' and allegorized via white women's bodies and their sexual integrity. In a broader context of right-wing populism's culture, **Simon Strick** examines the soft power of "Right-Wing World-Building" regarding its ordinary affect structures. He shows how a discourse of self-help and self-care (involving body-building, diet, and the maintenance of 'healthy' intimate relationships) time and again also (re)produces whiteness, while camouflaging or at least side-stepping the violence foundational for the right-wing projects of "world-building," a violence that only occasionally relates self-care to the project of maintaining the good health of the white race.

Akwugo Emejulu and Nicole Anna Schneider come to the discussion of populism from an angle that addresses social justice movements, feminist movements, and Black Lives Matter, probing bottom-up approaches of populist resistance. **Akwugo Emejulu**'s "Feminism for the 99%: Towards a Populist Feminism?" asks whether and how the constituent elements of populism can be subverted for the purpose of building a new internationalist feminist movement around issues of intersectionality. Such "a grassroots, anti-capitalist feminism," the author sees embodied in the political mobilization following the inauguration of Trump and in the worldwide Women's March in January 2017. The so-called F99-movement draws on the strategies of the Occupy-movement and joins forces with feminist groups in the Global South and North. Similarly fleshing out and analyzing a different kind of populist politics, **Nicole Anna Schneider** focuses on the role and rhetoric of 'the people' in the Black Lives Matter-movement. She discusses how processes of group formation become visible in its protest culture of signs, posters, and actions in the context of various events. Drawing on the works of Ernesto Laclau, Chantal Mouffe, and others, she provides a detailed analysis of photographs taken during the protests against police brutality and places them alongside those used by the media in the representation of the same events. Schneider describes the tensions between the wish for a more inclusive understanding of 'the people,' the efforts to produce discomfort on the part of 'the people' by raising awareness for anti-black violence, and the antagonistic positioning against a police force whose actions are per definition considered to be an institutional implementation of legitimate democratic rule.

Sascha Pöhlmann approaches the topic of populism by addressing its connection to popular culture. Discussing Walt Whitman's self-representation as a man of 'the people,' Pöhlmann points to the (failed) efforts of the poet to seek popularity by imagining 'the people' as his preferred audience. Whitman's paradigmatic failure of "missing the people," is echoed in a large variety of cultural productions, past and present, in different media formats, including comics, video games, film, and music. Pöhlmann's essay ultimately points to the ambiguous relationship between the popular and the populist: whereas popular culture claims widespread dissemination and acceptance, it also displays a resistance toward populism.

In the archive of populism, Italy is often addressed as one of the first sites to have experienced a resurgence of populism centering on a media-savvy populist leader. **Donatella Izzo** revisits this history from the angle of Marxist critique and television culture and links it to recent narratives as quasi-allegorical engagements with the question of leadership as the epitome of – or, one might say, as a substitute for – politics under the conditions of neoliberalism. Paolo Sorrentino's drama series *The Young Pope* serves as a poignant attempt to (re)articulate the narrative of leadership within a (political) theology. This use of the Pope as a trope also evokes an association between populism and Catholicism, a connection, which has been repeatedly theorized within Italian critical theory.

The two final contributions widen the scope of the volume once again to include analyses of populism and populist politics in Latin America. **Carlos de la Torre** situates Donald Trump's 2016-election as US President in a larger context of populist movements (and successes) in the Americas and Latin America specifically, where populists have been in power since the 1930s. Addressing right- and left-wing populist figures such as Juan Perón, Hugo Chávez, Evo Morales, and Rafael Correa, the author shows how populists in different Latin American countries have undermined democratic institutions and structures, and he anticipates serious challenges for the United States, its democratic system and its civil society under Trump. Taking this comparative angle into the present, **Ursula Prutsch** sheds light in her essay on recent developments in Brazil – and on Jair Bolsonaro's win in October 2018. She looks closely at Bolsonaro's campaign strategies as candidate (his aggressive social media usage and his self-fashioning as an outsider to politics) and at his political strategies and decisions as president. In her assessment of the Bolsonaro presidency, Prutsch draws comparisons with long-time Brazilian ruler Getúlio Vargas and US president Donald Trump.

The scope of this volume, thus, reaches from Germany, Italy, and European populisms more broadly to the United States and the Trump presidency, and, finally, to Latin America. The different faces and phases of populist politics bear resemblances as well as pronounced difference. Populism in a generic form does not exist. Typologies and definitions are helpful for a systematic understanding of the mechanisms of populist movements and leaders; historical context and cultural specificity inform and are part of populism's make-up.

Arguably, the sense of impending doom the TV series *House of Cards* projected and that I have referenced at the beginning of this introduction has not been banished. It has perhaps even been exacerbated by the record the Trump-presidency has produced – alongside other constellations elsewhere. Among other things, cultural imaginaries rehearse various scenarios of endings – or they revisit caesura of the past. By inversion, the title of Michael Moore's *Fahrenheit 11/9* seems to ask whether the election of Donald Trump is as devastating as were the terrorist attacks of 9/11. Once again, every single thing seems to become affected – in ordinary and extraordinary ways.

Versions of authoritarian populists may exist in unexpected places. Recently, Stephen Greenblatt has revisited Shakespeare's kings – pushing the allegorization in Shakespeare's texts far into our own time. Likewise, Shakespeare-productions have become conspicuous as sites of protest and political dissent with the presidency, especially when Julius Caesar (newly popular in American playhouses) bears a visual likeness to the president and is received as a "Shakespearian depiction of Trump" (Paulson et al.). Next to the historical drama, the genre of the dystopia is alive and well, once again. Canadian novelist Margaret Atwood, whose classic dystopian novel *The Handmaid's Tale* has had a huge comeback in the last couple of years (as a book, as a television series, as a graphic novel, and as reference in protest culture),[10] is publishing a sequel to it, *The Testaments*. In fact, gendered and racialized dystopian worlds abound in the pages of Louise Erdrich's *Future Home of the Living God* (2017), Naomi Alderman's *Power* (2017), Omar El Akkad's *American War* (2018), and John Lanchester's *The Wall* (2019). All of these stories produce a level of discomfort and fear that echoes the message of the flag hanging upside down.

The editors would like to express their profound gratitude to Susen Faulhaber for diligently proof-reading the entire manuscript, for checking on bibliographical references, for making the essays conform to the style sheet, and for producing the formatted final version.

Works Cited

Albright, Madeleine. *Fascism: A Warning*. London: William Collins, 2018.
Armstrong, Jennifer Keishin. "Why The Handmaid's Tale is so Relevant Today." *BBC* 25 April 2018 <http://www.bbc.com/culture/story/20180425-why-the-handmaids-tale-is-so-relevant-today>. Last accessed on 15 June 2019.
Associated Press. *Divided America: An AP Guide to the Fracturing of a Nation*. New York: Associated Press, 2016.
Bessire, Lucas, and David Bond. "The Rise of Trumpism." *Society for Cultural Anthropology* 18 January 2017 <https://culanth.org/fieldsights/series/the-rise-of-trumpism>.
Betz, Hans-Georg, and Stefan Immerfall. *The New Politics on the Right: Neo-Populist Parties and Movements in Established Democracies*. New York: Palgrave Macmillan, 1998.
Bloom, Peter. *Authoritarian Capitalism in the Age of Globalization*. Cheltenham/ UK: Edgar Elgar, 2016.
Brownstein, Ronald. "Trump's Rhetoric of White Nostalgia." *The Atlantic* 2 June 2016 <https://www.theatlantic.com/politics/archive/2016/06/trumps-rhetoric-of-white-nostalgia/485192/>. Last accessed on 15 June 2019.
Chira, Susan. "'You Focus on the Good': Women Who Voted for Trump, in Their Own Words." *The New York Times* 14 January 2017 <https://www.nytimes.com/2017/01/14/us/women-voters-trump.html>. Last accessed on 15 June 2019.
De Vries, Catherine E, and Isabell Hoffmann. "Die Macht der Vergangenheit: Wie Nostalgie die öffentliche Meinung in Europa beeinflusst." *eupinions / what do you think* 2018/2. Bertelsmann-Stiftung <https://www.bertelsmann-stiftung.de/

---

[10] See Armstrong.

fileadmin/files/BSt/Publikationen/GrauePublikationen/eupinions_Nostalgie.pdf>. Last accessed on 15 June 2019.

Frum, David. *Trumpocracy: The Corruption of the American Republic*. New York: Harper, 2018.

Heinisch, Reinhard C., Christina Holtz-Bacha, and Oscar Mazzoleni (eds.). *Political Populism: A Handbook*. Baden-Baden: Nomos, 2017.

Hinck, Ashley. *Politics for the Love of Fandom: Fan-Based Citizenship in a Digital World*. Baton Rouge: Louisiana University Press, 2019.

Judis, John B. *The Populist Explosion: How the Great Recession Transformed American and European Politics*. New York: Columbia Global Reports, 2016.

Kazin, Michael. *The Populist Persuasion: An American History*. Revised edition. Ithaca: Cornell University Press, 1998.

Klinkhammer, Lutz. "Einfache Antworten auf schwierige Fragen? Populismus heute und gestern." Berlin-Brandenburgische Akademie der Wissenschaften. Akademiegebäude am Gendarmenmarkt, Berlin, 20 June 2016. Panel discussion. <http://www.bbaw.de/veranstaltungen/2017/juni/populismus>.

Köppchen, Ulrike, "Europäische Sozialdemokratie in der Krise: Wir sind dann mal weg." *Deutschlandfunk Kultur* 6 November 2017 <https://www.deutschland funkkultur.de/europaeische-sozialdemokratie-in-der-krise-wir-sind-dann.976. de.html?dram:article_id=399966>. Last accessed on 15 June 2019.

Laclau, Ernesto. *On Populist Reason*. London: Verso, 2007.

Lovell, Joel. "Can the ACLU Become the NRA from the Left?" *The New York Times Magazine* 2 July 2018 <https://www.nytimes.com/2018/07/02/magazine/inside-the-aclus-war-on-trump.html>. Last accessed on 10 June 2019.

Manow, Philip. *Die politische Ökonomie des Populismus*. Berlin: Suhrkamp, 2018.

Miner, Qadira. "The Upside of Trump's Election: It Inspired My Generation to Fight Back." *The Guardian* 2 August 2018. <https://www.theguardian.com/us-news/2018/aug/02/trump-election-generation-z-teenagers-activism>. Last accessed on 15 June 2019.

Moffitt, Benjamin. *The Global Rise of Populism: Performance, Political Style, and Representation*. Stanford: Stanford University Press, 2016.

Mudde, Cas. "The Populist Zeitgeist." *Government and Opposition* 39.4 (2004): 541-63.

Müller, Jan-Werner. *What Is Populism?* New York: Penguin, 2017.

Norris, Pippa, and Ronald Inglehart. *Cultural Backlash: Trump, Brexit, and Authoritarian Populism*. Cambridge: Cambridge University Press, 2019.

Pallaver, Günther, Michael Gehler, and Maurizio Cau, eds. *Populism, Populists, and the Crisis of Political Parties: A Comparison of Italy, Austria, and Germany 1990-2015*. Bologna: Il mulino, 2018.

Paulson, Michael, and Sopan Deb. "How Outrage Built Over a Shakespearean Depiction of Trump." *The New York Times* 12 June 2017

<https://www.nytimes.com/2017/06/12/theater/donald-trump-julius-caesar-public-theater-oskar-eustis.html>. Last accessed on 15 June 2019.

Pierson, Paul. "American Hybrid: Donald Trump and the Strange Merger of Populism and Plutocracy." *The British Journal of Sociology* 68.1 (2017): 105-19.

Priester, Karin. "Right-wing Populism in Europe." Pallaver, et al. 45-61.

Rovira Kaltwasser, Cristobal, Paul Taggart, Paulina Ochoa Espejo, and Pierre Ostiguy (eds.). *The Oxford Handbook of Populism*. Oxford: Oxford University Press, 2017.

Stone, Gene. *The Trump Survival Guide: Everything You Need to Know About Living Through What You Hoped Would Never Happen*. New York: Dey Street Books, 2017.

Türmer-Rohr, Christina. *Mittäterschaft und Entdeckungslust*. Berlin: Orlanda, 1989.

Weale, Albert. *The Will of the People: A Modern Myth*. Cambridge: Polity, 2018.

Wodak, Ruth. *The Politics of Fear: What Right-Wing Populist Discourses Mean*. Los Angeles: Sage, 2015.

Wolf, Martin. "Donald Trump's Pluto-Populism Laid Bare." *Financial Times* 2 May 2017 <https://www.ft.com/content/69fe4862-2f20-11e7-9555-23ef563ecf9a>. Last accessed on 15 June 2019.

Populism and Modern Democracy – An Outline

Hans Vorländer

Many attempts have been made to define populism, of which only very few have been convincing. The most persuasive approaches to the phenomenon of populism seem to those that have attempted to analyze its manifestations within their particular historical, cultural, and political contexts (see Priester 2007; Beigel et al.). General and systematic definitions of the term have for the most part failed. And yet a way must be found to approach populism descriptively, analytically, as well as normatively that goes beyond its particular manifestations and seeks to determine the relationship between populism and democracy (see Taggart; Mény et al.; Decker 2003, 2005; Mudde et al. 2012; Hartleb; de la Torre; Diehl; Graf Kielmansegg). The current renaissance of populism necessitates such an approach, and recent studies have already pointed in this direction (see e.g. Müller; Mudde et al. 2017; Jörke et al.).

Many years ago, in reference to a well-known film, I wrote about "the good, the bad, and the ugly" in order to be able to differentiate between various populisms and their complex and ambivalent relationship to democracy (see Vorländer 2011a). Whether this heuristics is still fruitful for classifying contemporary phenomena from Trump and Orban to Brexit, the 'Patriotic Europeans,' and the Alternative for Germany warrants further examination. It should not be ruled out *a priori* that aside from bad populisms, which threaten democracy, and ugly populisms, which destroy it, there might also exist populist movements and actors that by touching the sore spots of democracy call attention to undesirable developments and shortcomings and in this way contribute to democracy's renewal. Populisms certainly are symptoms of a crisis of democracy. However, the problem is that they at the same time also intensify this crisis and thus put enormous pressure on liberal systems. I will begin with some rather elementary and phenomenological reflections before turning to the specific problem of populism and modern democracy within the current situation.

What Is Populism?

Populism and democracy both contain a central reference to the term 'people,' which makes their relationship to each other problematic. Populism could be read as if democracy were realized only through it. Democracy, as is generally known, is based on the sovereignty of the people; accordingly, populism is inscribed into democracy. It is an intrinsic phenomenon rather than one introduced from the outside. Populism moreover can pose a challenge to democracy by demanding of it to honor its promise of a 'true' and 'real' rule of the people. A different and more common perception of populism, however, is that it threatens the very core of democracy and eventually leads to its destruction. Here, populism figures as the pathological flip side of democracy, which expresses democracy's proneness to crisis and possibly also excess. It thus is not surprising that populism is regarded as a Hydra threateningly raising her ever-different head in different contexts. Those who so wish can study the ambiguities of the people's rule as far back as Athenian democracy's impressive practice of direct and immediate exercise of authority by the demos on the one hand, and its derailment by demagogues and political seducers who knew how to sway the masses on the other. The Athenians' remedy for the damage brought about by demagogues was ostracization: the seducers of the people were banned from their city.

More recently, discussions of populism regularly include references to rightist or extreme-right populisms in Europe (see Mudde; Decker et al.; Kriesi et al.). At times, individual politicians, regardless of whether they are on the right or on the left, are also called populists. This, however, is not the whole story. Historical studies have also related the term 'populism' to other contexts in which movements or parties emerged that allegedly had a 'populist' flavor. Thus at least three 'waves of populism' can be differentiated: agrarian populism, Latin American populism, and the contemporary populism of the New Right. Firstly, agrarian populism goes back to developments in 1830s America, when then-president of the United States Andrew Jackson was able to unite farmers, craftsmen, and small businessmen into a protest movement against big business, the banks, and emerging industrial structures and through this expansion of political participation initiated a (mass) democratization of the US political system. A similar case was the protest by farmers, workers, and so-called Greenbackers in the 1890s, which was directed mostly – if not exclusively – against the social disruption caused by industrial capitalism, and brought considerable electoral success to William Jennings Bryan and the Populist Party, later the People's Party, which were fighting, among other things, against the industrial monopolies of the so-called robber barons and an expansionist national monetary policy (see Goodwyn). Secondly, the nineteenth-century Russian intellectual movement of the Narodniks can also be counted among the forms of agrarian populism.

Latin American variants of populism, which have blossomed especially since the 1940s and 1950s and were at that time connected to the authoritarian regimes of Perón in Argentina and Vargas in Brazil, can be said to constitute the second wave of populism (see de la Torre et al.). Subsequently and until today, Latin American populism has at times also appeared in left versions, but it has always been embodied by strong leader figures: Meném, Collor, and Fujimori right up to Chavez, Morales, and Maduro. Since the 1970s, movements of the New Right have gained strength in various European states and in the Anglo-American world. Since then, populism has more and more been associated with parties on the right. Some of these parties are openly anti-democratic, while others hide their anti-democratic stance beneath a facade of bourgeois respectability. Some parties on the right position themselves as anti-immigrant and increasingly also anti-Muslim parties; many pose as protest parties and garner a significant portion of the electorate. Most of these parties, for example the Swiss People's Party (SVP), Austria's FPÖ, Italy's Lega Nord, the Netherland's Partij voor de Vrijheid (formerly Lijst Pim Fortuyn) under Geert Wilders, France's Front National under Jean-Marie and more recently Marine Le Pen, the new Scandinavian populist parties, and UKIP in the UK, have (or had) charismatic leaders who know (or knew) how to mobilize their constituencies and unite them under the party banner. At the same time, the populism of the New Right appeals to xenophobic, racist, and nationalist sentiments based on topics such as immigration, taxes, and crime.[1]

Recently, populism has also been successfully reaching for power and taking it first in Latin America, then in North America – more specifically in the United States –, and in the Czech Republic. In Austria, the FPÖ (Freedom Party of Austria) has for the second time come to power as part of a coalition government. In the United Kingdom, the populists, and not only those of UKIP, managed to mobilize voters for Brexit. In Western Europe, the coming into power of populists admittedly was prevented, as were further electoral gains by populist parties in Austria, the Netherlands, and France. But populists in office in Central and Eastern Europe have been working with brute consistency on a new model of democracy, which Hungarian prime minister Orban has called "illiberal democracy" (see Orban) and which constitutes the antithesis to the Western, pluralist, constitutional, checks-and-balances understanding of democracy. And, so as not to entirely lose sight of Germany: in these parts, through Pegida and the AfD (Alternative for Germany), a connection to international right-wing populism seems to have been established. Do these current phenomena still belong to the third wave of populisms or is this a new constellation, a fourth wave conducting a frontal assault on democracy as we know it? And lastly: What about left-wing populism, dignified

---

[1] The conceptual categorization of these and similar parties in the international and German literature on the subject varies between (Populist) Radical Right, Right Wing, Extremist, and Fascist. This is due to the problem of conceptual boundaries, which I attempt to solve in this article by gathering them all under the rubric of populism, with the exception however of the extreme and extremist right. It should be noted that populist groups on the right are often marked by a certain fluidity that reveals their function as bridge builders and partners in right-wing alliances, an issue which warrants further empirical analyses (see Mudde; Finchelstein; Minkenberg).

by intellectuals such as Laclau and Mouffe (see Laclau; Mouffe; Mouffe et al.; for an assessment thereof see Priester 2014; Möller) for breaking the alleged hegemony of 'neoliberalism' and practiced in France by Mélenchon and his movement La France Insoumise during the 2017 presidential election campaign? The Spanish Los Indignados, Podemos or the Greek Syriza, all both movements as well as parties, can also be counted among the left-wing populists.

The Modus Operandi of Populisms

Any generalizing definition – even a minimal definition – reaches its limits very fast. The question whether populism is an ideology or 'only' a style, a doctrine, rhetoric, conviction, or a polemical figure differentiating oppositional from governmental populism, the populisms of movements from those of politicians, temporary from enduring and legitimate from illegitimate populism can be answered either way, depending on which *a priori* definition is used to identify populist phenomena and in which contexts the respective tendencies, groups, or movements operate. This is a strong argument for abandoning general as well as minimal definitions in favor of a descriptive semantics that is historically open and at the same time context-sensitive, which is why it seems more accurate to always refer to populisms in the plural, as they differ in terms of substance, structures, as well as their historical, cultural, and institutional frameworks.

And yet the question may be asked what it is that different populisms have in common. Their commonality seems to be a specific political mobilization strategy that draws on recognizable semantics, symbolic references, and political constructions. Five characteristics can be pointed out that as the *modi operandi* of populisms provide them with a specific appearance and internal structure. First, all populisms explicitly refer to the 'people' and/or the 'common man' and sometimes also to the 'plain citizen.' They construct a people by resorting to the mechanisms of inclusion and exclusion. This is why, second, populisms constitute themselves by use of clear-cut fundamental binaries, with their rhetoric structured along basic differences such as 'us' and 'them,' 'over' and 'under,' 'inside' and 'outside;' the assertion of these differences becomes triadic whenever a middle-class populism defines itself against those 'above' and 'below'[2] or a right-wing populism against the establishment and foreigners. Third, categories such as 'they,' 'over,' 'under,' and 'outside' are used to construct collective, stereotyped entities whose function it

---

[2] Karin Priester (2007) most notably shows that modern, contemporary middle-class populism has a dual thrust. Another interesting question is whether the difference between a *populisme des modernes* and a *populisme des anciens* is also grounded herein (see Hermet; I am grateful for this reference to Alexandre Escudier).

is to provide meaning for and enable the establishment of an identity that is 'us.' The construction of this social and political entity, which is usually referred to as 'the people,' corresponds with the intentionally produced effect of the Other's exclusion and separation and of the difference between 'them' and 'us,' of in-group and out-group. Fourth, populisms operate on claims of homogeneity: Social, economic, cultural, and political differences are erased by the collective singular of 'the people' and the 'common man,' of 'us,' 'them' and so forth. Diversity, according to this logic, undermines the genuine expression of the 'true' will of the polity. Fifth, populisms establish a mobilizing structure of political entrepreneurship, usually a charismatic figure and his supporters – the movement –, or, to put it bluntly, of leader and followership. The leader is spokesman of the will of the people, which is imagined as homogeneous and exclusive. He or she is the medium through which the movement understands itself and finds its identity.

These feature descriptions of the m.o. of the phenomenon of populism are heuristically valuable, but they do not tell us anything about the relationship between populism and democracy yet. They could have neutral effects, they could be used within the framework of democratic structures and politics, but they could also, not least because of the basic convictions and dynamics operative within them, push beyond democracy and lead to a transformation or destruction of democratic structures and practices.

Populism as the Renewal of Democracy?

It was most notably Margaret Canovan who contributed with her work on the historical manifestations of populism to a change in the perception that populism per se poses a danger to democracy and constitutes a symptom of its degeneration. For Canovan (see Canovan 1981, 1999), populism is a positive challenge to democracy. She argues that democracy is based on a tension between stasis and movement which from time to time is dissolved by populist movements. Whenever democracies ossify, populisms re-galvanize them. Institutional mechanisms of stabilization face off with invigorating elements, i.e. popular movements. From this perspective, an alternative interpretation comes to the fore which breaks populism free from its veneer of reactionary conservatism, nativism, and racism. Populism gains the character of a radical political undertaking, a grassroots movement that reinvigorates a vertically segmented democracy. Populism becomes a vital and vitalizing element of democracy and can be categorically understood with Michael Oakeshott as a "redemptive politics of faith" (Canovan 1999: 8; Oakeshott 21-38). Populism 'cleanses' a democracy that has become rigid in its structures. Populism in this sense should be understood as democracy in movement.

Canovan's change of perspective opens up an important analytical perspective that helps explaining and interpreting the genesis and function of populisms within the framework of modern democracies. Modern 'Western' democracies have developed a complex network of institutions and procedures, of representative decision-making processes and direct civic participation, which was 'invented' within a historical constellation in the second half of the eighteenth century and which aimed at the reconciliation (and also restriction) of the sovereignty of the people with the protection of basic and human rights. Liberal or constitutional democracy ties (popular) sovereignty to the validity and guarantee of individual rights and through balancing mechanisms provides a means to limit power. At the same time, the political decision-making process takes place within the institutions and procedures of democracy through representation. The problem is that this model – which seemed to be promising self-determination, freedom, and stability in times of increasing societal differentiation and in this way claimed to be superior to the 'pure,' direct rule of the people – is itself delicate, too. It seems as if exactly those populisms seep through the cracks between democracy as an institutional decision-making system and democracy as a political way of life that create their momentum from the real or perceived opposition between the establishment and the people, between 'those up there' and 'us down here.' (see Vorländer 2011b, 2016).

Canovan thus has undoubtedly cast a fresh glance at the phenomenon of populism. At the same time, her theoretical approach is every bit as ambivalent as populisms themselves. Her declaring populism to be a force of democratic renewal shows her to be inspired by its progressive variants. While this is not historically wrong in view of the People's Party in the US at the turn of the nineteenth to the twentieth century and Theodore Roosevelt's 'Bull Moose' Party – and one could also add more recent forms of inclusive populism in Latin America – deducing from these examples that populism in general constitutes an element of democratic renewal can only be claimed by ignoring all other variants of populism. The history, not least the very recent history, of populist movements does show after all that populists – to put it as mildly as possible – are not exactly characterized by their high respect for the institutions and structures of democracy. Canovan all too speedily levels the difference between democracy and populism with her reading – which is certainly inspired by Hannah Arendt – of progressive, populist democracy in movement.

Thus Pegida, or 'Patriotic Europeans against the Islamization of the West,' which came into being a good four years ago, can for example be described as a right-wing populist movement of indignation, which alongside criticisms of Islam, xenophobia, and resistance against the immigration of refugees has publicly staged all kinds of disappointments and frustrations as invectives against 'politics,' 'politicians,' and 'the media' (see Vorländer et al. 2016, 2017, 2018). Slogans such as 'lying press' and 'traitor of the people' on the one hand and 'we are the people' on the other reflect a fundamental political alienation between civic life-world and politics as well as the media. On the one hand, the mediated public sphere and political institutions are perceived as alien, as instruments of a faux democracy; the representatives and decision-making processes of this system are regarded either as 'fossilized,' 'conceited,' or 'corrupt.' On the other, there are calls for a direct democracy in which the people are in charge and politicians act merely as weak and dependent 'employees' that are directly accountable to 'the people's will.' This vulgar understanding of democracy (Ernst Fraenkel) denies how complex, time-consuming, and compromise-based political opinion- and decision-making processes really are in a representative system and claims as a remedy the direct assertion of the 'unadulterated' will of the people via plebiscite. It consequently equates the job profile of elected officials with a simple 'down/up' model of 'we ask and order/you answer and deliver.' "And who doesn't deliver gets fired," as a Pegida supporter puts it; a people thus fires its representatives.

Populisms: An Expression of a Representational Deficit?

In view of contemporary populisms, the question now must be asked whether they should be described as good, bad, or ugly. Is a positive interpretation of the current movements acceptable? If populist attitudes and movements develop whenever representative democracy has lost its balance between its two pillars – democracy as a decision-making system and democracy as a way of life –, then indeed the argument about representational deficiencies might take hold, i.e. the argument about the poor or even complete lack of representation of parts of the population by the institutions and channels of publicly visible decision-making processes, parties, parliaments, and the media. Those who perceive themselves as having been left behind, excluded, or insufficiently listened to then become the segment which political entrepreneurs using the m.o. of populism capture and mobilize in order to stand up against the ossification of democracy, against exclusion and discrimination.

Trump and Farage, with considerable success, set themselves up as the spokesmen of socioeconomically disadvantaged groups and of those who felt culturally dominated. Marine Le Pen, as her father before her, has been able for a long time to forge a national front of resistance from the social, cultural, and religious tensions deriving not least from the immigration of people from the francophone Maghreb and other former colonies. Pegida has (also) given voice to the simmering resentment of that part of Saxony which has felt abandoned since reunification in 1990, and the Alternative for Germany (as well as Pegida) have similarly managed to transform widespread fears of losing control over the influx of migrants – fears that had not been part of the public discourse – into votes. All of these movements, it seems, brought something to light that had been latent but not visible. Populists entered the limelight and captured the discontented and unrepresented, gave them a voice, lambasted the corruption of the elites, accused politicians of treason, and equated the existing indignation with the 'will of the people.'

It is obviously difficult to call such populist movements good, especially as it can be seen that they make common cause with extreme right and extremist groups and that their main thrust – far beyond making visible problems of representation – is to attack the foundations of liberal democracy. At the same time, it cannot be denied that the current populist movements on the right demarcate lines of conflict of the present age that have led to divisions in Western societies and to disagreements within the European and transatlantic communities. These cleavages can be interpreted culturally and/or socio-economically, as a struggle about cultural identity in which ethnocentric and cosmopolitan attitudes and groups clash, or, broadly speaking, as a socio-economic struggle between the winners and losers of globalization.[3] In most cases, the populists have been able to fuse cultural, social, and economic factors as well as anti-European and nationalist-identitarian sentiments, and thus to create maximum political momentum.

These populisms can be described as good at best in regard to their effects, in particular if they are taken seriously as indicators of deficits within the representational system and if the forces of democracy know how to respond. Then populisms, as a reservoir of protest, could have an inclusive and transformative function for a democracy that has weakened in its responsiveness. If non-voters who have turned away from the established parties in resignation are re-integrated into the political process, then this is a gain for democracy. Granted, if such a populism of indignation is situative and temporary, then at the end of the day it does not necessarily have to pose a threat to democracy but instead can act as a rejuvenating therapy – provided that it has not antagonistically deepened the rifts in society and lastingly damaged the institutional foundations of and trust in democracy along the way.

The Phantasms of Populisms

However, this is true in many cases, as the mobilization strategies of populisms deploy a set of ideologemes that contradict the foundations of modern, liberal democracy. Orban's 'illiberal democracy' provides a counter-image to an open,

---

[3] For discussions of causes, lines of conflict etc. see e.g. Eribon; Hochschild; Merkel; Lilla; Rodrik; Vorländer 2016.

pluralistic society; it is based on notions that can be described as the three phantasms of homogeneity, authenticity, and immediacy, whose imaginaries aim toward the destruction of the institutions, principles, and procedures of modern, representative, and constitutional democracy. They blur the boundaries between good, bad and ugly populisms.

Populisms distrust institutions which possess a certain institutional autonomy and thus also immunity, such as the judiciary, constitutional courts, the media, or central banks. These, in the eyes of populists and their supporters, distort the will of the people. The same holds true for territorial divisions of power as they commonly exist in federatively organized states. This distrust against the institutions of liberal and constitutional democracy is furthermore accompanied by the curtailment and intentional denial of the constitutionally guaranteed rights of ethnic, national, cultural, and religious minorities. Diversity appears as bad because it undermines the notion of an inviolable and uniform will of the people. Negotiations, compromises, and deliberations then appear as diversionary maneuvers or cover-ups, and interfere with the immediacy of the relation between leader and people. Leaders of this kind today communicate with their followers directly – preferably by tweet –, and also govern directly – preferably by decree – both being preferred leadership tools of the US president.

The principle of immediacy thus replaces the civic, intermediary and mediated decision-making processes typical of representative democracy. In a representative democracy, political compromises are negotiated, and the principle of checks and balances prevents the arbitrary exercise of power. Populists on the other hand attempt to circumvent this so that the will of the people may become effective immediately and directly – embodied and executed by the leader.

Furthermore, the proclaimed will of the people is the only one granted legitimacy because it is deemed authentic in a double sense: as the expression of a socially united entity and as the expression of a specific political will. Usually, this social unity is deemed to have historical roots and to be locally or regionally bounded, a 'homeland' of an allegedly intact past that must be preserved or restored. The political will is also held to be authentic because it originates from the collective unity of the people and is embodied directly through the medium of the leader.

Populism at its core is based on the illusion of an intrinsic unity. The phantasm of an organic unity of the body politic (see Lefort) has the advantage of allowing one to assert the identity of a clearly and definitely defined political collective which can be positioned against the strenuous and lengthy democratic process. It generates a logic that eliminates the idea of difference and the Other from the vision of democracy. The illusions of unity, identity, and a political collective, which particularly in the German context is semantically coded as 'Volksgemeinschaft,' then also become the nexus of populism and totalitarianism.[4] Modern democracies, however, must insist on the fact that a plurality of values and interests can only be balanced *pro tempore* through necessarily conflictual decision-making processes. Democracy is based on the idea of an open society that is integrated on the political level case-by-case, whereas populism is based on the notion of a closed, homogeneous, historically or ethnically constituted collective unit that finds its direct expression in the allegedly uniform will of the people.

From the standpoint of modern, representative democracy, populisms thus are not to be trusted. Whether they were good, bad, or ugly, whether they had positive effects of renewal and revitalization or rather shook the legitimacy of democracy or even initiated an authoritarian-totalitarian transformation can usually be determined only in hindsight. At which stage we are at the moment is difficult to say. Findings will diverge from each other. In the US, the robustness of the institution of democracy is being put to the litmus test – with an uncertain outcome. In Central Europe – in Hungary, Poland, and the Czech Republic – tendencies toward a semi-authoritarian transformation of democratic structures can be discerned. In Western Europe, particularly in France, the populist flood seems to have been contained, at least for the time being. Yet the current metamorphoses of Western democracies still suggest that populism might become a "long shadow" (Arditi 20) because contemporary democracies themselves manifest developments that can be interpreted as a creeping populist transformation (see Vorländer 2011a, 2013; Mair; Decker 2003; Urbinati).

Populist Transformations of Democracy?

There are especially three developments that have to be mentioned here in conclusion: the new social media have caused a fundamental transformation of the public realm. While the shaping of public opinion had previously been strongly influenced by audio-visual and print media, now forms of internet communication have come to the fore. These operate faster and are able to organize political articulations and protest on demand as well as to generate eruptive shifts in the political mood. At the same time, hermetically closed networks are established which as shared echo chambers create communities of the like-minded that preempt dissent. Wherever rage, anger, and aggression, scandal-mongering and conspiracy theories shape opinion, the digital era seems to spawn a new political type – the democracy of indignation. The 'connected multitude' (Bernhard

---

[4] Finchelstein convincingly elaborates on the commonalities but also the significant differences between fascism and populism (see Finchelstein).

Pörksen) has power, but no institutional connection to the political decision-making system. Yet it puts pressure on representative processes to react more quickly and prove their legitimacy. The new populist movements on the left as well as the right usually have their origins online and only at a later stage occupied the streets and plazas. Social media in this context function as mobilizers of populisms.

This development is mirrored on the other side by a similarly profound transformation of the institutions of constitutional democracy, which today are much more responsive to the news cycle and attempt to react to current developments on the fly and in real time. This leads to a preference for fast and solitary decisions as well as to a presidential and at times almost autocratic leadership style that runs counter to the time-consuming logic of counseling and negotiation in representative decision-making processes as well as the necessary incorporation of democratic committees and institutions, and thus creates a backlash among those who are no longer listened to and represented. A democracy of the elites and populist revolts are two sides of the same coin.

Ultimately it is the signs of disintegration of the political basis or of the social infrastructure of democracy which as disruptions of the mediation between citizens and political decision-makers structurally facilitate populisms. Parties, unions, regulars' tables, and associations more and more lose their politically binding, organizing but also integrating character. In this way civil society loses important social and intermediary institutions that mediate between politics and life-world. The transformation of the party system, the loosening or dissolution of close social bonds at the same time leads to an almost absolute personalization of the political process. This is the hour of populist leader figures who know how to win over voters by directly addressing them through perfectly staged (social) media appearances.

The effects of these structural changes have made themselves felt for quite some time: The collapse of the established party system in Italy, which had existed since the post-war era – a strong Christian-democratic pillar on the one side and an equally strong socialist-communist formation on the other –, made possible the rise of Berlusconi and his party Forza Italia in the 1990s as well as more recently the Movimento Cinque Stelle under the leadership of Beppe Grillo. The populist right-wing Freedom Party of Austria has benefitted from the ossification of the Austrian party system, which found its expression in the consolidation of a grand coalition between the conservative Austrian People's Party (ÖVP) and the Social Democratic Party of Austria (SPÖ). The FPÖ could recently be prevented from garnering a majority on the national level only when ÖVP-frontrunner Sebastian Kurz, using populist strategies himself, ostentatiously distanced himself from his party's party line and effectively and successfully branded himself as a young and dynamic candidate of renewal and change. After the recent political scandal involving the FPÖ the new elections in September 2019 will prove whether his strategies continue to be successful.

And in France, a totally new formation, mind you: a movement 'en marche' could arise which dealt a death blow to the weakened parties of the left and right. It is not by chance that Macronism used populist tools and thus was able to charismatically stage the hyper-personalization of its messiah. The 'yellow west movement' has amplified a left-wing counter-populism, whose political clout Macron is presently trying to contain.

Whether these observations are indicative of a fundamental populist transformation of modern, representative democracy remains to be seen.

Works Cited:

Arditi, Benjamin. "Populism, or, Politics at the Edges of Democracy." *Contemporary Politics* 9 (2003): 17-31.

Beigel, Thorsten, and Georg Eckert. *Populismus*. Münster: Aschendorff, 2017.

Canovan, Margaret. *Populism*. Toronto: Junction Books, 1981.

---. "Trust the People! Populism and the Two Faces of Democracy." *Political Studies* 47 (1999): 2-16. doi: 10.1111/1467-9248.00184.

Decker, Frank. "The Populist Challenge to Liberal Democracy." *Internationale Politik und Gesellschaft* 3 (2003): 47-59.

---. "Notwendiges Korrektiv oder systemgefährdendes Übel? Die Herausforderungen der liberalen Demokratie durch den neuen Rechtspopulismus." *Populismus in Europa: Krise der Demokratie?* Ed. Rudolf von Thadden and Anna Hoffmann. Göttingen: Wallstein, 2005. 45-58.

Decker, Frank, Bernd Henningsen, and Kjetil Jakobsen (eds.). *Rechtspopulismus und Rechtsextremismus in Europa*. Baden-Baden: Nomos, 2015.

de la Torre, Carlos. *The Promise and Perils of Populism: Global Perspectives*. Lexington: University of Kentucky Press, 2015.

de la Torre, Carlos, and Cynthia J. Arnson. *Latin American Populism in the Twenty First Century*. Washington: Woodrow Wilson Center Press, 2013.

Diehl, Paula. "Demokratische Repräsentation und ihre Krise." *Aus Politik und Zeitgeschichte* 66.40-42 (2016): 12-17.

Eribon, Didier. *Rückkehr nach Reims*. Berlin: Suhrkamp, 2016.

Finchelstein, Federico. *From Fascism to Populism in History*. Oakland: University of California Press, 2017.

Fraenkel, Ernst. "Die repräsentative und die plebiszitäre Komponente im demokratischen Verfassungsstaat." *Zur Theorie und Geschichte der Repräsentation und Repräsentativverfassung*. Ed. Heinz Rausch. Darmstadt: Wissenschaftliche Buchgesellschaft, 1968. 330-85.

Goodwyn, Lawrence. *Democratic Promise: The Populist Moment in America.* Oxford: Oxford University Press, 1976.

Graf Kielmansegg, Peter. "Populismus ohne Grenzen." *Frankfurter Allgemeine Zeitung* 13 February 2017 (Nr. 37): 6.

Hartleb, Florian. "Populismus als Totengräber oder mögliches Korrektiv der Demokratie?" *Aus Politik und Zeitgeschichte* 62.5/6 (2012): 22-9.

Hermet, Guy. *Les Populismes dans le monde.* Paris: Fayard, 2001.

Hochschild, Arlie. *Strangers in their Own Land: Anger and Mourning on the American Right. A Journey to the Heart of Our Political Divide.* New York/London: New Press, 2016.

Jörke, Dirk, and Oliver Nachtwey. *Das Volk gegen die (liberale) Demokratie.* Baden-Baden: Nomos, 2017.

Kriesi, Hanspeter, and Takis Pappas. *European Populism in the Shadow of the Great Recession.* Colchester: ECPR Press, 2015.

Laclau, Ernesto. *On Populist Reason.* London: Verso, 2005.

Lefort, Claude. "Démocratie et représentation." *Métamorphoses de la représentation politique au Brésil et en Europe.* Ed. Daniel Pecaut and Bernardo Sorj. Paris: Broché, 1991. 223-32.

Lilla, Mark. *The Once and Future Liberal: After Identity Politics.* New York: Harper, 2017.

Mair, Peter. "Populist Democracy vs. Party Democracy." *Democracy and the Populist Challenge.* Ed. Yves Mény and Yves Surel. New York: Palgrave Macmillan, 2002. 81-98.

Mény, Yves, and Yves Surel (eds.). *Democracies and the Populist Challenge.* Basingstoke: Palgrave Macmillan, 2002.

Merkel, Wolfgang. "Kosmopolitismus versus Kommunitarismus: Ein neuer Konflikt in der Demokratie." *Parties, Governments and Elites: The Comparative Study of Democracy.* Ed. Philipp Harfst, Ina Kubbe, and Thomas Poguntke. Wiesbaden: VS, 2017. 9-23.

Minkenberg, Michael. *The Radical Right in Eastern Europe: Democracy under Siege?* London: Palgrave Macmillan, 2017.

Möller, Kolja. "Invocatio Populi: Autoritärer und demokratischer Populismus." Jörke and Nachtwey. 257-78.

Mouffe, Chantal. "The 'End of Politics' and the Challenge of Right-wing Populism." *Populism and the Mirror of Democracy.* Ed. Francisco Panizza. London: Lawrence & Wishart, 2005. 50-71.

Mouffe, Chantal, and Íñigo Errejón. *Podemos: In the Name of the People.* London: Lawrence & Wishart, 2016.

Mudde, Cas. *Populist Radical Right Parties in Europe.* Cambridge: Cambridge University Press, 2007.

Mudde, Cas, and Cristóbal Rovira Kaltwasser. *Populism in Europe and the Americas: Threat or Corrective for Democracy.* Cambridge: Cambridge University Press, 2012.

---. *Populism: A Very Short Introduction.* New York: Oxford University Press, 2017.

Müller, Jan-Werner. *Was ist Populismus?* Berlin: Suhrkamp, 2016.

Oakeshott, Michael. *The Politics of Faith and the Politics of Scepticism.* New Haven, CT: Yale University Press, 1996.

Orbán, Viktor. "Rede des ungarischen Premierministers Viktor Orbán vom 30. Juli 2014." http://www.kormany.hu/en/the-prime-minister/the-prime-minister-s-speeches/prime-minister-viktor-orban-s-speech-at-the-25th-balvanyos-summer-free-university-and-student-camp. Last accessed 31 January 2018.

Pörksen Bernhard, and Burkhard Müller-Ulrich. "Masse und Macht im Internet: 'Die vernetzten Vielen werden zur fünften Gewalt.' Interview in *Deutschlandfunk* (14 June 2015). <https://www.deutschlandfunk.de/masse-und-macht-im-internet-die-vernetzten-vielen-werden.694.de.html?dram:article_id=322593>.

Priester, Karin. *Populismus: Historische und aktuelle Erscheinungsformen.* Frankfurt/M.: Campus, 2007.

---. *Mystik und Politik: Ernesto Laclau, Chantal Mouffe und die radikale Demokratie.* Würzburg: Königshausen & Neumann, 2014.

Rodrik, Dani. *Populism and the Economics of Globalization.* Cambridge: Harvard University Press, 2017.

Taggart, Paul A. *Populism.* Buckingham: Open University Press, 2000.

Urbinati, Nadia. *Democracy Disfigured.* Cambridge/London: Harvard University Press, 2014.

Vorländer, Hans. "The Good, the Bad, and the Ugly: Über das Verhältnis von Populismus und Demokratie. Eine Skizze." *Totalitarismus und Demokratie: Zeitschrift für Internationale Diktatur- und Freiheitsforschung* 8 (2011a): 187-94.

---. "Der Wutbürger: Repräsentative Demokratie und kollektive Emotionen." *Ideenpolitik: Geschichtliche Konstellationen und gegenwärtige Konflikte.* Ed. Harald Bluhm, Karsten Fischer, and Marcus Llanque. Berlin: Akademie, 2011b. 467-78.

---. "Kritik, Krise, Szenarien: Zur Lage der Demokratie." *Zeitschrift für Politikwissenschaft* 2 (2013): 267-77.

---. "Wenn das Volk gegen die Demokratie aufsteht: Die Bruchstelle der repräsentativen Demokratie und die populistische Herausforderung." *Vielfalt statt Abgrenzung: Wohin steuert Deutschland in der Auseinandersetzung um Einwanderung und Flüchtlinge?* Ed. Bertelsmann Foundation. Gütersloh: Bertelsmann, 2016. 61-76.

Vorländer, Hans, Maik Herold, and Steven Schäller. *Pegida and New-Right Wing Populism in Germany*. London: Palgrave Macmillan, 2018.

---. "Entfremdung, Empörung, Ethnozentrismus: Was PEGIDA über den sich formierenden Rechtspopulismus verrät." Jörke and Nachtwey 138-59.

---. *Pegida: Entwicklung, Zusammensetzung und Deutung einer Empörungsbewegung*. Wiesbaden: Springer VS, 2016.

Populism in Germany and Abroad

Frank Decker

Since the mid-1980s, several Western European countries have witnessed the emergence of a new and novel family party whose moniker "right-wing populist" has become firmly established within both scientific and journalistic parlance. Initially, the arrival of these newcomers from the right (Front National, Lega Nord, Vlaams Blok, Freedom Party of Austria) and the electoral successes they celebrated were seen as a fleeting phenomenon that had always been a part of Western democracies – in a populist guise as well. The expectation that these challengers would sooner or later be cut back to size and disappear altogether from the party system was widespread. Subsequent trends would thoroughly disprove this assumption. Not only were right-wing populists able to defend and sometimes even expand their position on the political stage. The phenomenon now began to spread to other Western European countries as the new democracies of Central and Eastern Europe proved to be susceptible as well. In several countries in the region, right-wing populists have even gone on to become the center-right's primary political force, for example Poland's Law and Justice and Hungary's Fidesz (Giusto et al.).

After a largely uninterrupted ascent until the year 2000, the right-wing challengers' growth curve inched downwards until the mid-2000s before support subsequently once again rose quite markedly. Right-wing populism now emerged in countries that had previously been unaffected by it. Its short-lived downward trajectory can likely be attributed more to its own success than a diminished demand for right-wing populist messages within the electorate. Evidence for this theory can be found in the injection of populism into the established parties of the political "mainstream." Not only did they coopt topics previously championed by right-wing populist actors but they moreover embraced their political style as well. Left-wing populist parties and movements that could sometimes address voters' concerns in a more credible manner than their counterparts on the right experienced a simultaneous upswing. Two populist strains – also frequently present within a single party – are currently attacking Christian democratic-conservative and social democratic parties from both sides: a social populism that professes welfare chauvinist values and/or criticizes capitalism and an anti-Islamic-populism built upon a culturalist foundation (Heinisch et al.).

In Western Europe, the rise of right-wing populist parties can be divided into three phases: pioneering, main, and that of the late arrivals. The Progress Parties that emerged in Denmark and Norway at the beginning of the 1970s played the pioneering role. Both initially conceived of themselves as tax protest parties with an anti-welfare slant before discovering immigration as a key issue for their own electoral gain in the mid-1980s. In 1995, the Danish People's Party was formed as a spin-off from the Danish Progress Party. Along with the Swiss People's Party, the Danish and Norwegian representatives exhibit the highest degree of integration into their respective political systems among all Western European right-wing populist parties.

The 1980s saw the founding and breakthrough of those parties that have since constituted the hard core of European right-wing populism: The Front National in France, Vlaams Blok (later: Vlaams Belang) in Belgium, and Lega Nord in Italy. Having been founded in 1956, the Austrian Freedom Party (FPÖ) was transformed into a right-wing populist party by Jörg Haider during this period. The Front National had already been established by Jean-Marie Le Pen in 1972 but failed to make any significant headway until the early 1980s. No enduring success was to be achieved by the Republikaner in Germany, a party founded by CSU defectors in 1983 that obtained several spectacular election results at the state level (in Berlin and Baden-Württemberg) before once again disappearing into oblivion in the mid-1990s.

During the 1990s, right-wing populism would spread to virtually all corners of Europe. The initial late arrivals to the hard core were Forza Italia, a party established by Italian media mogul Silvio Berlusconi to unite different strains of the right, and the Swiss People's Party, firmly placed on a right-wing populist ideological footing by Christoph Blocher. The 2000s saw the emergence of the Dutch Lijst Pim Fortuyn, out of whose remnants Geert Wilders formed his Partij voor de Vrijheid in 2006, the United Kingdom Independence Party (UKIP), which had already been established in 1993 but did not achieve its electoral breakthrough until the 2009 European elections, the Finns Party – likewise founded in the 1990s as a successor to the Finnish Rural Party in 1995 – which came in third in the 2011 Finnish general election as it secured a fivefold increase of its share of the vote, and the Alternative for Germany (AfD), founded in 2013. In Sweden, where attempts by the right-wing populist New Democracy to establish themselves on the political stage had failed in the 1990s, the far-right Sweden Democrats were able to increase their share of the vote from 5.7 percent in the 2010 to 17.5 percent in the 2018 parliamentary election (Decker et al.).

The MoVimento 5 Stelle (Five Star Movement), founded in 2009 by Italian blogger and comedian Beppe Grillo, constitutes a special case in the world of European populism (Lanzone). While the party – without having a decidedly leftist profile – appears more at home within the left-wing populist family from a policy perspective, it did join UKIP and the Sweden Democrats in the right-wing European parliamentary group "Europe of Freedom and Direct Democracy" (EFDD). In the Italian parliamentary election of 2018 the party received 32.7 percent of the vote, coming in first before the governing Partito Democratico (18.7 percent) and the right-wing populist Lega (17.4 percent).

Causes and Reasons behind their Emergence

Populist parties and movements are a product of modernization crises. They occur in a given society when its "balance of economic necessities, the socio-structural distribution of power and cultural forms of consciousness are set in motion" (Dubiel 47; translation mine). If such a social change unfolds too rapidly or produces (overly) strong upheavals, certain parts of the population will lose their sense of orientation, accompanied by status anxiety, uncertainty concerning the future, and feelings of political alienation. Populists who have exploited such developments are by no means a modern phenomenon – case in point the Populist Party (which gave its name to the phenomenon) that emerged in the late nineteenth century in the United States or the Poujadists of the French Fourth Republic. These movements materialized in different eras though, while today's populisms are defined by their shared temporal background and their simultaneous expansion across large swathes of the political world. Since accelerated globalization confronts societies with similar problems, they also exhibit the same populist reactions brought about by the negative consequences of modernization (Decker 2006: 13-15).

- Economically, these consequences present themselves through increased wage competition as well as a gradual dismantling of the welfare state which has exacerbated polarization between the rich and poor. Increasing segments of the middle class feel threatened by social decline. Those affected by such anxieties do not necessarily have to suffer objective losses (in terms of income or employment). Far more crucial is a perceived deterioration based on expectations or on comparison to certain reference groups. Such feelings can also be common among winners, if they believe to be taken advantage of by other groups in the struggle for the allocation of wealth.
- From a cultural perspective, globalization serves to highlight differences in lifestyles and moral orientations. Since modern migratory movements – contrary to previous eras – are increasingly made up of people from a foreign cultural realm, previously homogeneous nations will sooner or later be transformed into multi-ethnic and multicultural societies. The injection of foreign elements is perceived by some parts of the native population as invariably leading to the loss of their own national culture. Moreover, this loss is exacerbated by the fact that individualization processes have severed other group affiliations.
- Social anxieties and alienation ultimately give rise to the sentiment of a lack of political representation among certain segments of society. Facing a proliferation in impediments concerning the utilization of its sovereign capability to act as a result of globalization, the state is no longer capable of readily compensating for this development through increases in efficiency. Lost

capabilities to pursue policies can be regained at least partially at the supra- and transnational level; however, precisely through this change, they are at the same time removed from mechanisms of democratic control and influence that have thus far been found exclusively at the level of the nation state.

Indications of a gradual deterioration in the potential of populist mobilization in the early 2000s were wholly reversed by the ubiquitous specter of Islamic terrorism that first came to the fore on September 11, 2001, sharp increases in the number of refugees since 2013 as a result of the civil wars in the Middle East, and worsening living conditions across vast parts of the African continent and the Balkans, as well as the financial and eurozone crisis that broke out in 2007. While anxieties and outright fears concerning Islam lent themselves to being exploited by far-right critics of immigration, the financial and eurozone crisis provided critics of the "neoliberal" modernization project – both on the left and right – with additional support. Its drawbacks had already become increasingly apparent in Europe during the 1990s, instigating an about-face even among those right-wing populist actors that had previously been pro-European such as the Lega Nord as these parties subsequently transformed themselves into some of the most ardent Eurosceptics instead. According to their line of argument, the European Union has come to represent all that is detrimental about modernization: material losses in wealth, a multicultural 'inundation' by foreigners, and a crisis of political representation. A concrete culprit for the usually rather abstract process of globalization has thereby been found.

The causes behind the emergence are reflected in the structure of the electorate of populist parties. Evidence to support the "losers of modernization"-thesis can be found both in terms of demographics as well as ideological preferences. Men, young and middle-aged cohort groups, as well as those with a low and medium level of formal education are overrepresented among their electorate. As "neoliberalism" began to be embraced by an ever-increasing share of policy makers in the 1990s, right-wing populism expanded its appeal beyond the entrepreneurial "petite bourgeoisie" into the working class and unemployed. The structure of its electorate therefore began to more closely resemble that of its left-wing populist and socialist competitors. In terms of policy preferences and general opinions, political dissatisfaction, xenophobic attitudes, and a lack of social trust, among others, have been shown to correlate with a readiness to vote for populist parties. As many voters of leftist parties also subscribe to conservative-authoritarian values, the electorates of both right and left-wing populists overlap in this instance as well (Ivaldi).

Shifting the spotlight towards individual parties highlights that along with the general causes several other – system and context-specific – factors warrant interpretation. Based on the classification as depicted above, country-specific differences should be at their most pronounced with respect to political conflicts, seeing as they are primarily rooted in historical, institutional, and cultural characteristics of a given political system. Case in point is Austria, a country in which the political cartel of the Social Democrats (SPÖ) and People's Party (ÖVP), usually euphemistically portrayed as merely guided by a desire for consensus, have played a key role in legitimizing the anti-establishment rhetoric employed by the FPÖ.

Economic and cultural factors also provide diverging data. Starting with Hitler's rise in the 1930s, the notion that far-right parties thrive primarily during periods of economic upheaval, when both unemployment and inflation are on the rise, has become commonplace in the social sciences. Assessing the electoral results of European right and left-wing populists since the outbreak of the eurozone crisis presents a different picture though. While leftist representatives such as Syriza, Podemos, or the Five Star Movement have mainly flourished in the crisis-hit countries of southern Europe, right-wing parties have on their part seen their electoral fortunes increase in countries that escaped the crisis relatively unscathed: Austria, Denmark, France, Germany, the Netherlands, and Sweden.

This, first of all, points to a difference in the dominant cleavage: In southern Europe, economics has trumped culture, in the more affluent north of the continent, cultural conflicts have taken precedence over economic ones (Rodrik). It secondly also exposes the ideological implications of the conflicting interests generated by the debt crisis. Criticism of austerity policies that supposedly reduced the southern periphery to subservient actors constrained by the orders of the so-called 'institutions' could be voiced in the most credible manner by the populist left, whereas the rejection of any form of transfer union that would rob EU member states of national responsibility and independence provided the populist right with the perfect theme.

Typology and Ideological Varieties

Populism can attach itself to different ideological and programmatic contents. While leftist forms of populism are primarily at home in Latin America, they constitute a recent phenomenon in southern Europe. The rest of Europe is – as illustrated – dominated by right-wing populism. Whether populism by itself contains ideological attributes is still a cause of disagreement. Its rigorous defense of the people against the elites emphasizes individual freedom and a simultaneous necessity for the inclusion into a shared community. This leads to a broad spectrum of policy positions that provides populism with the appearance of merely being a "thin" or hyphenated ideology. Addressee and ideological foundation of all forms of populism is the "people" as an ideal providing a sense of identity. Rather than recognize the complex nature of modern societies, populists emphasize moral values and virtues (Müller). What exactly constitutes the people depends on the ideological alignment.

Parties of the right primarily focus on national identity, while groups on the left are more likely to direct appeals to the social status of workers and the unemployed. Common to both movements is the portrayal of the specific interests of their voters as the 'true' will of the people.

The dominance of the right-wing variety of populism in Western Europe can be explained by empirical and theoretical reasons. The empirical explanation points to the increasing salience of the cultural (value-related) cleavage in party systems, a change that initially led to the rise of new social movements during the 1970s and the subsequent emergence of green (ecologist) parties before new populist parties – in the same vein as a 'postmaterialist' counterreaction from the right – took shape during the 1980s.

The theoretical explanation emphasizes the innate relationship between right-wing reasoning and populist ideology. First of all, the juxtaposition of the simple, common people and a disconnected elite is said to lend itself to also conceiving of the people as a homogeneous entity. The inherent exclusion at the horizontal level of individuals or groups in society not deemed to be part of the people is seen as a distinguishing feature of the right compared to the universalist principles of the left. Secondly, despite its anti-liberal and anti-pluralist inclinations, the core of populism is presented as containing an individualist approach that affirms personal responsibility and rejects the imposition of values at the hands of the government along with a collectively imposed "mandatory solidarity" (Lasch). And third, populism is portrayed as inherently backwards-looking, as it expresses a desire to preserve an anachronistic conception of society that has been rendered obsolete by modernization processes, romanticizing the past as a 'golden age.'

Out of the three arguments, the final one rests on the weakest foundations. Holding onto or preserving the past is by no means an exclusive domain of the right anymore (if it indeed ever was) but has by now also become a central objective of the left – take for example the fight to protect the environment and combat climate change or the preservation of a welfare state that has come under pressure as a result of international competition. While this points to certain potential common policy preferences among populists on the left and right, the two initial arguments, at the same time, highlight the scope of ideological positions found within the populist right.

Dutch political scientist Cas Mudde – whose comparative assessment of European right-wing populism still represents the best account in this field – equates the populist party family with the radical right. Nativism and authoritarianism are identified by him as the primary ideological components. Nativism stands for an illiberal (but not necessarily racist or ethno-nationalist) variety of nationalism that strives for a culturally as homogeneous as possible nation state, free from 'foreign' people and ideas. Threats to said homogeneity can emanate from conflicts that have arisen due to immigration or the presence of different nationalities/ethnicities within a country, a diverging approach that distinguishes most Western and Central-Eastern European representatives of the radical right from one another. The definition of authoritarianism on its part is in line with the classic socio-psychological understanding of the Frankfurt School which considers a desire to hold onto traditional moral values and the belief in a hierarchical order of society as the core of an authoritarian personality.

Mudde's definition builds upon the widely-held stance present in more recent research that argues for 'identity' to constitute the key theme of populism on the right. Its most important source remains the nation to this day, which is nonetheless no longer solely (or primarily) interpreted in an individual sense but is instead embedded in the notion of a common (Western) European cultural realm whose antithesis can be found in the primarily non-Western immigrant population. The problem of Mudde's definition is that it outlines the ideological core of populist identity politics too narrowly. On the one hand, parties like the Front National, Vlaams Blok/Belang, or the Sweden Democrats illustrate that right-wing populism can be closely associated with racist and extremist positions. At the same time though, it can also be incorporated into non-nativist notions of society and socially more liberal positions, demonstrated by Pim Fortuyn, whose criticism of Islam was solely based on the liberal and democratic values of the West – the separation of church and state, equality between men and women, and the freedom of sexual orientation.

The economic policies of right-wing populist actors are just as multifaceted as their 'identity politics.' During their initial emergence, virtually all representatives still pursued a 'neoliberal' path before protectionist positions began to gain the upper hand in most parties during the 1990s. Rather than dismantle the welfare state, calls were now made to defend, if not even expand it. Part of this strategy was to vociferously oppose European policies that were solely concerned with tearing down market barriers. This shift to the left on the one hand reflected the changing electoral base of these new parties of the right, while populist demands concerning social policies at the same time also lent themselves to being attached to the identitarian core topics of limiting immigration and their criticism of multiculturalism. Right-wing populists thereby managed to make inroads into the electorate of leftist parties or prevent the emergence of left-wing populist competitors altogether. The belief of one's own prosperity being threatened by the illegitimate utilization of the welfare state at the hands of a third party (be they immigrants or members of other ethnic groups), a stance known as 'welfare chauvinism,' has fallen and is falling on particularly fertile ground in countries with a robust economy that have a comparatively comprehensive welfare state.

Organizational Features

From an organizational perspective, populist challengers also display certain traits that differentiate them from representatives of the political mainstream. Today, the latter are usually subsumed under the banner of the 'electoral-professional party,' a term coined by Angelo Panebianco that represents a modernized version of the political party run by members and officials. The newcomers on their part can be separated into three organizational types that differ from the mainstream model, with a certain extent of overlap among them. Also taking a cue from Panebianco's terminology, the first type can be referred to as a charismatic party. A majority of both right and left-wing populists fall into this category. These parties tend to coalesce around a single individual who as head of the party usually also acted as the driving force behind its initial establishment. Institutional structures and democratic procedures take a backseat to the authority of the leader; loyal adherence is the guiding principle. The second organizational type, embodied by Silvio Berlusconi's Forza Italia, is established by a business person who provides a significant share of its funding while running the party like a conventional business enterprise. This type of entrepreneurial party places a smaller emphasis on ideology than its populist counterpart while nonetheless resembling it in a variety of other ways; it represents a specific form of the electoral party. The third type is the movement or framework party. Its organization is limited to a loosely associated network of activists, emanating from within society. Examples can be found in Beppe Grillo's Five Star Movement in Italy or Emmanuel Macron's République en Marche in France both of which at the same time exhibit certain traits of the charismatic type. In the United States, populist movements, which get along without a strong leader, have a long tradition. A recent case is the Tea Party.

That populism bears the hallmarks of a movement is, on the one hand, illustrated by the fact that its representatives generally are not spin-offs of existing parties but instead have their roots within society. At the same time, its movement character is also based on the ideological understanding of an anti-parties-party. Criticism of representative institutions and the promotion of providing the electorate with more avenues to directly decide on political matters represent two sides of the same coin in the populist interpretation of democracy. The emphasis placed on charismatic leadership also rests on the populist concept of a uniform will of the people that is apparently best represented by a single individual at the very top of the party. Relying on this figure is nonetheless risky as their initially perhaps untarnished reputation is bound to wither sooner or later. The importance of charisma for populism therefore has certain caveats. It is present during the party's initial emergence in particular – its founding and electoral breakthroughs are indeed usually owed to prominent leaders. Most parties have nonetheless been capable of not just surviving but actually prospering after the exit of said figures. In the wake of this institutional consolidation, their movement character weakened and their organizational form increasingly resembled that of mainstream parties.

In several countries, laws and regulations concerning the organizational structure of political parties impose a process of institutionalization anyway. German political activists, for example, lack the capacity to establish a party run by a single dominant leader provided with the ability to have the last word on all matters because the country's constitution and political parties act place stringent democratic requirements on a party's 'internal organization.' That the participatory rights provided to a party's rank and file obstruct the task of building a party organization in a controlled manner is illustrated by the publicly waged battles over the direction and personal makeup of the AfD that preceded its split in July of 2015. Internal democratic stipulations therefore present a bigger impediment to the potential success of this group of populist challengers than electoral laws or party financing provisions. This problem is exacerbated by the populists' plebiscitary understanding of democracy, which logically requires an application to its internal organization as well. A corollary of this, for example, is the AfD's preference for asking members rather than delegates to decide on a variety of matters. The model of having two or even three party leaders that stand on an equal footing is moreover an organizational element that has thus far only been employed by leftist parties in Germany (Greens and the Left Party).

The Belated Arrival of Right-wing Populism in the Federal Republic

For decades, Germany was a blank spot on the map of European right-wing populism. Both with a sense of astonishment and irritation Germans reacted to the rise of new right-wing parties in neighboring countries, a process that began in the 1970s. Their leaders quickly gained notoriety: Jean-Marie Le Pen, Jörg Haider, Silvio Berlusconi, Pim Fortuyn. The Federal Republic on the other hand appeared to be immune to this virus (Bornschier). Sporadic success at the ballot box of various right-wing parties did indeed occur but was limited to regional elections. These new challengers were neither able to pool their resources within an effective organizational structure, nor was any single group – for example the Republikaner that entered the political stage with relatively promising prospects in 1983 – able to achieve lasting success (Decker 2008).

The Alternative for Germany's (AfD) emergence has dramatically changed this dynamic. Having failed to cross the five percent-threshold by the slimmest of margins as a three-month-old party in the September 2013 federal election, it subsequently entered the European parliament as well as all state parliaments for which elections have been held since, in the process sometimes even obtaining robust double-digit figures. So it was no surprise, that the right-wing populists came in as the largest of the four opposition parties in the federal election of September 2017 with a 12.6 percent share of the vote.

Although the topic that has formed the basis for its recent success – the refugee crisis – was playing a less prominent role at the beginning of the election year, there is little reason to believe the AfD will disappear any time soon. Germany will therefore – at least in the medium-term future – have to get used to a political environment that has been present in neighboring countries for a number of years now as right-wing populism has become a common, sometimes even widely accepted feature of the respective countries' political systems.

If that is indeed the case, three questions present themselves: What are the reasons behind the AfD's success? Why has the party emerged at this moment in time? And does the AfD stand a chance of permanently establishing itself in the German party system beyond the 2017 election year?

Comparative research shows that it usually requires an initial spark, a certain "populist moment" (Goodwyn) for these parties or movements to emerge. In the AfD's case this role was played by the financial and eurozone crisis, which opened a 'window of opportunity' for a new eurosceptic party. Its core demands – a controlled dissolution of the currency union and rejection of any further European integration – perfectly lent themselves to the attachment of a broader right-wing populist platform that linked an opposition to the establishment (as the essential element of populism) to an antagonist stance concerning the topic of immigration and other socio-cultural policies.

Several circumstances assisted the AfD in this effort. First of all, it was able to build upon a number of organizations that had preceded it, from the disbanded anti-euro party Bund freier Bürger (Alliance of Free Citizens) to the conservative campaign network Zivile Koalition, established by one of the AfD's MEPs, Beatrix von Storch. The Sarrazin-debate in 2010 most certainly also played a role in paving the path for right-wing populism. It was triggered by a former SPD-politician and senator of the state of Berlin, who published a book that depicted the history of the integration of foreigners in the Federal Republic as a complete failure. Sarrazin's comments were dismissed by government and party officials (including Chancellor Angela Merkel) but seemed to fall on fertile grounds within parts of the electorate. The reception showed that xenophobic populist attitudes did not appear out of thin air with the arrival of the AfD.

Secondly, the programmatic course of the center-right CDU/CSU and FDP and their actions in government after 2009 opened a void in the party system. While the liberals could not play the role of a more eurosceptic actor in government after a referendum among its members narrowly backed the government's eurozone rescue policies, the Christian Democrats on their part abandoned long-held positions on family and socio-cultural policies under Angela Merkel (recognizing same-sex partnerships, the introduction of a gender quota in the boardrooms of German companies, or the support for a modern immigration law) that are now occupied by the AfD.

And third of all, the newcomer profited from presenting an outward appearance wholly rooted in the educated middle class as the party's most prominent defectors were all former Christian and Free Democrats; scholars themselves initially classified the party as "right-wing liberal or conservative" rather than already applying the "right-wing populist" label to it. A central role was played by Bernd Lucke who despite a lack of charisma represented the driving force behind the party's establishment and would as its leading figure become the AfD's most prominent public face during the party's initial ascent.

This enabled the AfD to overcome most of the restrictive conditions that have historically prevented right-wing populism from achieving a nationwide breakthrough in Germany (Decker 2016). Particularly conspicuous within the European context is the inability to mobilize the electorate on the basis of the issue of 'foreigners,' a policy area whose politicization had been avoided by all of the Federal Republic's parties (bar the Greens). This also applied to the SPD, whose support for a more restrictive asylum law in the early 1990s was contingent upon the passage of a modern immigration act, a provision it subsequently never delivered upon though.

Cultural conflicts of recognition brought about by the integration of migrants were therefore addressed discretely – preventing them from bursting out into the open was seen as paramount. Beneficial to this pursuit was the fact that the primarily Turkish Muslim migrants in Germany proved to be easier to integrate than their counterparts from the Maghreb in France for example.

The primary responsibility for rejecting changes to Germany's immigration law and a recognition that immigrants had now become an integral part of German society lay in the hands of the Christian democratic sister parties, a stance that caused both the eighties and nineties to be lost decades in terms of integration but admittedly also allowed the center-right to reliably defend its right flank against any challengers. Sharing the burden between the CDU and the at times openly populist Bavarian sister party CSU proved to be just as useful as the continued existence of national-conservative traditions within a strong right wing. In Eastern Germany, where the potential for right-wing populist success was and continues to remain higher than in the West despite or perhaps because of a smaller presence of foreigners, advances by the far right were hampered by the post-communist PDS that presented itself to voters as the real "protest alternative" in this part of the country.

Should these conditions now disappear or subside, right-wing populism will find a rather favorable environment in terms of the electorate. Considering the immense challenges and pressure to change which German society will face in future years and decades as a result of immigration, it would be rather surprising if a party critical of a migrant influx such as the AfD were incapable of exploiting these developments for its own electoral profit. Even after the government's restoration of some control over the influx of refugees entering the country, the party will therefore have plenty of thematic opportunities at its disposal. At the same time, it is capable of using its conservative socio-cultural positions to fill other representation gaps within the party system (Berbuir et al.).

One constraint that still distinguishes Germany from other European countries could nonetheless prove to be an obstacle for the AfD's path forward: the political and social stigmatization of right-wing extremism, a legacy of the Nazi era that continues to loom large over the country. The question whether right-wing populism's past weakness in Germany is in some way linked to the sometimes quite militant right-wing extremism that has seen a rise since the country's reunification has strangely enough not garnered much attention among scholars. At least from an organizational perspective, a connection appears self-evident. Precisely because of its stigmatization, right-wing extremists seek to use right-wing populist parties and movements as a politically presentable vehicle (Karapin). All attempts to establish a new far-right party in the Federal Republic have eventually fallen victim to these unwanted supporters – from the Republikaner, to the Bund freier Bürger, and the Schill-Party in Hamburg. Will the AfD suffer the same fate?

A closer look at the party's short history indicates it may potentially head down a similar path. Just as Bernd Lucke failed in his endeavor to prevent the radicalization of the AfD before Frauke Petry ousted him as co-chair, his successor suffered a similar fate as she left the AfD and the Bundestag party group shortly after the national election of September 2017 (for which she was an AfD-candidate). The problem of a blurring of the lines between the party and the extreme-right fringe of society is made particularly evident by the party leadership's handling of Björn Höcke, head of the AfD's Thuringia state branch and someone, who, as the leading figure of its nationalist wing, maintains open ties to the New Right, a movement found in the vicinity of the NPD. Infighting over leadership positions as well as disagreements concerning the future policy direction of the party and the less than professional appearance of the party's largely inexperienced cadre of officials and parliamentarians places additional strains on the AfD's public image.

Along with the demand-side opportunities, the power resources that have in the meantime been obtained by the AfD within the political and party systems nonetheless point towards a medium-term establishment of the party at the very least. Its parliamentary presence alone (the Bundestag, all 16 state legislatures and the European parliament) provides the party with a substantial organizational strength. At the same time, the AfD is not dependent on access to the traditional media to obtain support since it is able to address its voters directly through social networks. Combined, these two factors mitigate the need for a charismatic leadership figure at the head of Germany's populist radical right, an observation that qualifies the importance scholarly research into right-wing populism usually places on this aspect.

Impact and Strategies to Combat Populism

Populist challengers have had a lasting impact on the party systems of Europe's democracies. Usage of the 'protest party' label misses the staying power this phenomenon has shown. A more appropriate moniker would be to refer to these more recently emerged parties as 'mouthpieces of discontent' that serve to both expose and offset representation gaps present among established political actors. In this sense, and provided they move within constitutional boundaries, populists potentially fulfill a useful role for democracy.

The stipulation "potentially" is important. It indicates that the challenged parties have a variety of ways to respond to the challengers. This goes beyond the straightforward suggestion of "adaptation or isolation" that is so frequently cited. It, for example, makes a difference whether the style and methods of populism are adopted or if the incorporation extends to actual policy contents. Isolation does not preclude appropriating certain subject matters or even positions championed by the undesired competitors. A strategy of adaptation can, on the other hand, also coincide with fierce verbal attacks against populist actors (Decker 2004: 264-70).

Furthermore, what exactly do both isolation and adaptation refer to? Addressing the problems and topics that have been raised by challengers by no means suggests that established parties also share the answers or solutions proposed by the former. It is one of populism's defining features that it fails to provide any such answers. Or the complex nature of the problems at hand are completely ignored. When politicians and parties accuse one another of populism, they usually refer to this particular trait.

Populism's inability to draw up concrete and extensive policy proposals is not necessarily a drawback in the eyes of its supporters though (Downs). If that were the case, populist parties would only be able to maintain their credibility on the opposition benches. Reality has somewhat disproven this assumption. While the Pim Fortuyn List in the Netherlands and Freedom Party in Austria both hemorrhaged electoral support after their entry into government, the continued success of the Swiss People's Party illustrates that an opposition to European integration, skepticism towards immigration, and an anti-Islamic stance are compatible with being in government. Italy was also governed for a prolonged period by the right-wing populist alliance between Berlusconi's Forza Italia and the Lega Nord. While the Danish People's Party (DF) merely tolerated various liberal-conservative cabinets between 2001 and 2011, it nonetheless heavily influenced their policy direction. Its pressure brought about a tightening of immigration and asylum laws while acting as a catalyst for efforts to renationalize EU policies. A revival of the center-right alliance tolerated by the DF in 2015 (with the party having become the strongest representative of the center-right camp) could once again see the party increase its clout.

An alternative approach can be found in countries whose political players have formed a cordon sanitaire around populist competitors, keeping them at an arm's length on virtually every topic. Any sort of cooperation with the Sweden Democrats is for example eschewed in the Scandinavian country as even informal talks are out of the question. All established representatives have essentially entered a competition of disassociating themselves to the largest extent possible from the immigration and asylum policies of the right-wing challenger. If the intended goal was to put an end to the rise of the populist radical right in Sweden, the country's liberal approach proved just as much a failure as the Danish strategy of adaptation. The 2018 parliamentary election in Sweden saw the local right-wing populist matching the results of its counterparts in the neighboring Scandinavian countries as the Sweden Democrats obtained 17.5 percent of the vote.

What are the recommendations then concerning how to respond to the rise of populist radical right parties in light of the failure these differing strategies have shown themselves to be? Along with confronting the topic head on in the political arena, a recommendation that goes without saying, four objectives appear essential to tackle the root cause of these social and political problems:

First, both at the national and European levels there is a need for a brand of politics that puts a stronger emphasis on the economic and social cohesion of societies. An appreciation for the role the welfare state has played in guaranteeing this cohesion is increasingly lacking. This is particularly evident when focusing on international competition: As economies become more open to the outside world, not only do education and training (to withstand said competition) increase in value and importance but so does a safety net against the domestic risks competition invariably entails. Should politics fail to establish a society based on equal opportunities and fairness it will also not succeed in diminishing the potential of populism.

Populism must, second, be confronted on its home turf – the politics of values. This constitutes a particular challenge for social democrats whose understanding of values is of a more materialist nature. They can only recoup their losses, however, by challenging the far-right 'counter modernization' with a non-regressive model of a good society of their own that takes into account a widespread desire to belong present among the population. This applies in particular to immigration policies (Collier). Just as one needs to take on the perfidious right-wing populist approach of turning social conflicts into purely cultural or national ones, one should not fall victim to the temptation of reducing cultural differences (and how they are handled) to a purely social problem.

Politicians also need to make clear why, third, regulating markets at the European and transnational levels, while relinquishing national competences for this task (or at least expressing a willingness to), is nonetheless in the national interest. This challenge presents itself in the conduct with populists on both the right and left. A population that has grown increasingly weary of the European integration project can only be won back if the burden of the social and cultural side effects of events in the markets are no longer shouldered solely by domestic political institutions. In other fields – for example foreign and defense policy – the onus is on political elites to show more fortitude and move towards greater integration as public hostility is in this case not the reason for the continued persistence of approaching problems from a national perspective.

And fourth, parties must bring down barriers between themselves and the population at large. This requires an adjustment in how parties conceive of both representation and organization, thereby constituting a break from today's model of a top-down led party made up of members and officials. Another question to be considered is whether and how to complement representative party democracy through direct democratic means of participation – ensuring that right-wing populists are no longer the exclusive proponents of such reforms. Most of all, a new culture of listening and interaction is necessary. The indispensable engagement with the people that is central to any democracy does not require a politician to follow popular opinion but instead seeks to provide citizens with a voice. This entails knowing the everyday realities of voters or at least not making a conscious effort of avoiding them.

Works Cited

Berbuir, Nicole, Marcel Lewandowsky, and Jasmin Siri. "The AfD and Its Sympathisers: Finally a Right-Wing Populist Movement in Germany?" *German Politics* 24.2 (2015): 154-78.

Bornschier, Simon. "Why a Right-Wing Populist Party Emerged in France but not in Germany: Cleavages and Actors in the Formation of a New Cultural Divide." *European Political Science Review* 4.1 (2012): 121-45.

Collier, Paul. *Exodus. Immigration and Multiculturalism in the 21st Century.* London: Allen Lane, 2014.

Decker, Frank. "The 'Alternative für Deutschland.' Factors Behind Its Emergence and Profile of a New Right-wing Populist Party." *German Politics and Society* 34.2 (2016): 1-16.

---. "Populism in Germany: Right-wing Failures and Left-wing Successes?" *Twenty-First Century Populism. The Spectre of Western European Democracy.* Ed.

Daniele Albertazzi, and Duncan McDonnell. Basingstoke: Palgrave Macmillan, 2008. 119-34.

---. "Die populistische Herausforderung. Theoretische und ländervergleichende Perspektiven". *Populismus. Gefahr für die Demokratie oder nützliches Korrektiv?* Ed. Frank Decker. Wiesbaden: VS Verlag, 2006. 9-32.

---. *Der neue Rechtspopulismus*. Opladen: Leske und Budrich. 2nd ed. 2004.

Decker, Frank, Bernd Henningsen, and Kjetil A. Jakobsen (eds.). *Rechtsextremismus in Europa. Die Herausforderung der Zivilgesellschaft durch alte Ideologien und neue Medien*. Baden-Baden: Nomos, 2015.

Downs, William. *Political Extremism in Democracies. Combating Intolerance*. Basingstoke: Palgrave Macmillan, 2012.

Dubiel, Helmut. "Das Gespenst des Populismus." *Populismus und Aufklärung*. Ed. Helmut Dubiel. Frankfurt a.M.: Suhrkamp, 1986. 33-50.

Giusto, Hedwig, David Kitching, and Stefan Rizzo (eds.). *The Changing Faces of Populism. Systemic Challengers in Europe and the U.S.* Brussels/Rome: Foundation for European Progressive Studies et al. 2013.

Goodwyn, Lawrence. *Democratic Promise. The Populist Movement in America*. New York: Oxford University Press, 1976.

Heinisch, Reinhard, Christina Holtz-Bacha, and Oscar Mazzoleni (eds.). *Political Populism. A Handbook*. Baden-Baden: Nomos, 2017.

Ivaldi, Gilles. "Electoral Bases of Populist Parties". Heinisch, Holtz-Bacha, and Mazzoleni. 157-68.

Karapin, Roger. "Explaining Far-Right Electoral Successes in Germany. The Politicization of Immigration-Related Issues." *German Politics and Society* 16.1 (1998): 24-61.

Lanzone, Maria Elisabetta. "The Post-Modern Populism in Italy. The Case of the Five Star Movement". *The Many Faces of Populism: Current Perspectives*. Ed. Dwayne Woods, and Barbara Wejnert. Bingley: Emerald Group Publishing, 2014. 53-78.

Lasch, Christopher. *The Revolt of the Elites and the Betrayal of Democracy*. New York: W.W. Norton, 1995.

Mudde, Cas. *Populist Radical Right Parties in Europe*. New York: Cambridge University Press, 2007.

Müller, Jan-Werner. *What Is Populism?* Philadelphia: University of Pennsylvania Press, 2016.

Panebianco, Angelo. *Political Parties. Organization and Power*. Cambridge: Cambridge University Press, 1988.

Rodrik, Dani. *Populism and the Economics of Globalization*. CEPR Discussion Paper No. 12119, 2017.

"We the People": Popular Sovereignty, National Identity, and the Democratic Principle

Jürgen Gebhardt

After the breakdown of the Soviet empire, a jubilant West embraced the vision that "the movement toward democracy seemed to take on the character of an almost irresistible global tide moving from one triumph to the next" (Huntington 316). In the late twentieth century, the prevailing assumption was that the historical process of 'modernization' would bring forth a single homogenized political world that would be modeled normatively on the Western type of the constitutional democratic state, i.e., on liberal democracy. But this assumption turned out to be yet another case of failed political prophesy. The once self-assertive and strong willed Western democracies are undergoing a serious political upheaval that involves bitter partisan infighting and which is characterized by a populist refutation of the democratic consensus.

However, the populist movement is just one symptom of the manifold conflicts that trouble the United States and the European Union and which fuel centrifugal forces in the once politically unified West. Seen from this perspective populism is part of a growing trend toward national identity politics and the reassertion of national sovereignties in the transatlantic community as a whole. As such, populism threatens the role and the political agency of the West as a global actor in the evolving multi-polar political world of powerful and sovereign states.

In the remarks that follow, I will analyze the so-called populist complex – its origins, forms, and contents – from a theoretical and historical point of view. This will permit us to take a more precise approach to the question that concerns us here, popular government. With my historical argument, I hope to re-frame the Euro-Atlantic predicament in terms of its global setting. I will conclude my remarks with a few apodictically formulated historical reflections in order to trace the grave tensions within and among today's democracies back to their historical origins in the fundamental ideas of democratic political order: the 'people' and the 'nation.' For both now, and at critical junctures in the past, the notions of the 'people' and of the 'nation' have strongly shaped the cultural and institutional make-up of modern politics.

The Conundrum of a Specter

"A specter is haunting the world – the specter of populism" – proclaimed the editors of a 1969 collection of essays that covered manifestations of populism in various countries and regions (Ionescu et al. 1). The authors surveyed a whole set of social and political phenomena which they subsumed under the generic term 'populism.' Here, as elsewhere, the term referred to social, political, and ideological movements and organizations; sometimes it merely referred to forms of public agency – often negatively connoted. In the late twentieth and early twenty-first century, the term populism became one of the main political buzzwords (Mudde et al. 1). As far as mainstream social science is concerned, it is a well-known fact that populism is a genuine phenomenon of American politics, that indeed the term and its meaning originated in the course of the formation of one of the many third parties, the Populist (originally People's) Party, that emerged in the late nineteenth century at a critical moment in post-civil-war America. However, the term was soon generalized to denote the various movements of economic and political reform (right-wing or left-wing) that operated throughout the country.

"The populist philosophy," states a chronicler, "[…] boils down finally to two fundamental propositions; one, that government must restrain the selfish tendencies of those who profited at the expense of the poor and needy; the other, that the people not the plutocrats, must control the government" (Hicks 406).

Looking ahead briefly to the following section of my argument, let me state here that American populists responded critically to the existing system of representative government and proclaimed the political alternative of direct democracy. This response was modeled on the semi-direct democracy of Switzerland and established direct-democratic systems in many American states (Cronin 48-51). The current discourse on populism largely ignores the fact that the populist movement initiated the systems of direct democratic rule that thrive in America. In the United States populist politics are a living force that reaches into the highest levels of national politics. A closer look at the historical strands of American populism that go back to the American Revolution and the struggle over the institutional principles of a truly popular government will illuminate this point. Below, I will go into the history of populism's role in the United States in more detail. But for now, let us recall that in the 1960s and 70s, American students of populism were well aware of this tradition when they discussed the neo-populism of both the right and the left. For populism extended well beyond the southern racist and chauvinist positions of George Wallace and his third party; it also characterized the democratic politics of George McGovern. And it found expression again in the evangelical reform populism of President Jimmy Carter and, most recently, in the election of President Trump.

Political scientist Peter Lösche, a prominent analyst of American political culture, showed in his in-depth analysis of American populism, past and present, its self-contradictory character that prevents a clear-cut conceptual definition (Lösche 145). Indeed, he denied that the term 'populism' is a category of social science; it must be understood within its historical context and in this regard it needs to be carefully described (Lösche 142).

The Predicament of the European Project

However, others dropped Lösche's scholarly reserve when they found themselves confronted with the slow shift of the Western-European party system that had previously been dominated by a more or less stable balance between a right and a left political block. Up until the 1970s, and within the European community that was evolving along the lines of the super-national construct of the common market, it was believed that Europe "wouldn't see anything resembling American populism" (Judis 88). Yet things changed with the breakdown of the bipolar order and the crucial step of building a European Union that sought to include the Eastern and Central European states that had formerly been part of the Soviet Block.

However, before I deal with the specific problem of the European project's predicament that has emerged in the course of the last decades, let me take a brief look at the historical rise of so-called European populism.

In France and other Euro-States (Germany being the exception), small rightist and leftist parties have always existed. They criticized the European enterprise that, according to them, for economic and social reasons distanced itself in principle from a Europe based on a nation-centered historical system of independent states. The critics insisted on the need for the self-assertion of national traditions. In a way, this national sentiment took up President de Gaulle's dictum of "L' Europe des patries" which postulated interstate cooperation – mainly between France, West Germany, Italy, and the Benelux states – under the condition of preserving the respective states' national sovereignty. Consequently, in 1963, De Gaulle prevented the entrance of Britain into the European Community. In retrospect, the tension between building a European Union and the resurgence of national sentiments in its member states brought forth political formations that claimed to speak for the true interests of 'the people,' asserting that the people had been more or less disenfranchised in the Union's institutional setup. In particular, this charge was made when it became clear that the Union carried on a policy of open borders.

Confronted with this new nationalist phenomenon, mainstream social science and the political establishment turned to the American derived term of 'populism' in search of a conceptual framework that could adequately deal with this conglomerate of new parties. Yet in Europe, and from the very beginning, leftwing and centrist politicians, the media, and academics used the term pejoratively (Judis 89). Since the early twenty-first century, much of the literature devoted to the empirical and theoretical analysis of populism has attempted to develop a theoretical framework to explain its various forms. Of course, behind these efforts looms the memory of the mass movements of National Socialism, Fascism, and Communism.

The central perspective of the European theoretical and practical discourse on populism contrasts it with the liberal pluralist rights-based representative democracy, which is taken to be the dominant form of the European democratic systems and of most of the approximately forty Western-type polities. The public discourse on populism views it as a threat to democracy per se and sees it as a force that tends to undermine the present political culture. However, strangely enough, a survey of the growing literature on European populism reveals that it actually understates the nationalist aspect. It plays down the growing misgivings of parts of the electorate worried about the unlimited power of party elites and bureaucrats that excludes citizens from participating in decision-making on major issues. This exclusion is a problem in both individual states and in the European Union as a whole. Thus, it is no accident that populist politicians prefer – and make use of – the direct-democratic institution of mandatory and optional popular referenda in constitutional and territorial matters; an option that is available in a number of European democracies. For indeed, the historical record shows that most critical decisions concerning the future of the European Union were made in popular votes: the failure of a European constitution in 2005 was the result of negative referenda in France and the Netherlands, and the UK's 'Brexit' was also decided in a referendum. These facts make it clear that, historically, within the political culture of the European Union, the existing constitutional device of popular referenda has played a role in national decision-making and that this role extends well beyond the agenda of populist parties. Moreover, there is the particular case of the expansion of the Union. The belief that the enlargement of membership after the break-up of the Soviet Block would also consolidate the post Lisbon-Union turned out to be highly problematic. For the East-central and Southeastern countries, there was indeed but one option: join Western Europe on the latter's terms. And the new members celebrated what they called the "return to Europe" (Judd 70). However, it must also be borne in mind that for these states, emancipation from Soviet rule meant first of all the restitution of their own national identities. After all, the potential loss of nationhood had been a constant threat from the very beginning of their national existence. And the traumatic experience of such loss continues to influence their political thinking. For Poles, Czechs, and Hungarians, the return to Europe signaled the return to the historical and cultural world to which they had once belonged. Therefore, their newly acquired national self-assertiveness also valued the support of a populist vision of national self-determination. In sum: all this added up to the centrifugal national forces in the European Union in the past decades (Gebhardt 2013: 387).

Beyond a doubt, the European elites have missed the opportunity to transform the original confederation of the founding states of the European market-society into a federal union under a European constitution. And after the constitutional project had failed, in 2007 the Lisbon treaty changed the European Union into a legal entity. But it retained the constitutional hybridism of a treaty-based alliance of states that had failed to come to grips with the fundamental principle of popular sovereignty – the very foundation of modern political order. It is therefore no wonder that the decline of European communitarian and civic-political culture induces citizens in times of crisis to seek shelter under the umbrella of a national sovereignty that safeguards the interests of the people. This is the promise that is at the root of the present success of populist governments and parties in Europe.

Benjamin Barber has described this pointedly: "The crisis of liberal democracies is expressed most pungently in the claim that the world has become ungovernable, that no leader or party or constitutional system can cope with the welter of problems that afflict large industrial societies." But, "if the world has become ungovernable how can men be expected to govern themselves? How can they ask that their representatives govern them well?" And Barber concludes: "unless it takes a participatory form of democracy, democracy will pass from the political scene along with the liberal values" that made it possible (Barber xii-xiv).

In Search of the People – the Historical Quandary of Democracy

Barber's skeptical observation identifies the issue at stake: The problem is not the recent chameleon-like and omnipresent challenges of populists to the dominant model of Western representative democracy; rather the crucial point is the dilemma of popular government itself or, more generally, the idea of a democratic order.

As I pointed out above, the American populists acted within a political tradition that reaches back to the political upheaval of President Jackson's appeal to the 'common man': The populist battle cry of the 1890s was Jacksonian: "bring back the government to the people." In the last analysis, it reflected the fundamental conflict that dates from the country's founding, namely the question of how a truly republican order of civic self-government should be established.

Alexis de Tocqueville announced the "great democratic revolution" and the beginning of the overthrow of the old political world. And indeed the transatlantic democratic revolutions between 1649 and 1789 brought forth the political evocation of a novel vision of order. This vision is inherently bound up with the interrelated principles of the people – popular sovereignty – and with the idea of the nation – a state that institutionally frames the communitarian existence of the people. Tocqueville celebrated the founding of the American republic as the first and principally original form of democratic order. Here, the citizens rule themselves since they are the original fountain of power. This was the beginning of the "Novus ordo seclorum" that the founders of the American republic had proclaimed and placed on the Great Seal of the new nation in 1782 (U.S. Department of State 5). However, the 1776 revolutionary Declaration of Independence and the Constitution of 1788 actually refer back to the thought and action of the episodic and short-lived seventeenth century Commonwealth of England. This was the archetypical foundation of modern revolutionary constitutional republicanism and the pivotal event in the history of the democratic revolution. In January 1649, the so-called 'rump parliament' of heterodox Christians and republicans under the protection of the 'Bible reading' New Model Army and its charismatic leader Oliver Cromwell, "resolved that the Commons of England, in Parliament assembled, do declare, that the people are, under God the original of all just power; and do also declare that the Commons of England assembled in Parliament, being chosen by, and representing the people have the supreme power in this nation" (Kenyon 324). The Divine Right of the king was denied. King Charles I was brought before the High Court and beheaded and the king's Divine Right was replaced by the Divine Right of the people. The sectarian background of the original idea of popular sovereignty is in the famous prologue to Wycliffe's fourteenth-century translation of the Bible: The Bible is for the government of the people by the people and for the people. These words of course returned in the same symbolic formulation in Abraham Lincoln's Gettysburg Address of November 1863.

The American Revolution was not a reenactment of 1649. But the memory of this tradition resurfaced in the Declaration of Independence. Its argument followed the accusation and judgment against Charles I. However, in 1776 the High Court of Justice of 1649 was replaced by the 'the Supreme Judge of the World.'

The revolutionary establishment of constitutional government in the thirteen former colonies was marked by the controversy over the political meaning and consequence of the 'great republican principle of popular supremacy.' This debate continued in the conflict between Federalists and Anti-Federalists over a national constitution that would enable the Americans to act internationally in the concert of nations. Anti-Federalists opted for the status quo of an alliance of small agrarian republics that alone – they believed – could guarantee immediate political self-determination: every citizen "a participator in the government of affairs" (Jefferson 99). Both parties determined citizenship by manhood suffrage. But the Federalists did not define the civic body politic in terms of local community but in terms of a national body politic: Providential design provided for "one united people, a people descended from the same ancestors, speaking the same language, professing the same religion, attached to the same principles of government, very similar in their manners and customs" (Hamilton et al. 2: 7). As a consequence, they argued "that in a democracy, the people meet and exercise the government in person; in a republic they assemble and administer it by their representatives and agents. A democracy consequently, must be confined to a small spot. A republic may be extended over a large region" (Hamilton et al. 14: 63).

This was the birth of the concept of "representative democracy," a term coined by Alexander Hamilton. More extreme opponents suspected that the thirteen free republics were to be consolidated into a compound of monarchy and aristocracy, and that the president would become a military king (Kenyon xlix). This suspicion, which was to spawn so-called populist activities, was not completely unfounded.

Aside from accepting states into the Union that were ruled by an oligarchy of slave owners and thereby depriving non-whites of their civic rights, the constitutional framework limited direct election to the House of Representatives and stipulated indirect elections for the other offices of government. The attempts to establish direct democracy undertaken by later populists brought about the direct election of the members of the second house, the Senate, and introduced the system of Presidential primaries. However, they failed to abolish the Electoral College. (Had they succeeded in doing so, the populist Trump would not have won the 2016 presidential election).

The enduring success of this novel political model of representative democracy in the United States absorbed the direct-democratic basis of a latent populism. And it reminded the governing elite that the streams of national power ought to flow immediately from 'the people' – the pure and original fountain of legitimate authority (Hamilton et al. 22: 111).

But the ultimate challenge to representative democracy took place elsewhere. It was posed by the final stage of the great Atlantic Revolution in France between 1789 and 1804. Following the revolution of 1789, France underwent a series of constitutional experiments ranging from the Girondist system in 1791 of a constitutional monarchy sustained by a unitary national representative assembly, to the Jacobin democratic dictatorship, the so-called bourgeois interim semi-democratic directorial regime, and finally to Napoleon's plebiscitarian empire.

Underlying this power struggle was a historically significant metamorphosis of the idea of popular sovereignty. It first manifested itself in the alternative brought forth in the Jacobin experiment which defined the 'gouvernement revolutionnaire' as the antithesis of the 'gouvernment constitutionel' with its 'representative despotism' of parliament that a priori obscures the *single* will of the people. For parliament does not pursue the ultimate revolutionary intention of transforming man and the world in accordance with the messianic project of delivering the world from evil: "The goal of the constitutional government is to maintain the republic, the goal of the revolutionary government is to establish the republic" (Grab 215).

This latter idea of the rule of the people that is guided by the 'true interpretation' of the people's will led to the notion that a democratic dictator is the true interpreter of the 'public good.'

Still, even this option does not exhaust the revolutionary potential of the democratic principle. And, in fact, the revolution culminated in the democratic Caesarism of Napoleon Bonaparte. In recognition of popular sovereignty, he made use of the plebiscite to legitimize his coup d'état by appealing to the French people in 1799. He returned to the plebiscite in 1802 in order to make himself consul for life, and again in 1804 to make himself Emperor of France. Thus, the bonapartist regimes of Napoleon I and Napoleon III brought forth a third form of implementing the democratic principle. Tocqueville called it a one-man despotism that rests on a democratic foundation (Tocqueville 154). It legitimizes a government by calling on the will of the people in a plebiscite. This type of plebiscitary-democratic rule was established in Latin America by Simon Bolivar and has continued in various shapes to dominate the modern political landscape.

Epilogue: Max Weber – a Theorist of Populism Avant la Lettre

There is some historical evidence that the fundamental modern principle of democratic legitimacy is inherently tied up with multifaceted forms of the populist syndrome.

Reflecting on German political turmoil in 1918, the skeptical Max Weber recognized a Caesarist-plebiscitarian element in all modern mass democracies.

> Active democratisation of the masses means that the political leader [...] uses the means of mass demagogy to gain the confidence of the masses and their belief in his person, and thereby gains power. Essentially this means that the selection of the leader has shifted in the direction of Caesarism. Indeed every democracy has this tendency. (Weber 220-1).

Weber explicitly refers to the American presidential system. The parties are forced by the 'Caesarist' features of mass democracy to submit to the leadership of political strongmen that show themselves capable of winning the trust of the masses. Major concessions to the Caesarist principle of leadership selection resting on the trust of the masses (even in the United States and England) prepare the way to pure forms of Caesarist acclamation – a prophecy by Weber that became true before long. Weber diagnosed: "A Caesarist leader can rise, be excluded and fall without the danger of a domestic catastrophe occurring" – provided that governmental power is effectively shared by strong and powerful representative bodies [like the English parliament or the American Senate] and by a responsible public administration which together maintain political continuity and ensure that the constitutional guarantees of civil order are preserved (Weber 227-8). On the other hand, Weber points out, "mistrust of the impotent and, for this very reason, corrupt parliaments in the individual states in America has led to the extension of direct legislation of the people." However, under the conditions of a "pure plebiscitarian democracy [...] the power of money and the leverage of the demagogic apparatuses supported by it would assume colossal dimensions in any mass state ruled exclusively by popular elections and popular referenda" (Weber 226).

Before too long, Weber's critical view of the Caesarist-plebiscitarian potential of modern democracy was confirmed by the rise of the dictatorships of the totalitarian extremes. Moreover, Weber's empirical analysis concluded that the 'populist' moment *per se* is concomitant with the Caesarist tendencies that threaten to undermine the constitutional order of parliamentary government. The preservation of this order depends on the rational ethos of civic leadership and on stable representative institutions. Since Weber's time, political conditions have changed radically, but his insights still contribute to our understanding of the democratic age.

'We the people' proclaims the historic vision of the primordial power of the people embodied in the democratic idea. As such, it has spread over the entire world. Populism was and is the unruly child of modern mass democracy. Resurgent populisms have been the noisy combatants in power struggles over the democratic principle. This struggle is now worldwide.

Works Cited

Barber, Benjamin. *Strong Democracy: Participatory Politics for a New Age*. Berkeley: University of California Press, 1984.

Cronin, Thomas E. *Direct Democracy: The Politics of Initiative, Referendum, and Recall*. Cambridge /Mass.: Harvard University Press, 1989.

Gebhardt, Jürgen. "The Predicament of the European Project." *Analysen nationaler und supranationaler Politik: Festschrift für Roland Sturm*. Ed. Heinrich Pehle and Klaus Brummer. Berlin: Opladen, 2013. 383-96.

---. "Das Plebiszit in der Repräsentativen Demokratie." *Direkte Demokratie: Beiträge auf dem 3. Speyerer Demokratieforum vom 27. bis 29. Oktober 1999 an der Deutschen Hochschule für Verwaltungswissenschaften Speyer*. Ed. Hans Herbert v. Arnim. Berlin: Duncker & Humblot, 2000. 13-26.

---. *Americanism: Revolutionary Order and Societal Self-Interpretation in the American Republic*. Baton Rouge: Louisiana State University Press, 1993.

Grab, Walter (ed.). *Die Französische Revolution: eine Dokumentation*. München: Nymphenburger Verlagshandlung, 1973.

Hamilton Alexander, James Madison, and John Jay. *The Federalist Papers*. Ed. Garry Wills. New York: Bantam Books, 1982.

Hicks, John D. *The Populist Revolt: A History of the Farmer's Alliance and the People's Party*. Lincoln: University of Nebraska Press, 1961.

Huntington, Samuel P. *The Third Wave: Democratization in the Late Twentieth Century*. Norman: University of Oklahoma Press, 1991.

Ionescu, Ghiţa, and Ernest Gellner (eds.). *Populism: Its Meaning and National Characteristics*. New York: Macmillan, 1969.

Jefferson, Thomas. *The Political Writings of Thomas Jefferson: Representative Selection*. Ed. Edward Dumbauld. New York: Liberal Arts Press, 1955.

Judis, John B. *The Populist Explosion: How the Great Recession Transformed American and European Politics*. New York: Columbia Global Reports, 2016.

Judt, Tony. *A Grand Illusion?: An Essay on Europe*. New York, 1966.

Kenyon, Cecilia (ed.). *The Antifederalists*. Indianapolis: Bobbs-Merrill, 1968.

Lösche, Peter. *Politik in USA: Das Amerikanische Regierungs- und Gesellschaftssystem und die Präsidentsschaftswahl 1976*. Opladen: Leske, 1977.

Mudde, Cas, and Cristobal Rovira Kaltwasser. *Populism: A Very Short Introduction*. Oxford: Oxford University Press, 2017.

Müller Jan-Werner. *Was ist Populismus?: Ein Essay*. Berlin: suhrkamp, 2016.

Priester, Karin. *Rechter und Linker Populismus: Annäherung an ein Chamäleon*. Frankfurt: Campus, 2012.

Stewart, John Hall (ed.). *The Documentary Survey of the French Revolution*. New York: Macmillan, 1951.

Tanner J. R. *The English Constitutional Conflicts of the Seventeenth Century, 1603-1689*, Cambridge: University Press, 1960.

U.S. Department of State – Bureau of Public Affairs, The Great Seal of the United States, Publication Nr. 10411, Washington D.C. 1996

Weber, Max. *Political Writings*. Ed. Peter Lassman, and Ronald Speir. Cambridge: University Press, 2003.

US-Populism in the Late Nineteenth Century

Michael Hochgeschwender

At first glance, it seems relatively easy to place populism in the history of US political culture. After all, the concept developed in the USA. With the election of Donald Trump, a 'populist,' to the US presidency in 2016, it appears that populism has had an unexpected comeback at the highest level of government and in broad sections of society (see Robin; Hochschild; Stoll; Vance; Packer; Isenberg 291-323; Judis; McNichol Stock). If one wants to trace the roots of this development, one must revisit the American history of the late nineteenth century. In the 1890s in particular, a movement emerged in the United States of America which was itself populist and from whose self-designation all other populist movements have been derived ever since (Mudde et al.; White; Müller; Priester 2007, 2012). Even in interpretations of genuinely American populism in the narrower, strictly epoch-specific sense, however, historians do not agree as to whether and to what extent this late nineteenth century movement was the model for similar ideological and sociocultural formations in the history of the United States, let alone for a trans-historical systematic political concept. In the 1890s and shortly afterwards, during the Progressive Era (Chambers; McGerr; Flanagan; Lears), populism was seen as a modernizing movement (Hicks; Woodward; Miller; Wilentz), whereas in the 1940s and 1950s it was characterized by consensus-liberal historians such as Richard Hofstadter, under the influence of national socialism and the communist persecution under the Republican senator Joseph McCarthy during the early years of the Cold War, as a proto-fascist movement of anti-intellectual rural radicalism (Hofstadter 1964: 148-57, 1967: 154-60). The liberal consensus historians constructed a politically powerful and for a large constituency convincing progressive tradition reaching from Thomas Jefferson and Andrew Jackson to Franklin Delano Roosevelt and the New Deal. In contrast to this tradition, populism served as the defining and anti-American Other. It was only recently that the historical agrarian populists experienced a rehabilitation that clearly distinguished them from populism in a trans-historical sense (Postel). But it was not only in historiography that it was difficult to classify populism consistently.

Part of the problem can be attributed to the different supporters of the movement itself. They were multifarious and multifaceted. Notoriously xenophobic racists and fanatical anti-Catholics such as Thomas Watson stood next to the pacifist fundamentalists and idealists of the *Common Man* such as William Jennings Bryan; self-confident, progress-oriented agrarians from the West stood alongside frustrated southerners. Race, tradition, and religion could be but did not have to be a source of identity and resentment. These populisms, in their ideological-cultural derivations or in their political and social aims, cannot easily be identified as having a common denominator. For this reason, we shall first look at populism in the narrower sense and its specific contexts of conception in the nineteenth century, before a further step is taken towards an examination of populism in American political culture at large. After all, the concept of populism in the United States of America underwent a profound change towards the trans-historic concept as that which is now in use.

The rise of populism happened during a time of dramatic and rapid socio-economic change in the United States (Edwards; Brands; White; Lears). With the end of the Civil War in 1865, the model of a slave-holding, semi-fluid cotton economy in the South also came to an end, while the transformation into an intensive meat and wheat producing agriculture was initiated in the Midwest and the West. This change was accompanied by substantial domestic and foreign capital investments, in particular from the United Kingdom, which led to the phenomenon of industrialized mass production by large landowners, often organized in joint stock companies. Many landowners were no longer living on the spot but could be represented by paid managers at the farms. This absentee ownership had existed already in the run-up to the American Revolution in the eighteenth century, but after 1865 it increased dramatically, resulting in various conflicts with old-established small and medium-sized landowners, which were not infrequently carried out by force.

The bloody ranch wars in the West between 1865 and 1920 were also called the *Civil War of Incorporation* (Brown). Since the agricultural industry was closely intertwined with the railways' interests, a kind of cartel system developed between the railway and agricultural oligopolies in the agricultural sector, which favored large agglomerations, particularly regarding the transportation costs for smaller landowners. This capital-intensive co-operation was supported by the major banks of J.P. Morgan, Thomas Ryan, and Kuhn, Loeb & Co., since the capital markets clearly favored a mixed agricultural economy which was less susceptible to crises than the anarchic market conditions of the previous phase. This applied not only to agriculture but also to the emerging industry and was followed by a take-off phase after the Civil War. The transition from proto- and early industrialization to high industrialization was primarily driven by railway construction, the associated steel industry, and by the new chemical and oil industries. Despite setbacks during the world economic crisis from 1873 to 1896, which was socially dramatic in the 1890s, the United States' share of world industrial production and world trade rose sharply. New York became, alongside London, a leading financial center, and Wall Street became a layman word. Next to the German Reich, the United States had the most dynamic global economy. Since the 1870s, the big banks, aided by mergers, emerged as efficient oligopolies and monopolies in a whole series of production segments.

Standard Oil of New Jersey, U.S. Steel, Pullman and other companies dominated the markets and barely allowed any external competition. These overcapitalized giant firms were organized using state-of-the-art Fordist and Taylorist insights and methods so that their production and sales processes remained efficient in the medium term despite the lack of competition in the markets.

It was not until the 1920s that they became overwhelmed by the sheer weight of their own size and their inherent bureaucratism, and lost their dominant position (Kolko). In the 1890s, however, they almost totally dominated the economic scene in the United States. In particular, financial capital and large-scale industry implemented an exceptionally restrictive monetary policy linked to the gold standard, which on the one hand was anti-inflationary and, as large parts of international business were traded over gold currencies, favored global trade, but, on the other hand, made small business loans difficult to get due to the high interest rates, which in turn accelerated the ongoing concentration and consolidation processes of the markets. In the Senate, the interests of the wealthy and super-rich, who also had the ultimate say in individual states and cities, dominated the federal level. Thus, the United States was a republic in that it was formally democratically organized, but in fact, it was dominated by a few oligarchs.

Against this background, the elite experienced a wealth of unsolved problems: the social issues of high industrialization and the associated transformation of values and lifestyles; the integration of migrants, including Jews, Catholics, and Asians, all of whom were not very familiar with traditional American Protestant traditions; corruption, election fraud and violence, especially the massive, ritualized lynching of African Americans in the continually violent South; inadequate social security measures, workplace accidents, insufficient fire protection, and lack of competition in the markets. While a number of ameliorative measures existed at the local level, the feeling that the ruling elites did little or nothing to meet the interests of the majority, socially, culturally, and economically, was widespread. Reformers of all kinds in urban and rural areas, from utopians to hardline policymakers, arose and criticized the obvious omissions.

In these contexts, the appearance of populists is found as well. They dominated the rural reform movements, while liberal progressivists, socialists, and trade unionists indicated the tone in the cities. This does not mean that populism differed qualitatively from the urban reformers in its claim to progress. In many cases, co-operation and the perception by urban critics of the established system did not detract from the populists. They were by no means more backward, xenophobic, racist, or nationalist than the Progressivists, among whom there was a proper share of extremist racist and xenophobic attitudes. White Supremacy, for example, was not a reactionary slogan between 1890 and 1910, but a progressive, scientifically empirical fact in a highly imperialistic world system, which was able to convince Populists and Progressives alike.

There was, yet, one decisive difference between the Populists and their Progressivist fellow-reformers. As Richard White has convincingly argued, the progressivist liberal elites were pretty unsure about how to treat the majority of the people, including immigrants and the working-class. Seen through the lenses of elitist liberalism, as for example in magazines such as *The Nation*, *The Atlantic Monthly*, or *The North American Review*, bulwarks of social and academic liberalism, powerful kinship networks, such as the Boston Brahmins and the New York or Philadelphia High Society viewed the masses as corrupt, uncivilized, as dangerous and riotous mobs. The latter was the inferiorized Other of the intellectual elites. Thus, the same kind of social disciplination in the august traditions of enlightened bureaucratic paternalism that was used to control the masses of the presumably uncivilized peoples in the far-away colonies under the heading of a civilizing mission had to be used to control the unruly (White 172-81). Especially the party machines of the Democratic Party, predominantly Tammany Hall in New York City with its large Irish-Catholic constituency (Golway), served as a case study for the corrupting influences of the vulgar masses. Social Darwinism, eugenics (Black), and the evolving, rather haughty and aristocratic social sciences – together with the courts that were dominated by liberals – provided the answer: Technocracy, a rigid rule of liberal property laws, and meritocratic expertise were supposed to overcome the weaknesses of democracy.

Therefore, the overall distinction between Progressivism (Lessoff) and populism might be interpreted as the expression of an underlying but nonetheless powerful incompatibility between the traditions of elitist enlightened liberalism with its pathos of truth, virtue, and social responsibility of the ruling classes on the one hand, and the voluntarist egalitarianism of mass-participatory democracy on the other hand. The fierce anti-elitist rhetoric of William Jennings Bryan and the advent of Thomas Watson may become intelligible through these conflicting dialectics. Bryan's monumental fight against Darwinism and Social Darwinism, for instance in the context of the so-called 'Monkey Trial' in Dayton, Tennessee, makes only sense, when it is seen as a struggle against elitist conceptions of a non-democratic republic of social engineers and technocrats in the sense that liberal ideologues tended to frame modern societies (Conkin; Kazin).

Institutionally and ideologically, the populists were led back to the *Granger* movement (also known as patrons of Husbandry) as well as to the *Greenbackers* (Postel 32-78). The *Grangers* were closely associated with liberal-progressive reformers, advocating women's suffrage, the direct election of senators, and the typically Protestant anti-alcohol movement (Creech; Welskopp). First and foremost, however, the goal was a legislation that would benefit farmers in the Midwest, such as the regulation of rail tariffs in favor of small-scale producers and the regulation of hay-making.

There is already something to be seen here which would later be a characteristic of the Populists: confidence in the constitutional and regulatory power of the state. *Grangers* and Populists vehemently turned away from liberal market dogmatism and the liberal belief in a pure post-war state. To a certain extent, their positions resembled those of reformists like John Stuart Mill, the British *Fabian Society*, or the German cathedral socialists and later the Catholic, neo-scholastic ultramontane social critics of the solidarist school around P. Heinrich Pesch, SJ (Hochgeschwender 2012), who were proponents of interventionism on the part of the state in the socioeconomic realm in order to master the social problems of high industrialization without a socialist revolution in the Marxist sense. The *Grangers* advocated private ownership and a capitalist market society but with state intervention in favor of small-scale producers and with an intensive democratization of the political enterprise. While the *Grangers* were successful as a lobbying organization for small farmers in the pre-political area, the *Greenback Labor Party*, which was also active as the *Reform Party* in Wisconsin and even had the governorship there, served as a direct political arm of the farmers between 1874 and 1889. In fact, it was a coalition of small farmers, workers, democrats, and reform-oriented Republicans in the Midwest.

The *Greenbackers*, therefore, had a wider social base than the *Grange*, but their goals were more limited. In essence, they had only one goal: the abolition of the deflationary currency on the basis of the gold standard in favor of a non-gold-covered, inflationary paper currency, as there had been during the Civil War. By 1875 with the *Species Act*, however, the expansion of money had been withdrawn, which was perceived to be in favor of New York's financial capital and small-scale producers (Pollack; Ritter). The struggle for the currency would accompany all radically egalitarian movements in the United States from the late nineteenth century onwards.

Parallel to the early disintegration of the ideologically monomaniac *Greenbackers* and the partial direct succession of the *Grange* was the rise of the Farmers' Alliances, from which the Populist Party developed. It is true that the first all-white, southern alliances were founded in 1875 and their racially mixed, i.e. non-segregated, mid-western counterparts were established a year later on the basis of the old *Grange*. However, they did not receive mass support until the mid-1880s, with around 50,000 supporters in the South and over 100,000 in the Midwest. In 1886 the founding of the *Colored Farmers' National Alliance and Cooperative Union* took place with over 1.2 million members (Leikin).

The quantitative growth of the alliances was first and foremost a consequence of the aggravating agrarian crisis in the 1880s. In this context, it was no coincidence that all three alliances took over the essential elements from the *Grange's* stance and, moreover, took up the monetary policy of the *Greenbackers*. In this case, the farmers' movements were similar to other urban reform movements. To this extent, they also stood on the side of liberal democratic, emancipatory, and participatory progress as well as science and enlightenment. The alliances as an educational movement were explicitly meant to convey to their members not only the latest findings of modern agricultural sciences, but also scientific knowledge, including the evolution theory of Charles Darwin, social Darwinism, and eugenics. In addition, they were enthusiastic about technical advances, such as those in communications technology, for new industries and agricultural sciences at new universities. In all these aspects, the alliances took the socialist, liberal-progressive, and Catholic societies of their epoch as their model. But, unlike Catholics, they placed themselves unconditionally in the service of the modernization of the economy, politics, and society.

This, however, did not exclude the active participation of Evangelical Protestants. In the 1880s and 1890s, there was still a closed anti-Darwinist-fundamentalist front in rural Evangelicalism. Evangelical farmers were as much attracted to the religious rhetorical fire of the early populists as to their passionate struggle against alcohol in the national abstinence and prohibition movement, which was the last joint project of progressive and evangelical society reformers. Last but not least, this ideological aspect of alliance-populism attracted the wives of farmers. Prohibition was a central concern for Protestant women. Finally, there were still remains of postmillennialist evangelicalism, which had emphatically pushed for social reforms from the 1830s up to the women's movement (Hochgeschwender 2007).

A peculiarity, however, distinguished populism from other reform movements: its political semantics. No other movement was so intensely supported by the moral dichotomy of the elites with their 'special interests' in the community, and the common man, who, intrinsically democratic, was solely committed to the common good. This was by no means the language of the Marxist class struggle or of a modern political economy but an expression of a traditional moral economy which had always been the object of the pre-modern era (Ashworth). Thomas Jefferson, one of the founding fathers of the republic, took advantage of the revolutionary era but radically modified it at two specific points. Jefferson had known the country ideology, a form of classical virtue republicanism, which was originally conceived by the Tory-thinker Lord Bolingbroke in the 1720s and directed against the alliance of the Hanoverian kings with the Whigs. Free landowners, according to Jefferson, thus served primarily as a *common good*, while thinking less of the simple *common man* as the bearer of this ideal but rather of the educated enlightened elites of his time. The poor, on the other hand, were the bearers of the special interests as they had nothing but the expropriation of the propertied and were, therefore, virtuous classes, especially when they lived and worked in cities and had no morally perfect land holdings (Hochgeschwender 2016). Only Andrew Jackson in the 1820s and 1830s changed this. From then on, the *common man* became the mythical bearer of the *common good*, while the elites were denounced as a champion of selfish, corrupt, even despotic *special interests*. Jackson also expanded Jefferson's premodern moral economy in the fight against the central bank, the *Second Bank of the United States*, under the highly liberal Nicholas Biddle (Pessen).

Jefferson and Jackson themselves introduced economy as a simple core system in which small-scale producers, retailers, and small consumers entered into a direct exchange in a face-to-face society that guaranteed mutual justice. Banks, industry, abstract markets, all of this could not play a more important role for moral reasons. This was classic *producerist capitalism*. In fact, both Jefferson and Jackson pushed ahead with the capitalist industrialization of the United States but hindered the organizational expansion of accompanying institutions, such as a central bank. A side effect of the moral understanding of politics were both heated, partly violent campaigns, since it was always good against evil, the 'stood down' against the 'up there.' The opponents were denounced as monarchist aristocrats and despots, as traitors and popular enemies.

This idea of the primacy of the simple man was also rooted in the theoretically still unresolved question of the expert's position in mass-democracy and in the equally uncontrolled tension between mass-participatory-democratic egalitarianism and liberal individualism in the intellectual legacy of the Enlightenment. Thus, Bryan and the populists were not liberals, but radical democrats, with all their intellectual and socioeconomic consequences. But they were not antimodern.

In 1892 the alliances changed into the *People's Party* and tried to get directly from the pre-political space to the political space in the succession of the *Greenbackers*. They succeeded, despite or because of the support of the prominent Bryan, but only at the individual level, regionally and locally. Gradually, the populists merged with the Democratic Party after the end of the world economic crisis in 1897. In this context, the populists of the South then moved increasingly into the conservative-racist camp, in league with a resurgent Ku Klux Klan and its racist fundamentalism. This was connected with the perfectly accurate perception of the Progressivists as representatives of an elitist reform policy, which was clearly antidemocratic in its social engineering wing. The semantics and the content of populism were now increasingly interpreted as reactionary by progressive and liberal historians. Even the party program of 1892 (the Omaha platform), which had then carried the divergent, boldest reforms of the populists to the national public in a systematic and precise way, became, after the defeat of the party and against the background of national socialism and *McCarthyism* of the 1940s and 1950s, proto-fascist. Joseph McCarthy, a notorious figure in 1950s American politics, despite his rhetoric and electorate, was not a populist and neither did his electorate have a populist background. On the one hand, he defended a radical, alarming anti-Communism but, on the other hand, he supported the interests of conservative Catholic and Jewish minorities, who felt as repelled by the populists as by the Anglo-

Saxon Protestant elite of the United States. However, in the scientific-academic debate with McCarthy and his supposedly populist prehistory, the transhistorical concept of populism, which today dominates political discussions, and which applies to Donald Trump, provides the political semantics of the moral dichotomy of elites and *common man* populism, while its policy serves the interests of the accused elite. The socioeconomic crisis in the United States in the late nineteenth century is closely comparable to the current socio-economic crisis, which after the world economic crisis of 2008 and after decades of neoliberal redistribution policy reveals how ruthless financial capital and large industry can subordinate the state to its interests, while the economic and political participation opportunities of the people are systematically minimized. This new populism is, compared with the real-historical phenomenon of populism in the 1880s and 1890s, a simplistic but productive misunderstanding that undermines semantic continuities. Possibly, a populist, modernizing critique of the present, often backward-looking 'populism' is needed; without the original and – considering the events of the twentieth century – naive confidence of egalitarian populism in the moral superiority of the common people, it might still be reproducible today.

Works Cited:

Ashworth, John. *Slavery, Capitalism, and Politics in the Antebellum Era, vol. I: Commerce and Compromise, 1820-1850*. Cambridge: Cambridge University Press, 1995.

Black, Edwin. *War against the Weak: Eugenics and America's Campaign to Create a Master Race*. New York: Four Walls Eight Windows, 2003.

Brands, Henry W. *American Colossus: The Triumph of Capitalism, 1865-1900*. New York: Doubleday, 2010.

Brown, Richard Maxwell. "Violence." *The Oxford History of the American West*. Ed. Clyde A. Milner II, Carol A. O'Connor, and Martha A. Sandweiss. New York: Oxford University Press, 1994. 393-425.

Chambers II, John Whiteclay. *The Tyranny of Change: America in the Progressive Era, 1890-1920*. New Brunswick: Rutgers University Press, 2001.

Conkin, Paul. *When all the Gods Trembled: Darwinism, Scopes, and American Intellectuals*. Lanham: Rowman & Littlefield, 1998.

Creech, Joel. *Righteous Indignation: Religion and the Populist Revolution*. Urbana: University of Illinois Press, 2006.

Edwards, Rebecca. *New Spirits: Americans in the Gilded Age*. New York: Oxford University Press, 2006.

Flanagan, Maureen. *America Reformed: Progressives and Progressivisms, 1890s - 1920s*. New York: Oxford University Press, 2007.

Golway, Terry. *Machine Made: Tammany Hall and the Creation of Modern American Politics*. New York: Liveright Books, 2014.

Hicks, John D. *The Populist Revolt: History of the Farmer's Alliance and the People's Party*. Minneapolis: University of Minnesota Press, 1931.

Hochgeschwender, Michael. *Die Amerikanische Revolution: Geburt einer Nation, 1763-1815*. München: C.H. Beck Verlag, 2016.

---. "Sozialer Katholizismus in den USA." *Tradition und Erneuerung der christlichen Sozialethik in Zeiten der Modernisierung*. Ed. André Habisch, Hanns Jürgen Küsters, and Rudolf Uertz Freiburg/Breisgau: Herder, 2012: 186-223.

---. *Amerikanische Religion: Evangelikalismus, Fundamentalismus, Pfingstlertum*. Frankfurt/Main: Suhrkamp, 2007.

Hochschild, Arlie Russell. *Strangers in Their Own Land: Anger and Mourning on the American Right*. New York: New Press, 2017.

Hofstadter, Richard. *Anti-Intellectualism in American Life*. New York: Vintage Books, 1967.

---. *The Paranoid Style in American Politics and Other Essays*. New York: Harvard University Press, 1964.

Isenberg, Nancy. *White Trash: The 400-Year Untold History of Class in America*. New York: Viking Books, 2016.

Judis, John B. *The Populist Explosion: How the Great Recession Transformed American and European Politics*. New York: Columbia Global Reports, 2016.

Kazin, Michael. *A Godly Hero: The Life of William Jennings Bryan*. New York: Anchor Books, 2006.

Kolko, Gabriel. *The Triumph of Conservatism: A Reinterpretation of American History, 1900-1916*. New York: Free Press, 1977.

Lears, T. Jackson. *Rebirth of a Nation: The Making of Modern America, 1877-1920*. New York: HarperCollins, 2009.

Leikin, Steve. *The Practical Utopians: American Workers and the Cooperative Movement in the Gilded Age*. Detroit: Wayne State University Press, 2005.

Lessoff, Alan. "American progressivism: Transnational, Modernization, and Americanist Perspectives." *Fractured Modernities: America Confronts Modern Times, 1890s to 1940s*. Ed. Thomas Welskopp and Alan Lessoff. München: Oldenbourg, 2012. 61-79.

McGerr, Michael. *A Fierceful Discontent: The Rise and Fall of the Progressive Movement in America*. New York: Oxford University Press, 2005.

McNichol Stock, Catherine. *Rural Radicals: From Bacon's Rebellion to the Oklahoma City Bombing*. New York: Penguin Books, 1997.

Miller, Worth Robert. "A Centennial Historiography of Populism." *Kansas History* (1995): 54-69.

Mudde, Cas, and Cristóbal Rovira Kaltwasser. *Populism: A Very Short Introduction*. New York: Oxford University Press, 2017.

Müller, Jan-Werner. *Was ist Populismus? Ein Versuch*. Berlin: Suhrkamp, 2016.

Packer, George. *The Unwinding of America: An Inner History of the New America*. New York: Farrar, Straus and Giroux, 2016.

Pessen, Edward. *Jacksonian America: Society, Personality, and Politics*. Urbana: University of Illinois Press, 1985.

Pollack, Norman. *The Humane Economy: Populism, Capitalism, and Democracy*. New Brunswick: Rutgers University Press, 1997.

Postel, Charles. *The Populist Vision*. New York: Oxford University Press, 2007.

Priester, Karin. *Rechter und linker Populismus: Annäherungen an ein Chamäleon*. Frankfurt/Main: Campus, 2012.

---. *Populismus: Historische und aktuelle Erscheinungsformen*. Frankfurt/Main: Campus, 2007.

Ritter, Gretchen. *Goldbugs and Greenbacks: The Anti-Monopoly Tradition and the Politics of Finance in America*. Cambridge: Harvard University Press, 1990.

Robin, Corey. *Der reaktionäre Geist*. Berlin: Ch. Links Verlag, 2018.

Stoll, Steven. *Ramp Hollow: The Ordeal of Appalachia*. New York: Hill and Wang, 2017.

Vance, James D. *Hillbilly Elegie: Die Geschichte meiner Familie und einer Gesellschaft in der Krise*. Berlin: Ullstein, 2017.

Welskopp, Thomas. *Amerikas große Ernüchterung: Eine Kulturgeschichte der Prohibition*. Paderborn: Ferdinand Schöningh Verlag, 2010.

White, Richard. *The Republic for which it Stands: The United States during Reconstruction and the Gilded Age, 1865-1896*. New York: Oxford University Press, 2017.

Wilentz, Sean. "Populism Redux." *Dissent* (Spring 1995): 149-53.

Woodward, C. Vann. *Tom Watson, Agrarian Rebel*. Savannah: Beehive Press, 1938.

Understanding the Trump Win: Populism, Partisanship, and Polarization in the 2016 Election

Jack Zhou, D. Sunshine Hillygus, John Aldrich

In the immediate wake of the 2016 United States presidential election, Donald Trump's surprising victory was often framed as the comeback of American populism from the heady days of the late-1800s. Headlines depicted his election as "riding a populist wave" (Hook et al.) and heralding "the rise of white populism" in American politics (Taub). Further analyses tied his ascendance to other recent phenomena like Brexit and the strong presidential candidacy of France's Front National leader Marine Le Pen as part of a "global populist wave" (Witte et al.).

Trump's populist bonafides were seemingly clear: he was a political outsider who belittled more traditional Republicans such as Jeb Bush and Marco Rubio. His rhetoric was nationalistic in the extreme and he both implicitly and explicitly denigrated "outsiders." And perhaps most viscerally, he attracted large crowds for his bombastic speeches and rallies that provided increased visibility and popularity to his strongman showmanship. In contrast, Trump's Democratic opponent in the general election, Hillary Clinton, was characterized as the arch-establishment candidate: a political legacy and favorite of the Democratic elite. It is no wonder that the prevailing narrative of the campaign was one of Trump being unexpectedly lifted to the presidency by a blue-collar rural white uprising, a movement that rejected past electoral precedent and sought to retake control of their country (Swaine).

While the campaign rhetoric had clear populist allusions, it remains unclear if that was the primary driver for Trump's surprising victory. In other words, was a "comeback of populism" among the American electorate what explained the outcome of the 2016 US presidential election? Or are the predictors of voting behavior in 2016 largely the same "fundamental" factors that matter in every presidential elections – partisan identity, ideology, and evaluations of the state of the economy? To preview the empirical evidence, the 2016 presidential election looked more like an ordinary than extraordinary election. It was, in large part, not a "return" of populism, as neither personal economic anxiety nor authoritarian attitudes were relevant to electoral choice. Anti-immigrant and racial attitudes offered some additional explanatory power beyond the fundamentals, but even these are factors that have a long history of relevance in American elections.

How Much did Populism Matter in 2016?

Populism, in its linguistic roots, refers to an ideology of "the people." While this seems clear enough, measuring the effect of populism is difficult as the concept, though frequently invoked by media and commentators, is not well-defined. As Mudde and Kaltwasser point out, populism can encompass "such diverse phenomena as a cross-class movement, an irresponsible economic program, or a folkloric style of politics" (493). Depending on context, populism can be a pejorative and demagogic term, or it can signify an appeal to virtue and to the "common man."

There are, however, some commonly-cited components of populism in political science research that can be used to specify the complex concept. Mudde (2007) claims that populism boils down to three core features: anti-establishmentarianism, authoritarianism, and nativism. Populism highlights the virtue of "the pure people" over "the corrupt elite," be they government figures, big business, big media, the rich, or the intelligentsia. Populists exhibit authoritarian leanings by congregating towards charismatic leaders who are seen as representing the interests of the people. Additionally, populists draw on nationalistic feelings.

The politics of the 2016 US election, however, may find this conceptualization too restrictive. More holistically, populism can be thought of as containing three dimensions: a socioeconomic dimension, a political dimension, and a cultural dimension. The socioeconomic dimension captures the idea that a "people" (usually a national people) should be economically self-sufficient and that economic prosperity should be shared by the common person as opposed to merely the purview of societal elites (Formisano). Socioeconomic populism is a common element of Latin American populist movements, though even here the term is wide-ranging, applying to free-marketeers like Peru's Alberto Fujimori as well as critics of neoliberalism like Venezuela's Hugo Chávez (Mudde et al.). As different a pair of leaders as they were, they shared an appeal to the populace and took power by beating elites who had long run the nation in politics, business, and the media. Their common rationale was that these elites had ignored the just economic grievances of the people and instead rewarded those who already had much.

In the 2016 US election, socioeconomic populism was often branded as "economic anxiety," or the sense that segments of the American public were being left behind by the economic recovery and job creation since the Great Recession. According to some commentators, personal economic anxiety spurred voters "who feel threatened by globalization, who question the benefits of 'free trade' that political leaders have peddled for decades and who believe distant elites control the economy in ways detrimental to their lives and prospects" (Collinson). This term became somewhat of a meme in the latter stages of the campaign as commentators alternately pointed to it as the reason for Trump's win (e.g., Levitz) or a media construction reflecting more fiction than fact (e.g., McElwee et al.).

The political dimension encompasses Mudde's elements of authoritarianism on the one hand and anti-establishment sentiment on the other. In particular, populism is grounded in a fundamental division between two supposed groups: the "ordinary people" who are considered homogenous and "decent" in juxtaposition with elites who are corrupt and the source of societal harm. This in-group versus out-group formulation can be traced back to early agrarian populist movements in which rural folk – considered authentic, grounded, and "morally healthy" – were suspicious of urban industrialization (Mudde et al.).[1] In modern terms, this notion has evolved into a disenchantment with authority figures (particularly in the national government) and a distrust of the urbane political class.

The cultural dimension of populism has been variously described as nativist or xenophobic, emphasizing the concept that "the people" is tied to a mutual national origin – a homogenous body (Mudde et al.).[2] In his presidential campaign, for instance, Trump often denigrated foreign influences such as Mexicans, Muslims, and the Chinese (e.g., BBC News).[3] The conceptual primacy that "the people" is a homogenous body means that the definition of "the people" can be further restricted to exclude all groups who do not share their identity, including non-foreign racial and ethnic minorities. Consequently, populist movements, in their advocacy of a monocultural identity, can fall into the racial resentment and intolerance of multiculturalism recently seen in Western Europe (Oesch).

---

[1] This depiction in American politics can be traced even farther back to the divisions between Jeffersonian Republicans and Hamiltonian Federalists, America's first two parties. Jefferson held his "ideal citizen," the yeoman farmer, in the role of the virtuous common man versus the societal elites of colonial and early republican America, represented by those engaged in interstate commerce, who were at the center of Hamilton's economic policies.

[2] The subject of how race intersects with the cultural dimensions of populism is not fully explored in the populism literature. In particular, the cultural aspects of populism are more often than not equated to nativism or xenophobia of immigrants, in part because much of the literature is generated via comparative research in Europe where these trends are more prevalent. However, this framework sometimes ignores the case of non-immigrant minority groups, for instance, African-Americans in the United States, and whether they are as "othered" by the in-group "people" as immigrants. The closest European analogue may be the Roma people, who are similarly seen as outside the conventions of the majority and "oscillating between the poles of potential re-educability and potential dangerousness" (Picker et al.).

[3] Given the particular context of the 2016 election and the tenor of Trump's presidential campaign, which featured numerous negative interactions with black communities and individuals (e.g., Diamond; Wang), racial resentment might arguably be a marker of populism in 2016. On the other hand, racial attitudes have long played a prominent role in US presidential elections.

Alternative View: the Standard Predictors

While the populist case for Trump's presidential victory has dominated electoral postmortems, this presumes that the 2016 election was so extraordinary in form and outcome that populism is the best (or only) explanation for how the election played out the way that it did. However, is this fundamental assumption about the election accurate? Was this election really that different from those in the past?

Over the past half century, political scientists studying American elections have built a robust conceptual toolbox to characterize how voters make their decisions. The set of concepts have been developed from the study of individual citizens and their attitudes, beliefs, and values as they decide whom to support and whether to turn out to vote. Election forecasting modelers like to use the terminology of "fundamentals" to describe the core variables that are important in their prediction models, election after election. We adopt that terminology here, but use it to cover variables considered important both at the level of the voter and that of the party, candidate, and outcome.

Chief among these fundamentals is political party identification. An individual's identification with a political party has reigned as the primary and most powerful engine for both direct and indirect determination of vote choice since the early 1960s (Campbell et al.).[4] In short, the vast majority of Democrats have always voted for Democratic candidates and Republicans for Republican candidates. This reflects party identification's critical role in political socialization and political evaluations. In addition, it has proven to be extremely stable over time. Adults, once they establish a party loyalty, tend to crystallize their identification over the course of their lives. While there may be disagreement about just what the concept means, there is no disagreement over the basic patterns (e.g., Fiorina; Achen; Bartels).

The second fundamental variable is political ideology, which predicts voting behavior in tandem with party identification and has taken an increasingly larger role in American elections due to growing partisan polarization over time. While the American system has long been dominated by two major parties, these two parties have moved increasingly farther apart since 1980 as each has drifted in their respective ideological directions – the Democratic Party to the left and the Republican Party to the right (Abramowitz et al.). Consequently, the two parties have increasingly differentiated themselves from each other, which is reflected in the policy positions they choose to support and the candidates they choose to run. In light of this ongoing trend of partisan polarization, voting in US presidential elections tends to boil down to a simple "us versus them" decision, in which liberal

---

[4] Campbell et al. were clear that party identification was only an indirect determinant of the vote, but many other have gone on to use it as a direct explanatory variable for the vote, considering it part of the triumvirate of parties, candidates, and issues that directly determine the outcome.

voters back liberal candidates and liberal candidates are almost always Democrats. Similarly, conservative voters will consistently choose to support conservative candidates, meaning they vote Republican because virtually no Democratic candidate is more conservative than their Republican opponent. Thus, "us versus them" increasingly means party peers and ideological compatriots are bundled together as the "us." Indeed, it might be said that an electorate originally viewed as all but "innocent" of ideology (Kinder; Kinder et al. 2017) in the 1950s and 1960s is now perhaps not very sophisticated in its ideological understandings but ideological nonetheless.

The last fundamental is voters' evaluation of recent economic conditions, which relate strongly with the sitting president's approval rating. Put simply, if people think the economy is trending upwards, that favors the in-party candidate and vice versa. This is a matter of some considerable debate in election forecasting models on just what aspect of the economy to use as pre-election measure. In survey research, the industry standard is to use measures of how the voter thinks the economy is doing currently compared to previously. For instance, a standard measure is how the voter thinks the national economy has fared over the last year as a whole (sometimes called "sociotropic voting").[5]

While it is difficult to conduct a formal test of populism in the 2016 US presidential election given how imprecise the concept is, we can begin to assess the role of populism in the election using post-election survey data and statistical modeling. In doing so, it is also possible to analyze whether populism or more traditional predictors of voting choice played a larger role in voters delivering Trump to the Oval Office.

Data/Methods

For data, we draw upon the 2016 American National Election Study (ANES) time series study, a nationally-representative survey project that offers extremely high-quality political attitudinal and behavioral data, a wide breadth of questions, and comparability over time with past iterations of the ANES. The 2016 ANES was funded by National Science Foundation grants awarded to the University of

---

[5] Another fundamental in forecasting models, yet not relevant in this case study, is incumbency; incumbent presidents enjoy numerous advantages over challengers. However, in term-limited years, voters may wish to flip party control of the White House in order to foster political change, particularly if the party in charge is doing poorly on other fundamentals. Besides considering presidential approval measures, survey researchers rarely seek to measure anything that could be considered "incumbent party fatigue." Forecasting models are inherently using aggregate measures of elections over time, so they can include this, *en passant*, while survey-based models of an election are inherently cross-sectional, in which incumbency is a fixed constant.

Michigan and Stanford University. Data collection for the 2016 ANES was provided by Westat, Inc.

The 2016 ANES included 4,271 total respondents who were interviewed in two waves, one before the election and the other immediately after.[6] Data in this study are weighted to include both pre-election and post-election responses from both survey mode types.[7]

Given that we aim to analyze why Trump won the 2016 US presidential election, our dependent variable is a dichotomous choice between whether voters voted for Donald Trump or Hillary Clinton. We explore how well the fundamentals – i.e., the continuously relevant forces – predict voter behavior in 2016 in comparison to populism measures. We add the three dimensions of populism to the set of fundamentals. A final set of variables are the mostly demographic controls, such as race, gender, age, and education, which set the context in which the fundamentals and the various elements of populism play out.

To operationalize populism within the scope of the election, we include measures of its socioeconomic, political, and cultural dimensions. In terms of socioeconomics, we include a measure of personal economic anxiety, i.e., the degree to which the respondent worries about his or her current financial situation. This is measured on a five-point scale, which has been normalized to a 0-1 scale, as were all subsequent independent variables to promote comparability of effect size.

The political dimension is measured by two sets of variables. One is a long-running ANES series of questions that have become the standard measure of the respondents' authoritarian tendencies: the child trait index, which is composed of four related questions asking for choices between sets of desired traits for child-rearing (Feldman et al.). These include whether a child should preferably demonstrate curiosity or good manners, and a choice between whether a child should be obedient or self-reliant.[8] Following Inglehart and Norris, anti-establishment attitudes were measured by whether the respondent agrees or disagrees with the notion that most politicians are trustworthy.

Finally, the cultural dimension has two indexes: one for racial resentment and one for anti-immigrant animus. The racial resentment index is a long-standing

---

[6] Respondents were probabilistically sampled from all 50 US states and the District of Columbia to be representative of US citizens age 18 or older. These respondents were surveyed using two modes of data collection: in-person surveying (n=1,181) via live interviewers in respondents' homes and online surveying (n=3,090) using a web-based platform. The per-election wave was conducted September 7 – November 7, 2016. The post-election wave was conducted November 9, 2016 through January 8, 2017.

[7] The American Association for Public Opinion Research (AAPOR) minimum response rate for the pre-election wave was 50 percent for in-person respondents and 44 percent for online respondents; the re-interview rate for the two modes were 90 percent and 84 percent, respectively.

[8] Cronbach's alpha for this index was 0.65, representing reasonable internal reliability.

concept in American political science research, and consists of four questions that gauge a respondent's recognition of existing racial inequities and support for a more equitable society (Kinder et al. 1996).[9] The index for anti-immigrant animus was constructed from seven items newly imported into the ANES from the Comparative Study of Electoral Systems, a cross-national survey project run by the University of Michigan and GESIS Leibniz Institute for the Social Sciences. These seven items assess different attitudes about the role of immigrants in American society and what it means to be truly American.[10]

In all cases, variables were coded such that the more populist opinion (e.g., greater anti-immigrant animus) was reflected with a higher numerical value.

In addition to the populist items, we control for age, race, gender, education, religiosity, and income level. The fundamentals include partisanship, ideology as well as a measure of retrospective voting, by the commonly-used measure of the respondent's evaluation of the state of the economy and whether it has improved or declined over the past twelve months. Except for age and income level, all of these measures were transformed to fit a 0-1 scale. Race, gender, education, religiosity, and partisanship (treating leaners as partisans) were treated as dummy variables. Ideology was normalized to fit the 0-1 scale from the standard seven-point scale. Age is a continuous variable and income level is an ordinal variable.

We ran a series of four stepwise logit models to evaluate which considerations best predict vote choice in the 2016 US presidential election. The first model includes all demographic variables as well as the traditional measures of party identification, political ideology, and evaluations of the state of the economy. The second introduces the variable of personal economic anxiety. The third includes the political measures of populism: authoritarian leanings and whether politicians are generally untrustworthy. The last, fully-specified model brings in the cultural measures of populism in the form of the racial resentment index and the anti-immigrant animus index.

Results

Our results suggest that Trump's election may not have been as populist as it initially seemed, or perhaps it is only populist in a narrow uni-dimensional sense. While the cultural measures of racial resentment and anti-immigrant animus are strong predictors of voting for Trump, the socioeconomic and political measures of populism – distrust of politicians, authoritarian leanings, and personal economic anxiety – provide little explanatory value after controlling for demographics and the

---

[9] Cronbach's alpha for this index was 0.85, representing excellent internal reliability.
[10] Cronbach's alpha for this index was 0.84, representing excellent internal reliability.

fundamental variables of partisanship, ideology, and evaluations of the state of the economy. The full set of regression tables may be found in Appendix 2.

We start with a descriptive look at the continuing pull of the fundamentals in vote choice in 2016 compared to previous years. Instead of the electorate responding to the full range of populist appeals, the fundamentals, particularly those of party identification and political ideology, seem to hold in predicting how individuals decide which candidate to support – Republicans and conservatives tended to vote for Trump no matter what. This finding of party loyalty in the 2016 election reflects a steady trend in American political history that has strengthened over the past few decades. As shown in Table 1, the likelihood that a voter will vote with his or her partisan identity has held around 90 percent (or higher) going back to the Reagan era.

The data also show a continuing effect of ideological identification – liberals supporting Democrats, conservatives supporting Republicans – going well back into the era of partisan polarization. As the two major American political parties began to align more clearly with these opposing political ideologies from the 1980s onward, voters sorted themselves and cast their ballots accordingly (Abramowitz et al.; Levendusky). Over the past four elections, political ideology has been as strong a force as party identification in determining how voters select their choice for president.

Additionally, the 2016 election falls right in line with past presidential elections in terms of how retrospective evaluations of the state of the economy relate to incumbent party vote choice. Voters who perceive the national economy as improving over the year prior to the election are overwhelmingly likely to vote for the incumbent president – up to 87.1 percent for Obama's re-election bid in 2012. Even when the sitting president is not running for re-election, the candidate from the incumbent's party still receives a sizable (though diminished) boost simply by representing continuity.

Similarly, voters who hold pessimistic evaluations of the state of the economy tend to look away from the incumbent's party when it comes to voting for President; these voters appear open to a changeover in power and new economic policies. Consequently, the relationship between voting behavior and party identification, political ideology, and economic evaluations look only marginally different in the 2016 presidential election than in previous years. There appears to be little room for populist appeals to have moved voters in 2016 away from how the fundamentals already would have led them to vote.

Table 1: Partisan loyalty in US presidential elections 1980-2016.

	Partisanship		Ideology		Economic evaluations	
Election Year	Democrats voting Democratic	Republicans voting Republican	Liberals voting Democratic	Conservatives voting Republican	"Gotten better" voting incumbent	"Gotten worse" voting incumbent
1980	72.5%	88.3%	70.7%	79.5%	48.7%	35.2%
1984	77.7%	94.7%	76.8%	84.9%	79.2%	20.3%
1988	82.4%	91.6%	87.0%	84.7%	76.2%	34.0%
1992	82.1%	73.0%	83.3%	69.3%	71.1%	25.8%
1996	89.1%	82.6%	86.4%	76.9%	70.8%	27.9%
2000	91.6%	90.9%	80.6%	84.2%	67.3%	29.0%
2004	92.0%	94.0%	93.9%	87.7%	85.6%	19.6%
2008	90.0%	92.3%	94.5%	88.4%	68.9%	42.9%
2012	93.6%	91.9%	95.7%	89.2%	87.1%	18.7%
2016	89.3%	87.4%	88.2%	79.7%	77.6%	20.2%

Note: Data from ANES Cumulative File and 2016 ANES. Democrats and Republicans in this table do not include "leaners," or independents who lean towards one party. Liberals and conservatives also do not include "slight ideologues." "Gotten better" and "Gotten worse" indicate whether the respondent thinks the economy has improved or degraded over the preceding twelve months, respectively.

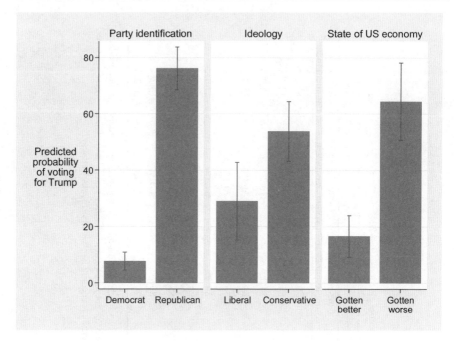

Figure 1: Predicted probability of vote choice (Fundamentals)[1]

Figure 1 shows that the established fundamentals of political science's explanations of vote choice were all strong predictors in the 2016 election. For instance, simply being a Republican, absent all other considerations, meant that a voter had a 76 percent chance of voting for Trump while being a Democrat shrank that likelihood down to under 8 percent. It is important to keep in mind that the predicted probabilities of voting for Trump in this and the following figures have been estimated from models controlling for a host of political, social, and demographic characteristics, including the three dimensions of populism just described (and reported in Appendix 2), and are not simply bivariate relationships with vote choice.

Note that the economic evaluations variable measures fundamentals-based retrospective voting and not the socioeconomic dimension of populism. Essentially, economic evaluations are more a referendum on the Obama administration and its policies than a gauge of personal economic anxiety. To illustrate this point, the variable more strongly correlates with the survey item "has the government done a

---

[1] Note: Predicted probabilities are estimated from fully-specified vote choice model. Predicted probabilities for individual variables shown after setting all other explanatory variables at their mean values. Error bars represent the 95% confidence interval for each predicted probability. Evaluations of the state of the economy were measured on a 5-point scale.

good or bad job in the last eight years" (r = 0.41) than concern about one's personal financial situation (r = 0.14). Consequently, it is quite reasonable that a voter who considers the Obama administration to have been a failure votes for Obama's political opposite than someone seen as a key Obama ally. This desire for a change in political direction from one administration to the next is a common thread in American presidential elections (Wlezien et al.).

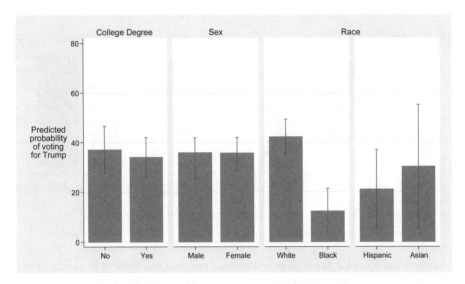

Figure 2: Predicted probability of vote choice (Demographics) [2]

Figure 2 shows that demographic characteristics did not matter much for respondents in determining which candidate to support. The one major exception was the race of the respondent. For example, while Trump did particularly well with the non-college educated (Galston et al.), having a college degree by itself was not a strong predictor of vote choice. Neither was sex in the fully-specified model, even though Clinton was the first major-party female presidential candidate in US history. Race, however, turned out to be a powerful voting predictor, with minorities considerably opposed to Trump.

---

[2] Note: Predicted probabilities are estimated from fully-specified vote choice model. Predicted probabilities for individual variables shown after setting all other explanatory variables at their mean values. Error bars represent the 95% confidence interval for each predicted probability.

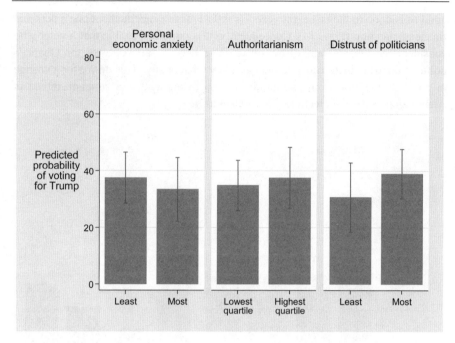

Figure 3: Predicted probability of vote choice (Socioeconomic and political populism)[3]

As shown in Figure 3, the socioeconomic and political measures of populism turned out to be unimportant predictors of vote choice. Their components – personal economic anxiety, authoritarian leanings, and distrust of politicians – all turned out to have no statistically nor substantively significant effect on the vote in the fully-specified model. In other words, these populist considerations did not appear to play much of a role in determining whether a voter cast a ballot for Trump or Clinton.

The cultural measures of populism included in the model, however, were strong predictors of how voters made their presidential decision in 2016. Figure 4 shows that racial resentment and anti-immigrant animus are both related to vote choice, in each case with the more populist sentiment (i.e., greater racial resentment or anti-immigrant animus) corresponding with a higher likelihood of voting for Trump, even after controlling for respondents' race. Whether these effects should be considered markers of populism is ambiguous. Clearly, racial attitudes and otherness mattered in this election. Racial resentment, however, has consistently been strongly related

---

[3] Note: Predicted probabilities are estimated from fully-specified vote choice model. Predicted probabilities for individual variables shown after setting all other explanatory variables at their mean values. Error bars represent the 95% confidence interval for each predicted probability. Economic anxiety was measured on a 5-point scale. Authoritarianism was a 5-point index based on four individual items. Distrust of politicians was measured on a 5-point scale.

to vote choices, and to that extent is essentially a fundamental factor explaining American voting behavior throughout history; anti-immigrant animus, meanwhile, has also often been important in American elections (Kinder et al. 1996).

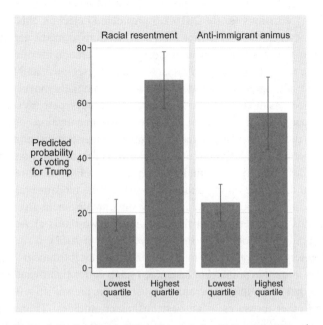

Figure 4: Predicted probability of vote choice (Cultural populism)[4]

Discussion

From these results, racial resentment, political ideology, anti-immigrant animus, party identification, and evaluations of the state of the economy were all strong predictors of voting for Trump in 2016. Notably missing from this tally of significant explanatory variables, however, were the socioeconomic and political measures of populism we tested. For the most part, the tried-and-true variables of party identification, ideology, and the economy tended to hold fast even after accounting for the populist items. Note that these results endure even when changing the dependent variable in the models from vote choice to post-election feeling

---

[4] Note: Predicted probabilities are estimated from fully-specified vote choice model. Predicted probabilities for individual variables shown after setting all other explanatory variables at their mean values. Error bars represent the 95% confidence interval for each predicted probability. Racial resentment was a 17-point index based on four individual items. Anti-immigrant animus was a 31-point index based on seven individual items.

thermometer ratings of Trump, or how favorably respondents thought of him. In other words, our findings are not the result of Clinton being Trump's opponent in the election, but about Trump directly.

Although racial resentment and anti-immigrant animus do appear to have played a part in voting decisions for the 2016 US presidential election, this election does not appear to be as extreme an outlier from past elections as media narratives would suggest. Again, race has long been an important consideration in American politics. The race of the respondent is strongly related to racial resentment and fairly strongly related to anti-immigration attitudes.[5] What is potentially novel in the 2016 presidential race was the import of anti-immigrant attitudes, perhaps suggesting that Trump's campaign rhetoric and nativist appeals had some traction.

Outside of these cultural measures of populism, wider populist attitudes may not have been what separated Trump and Clinton voters in the election. While other populist attitudes certainly exist among the American public, measures of populism do not seem to divide the voting public as clearly as the fundamental variables. As an illustration, the American public is widely anti-establishment given the abysmal approval ratings for governmental figures – nearly two-thirds of Americans have unfavorable opinions of Congress (Pew Research Center 2017).

Trump voters did appear to hold stronger anti-establishment attitudes than Clinton voters on certain points. For instance, Trump voters significantly agreed with the statement that "the will of the majority must always prevail" ($\beta = 0.73$, $p < 0.00$). However, on other measures of anti-establishment attitudes, Trump and Clinton voters appear remarkably similar. For example, Trump voters and Clinton voters were statistically indistinguishable in their opinion that "it doesn't make a difference who is in power." Similarly, there was also no significant difference between Trump and Clinton voters when asked if they agreed with the statement "people like me don't have any say about what the government does."

On still other items, however, Clinton voters actually expressed greater anti-establishment attitudes than did Trump voters. This may not come as a complete surprise given that her primary opponent, Senator Bernie Sanders, inflamed swaths of the Democratic base with his anti-financial elite campaign rhetoric, tapping into a vein of populist sentiment among likely Democratic voters. For instance, when asked if they agreed with the statement that "most politicians only care about the interests of the rich and powerful," Clinton voters concurred by a significantly higher degree than Trump voters ($\beta = -0.26$, $p < 0.00$). Clinton voters were also much more

---

[5] The weighted mean value of racial resentment for whites (on a 0-1 scale) was 0.58. For non-whites, the weighted mean was 0.43. The weighted mean value of anti-immigrant animus for whites (on a 0-1 scale) was 0.53. For non-whites, the weighted mean was 0.5. The weighted correlation between racial resentment and anti-immigrant animus among the entire sample was 0.51.

inclined to say that they were unsatisfied with the way democracy works in the US than Trump voters ($\beta = -0.29$, $p < 0.00$), a common measurement of populism in political science studies (Inglehart et al.). However, given the timing of this survey question, this last measure may be more likely an expression of dismay with the election results than a true populist sentiment.

On the whole, Republicans, conservatives, whites, and those with negative evaluations of the state of the economy under Obama voted for Trump; Democrats, liberals, people of color, and those with positive economic evaluations voted for Clinton. Thus, American voters in 2016 generally acted the way they would have been expected to act in any other election, regardless of the specific 2016 candidates. Despite Trump's provocative campaign, he was able to hold onto the Republican base provided for him by the party's nomination. ANES data show that 88 percent of Mitt Romney voters in 2012 ended up voting for Trump in 2016. For comparison, 82 percent of Obama voters in 2012 voted for Clinton in 2016. Political scientist Larry Bartels (2016), using preliminary vote returns data, estimated that the weighted correlation between the 2012 and 2016 elections was 0.93.

The Trump win came as a shock to so many commentators and analysts obfuscates the structural conditions surrounding the election. The fundamentals leading into the election suggested that the race was likely to be close, well-contested, and a near toss-up between the two party's candidates, whomever they were (Lewis-Beck et al.).

Further, the rate of polarization in American politics has greatly shaped politics over the last decades. Partisan polarization got underway with the election of Reagan and a Republican Senate in 1980, increased until the Republicans became fully competitive in congressional elections in 1994, and has continued to rise dramatically during Obama's time in office. The ongoing trend of partisan polarization has contributed to a multitude of potentially troubling normative outcomes, including more hostile views of elections (Miller et al.) and partisan intractability over issues like climate change (Zhou). The resulting "bundling" of fundamentals such as party and ideology (see Table 1) tend to freeze fundamentals even more firmly into place.

The other fundamental predictors of American presidential elections also pointed towards 2016 being a toss-up election. Given relatively anemic GDP growth in the early parts of 2016 – including the weakest quarterly growth rate in two years in the first quarter of the year – economic indicators did not tilt the race toward either Trump or Clinton (Masket). In terms of public perceptions, both candidates were seen as seriously flawed. Though these negative opinions of Trump and Clinton were mostly held by opposing partisans, even their own respective supporters feared that their candidate would make serious mistakes if they were to take power (Pew Research Center 2016).

The results of Election Night may have come as a surprise to so many observers because mainstream election coverage in the latter part of the campaign insisted Clinton had the election wrapped up (e.g., Kilgore). By mid-October, the Princeton Election Consortium had Clinton's chances of winning at 97 percent, HuffPost at 93 percent, and PredictWise at 90 percent. On the day of the election, the *New York Times*' *The Upshot* blog projected that Clinton had an 85 percent chance of success. Consequently, Trump's win ran completely counter to the established narrative of the election, charging in as a deflating dose of reality. In the end, even Trump's bombastic personal style was not enough to push the election away from the fundamentals and past precedent.

While the overall populist explanation does not appear to pan out in this analysis of Trump's victory, the strong effects of racial resentment and anti-immigrant animus in our models does perhaps support a narrower populist interpretation of the 2016 US election. Populism can be characterized as appealing to a homogenous in-group identity versus a homogenous out-group identity (Mudde). Therefore, if populism is meant to capture an ideology of "the people," it is important to characterize who are included into this moral entity and who are excluded as outsiders. In the case of Trump, his rhetoric frequently scorned minorities of many ethnic backgrounds, national extractions, and religious beliefs with little distinction between them other than that they were not part of the America he wanted to make great again. Consequently, while economic anxiety may not have played a role in Trump's election, cultural anxiety may well have.

Conclusion

In light of these findings, why were so many outside observers so quick to claim populism as the explanation for Trump's success? The answer may boil down to Trump's rhetoric, which was oftentimes explicitly and exceptionally populist-laden. For instance, his campaign was typified by gory public battles with the mainstream media (Kludt et al.), extensive use of social media to speak directly to the public (Keith), and exhortations to his supporters to "Make America Great Again," a paean to a downtrodden public desiring to retake the reins to their country. These sorts of comments – along with his alleged transgressions against women and circus-like rallies – drove the narrative that Trump's electoral result, win or lose, would be on the back of populist sentiment. That analysts and commentators were surprised by his victory in the Electoral College made them even more certain that the public reacted to his populist appeals, despite his loss in the popular vote.

However, this narrative of a populist revival is not supported by the political behavior of how people actually voted in the 2016 election. Although Trump's extreme rhetoric and temperament bucked traditional political norms, the data suggest that all of the populist flavor and sometimes-bizarre distractions of his campaign did not fundamentally change the way that voters behaved and were not what ultimately got him elected. While his rhetoric created a storyline that was different from previous elections, voter behavior and attitudes were not terribly different from past precedent. Additionally, even the observed attitudes that could be attributed to populism – racial resentment and anti-immigrant animus – may not be anything new as racial attitudes and otherness have long factored into American elections. In other words, Trump may not have heralded the comeback of populism as much as it seemed in popular culture.

With that said, we offer that caveat that just because the electorate might have behaved in fairly ordinary ways does not mean that Trump's presidency will be conventional in any sense. In fact, recent protests and the intensity of civil dissatisfaction with his administration may well spur further cries of a populist movement, now from the opposing side.

Works Cited

Abramowitz, Alan I., and Kyle L. Saunders. "Ideological Realignment in the U.S. Electorate." *The Journal of Politics* 60.3 (1998): 634-52.

Achen, Christopher H. "Parental Socialization and Rational Party Identification." *Political Behavior* 24.2 (2002): 151-70.

Bartels, Larry M. "2016 was an Ordinary Election, not a Realignment." *Washington Post* 10 November 2016 <https://www.washingtonpost.com/news/monkey-cage/wp/2016/11/10/2016-was-an-ordinary-election-not-a-realignment/>.

---. "Beyond the Running Tally: Partisan Bias in Political Perceptions." Political Behavior 24.2 (2002): 117-50.

BBC News. "Trump Accuses China of 'Raping' US with Unfair Trade Policy." *BBC News* 2 May 2016 <http://www.bbc.com/news/election-us-2016-36185012>.

Campbell, Angus, Philip E. Converse, Warren E. Miller, and Donald E. Stokes. *The American Voter*. Chicago: University of Chicago Press, 1960.

Collinson, Stephen. "How Trump and Sanders tapped America's economic rage." *CNN* 9 March 2016 <http://www.cnn.com/2016/03/09/politics/sanders-trump-economy-trade/index.html>.

Diamond, Jeremy. "Trump: Black Lives Matter has Helped Instigate Police Killings." *CNN* 19 July 2016 <http://www.cnn.com/2016/07/18/politics/donald-trump-black-lives-matter/index.html>.

Feldman, Stanley, and Karen Stenner. "Perceived Threat and Authoritarianism." *Political Psychology* 18.4 (1997): 741-70.

Fiorina, Morris P. "An Outline for a Model of Party Choice." *American Journal of Political Science* 21.3 (1977): 601-25.

Formisano, Ronald P. *The Tea Party: A Brief History*. Baltimore: Johns Hopkins University Press, 2012.

Gallup. "Presidential Approval Ratings -- Barack Obama." *Gallup* 2017 <http://www.gallup.com/poll/116479/barack-obama-presidential-job-approval.aspx>.

Galston, William A., and Clara Hendrickson. "The Educational Rift in the 2016 Election." *Brookings* 18 November 2016 <https://www.brookings.edu/blog/fixgov/2016/11/18/educational-rift-in-2016-election/>.

Hook, Janet, Colleen McCain Nelson, and Beth Reinhard. "Donald Trump Elected President, Riding Populist Wave." *Wall Street Journal* 9 November 2016 <https://www.wsj.com/articles/donald-trump-rides-populist-wave-1478678410>.

Inglehart, Ronald F., and Pippa Norris. "Trump, Brexit, and the Rise of Populism: Economic Have-Nots and Cultural Backlash." *Harvard Kennedy School Faculty Research Working Paper Series*. August 2016 <https://research.hks.harvard.edu/publications/getFile.aspx?Id=1401>.

Keith, Tamara. "Commander-In-Tweet: Trump's Social Media Use and Presidential Media Avoidance." *NPR* 18 November 2016 <http://www.npr.org/2016/11/18/502306687/commander-in-tweet-trumps-social-media-use-and-presidential-media-avoidance>.

Kilgore, Ed. "Some People are now 100 Percent Sure Hillary Clinton will Win." *New York Magazine* 18 October 2016 <http://nymag.com/intelligencer/2016/10/will-hillary-clinton-definitely-win-the-election.html>.

Kinder, Donald R. "Diversity and Complexity in American Public Opinion." *Political Science: The State of the Discipline*. Ed. Ada W. Finifter. Washington, DC: American Political Science Association, 1983. 389-425.

Kinder, Donald R., and Nathan P. Kalmoe. *Neither Liberal nor Conservative: Ideological Innocence in the American Public*. Chicago: University of Chicago Press, 2017.

Kinder, Donald R., and Lynn M. Sanders. *Divided by Color: Racial Politics and Democratic Ideals*. Chicago: University of Chicago Press, 1996.

Kludt, Tom, and Brian Stelter. "'The Blacklist': Here are the Media Outlets Banned by Donald Trump." *CNN* 14 June 2016 <http://money.cnn.com/2016/06/14/media/donald-trump-media-blacklist/index.html>.

Levendusky, Matthew. *The Partisan Sort: How Liberals Became Democrats and Conservatives Became Republicans*. Cambridge, UK: Cambridge University Press, 2009.

Levitz, Eric. "New 2016 Autopsies: It was the Obama-Trump Voters, in the Rust Belt, with the Economic Anxiety." *New York Magazine* 2 May 2017 <http://nymag.com/daily/intelligencer/2017/05/it-was-obama-trump-voters-in-the-midwest-with-econ-anxiety.html>.

Lewis-Beck, Michael S., and Charles Tien. "The Political Economy Model: 2016 US Election Forecasts." *PS: Political Science & Politics* 49.4 (2016): 661-63.

Masket, Seth. "A Weird Election to Forecast." *Pacific Standard* 16 May 2016 <https://psmag.com/news/a-weird-election-to-forecast>.

McElwee, Sean, and Jason McDaniel. "Economic Anxiety didn't Make People Vote Trump, Racism did." *The Nation* 8 May 2017 <https://www.thenation.com/article/economic-anxiety-didnt-make-people-vote-trump-racism-did/>.

Miller, Patrick R., and Pamela Johnston Conover. "Red and Blue States of Mind." *Political Research Quarterly* 68.2 (2015): 225-39.

Mudde, Cas. "The Populist Radical Right: A Pathological Normalcy." *West European Politics* 33.6 (2010): 1167-86.

---. *Populist Radical Right Parties in Europe*. Cambridge: Cambridge University Press, 2007.

Mudde, Cas, and Cristóbal Rovira Kaltwasser. "Populism." *Oxford Handbook of Political Ideologies*. Ed. Michael Freeden and Marc Stears. Oxford University Press, 2013. 493-512.

Oesch, Daniel. "Explaining Workers' Support for Right-Wing Populist Parties in Western Europe: Evidence from Austria, Belgium, France, Norway, and Switzerland." *International Political Science Review* 29.3 (2008): 349-73.

Pew Research Center. "Public Dissatisfaction with Washington Weighs on the GOP." *Pew Research Center* 17 April 2017 <http://www.people-press.org/2017/04/17/public-dissatisfaction-with-washington-weighs-on-the-gop/>.

---. "Clinton, Trump Supporters Have Starkly Different Views of a Changing Nation." *Pew Research Center* 18 August 2016 <http://www.people-press.org/2016/08/18/2-perceptions-of-the-presidential-candidates/>.

Picker, Giovanni, and Gabriele Roccheggiani. "Abnormalising minorities. The State and Expert Knowledge Addressing the Roma in Italy." *Identities* 21.2 (2014): 185-201.

Swaine, Jon. "White, Working-Class and Angry: Ohio's Left-Behind Help Trump to Stunning Win." *The Guardian* 9 November 2016 <https://www.theguardian.com/us-news/2016/nov/09/donald-trump-ohio-youngstown-voters>.

Taub, Amanda. "Trump's Victory and the Rise of White Populism." *New York Times* 9 November 2016 <https://www.nytimes.com/2016/11/10/world/americas/trump-white-populism-europe-united-states.html>.

Wang, Amy B. 2016. "Trump Booted a Black Man from his Rally and Called him a 'Thug.' Turns Out he is a Supporter." *The Washington Post* 29 October 2016 <https://www.washingtonpost.com/news/the-fix/wp/2016/10/29/trump-booted-a-black-man-from-his-rally-and-called-him-a-thug-turns-out-he-is-a-supporter/>.

Witte, Griff, Emily Rauhala, and Dom Phillips. "Trump's Win may be just the Beginning of a Global Populist Wave." *The Washington Post* 13 November 2016

<https://www.washingtonpost.com/world/trumps-win-may-be-just-the-beginning-of-a-global-populist-wave/2016/11/13/477c3b26-a6ba-11e6-ba46-53db57f0e351_story.html>.

Wlezien, Christopher, and Robert S. Erikson. "The Timeline of Presidential Election Campaigns." *The Journal of Politics* 64.4 (2002): 969-93.

Zhou, Jack. "Boomerangs versus Javelins: How Polarization Constrains Communication on Climate Change." *Environmental Politics* 25:5 (2016): 788-811.

Appendix 1: Question wordings for non-demographic items

Economic perceptions: *"Would you say that over the past twelve months, the state of the economy in the United States has [gotten much better, gotten somewhat better, stayed about the same, gotten somewhat worse, or gotten much worse / gotten much worse, gotten somewhat worse, stayed about the same, gotten somewhat better, or gotten much better]?"*

Economic anxiety: *"So far as you and your family are concerned, how worried are you about your current financial situation? [Extremely worried, very worried, moderately worried, a little worried, or not at all worried / Not at all worried, a little worried, moderately worried, very worried, or extremely worried?]"*

Authoritarianism: 1) *"Please tell me which one you think is more important for a child to have: Independence or respect for elders,"* 2) *"(Which one is more important for a child to have:) Curiosity or good manners,"* 3) *"(Which one is more important for a child to have:) Obedience or self-reliance,"* 4) *"(Which one is more important for a child to have:) Being considerate or well behaved"*

Distrust of politicians: *"'Most politicians are trustworthy.' (Do you [agree strongly, agree somewhat, neither agree nor disagree, disagree somewhat, or disagree strongly / disagree strongly, disagree somewhat, neither agree nor disagree, agree somewhat or agree strongly]?)"*

Racial resentment: 1) *"'Irish, Italians, Jewish and many other minorities overcame prejudice and worked their way up. Blacks should do the same without any special favors.' Do you [agree strongly, agree somewhat, neither agree nor disagree, disagree somewhat, or disagree strongly / disagree strongly, disagree somewhat, neither agree nor disagree, agree somewhat, or agree strongly] with this statement?"* 2) *"'Generations of slavery and discrimination have created conditions that make it difficult for blacks to work their way out of the lower class.' (Do you [agree strongly, agree somewhat, neither agree nor disagree, disagree somewhat, or disagree strongly / disagree strongly, disagree somewhat, neither agree nor disagree, agree somewhat, or agree strongly] with this statement?"* 3) *"'Over the past few years, blacks have gotten less than they deserve.' (Do you [agree strongly, agree somewhat, neither agree nor disagree, disagree somewhat, or disagree strongly / disagree strongly, disagree somewhat, neither agree nor disagree, agree somewhat, or agree strongly] with this statement?)"* 4) *"'It's really a matter of some people not trying hard enough, if blacks would only try harder they could be just as well off as whites.' (Do you [agree strongly, agree somewhat, neither agree nor disagree, disagree somewhat, or disagree strongly / disagree strongly, disagree somewhat, neither agree nor disagree, agree somewhat, or agree strongly] with this statement?)"*

Anti-immigrant animus: 1) *"And now thinking specifically about immigrants. (Do you [agree strongly, agree somewhat, neither agree nor disagree, disagree somewhat, or disagree strongly /disagree strongly, disagree somewhat, neither agree nor disagree, agree somewhat or agree strongly] with the following statement?) 'Immigrants are generally good for America's economy.'* 2) *"(Do you [agree strongly, agree somewhat, neither agree nor disagree, disagree somewhat, or disagree strongly /disagree strongly, disagree somewhat, neither agree nor disagree, agree somewhat or agree strongly] with the following statement?) 'America's culture is generally harmed by immigrants.'"* 3) *"(Do you [agree strongly, agree somewhat, neither agree nor disagree, disagree somewhat, or disagree strongly /disagree strongly, disagree somewhat, neither agree nor disagree, agree somewhat or agree strongly] with the following statement?) 'Immigrants increase crime rates in the United States.'"* 4) *"Some people say that the following things are important for being truly American. Others says they are not important. How important do you think the following is for being truly American... [very important, fairly important, not very important, or not important at all / not important at all, not very important, fairly important or very important]? To have been born in the United States,"* 5) *"(How important do you think the following is for being truly American... [very important, fairly important, not very important, or not important at all / not important at all, not very important, fairly important or very important]?) To have American ancestry."* 6) *"(How important do you think the following is for being truly American... [very important, fairly important, not very important, or not important at all / not important at all, not very important, fairly important or very important]?) To be able to speak English,"* 7) *"(How important do you think the following is for being truly American... [very important, fairly important, not very important, or not important at all / not important at all, not very important, fairly important or very important]?) To follow America's customs and traditions"*

Appendix 1: Regression table of vote choice models

	Model 1 (Baseline)	Model 2 (Socioeconomic)	Model 3 (Political)	Model 4 (Cultural)
Age	0.01	0.01	0.01	0.00
	(0.01)	(0.01)	(0.01)	(0.01)
Black	-2.02***	-2.02***	-2.14***	-1.57*
	(0.38)	(0.38)	(0.39)	(0.44)
Hispanic	-1.42***	-1.42***	-1.50***	-1.17*
	(0.44)	(0.43)	(0.45)	(0.47)
Asian	-0.73	-0.73	-0.79	-0.61
	(0.55)	(0.55)	(0.54)	(0.62)
Other race	-0.22	-0.26	-0.17	-0.18
	(0.57)	(0.58)	(0.57)	(0.56)
Female	0.11	0.10	0.12	0.07
	(0.21)	(0.21)	(0.21)	(0.21)
College	-0.76**	-0.75**	-0.55*	-0.15
	(0.25)	(0.25)	(0.26)	(0.31)
Religiosity	0.61*	0.61*	0.55*	0.47
	(0.25)	(0.25)	(0.26)	(0.28)
Income	-0.02	-0.02	-0.02	-0.01
	(0.02)	(0.02)	(0.02)	(0.02)
Democrat	-2.12***	-2.11***	-2.17***	-2.20***
	(0.33)	(0.33)	(0.32)	(0.36)
Republican	1.67***	1.69***	1.72	1.56***
	(0.30)	(0.30)	(0.30)	(0.32)
Ideology	3.84***	3.87***	3.47***	3.09***
	(0.61)	(0.62)	(0.61)	(0.80)
Economic evaluations	2.93***	2.83***	2.74***	2.11***
	(0.45)	(0.45)	(0.44)	(0.51)
Economic anxiety		0.37	0.22	-0.10
		(0.38)	(0.37)	(0.39)
Authoritarian			1.37***	0.54
			(0.35)	(0.43)
Politicians untrustworthy			0.76*	0.45
			(0.38)	(0.41)
Racial resentment				3.83***
				(0.60)
				2.71***

Anti-immigrant animus				(0.75)
Constant	-3.16	-3.34	-4.27	-6.63
	(0.62)	(0.67)	(0.81)	(0.91)
n=	2629	2629	2628	2627
McKelvey and Zavoina's R-sq	0.74	0.74	0.75	0.81

Note: Coefficients expressed in log-odds given logit regression specification. Coefficients are weighted using the full sample weight provided by the ANES. Standard errors are in parentheses. * $p < .05$, ** $p < .01$, *** $p < .001$. All items are measured on a 0-1 scale except for Age (continuous) and Income (ordinal).

#BasketofDeplorables: Digital Imagined Communities, *Twitter*-Populism, and the Cross-Media Effects of Popular Political Social Media Communication in the 2016 US Presidential Election

Laura Vorberg

> In this global environment, idealized views of populism as an unmediated or direct phenomenon that exists between the leader and 'the people' must be abandoned, and its intensely mediated nature needs to be addressed and explored. (Moffitt 3)

> The forgotten men and women of our country — people who work hard but no longer have a voice: I am your voice. (Donald J. Trump in his Nomination Acceptance Speech at the Republican National Convention 2016, 21 July 16, Cleveland, Ohio)

> The construction of the popular is always the site of an ongoing struggle; its content as well as its audience varies from one historical period to another. It is a domain in which different meanings and values, many of them with powerfully constituted political inflections (whether dominant, subordinate or oppositional) confront and mix with each other. (Grossberg 77)

On September, 16 2016, Republican presidential nominee Donald J. Trump took stage to the choir-part of the song "Do You Hear the People Sing?" from the Broadway musical adaption of Victor Hugo's nineteenth century novel *Les Misérables* at a campaign rally in Miami, Florida. While Trump entered the sparsely illuminated scene and applauded his audience, cheering supporters waving "Trump" and "Make America Great Again" signs, an edited version of a 2012 Hollywood movie adaption poster of the musical was displayed on a large video screen behind the candidate (fig. 1). The image, originally an illustration of a crowd of rioting French Republicans during the Paris uprising of 1832, had been modified and infused with civil-religious US symbolism in the spirit of the event: The red flag of the insurgents in the center had been exchanged with the stars and stripes, a French state flag on the left was superseded by a blue Trump banner and in addition, a bald eagle soared up to the sky. In place of the original movie title on the bottom, the altered projection displayed the words "Les Deplorables."

Figure 1: Deplorable Entrance: Trump Takes Stage to 'Les Mis' Song (Source: https://www.businessinsider.com/trump-les-miserables-deplorables-miami-2016-9)

While the music was gradually faded out, cheers became louder and mixed in with supporters' "USA, USA"-shouts, Trump took his place behind the podium. After having silenced the euphoric visitants by means of gestures, he drawled his matching opening greeting: "Welcome to all of you deplorables." The same evening, the creator of the movie poster modification, a political blogger who had posted the photo-shopped image on reddit.com first, commented on the rally and answered to a short video of Trump's stage entrance on Twitter: @NukingPolitics "Thank you @realDonaldTrump for using my meme to stick it to Hillary and her ilk. #MAGA We are just gonna keep winning" (Martosko). Likewise, the creators of the stage musical expressed their views on Trump's usage of their audio material, criticizing him for using "Do you Hear the People Sing?" without permission, yet also acknowledged, that songs from *Les Miserablés* had been used by political and social movements around the world time and again for more than thirty years (Alberge).

Whether assessed as an odd appropriation or his most dramatic stage entrance to date, Trump's performance, in which he stylized himself as leader of 'the deplorables,' yet again earned him broad social and news media attention. Trump's populist one-man show in Miami was the finale of a series of popular discursive reiterations and re-negotiations of the term 'deplorables' that had preceded the campaign event and that Trump could ultimately take advantage of for his self-presentation in Florida. While the expression 'deplorables' had originally been used as a pejorative collectivization for Trump supporters by Democratic candidate Hillary Clinton during a private fundraising event on September 9, social media publics, especially Twitter users, engaged in a process of creative reappraisal and reinterpretation of the Clinton statement in the following week. The adoption of the term that took place bit by bit in the digital realm in the course of this social media discourse resulted in a conversion of meaning of 'deplorables,' turning the original denigration into a positively connoted signifier for a collective self-designation of the pro-Trump electorate. This article examines how the performative communication dynamics on Twitter that resulted in a popular community building of 'deplorables,' were initially kicked off under the hashtag '#basketofdeplorables' and how they proceeded discursively in the networked public sphere, functioning as the starting point for a broader cross-media populist group formation that transcended the limited communicative environment of social media audiences. Within this context, the focus is going to be on the question how user-based popular-cultural processings of political occurrences, such as memes and similar forms of both textual and pictorial viral phenomena distributed and circulated on social network sites, operate as means of an affective communitization. To understand how and why this particular case of community building took place on Twitter and why it must not only be understood as 'popular' but also 'populist,' in the first instance, the network's specific inbuilt modes of communication as well as exemplary user posts (those of the '#basketofdeplorables' discourse) will be considered. By subsequently connecting and extending Benedict Anderson's concept of the 'imagined community' and Ernesto Laclau's work on populism, I will argue that the discursive popular renegotiation and appropriation of the 'deplorables' label on Twitter can be contextualized as an example of a collective community fantasy emerging in the digital sphere and, based on this, as an e/affective presencing of a unified populist group identity, widely observable in the general public to which Trump subsequently presented himself as a leader and voice. By examining the discussion under the hashtag '#basketofdeplorables' as paradigmatic example of popular political Twitter discourse, I will illustrate that the performative emergence of imagined communities on Twitter is especially driven forward by the distribution and circulation of memes and other viral expressions because these popular semantics are hyper-connective, quick to comprehend, easy to quote, and emotionally appealing and thus foster the inclusion of audiences into political publics. Concomitantly, Twitter must be regarded as a particularly suitable medium for such affective political communitization processes due to its unique inbuilt functional mechanisms in general and as an advantageous instrument for populist leaders in particular, since it can be used to create an illusion of speaking to 'the people' directly. As will be emphasized throughout the argumentation, both popular and populist Twitter posts and discourses can nevertheless only gain extensive social and political importance as well as durability, if they exceed the narrow sphere of the social network and are additionally covered by mass media and therefore made visible for broader publics.

On Friday, September 9, 2016, presidential candidate Hillary Clinton hosted the "LGBT for Hillary Gala," a private fundraiser in Manhattan, having invited the press. That night, in her campaign speech, Clinton criticized the offensive rhetoric of the Trump campaign and, in doing so, made a controversial statement about his supporters:

> You know, to just be grossly generalistic, you could put half of Trump's supporters into what I call the 'basket of deplorables.' Right? They're racist, sexist, homophobic, xenophobic, Islamophobic—you name it. And unfortunately, there are people like that. And he has lifted them up (Chozick).

While applause and laughter of the event attendees indicated approval of Clinton's use of the basket metaphor by the audience present, the ensuing extensive TV- and press-coverage on the speech quickly sparked public uproar and controversy. While Clinton declared in the subsequent part of her speech that the other half of Trump supporters were not racist but felt as if they had arrived at a dead end and thus were, "people we have to understand and empathize with as well" (Chozick), the moderate part of her talk received little public attention. In TV-, press- and Twitter-statements, both Republicans and Democrats, including Mike Pence and Paul Ryan, strongly disapproved of the expression 'basket of deplorables' as affront to the American working class. Over the day, Donald Trump posted two tweets on his official account 'realDonaldTrump' in which he criticized Clinton's statement as "SO INSULTING to [his] supporters" (@realDonaldTrump, 10. Sept. 2016, 05:47) and reminiscent of Mitt Romney's inappropriate and consequential 47% remark during the 2012 election season (@realDonaldTrump, 10. Sept. 2016, 16:37). At that point of the 2016 presidential election campaign, over 40 million followers had subscribed to Trump's account and thus always received his latest Twitter-statements. Both of his posts from September 10 received about 40.000 likes and 15-20.000 retweets each. While Trump himself had not used any hashtag to mark his own tweets on the incident, the day after, by Saturday morning, the hashtag '#basketofdeplorables' had become trending topic number one on the social network 'Twitter' (Chozick). The feature of 'hashtagging' is among the most common communication practices habitually used in social network communication, not only, but prominently on Twitter. To understand the consecutive discursive negotiation of '#basketofdeplorables,' Twitter's key operating principles such as hashtags and trending topics along with further distinctive elements of communication of the microblogging service must be considered briefly to begin with.

'Hashtagging,' the practice of marking an annotation of the topic of a tweet, generates a searchable, if selected also chronological, feed of tweets relating to this particular topic (Zappavigna 36). A 'tweet' is a user's short text-, image-, or video-posting, displayed as public and searchable if the user does not actively choose to make his or her account private (Zappavigna 3). If it is currently used in a large number of tweets, hence repeated over and over again, a hashtag shows up as 'trending topic' on the Twitter search page. Trending topics emphasize immediacy and are supposed to "help people discover the 'most breaking' news stories from across the world" (Zappavigna 18) as has been declared by Twitter officials. However, as media scholar José van Dijck and Thomas Poell emphasize, this statement must be perceived with care like most of the company's official self-descriptions, since "Twitter's Trending Topics are algorithms that push some topics and devaluate others" (Van Dijck et al. 7). Even if the network's image campaign suggests the opposite, trends are anything but objective: "Specific algorithms that inform these practices [following and trending] are presented as neutral, but in fact apply filtering mechanisms to weigh and select user contributions and tweet content" (Van Dijck 69). This observation is all the more important since the social and political impact of networked communication can be tremendous: "Trending conversations, in particular, present a stage that people can claim to render a personal thought public. As privately motivated actions attain a public orientation, they are infused with political potential *and* personal style. Style is performance and performance is power" (Papacharissi 110). The very fact that trending conversations provide a stream of user posts in which 'breaking news' are discussed, implies that networked publics on Twitter are now readily observed as real-time indicator of public opinion by all major news outlets and that social media discourses regularly feed into the news of the day. As van Dijck summarizes: "Twitter presents itself as [...] the online underbelly of mass opinions [...]" (69). Furthermore, today, news media journalists also keep an eye on politicians' official social network accounts since they can conveniently incorporate short tweets on current developments into their coverage as quotes (Van Dijck et al. 7). Moreover, public figures such as politicians and celebrities are already among the most powerful communicative authorities in social networks, since, "[i]n spite of the platform's egalitarian image, some people on Twitter are more influential than others, partly because the platform tends to be dominated by few users with large followings, partly because the platform assigns more weight to highly visible users" (ibid. 7). A large number of followers who regularly observe posts from a user that they have subscribed to increases the chance for posts from this account to be retweeted. The practice of 'retweeting' denotes a republishing of another user's tweet within one's own tweet, which can significantly amplify the reach of a message and, importantly, give rise to an emotional sense of shared conversational context (Zappavigna 35-6). Another way of increasing the scope of a posting on Twitter is by 'addressing' or 'mentioning'. By explicitly (using an @-sign before the name of another account in one's own tweet) or implicitly referring to another user/account, those who follow the mentioned user will automatically see the tweet.

Taking these interdependencies into consideration, it is not surprising that both the Twitter-negotiation of '#basketofdeplorables' as well as Donald Trump's Twitter reactions were quickly reported on by all leading online newspapers soon after the hashtag started trending. CBS news online for instance reported on Saturday morning, that "[o]utrage spread on Twitter immediately after Clinton's 'basket of deplorables'-line" (Flores) and issued images of Trump's tweets on the matter as well as tweets from his family members. Indeed, postings that expressed outrage at Clinton, accusing her of disrespect and hypocrisy, clearly dominated the initial stage of the trending period. Tweets such as @BarbaraJean_s "HRC should know better than refer to supports of any one or thing as #basketofdeplorables huge misstep not inclusive" and @realJamesCrane "number 1 i think it's absolutely disgusting for a presidential candidate to insult half of americans #BasketOfDeplorables" are only two examples of numerous expressions of critique that became more and more by second. They were contrasted by a relatively small number of affirmative postings gathered under the same hashtag which approved of Clinton's remark or even considered it as being too lenient regarding the number of racist, sexist, and misogynistic voters in the Trump camp, such as a tweet by @DonovanCaylor, who thereby addressed Hillary Clinton's official account: "@HillaryClinton was indeed wrong to say that half of Trump supporters were a #BasketOfDeplorables. I'm pretty sure she meant ALL of them." For the most part, this early stage of trending was characterized by text-based tweets that read as affectively charged expressions of users' opinions and can roughly be assigned to either one of two antagonistic camps. Yet the tweets that defended Clinton's statement were outnumbered by disapproval and uproar so clearly, that the majority of US news media almost exclusively portrayed public opinion on the issue as a wave of collective indignation. The practice of observing social networks on the basis of quantity and drawing conclusions about a prevalent public opinion thereof was daily press routine during the 2016 US election season. This method is problematic in a number of ways. First of all, it is unclear by what means Twitter's trending algorithms are programmed in the first place, since the network is under pressure to make content profitable, as Van Dijck emphasizes: "[…] Twitter's pipelines do not just transport streams of live tweets; neither the platform nor its users are simple carriers of information" (69). Secondly, automated accounts or so-called 'propaganda-bots,' algorithms that are masked as human, are increasingly implemented strategically by different interest groups in order to influence network discourses. By use of prefabricated text templates, such bots can duplicate and reproduce opinion posts (Breitenbach 46). Thereby, the course of a political discourse can be manipulated, even more by the intervention of third party actors. Therefore, whether and to what extend the postings grouped together under the hashtag '#basketofdeplorables' actually corresponded to real people's opinions is more than questionable and impossible to verify. With regard to the consecutive steps of popular renegotiation in the '#basketofdeplorables' discourse up to the emergence of an imagined collective of Trump supporters, the question of real authorship and authenticity is of secondary importance for the process of digital community construction in principle. Nevertheless, considering the political impact of social media trends today, growing evidence that the official campaigns, nonofficial supporter groups and Russian hackers influenced all sorts of discourses in the 2016 election is clearly alarming.

By Saturday afternoon, Clinton actually issued a statement via her social media accounts in which she apologized for having been, "grossly generalistic," regretting that she had labeled half of the Trump supporters as *deplorables* (@HillaryClinton, 10. Sep. 2016). At that point, '#basketofdeplorables' was still trending, but after the purely textual postings of critique, image-based commentary, that is, memetic-media, had clearly began to dominate the conversation. In his study *The World Made Meme*, Ryan M. Milner defines memes as "linguistic, image, audio, and video texts created, circulated, and transformed by countless cultural participants across vast networks and collectives. [...] They're used to make jokes, argue points, and connect friends. [...]" (1). Importantly, Milner also highlights the importance of irony and humor for mimetic re-appropriation (30). Their humorous appeal is one of the criteria that qualifies memes as 'spreadable media' according to Henry Jenkins et al. In contrast to the concept of 'viral media' that is commonly used to describe how content spreads on social networks like a contagious disease and thereby assigns a passive role to users who are virtually infected with a trend, Jenkins et al. introduce the idea of 'spreadable media' that highlights that people make active decisions when they decide to share, reframe, and remix media content in the social network sphere (20). Within the scope of their study, they list particular types of content that are more spreadable than others: "These include the use of shared fantasies, humor, parody and references, unfinished content, mystery, timely controversy, and rumors" (202). With regard to the criterion of 'timely controversy', not surprisingly, Clinton's statement already ignited a Twitter trend before it was turned into memes, but precisely its controversial character also made '#basketofdeplorables' likely to be transferred into a memetic discourse, since memes highlight controversial issues and thereby appeal to emotions (Heiskanen 2). The first memes that were posted under the hashtag 'basketofdeplorables' were mainly images with captions, photoshopped pictures, and font graphics. Most of these early memes followed the Clinton-critical discourse that had been expressed in previous, purely textual tweets and ironically inverted the insult, for example by photoshopping the heads of Clinton and other Democrats into a wooden basket, or attacked Clinton aggressively, such as a font graphic that simply stated: "Hillary Hates the American Working Class." Similar to the principle of trending topics, the assertiveness of a meme is first and foremost dependent on the scope of its distribution that guarantees extensive visibility (Breitenbach 36-7). Therefore, the reiteration through retweets may give memes public prominence and ensures that a meme can be re-used and re-mixed within different contexts. During the 2016 US election season, this sort of memetic negotiation of controversial statements was not unusual and happened almost on a daily basis. As Milner argues, in the digital age, memes have become a common form of mediated remix, play, and commentary and are highly significant with respect to the emergence and/or negation of major political moments: "Memetic media are premised on participation by re-appropriation, on balancing the familiar and the foreign as new iterations intertwine with established ideas. In this way, small strands weave together big conversations that are increasingly prominent, vibrant and instantaneous" (3). As shown below, the popular cultural processing of Clinton's 'deplorables'-gaffe through meme circulation on Twitter, in effect, resulted in a political act of collective re-appropriation of the term and a performative process of digital community formation.

Within a very short time after the first Clinton-critical memes had begun to circulate on Twitter under '#basketofdeplorables' on September 10, simultaneously, a second line of discourse began to evolve under the same hashtag, triggered through memetic reappraisal. While there were still some new posts in which the hashtag was used to designate that people considered Clinton's comment as insulting and derogatory, the number of tweets in which 'basketofdeplorables' was reinterpreted into/as a positive identity through self-attribution grew steadily. Textual posts such as @UsherJenn "Proud to be in a #BasketOfDeplorables" or @AUFemmeFBFan "Honored to be in the #BasketOfDeplorables with you! ;D" became more frequent among Trump supporters. Most of these tweets also contained pictures, especially group images and selfies of people of all races, gender and income groups who designated themselves as deplorables in the captions.[1] These included, for example, a collage of selfies of African Americans wearing Trump shirts or holding "Make America Great Again"-signs above their heads or a group of soldiers claiming that Hillary had "just lost the election" due to her statement. Even this process of re-appropriation was both accompanied and propelled by all sorts of humorous memes of which a significantly high share referred to already well-known phenomena of popular culture. While new memes can become familiar expressions of popular discourse if they fulfill the criteria of longevity and rise to public prominence, many memes also function as intertextual references to other, often already well-established popular cultural phenomena such as movie stills, logos or iconic images. In this case, they require a certain prior knowledge of the original context to be legible:

---

[1] The images were presumably showing the authors behind the posts. Whether these pictures are authentic, that is to say, whether the people depicted are those who posted the tweets and/or whether they really supported Trump is impossible to say.

[T]he basic assumption is that recipients need to "get" the meme in order to be in on the joke; if not, the meme loses its potential. For this reason, Internet memes are more powerful when distributed within a peer group of already likeminded users. (Heiskanen 2)

The degree to which memes are pre-conditional varies considerably. Some of the most visible and retweeted postings that emerged in the process of reinterpretation of '#basketofdeplorables' contained memes that playfully incorporated the expression into images from Hollywood movies with a matching description. For example, one meme showed a close-up shot of a main character from the Stephen Spielberg movie *Jaws*, humorously modifying the well-known quote "I think we gonna need a bigger boat" by replacing it with "We're gonna need a bigger basket" (fig. 2).

Figure 2: 'Bigger Basket'-Meme (Source: @AntonCleav *Twitter*, url no longer available)

Memes like this one which refer to a popular blockbuster movie appeal to a relatively wide audience. They reflect an ongoing trend of the use of all sorts of popular semantics in the political realm that could already be observed in the pre-digital era but has clearly reached its peak over the last decade due to the high popularity of many-to-many communication networks. Since they fulfill an important role in the performative communitization of (networked) collectives, it is short-sighted to consider popular semantics as a simple trivialization of political discourse in public debates. As Benita Heiskanen emphasizes:

Indeed, we would be remiss in considering popular culture related to electoral politics as just 'entertainment,' for it has an important role in meaning-making and in reflecting ongoing political trends. Most people around the world likely spend more time following popular culture than partisan political debates, but in the United States, in particular, where voter turnout is relatively low, popular culture has an absolutely central role in representations of political phenomena. (3-4)

Not least the general surprise of both scholars and the leading press on election day 2016 proves that the importance of popular semantics for the outcome of the Trump vs. Clinton race was significantly underestimated. Indeed, forms of the popular such as memes fulfill an important inclusionary function in politics. As the sociologist Urs Stäheli explains, the popular runs parasitically through all areas of society and can be understood as a discursive strategy of inclusion (283). For liberal democratic systems, the inclusion of a political audience is especially important in times of elections since voters are needed to keep democracy alive. Drawing on Judith Butler's notion of the performative, Stäheli describes the benefits of popular semantics in political communication as follows:

(Thus), the popular has two important dimensions [...]: it is, firstly, the construction of the becoming of a unity ('the people') and it produces, secondly, a de-unifying effect precisely by offering 'hyper-connectivity' (i.e. access and comprehensibility). (279)

In other words, the use of popular semantics particularly fosters the performative emergence of political collectives since they work as a low-level, complexity-reduced entry point into political discourse and are at the same time emotionally appealing. In spite of this general tendency towards all-inclusion, it is important to highlight that the construction of a unity automatically also implicates different moments of exclusion, for example, if one rejects the political identity of the collective, or through a lack of knowledge of how to use social media or simply a lack of access. Performative processes of affective communitization by use of popular semantics are obviously not limited to the digital realm, but they are clearly facilitated by network technologies, as Zizi Papacharissi explains in her study *Affective Publics*:

On a primary level, social media facilitate engagement in ways that are meaningful. Most notably, they help activate latent ties that may be crucial of the mobilization of networked publics. [...] On a secondary level, networked publics are formed as crowds coalesce around both actual and imagined communities. (20)

In contrast to Stäheli, Papacharissi thus distinguishes two stages of affective inclusion. Firstly, drawing on the terminology of danah boyd, the general emergence of 'networked publics,' publics that are restructured by and constructed through networked technologies (boyd 39). Secondly, a more specific communitization and fantasy of a collective identity which can be explained with Benedict Anderson's famous concept of the 'imagined community.' While Anderson discusses the role of 'imagined communities' within the broader scope of nationalism and nation building, its constitutive characteristics are equally adaptable to and even particularly suitable for the emergence of different types of political units in the digital realm. According to Anderson, an 'imagined community' is imagined, because its members "will never know most of their fellow-members, meet them, or even hear of them, yet in the minds of each lives the image of their communion" (49). While some of its members may actually be subjected to inequality and exploitation, the fantasy of this community is based on a feeling of equality, "conceived as a deep, horizontal comradeship" (51). It is however not to be understood by its lack of genuineness but must be defined and distinguished by the *style* in which it is imagined (49). Importantly, Anderson highlights the significance of media evolution and language for the emergence of political 'imagined communities' such as the nation since media enable both a communicative detachment from spatial proximity of its members and enable temporal transversality (52). In this respect, it seems obvious that especially social media take this process of instantaneous and location-independent community formations to the next level. In the digital age, global political communities can emerge performatively ad-hoc through social networks and can gain extensive visibility and social importance through transnational cross-media coverage.[2] That way, the discursive re-negotiation of '#basketofdeplorables' from a degrading statement to a positively loaded label of group identity by means of popular memes resulted in the performative affective presencing of an imagined community: the community of 'deplorables.' Unified under this label were all those who identified as victims of Clinton's insult and subsequently took the opportunity to give a whole new meaning to the term. The sheer size of the United States precludes that all members of the community of Trump supporters who identified as 'deplorables' on Twitter could have ever met their fellow members in real life, but the mental image of a group looking in the same direction and the feeling of comradeship constituted a shared political imaginary. Even though all sorts of social inequalities among the heterogeneous group members prevailed, the performative process of collective unification under one symbolic name concealed those social differences and created a feeling of being in the same boat, or, literally, the same basket.

---

[2] *Occupy Wallstreet* is a prominent example.

With regard to political communitizations, Twitter is the prevailing social network. Papacharissi particularly mentions Twitter as a network that facilitates the construction of imagined communities like the 'deplorables':

> Language is an essential enabler of performativity as it both describes and communicates a form of doing. For a textually based platform like Twitter, language is employed to convey both verbal and non-verbal performative gestures. [...] In this manner, performativity enables reproduction and remixing of dominant and other narratives, thus presencing their political potential. (97)

The use of both text- and image-based popular semantics such as memes in processes of community building works best, if it is accompanied by humor which "is a vehicle by which people articulate and validate their relationships with those with whom they are on the joke" (Jenkins et al. 204). However, it should be noted that Twitter is not only an especially suitable medium for the performative presencing of political collectives with regard to its textual contents but notably also because of its inbuilt functional modes of communication as described above. Due to its mechanisms of following, retweeting, hashtagging, and mentioning, based on reiterating, annotating and cross-referencing, the technology of Twitter is itself inherently performative already since any identity constructed in performative processes is generated through naming and stabilized through ongoing discursive repetition. As a matter of fact, in her study of Twitter discourses, Michele Zappavigna also concludes that the rise of the social web marks a turning point in digital communication since information sharing becomes less important while enacting social relationship becomes essential:

> In this way microblogging can be seen as an ongoing performance of identity. Perhaps another significant explanatory factor is the human desire for affiliation: we exist within communities of other voices with which we wish to connect. The stances we adopt and observations and evaluations we share exist relative to the meaning-making of the other members of our social network and to all other potential networks of meaning. In other words, we perform our online identities in order to connect with others (38).

Against this background, it is understandable that Twitter has been a popular tool for campaign communication in the US throughout the last decade. It is equally comprehensible that the calculated interference or even manipulation of such digital discourses was just a matter of time. While it is impossible to tell if social bots helped to multiply some of the postings and thus kept #basketofdeplorables trending, members of the Trump team and family got involved in the subsequent memetic negotiation. While memes such as the *Jaws* image are hyper-connective and inclusionary since they work on the basis of broad pop-cultural knowledge and are legible for a broad range of users, Donald J. Trump Jr. posted a meme on his Instagram account on September 11 that referred to a relatively well-known action movie but moreover included symbolism of the alt-right (fig. 3). It soon became one of the memes that circulated most frequently on Twitter as re-tweets or re-posts under the hashtag 'basketofdeplorables.' The post was a photoshopped poster of the 2010 movie *The Expendables* written by and starring Sylvester Stallone and other action film actors such as Jason Statham and Mickey Rourke. In the meme, the heads of the original actors who played a group of elite mercenaries on a mission to overthrow a Latin American dictator had been replaced with faces of the members of the GOP, the Trump Family, Roger Stone and Pepe the Frog while the original movie title had been changed to *The Deplorables*. In the center, Donald Trump, wearing a military beret, prominently replaces Sylvester Stallone as group leader. In the accompanying commentary that was also hashtagged with 'basketofdeplorables,' Trump Jr. stated that he was "honored to be grouped with the hard working men and women of this great nation that have supported @realdonaldtrump and know that he can fix the mess created by politicians in Washington. He's fighting for you and won't ever quit. Thanks for your trust!" (donaldjtrumpjr, Instagram, 11 September 2016).

Figure 3: 'The Deplorables'-Meme (Source: www.instagram.com/donaldjtrumpjr)

Apart from the prior pop-cultural knowledge concerning the movie that was needed to understand the reference, this meme also required a more specific type of insider group knowledge to be completely legible. 'Pepe the frog' was a popular meme that had been appropriated by the alt-right and was prominently used by Trump supporters and even Trump himself throughout the 2016 campaign. Interestingly, Donald Trump Jr.'s post entailed a broad discussion in the mass media with respect to the meaning of pepe and even incited a post on Hillary Clinton's campaign blog that discussed the image but was mocked for failing to understand its meaning. As a symbol whose proper meaning could only be understood with insider knowledge, 'pepe the frog' was frequently used by the pro-Trump community to distance itself from political opponents and keep them out of the debate. Thus, while most memes are all-inclusive in principle since they work with intertextual references to popular semantics, the deplorables-meme posted by Trump Jr. also excludes those who are not part of a specific political peer group already since some elements cannot be understood by those who are not familiar with the symbolism of the alt-right. While the early stages of digital discursive reappraisal of the 'basketofdeplorables'-incident proceeded in a general networked public, or, in Stäheli's terms, fostered the inclusion of a general audience (282), the political appropriation of the term 'deplorables' and emergence of an imagined community was triggered through humorous pop-cultural remixing. With the posting of Trump Jr.'s deplorable-meme and its ensuing spreading on social networks, the digital performative communitization process turned from 'popular' and all-inclusive to 'populist' and thus only partially inclusive. On Twitter, in the following days, a wide range of new 'deplorables'-memes was posted consecutively under the 'baskeofdeplorables' hashtag, among them the aforementioned '*Les Deplorables*'-meme as well as numerous variations and memes that linked the self-designation 'deplorables' to the first words of the constitution, "We, the People" (fig. 4).

Figure 4: 'We, the People'-Meme (Source: @iquesi, *Twitter*, https://twitter.com/iquesi)

Ernesto Laclau's concept of 'populism' is useful to understand how populist group identities, that is, political groups that conceive themselves as the legitimate unity of 'the people,' emerge performatively within discourses.³ Whereas his approach has been criticized for being too narrowly focused on linguistic forms of discursive performative processes, Jon Simons emphasizes that Laclau's ideas are equally transferable to mass media and popular culture (202). While the general formation of 'imagined communities' can, but does not have to, come along with the articulation of political demands, populist communitization works particularly through a transformation of different, previously rejected political demands into a logic of equivalence (96). Those who are involved in the emergence of a populist community may have little in common with regard to their social situation and even less with regard to their individual political demands, but what they share is the idea that those demands have been rejected by the government in place. The feeling of having been rejected and thus being *excluded* from legitimate political discourse is what creates the conditions of a new populist group formation, a performative process of *inclusion* through the equivalent articulation of heterogeneous demands in discourse and a self-perception of the group as being identical to a legitimate whole of 'the people' (74). As a consequence, the identity that is constituted in discourse must become, *intentionally* poorer in order to embrace all kinds of different demands (96). Therefore, the name of the community that emerges, and thus its self-designation and identification, is "a tendentially empty signifier" (131). As Simons explains: "Unfulfilled political demands are transferred to the empty signifier or partial object, becoming 'the rallying point of passionate attachments' and the locus of popular identity [...]" (208). In that manner, in the final stage of its digital re-interpretation and appropriation, the term 'deplorables' functioned as an affectively loaded empty signifier for a populist imagined community formation of Trump supporters who conceived themselves as legitimate totality of '(We,) the people.' To understand the notion of performative populist community formation solely by means of Laclau's formalistic approach, however, does not help much when it comes to the analysis of the performative emergence of specific populist communities, since it does not offer any tools to analyze the content of populist discourses. Moreover, as has often been criticized, Laclau's broad definition of 'populism' includes all kinds of political communitizations and deprives the term of any historical specificity or potential for critique. Hence, several scholars who explore the emergence of contemporary populism have argued for an approach which recognizes that 'style' and 'content' are inherently linked (Stegemann 14; Moffitt 40). With regard to the digital discourse on '#basketofdeplorables,' it could

---

³ While Laclau uses the term 'popular' when he talks about populist communitization processes, I differentiate 'popular,' referring to popular culture, and 'populist,' referring to populism for the sake of clarification.

be observed that populist communitization of 'the people' works particularly well by re-use, remix, and repetition of popular semantics, yet since the formation of a populist group is not all-inclusionary but simultaneously strictly exclusionary, a comprehensive approach to populism must take the use of particular political symbols and codes into consideration. After Donald J. Trump Jr. had used the figure of 'pepe the frog' in his deplorable meme, many Twitter users also incorporated the alt-right symbol into their own deplorable memes (fig. 5).

Figure 5: 'Les Dep'-Meme (Source: @El_Chorro, *Twitter*, https://twitter.com/el__chorro)

While hyper-connective popular memes had dominated the 'basketofdeplorables' discourse earlier, they were now increasingly replaced by memes that were pre-coded with right-wing political symbolism and thus only partially inclusive. A common notion about contemporary populism is that it implies the separation of society into two antagonistic camps, that is, 'the people' and 'the corrupt elite' (Mudde et al. 6). In the light of this demarcation, the popularity of the 'Les Deplorables'-meme and its emulations becomes comprehensible. Through the conversion of 'misérables' into 'deplorables,' the notion of a people suppressed by the state, unified by a legitimate and eventually violent rebellion against the government mirrors the self-conception of the populist digital imagined community of Trump supporters.

As conspicuous and as durable the trending of #basketofdeplorables and its respective discursive negotiation might have been, it is doubtful that the imagined populist community of 'deplorables' would have 'survived' in the digital semi-public realm exclusively in the long run. To become a long-term group identity, both far-reaching and long-lasting public visibility as well as a leader figure were essential. While visibility of the community was initially guaranteed through mass media coverage on the trending topic '#basketofdeplorables,' the interest of the press and TV reporting would have most likely weakened quickly after the disappearance of the Twitter trend. The fact that the digital imagined community of 'deplorables' was transferred into a broader cross-media populist group identity is due to the fact that Trump, in line with his son's 'deplorable' meme, subsequently stylized himself as the representative leading figure – representative of 'the people.' Importantly, as Benjamin Moffitt has summarized, populism scholars all agree on the centrality of a leader for populist movements as a figure who is responsible for bringing 'the people' together, either spatially or symbolically. While social media networks such as Twitter offer the illusion of direct communication between the leader and 'the people' by providing a 'semblance of immediacy' (Moffitt 88; Arditi 68), the presencing of a unified populist community is ultimately dependent on the verification of the representative claim through a wider media public:

> However, perhaps just as important as being accepted by your constituency in the form of 'the people' is the reception and coverage you receive from other audiences – particularly in regards of being perceived as being in touch with or representing 'the people'. [...] We know that the wider audience matters because the kinds of events noted above – rallies, online displays of support, elections and so forth – are not just aimed at pleasing 'the people' but are often designed to be broadcast and disseminated (that is, mediated) to wider audiences. [...] So while the wider audience may not personally accept the populist's claim to speak for 'the people' – that is, they may see the populist leader offering the claim as a charlatan – what they *do* need to 'buy' is the idea that the populist's claim to speak for 'the people' *resonates with those people.* (Moffitt 110)

When Donald J. Trump entered the stage to the sounds of "Do You Hear the People Sing?" with the 'Les Deplorables'-meme on the screen behind him at his presidential campaign rally on September 16, 2016, one week after Hillary Clinton's 'basketofdeplorables'-gaffe, his performance combined his own adoption of the role of the leader and voice of the populist imagined community of 'deplorables' and the public 'rendering present' of 'the deplorables' as unity of 'the people' and therefore legitimate holders of sovereignty (Moffitt 43). Summarizing the essence of the populist conflict of the people vs. the elite, the lyrics of the 'Les Miserables' song perfectly matched the occasion: "Do you hear the people sing, singing the songs of angry men? It is the music of the people who will not be slaves again! When the beating of your heart echoes the beating of the drums, there is a life about to start when tomorrow comes!" As all popular semantics that have been examined throughout this study, the song supported the affective communitization of the 'deplorables'- community. As Lisbeth van Zoonen points out in her study on politics and popular culture:

> We can conclude that when popular music claims an explicit political role for itself, it is usually in association with social movement politics, constructing and confirming the sense of togetherness around a particular shared concern (49).

By making use of the same products of popular culture that had fostered the performative emergence of a populist community-fantasy in the digital sphere and thus 'speaking the language' of 'the people,' in his performance in Miami, Trump thus ultimately validated the term 'deplorables' as empty signifier for the collective identification of his supporters that would take him to power a few weeks later. One year after election day 2016, he posted a photo of himself and parts of his team on board of Air Force One and a concomitant commentary: @realDonaldTrump "Congratulations to all of the 'DEPLORABLES' and the millions of people who gave us a MASSIVE (304-227) Electoral College landslide victory!"

Works Cited

@AUFemmeFBFan "Honored to be in the #BasketOfDeplorables with you! ;D" *Twitter*, 10. Sept. 2016. url no longer available

@BarbaraJean_s "HRC should know better than refer to supports of any one or thing as #basketofdeplorables huge misstep not inclusive" *Twitter*, 10. Sept. 2016. url no longer available.

@DonovanCaylor "@HillaryClinton was indeed wrong to say that half of Trump supporters were a #BasketOfDeplorables. I'm pretty sure she meant ALL of them." *Twitter*, 10. Sept. 2016. url no longer available

@HillaryClinton "'I won't stop calling out bigotry and racist rhetoric in this campaign.' – Hillary" *Twitter,* 10. Sept. 2016, <https://twitter.com/HillaryClinton/status/774671254850772992>

@realDonaldTrump "Wow, Hillary Clinton was SO INSULTING to my supporters, millions of amazing, hard working people. I think it will cost her at the Polls!" *Twitter*, 10. Sept. 2016, 05:47, <https://twitter.com/realdonaldtrump/status/774590070355529728>

@realDonaldTrump "Hillary Clinton just had her 47% moment. What a terrible thing she said about so many great Americans!" *Twitter*, 10. Sept. 2016, 16:37, <https://twitter.com/realdonaldtrump/status/774753598970466304>

@realDonaldTrump "Congratulations to all of the 'DEPLORABLES' and the millions of people who gave us a MASSIVE (304-227) Electoral College landslide victory!" *Twitter*, 8. Nov. 2017, 10:17, <https://twitter.com/realdonaldtrump/status/928325667556548608>

@realJamesCrane "number 1 i think it's absolutely disgusting for a presidential candidate to insult half of americans #BasketOfDeplorables" *Twitter*, 10. Sept. 2016. url no longer available

@UsherJenn "Proud to be in a #BasketOfDeplorables" *Twitter*, 10. Sept. 2016 url no longer available

Alberge, Dalya. "Donald Trump upsets Les Misérables creators by playing song at rally." *The Guardian* 19 September 2016 <https://www.theguardian.com/us-news/2016/sep/19/donald-trump-upsets-les-miserables-song-rally-cameron-mackintosh>.

Anderson, Benedict. *Imagined Communities: Reflections on the Origin and Spread of Nationalism*. London & New York: Verso, 1983.

Arditi, Benjamin. *Politics on the Edges of Liberalism: Difference, Populism, Revolution, Agitation*. Edinburgh: Edinburg UP, 2007.

boyd, danah. "Social Network Sites as Networked Publics. Affordances, Dynamics, and Implications." *A Networked Self. Identity, Community and Culture on Social Network Sites*. Ed. Zizi Papacharissi. New York: Routledge, 2011. 39-58.

Breitenbach, Patrick. "Memes. Das Web als kultureller Nährboden." *New Media Culture. Mediale Phänomene der Netzkultur*. Ed. Christian Stiegler, Patrick Breitenbach, and Thomas Zorbach. Bielefeld: Transcript, 2015. 29-50.

Chozick, Amy. "Hillary Clinton Calls Many Trump Backers 'Deplorables,' and G.O.P. Pounces." *The New York Times* 10 September 2016 <https://www.nytimes.com/2016/09/11/us/politics/hillary-clinton-basket-of-deplorables.html>.

"Deplorable Entrance: Trump Takes Stage to 'Les Mis' Song." *YouTube*, uploaded by *Bloomberg Politics*, 16 September 2016, <https://youtu.be/TEiTKloMgBg>.

donaldjtrumpjr, instagram, 11 September 2016, <https://www.instagram.com/p/BKMtdN5Bam5/?utm_source=ig_embed>.

Flores, Reena. "Hillary Clinton: Half of Donald Trump Supporters in 'Basket of Deplorables'." *CBS News* 10 September 2016 <https://www.cbsnews.com/news/hillary-clinton-half-donald-trump-supporters-basket-of-deplorables/>.

Grossberg, Lawrence. *We Gotta Get Out of This Place: Popular Conservatism and Postmodern Culture*. New York & London: Routledge, 1992.

Heiskanen, Benita. "Meme-ing Electoral Participation." *European Journal of American Studies*. Vol. 12, No. 2. (2017): 1-26. <http://journals.openedition.org/ejas/12158>.

Jenkins, Henry, Sam Ford, Joshua Green (eds.). *Spreadable Media: Creating value and Meaning in a Networked Culture.* New York and London: New York UP, 2013.
Laclau, Ernesto. *On Populist Reason.* London & New York: Verso, 2005.
Martosko, David. "Trump accused of inciting violence against Hillary AGAIN: Donald under fire after urging Clinton guards to drop their guns and 'see what happens' as he makes her Deplorables 'insult' his new slogan." *Daily Mail* 17 September 2016. <http://www.dailymail.co.uk/news/article-3793718/LES-DEPLORABLES-Trump-floors-cheering-Miami-crowd-enters-Broadway-anthem-speaks-giant-Les-Mis-video-screen-art.html>.
Milner, Ryan M. *The World Made Meme: Public Conversations and Participatory Media.* Cambridge & London: The MIT Press, 2016.
Mudde, Cas, and Christóbal Rovira Kaltwasser. *Populism: A Very Short Introduction.* New York: Oxford UP, 2017.
Moffitt, Benjamin. *The Global Rise of Populism: Performance, Political Style and Representation.* Stanford: Stanford UP, 2016.
Papacharissi, Zizi. *Affective Publics. Sentiment, Technology, and Politics.* New York: Oxford UP, 2015.
Simons, Jon. "Mediated Construction of the People: Laclau's Political Theory and Media Politics." *Discourse Theory and Critical Media Politics.* Ed. Lincoln Dahlberg and Sean Phelan. Basingstoke: Palgrave Macmillan, 2011. 201-21.
Stegemann, Bernd. *Das Gespenst des Populismus: Ein Essay zur politischen Dramaturgie.* Berlin: Theater der Zeit, 2017.
Stäheli, Urs. "The Popular in the Political System." *Cultural Studies* Vol. 17.2 (2003): 275-99.
Van Dijck, José. *The Culture of Connectivity. A Critical History of Social Media.* New York: Oxford UP, 2013.
Van Dijck, José, and Thomas Poell. "Understanding Social Media Logic." *Media and Communication.* 1.1 (2013): 2-14.
Van Zoonen, Liesbet. *Entertaining the Citizens. When Politics and Popular Culture Converge.* Lanham: Rowman & Littlefield, 2005.
Zappavigna, Michelle. *Discourse of Twitter and Social Media: How We Use Language to Create Affiliation on the Web.* London et al.: Bloomsbury, 2012.

Jobs, Free Trade, and a Conspiracy: Trump's Use of Producerism

Michael Oswald

> It's going to be unbelievable.
> I will be the greatest jobs president
> that God ever created, believe me.
> (Trump 2016m)

Jobs, Free Trade, and a Conspiracy

Job creators, losers, the corrupt government, the rigged system – Donald Trump used these terms often in his election campaign. Yet these are not mere phrases, they appear to be of a strategic nature because they rehearse a well-known cultural narrative. It is actually one of the oldest narratives of American populism: the narrative of producerism. Producerism is part of a right-wing conspiracy theory which seeks to undermine the state, and it divides society into two camps. According to the narrative, productive people are betrayed by the government and political liberals, who are ousting the wealth of the productive people. It is especially directed against taxation and regulation, and, with its anti-government stance, it also reinforces anti-statism (see Stone 2012: 166f.).

In Donald Trump's case, another important feature of producerism is that it offers a chance to make clever use of the role of the job-creator. It not only introduces a hero, it also suggests a bond between businesspeople and employees as they supposedly face common enemies: the government and the political establishment. Producerism also legitimizes the idea of tax cuts for businesspeople and makes such a proposal attractive for employees – the promised tax cuts will in turn increase their wages, so the narrative goes. With that, it produces a very specific interpretation of the relationship between the economy and the need for taxation.

In this paper, I want to shed light on the producerist narrative the president used in his campaign speeches in order to conjure up an image that resonates with a constituency whose grievances boil down to Washington's mismanagement of national affairs. By using the approach of producerism as a heuristic and the method of triangulation, 187 speeches of Donald J. Trump were coded in order to show a strategic pattern that was based on producerist sentiments. This is a powerful rhetoric and potentially a winning strategy because it frames pressing problems in terms that are directed against the establishment and especially the Democratic Party. The quotations used in the text can be seen as exemplary for all the speeches examined in this sample, as they are quite similar and often interchangeable.

Narrative Analysis

Narratology and narrative analysis are at the center of literary studies but have also been adopted by other disciplines, such as political science. Narrative analysis received particular emphasis by Deborah Stone who introduced the analysis of causal narratives (1989, 2012). Many other modes of analysis fail to recognize any content beyond the one that is manifest. The focus on narratives allows for a symptomatic reading, i.e. a deconstruction of communication strategies, bringing their latent elements to the fore and showing that there is usually more than what the content reveals at first glance (Van Gorp 72). Narrative analysis can provide insights into specific patterns in communication, which are usually embedded in larger societal contexts and which are sometimes shaped according to overall strategies.

Narrative Structure and Rationality

Societies are characterized by and rely on numerous narratives. These are well-known stories or parables, which often provide explanations of why certain things are the way they are – or "how the world works" (Stone 2012: 158). They also convey a deeper meaning and affirm different ways of life, beliefs, meanings, achievements, certain expectations, ideas, and values (Arnold 8; Berlet 2012b: 49). Through narrative strategies, a specifically constructed reality and new interpretations of political situations are conveyed. These are interwoven with subjectivity, identity, and ideology (McClure 191; Hajer 63).

Fisher sees a particular form of rationality in narratives. The central criteria for rationality are narrative probability and narrative fidelity. Both categories relate to the coherence and integrity of a narrative (Fisher 1987). According to Fisher, reality can only be communicatively constructed in a successful way if (1) the reality of the recipient is reflected in certain traits of a narrative, and (2) if the explanation or the reasons given are not rejected as implausible. Therefore, a narrative must be structurally meaningful not only in itself but also in a larger context (Fisher 1985: 297; 1984: 9). Fisher subsumes the narrative probability into three categories:

- **Argumentative or structural coherence**, in which the standards of formal and informal rationality are to be considered.
- **Material coherence**, which connects one story to other related stories. The latter are often as consistent as the former but often disregard essential questions, arguments, and facts – or exhibit a different framing.
- **Characterological coherence**, which stands for the reliability of the character and credibility of the narrators and actors. This is important because the actions and decisions of a person reflect their values (Fisher 1987: 47).

Narrative fidelity concerns the validity and credibility of a story. First of all, it addresses the question of whether 'good reasons' have been provided in order to be persuasive and to show the validity of claims in the narrative. Furthermore, fidelity is a measurement for resonance – does the story resonate with narratives the audience already knows and believes in (Fisher 1987: 47, 64, 194)? The narrative fidelity can therefore also be used as a reference for the correlation of a message with existing narratives, meanings, values, and norms of a society: the higher this correlation, the higher the recognition value and perceived cultural legitimacy (Williams 107; Benford 692).

Narratives structure the way people think and provide them with beliefs and attitudes. In this way, they structure specific discourses. The overall picture that is painted in a narrative encompasses far more than what is told in the story (Gadinger et al. 21; McClure 191). Especially the causality mechanisms in narratives play an important role for the interpretation of the problem depicted. Causal narratives are not only linked to specific issues but also to the question of what triggered them. Interpretations of political problems are constantly generated, changed, and fought over. Narrative story-lines and symbols help to form these framings even though it seems as if the communicators are merely describing facts (Stone 1989: 282). Therefore, narratives work well to convey a specific (new) definition of social problems. In particular, when the problematic features of reality correspond with traditional narratives, they can be used for framing the situation in a way beneficial for the narrator (Entman 164).

In causal interpretations, problems are depicted as a consequence of human action. In these stories, one group of people inflicts damage upon another. Thus, the perpetrators are identified as being responsible for the suffering of the victim group (Stone 1989: 283, 299). Correspondingly, narratives allocate and assign responsibility and establish heroes, villains, and innocent victims in these stories (Stone 2012: 158). According to Stone, there are usually two types of narrative structures in politics: narratives of decline and narratives of power. Both are characterized by certain causal connections between actions and consequences.

Causalities in Narratives

Narratives of decline portray a crisis or a scenario of an imminent catastrophe or unstoppable decay. Communicators may use facts and figures selectively to support their arguments concerning decline. They mostly use statistics of rising crime rates and poverty (Stone 1989: 138, 142; Stone 2012: 160-5). Among such narratives of decline are stories of prevented progress, in which specific individuals or groups are blamed for the deterioration of the situation (Stone 2012: 161f.). Another version of that narrative is that change – either an improvement or decline – is only an illusion (Stone 2012: 165; Stone 1989: 142).

In a narrative about power and control, a bleak situation that used to be accepted is contrasted with a possibility of change through human agency (Stone 2012: 165f.). These kinds of narratives often appear in the form of conspiracy theories in which a person or group of people is not only responsible for an act or an omission but also has a hidden agenda – at least in so far as the repercussions of the action were knowingly tolerated. In this version, those responsible are a few influential individuals who acted to their own advantage (Stone 2012: 166f.; 1989: 290).

According to Stone, the various forms of narratives can be categorized into four distinct types with specific causal dependencies: an intentional act (direct control of the actor), a mechanical cause (indirect control exercised by an intervening actor), an unintended cause (control by intervening conditions) or an unfortunate coincidence (accident, total absence of human control) (Stone 1989: 299). This list can be categorized in a four-field panel with corresponding dependencies:

		Consequences	
		Intended	Unintended
Actions	Unguided	Mechanical Cause	Accidental Cause
Actions	Purposeful	Intentional Cause	Inadvertent Cause

Figure 1: Categorization of narratives (Source: own depiction according to Stone)

In the lower left box, a specific person or a group of people intend their actions to have certain consequences. Because these are conscious actions, the narrative can be constructed as one of oppressors and victims. These stories are quite often close to conspiracy theories. Inadvertent causes are consequences of human actions which were not intended. These types of narratives often accompany the socially detrimental effects of well-intended policies (Stone 1989: 285). Mechanical causes cannot be traced back to an intention; however, in such narratives, the consequences of an indirect action have come to pass – for example by other people or by machines (Stone 1989: 286).

While one side in a political conflict tries to push a problem into the realm of intent, the other side tries to create the opposite impression. There are numerous narrative strategies that help to transfer the responsibility to certain people or groups (Stone 1989: 289). With such narratives

- a social order can either be changed or protected.
- causal agents can be identified, and responsibility can be attributed to certain political actors.
- actors can legitimize and empower themselves as a remedy for the problem.

If (groups of) people are in a similar unequal and oppressive relationship to an actor, new alliances between them can be created or existing ones can be restructured. Thus, common categories of victims are created through causal narratives (Stone 1989: 295, 299).

Donald Trump's Use of Producerism

Producerism in Trump's Campaign

The US-American producerist narrative can first be detected in the political discourse of Revolutionary America. It claims that parasites are feeding off the productive colonial subjects' hard-earned money. Clearly, the narrative back then was aimed against the British. This anti-aristocratic producerism was advocated by Thomas Jefferson and other influential statesmen and intellectuals and it served the revolutionary campaign well. The narrative was popularized in the early nineteenth century – in the politics of the Jeffersonian and Jacksonian eras – and in the course of time, it became widespread among the American public (Wilentz 69). The 1800s were the time when taxation became an issue amongst farmers and artisan working-class organizations. When the government started taxing farmers, some of them framed this as an act similar to a confiscation of their earnings. They started to accuse the government of robbing them of their belongings. The farmers and workers saw themselves as 'producers' who create goods, whereas politicians, bureaucrats, and the needy only consumed. The latter were seen as 'takers.' The producers represented themselves as being clamped into the vise between corrupt political elites at the top and lazy, sinful 'parasites' on the 'bottom' (Guardino et al. 540; Berlet 2012a: 568). This is why the producerist narrative dichotomizes society into two camps – productive people and 'parasites' (Peck 529f.; Berlet 2012a: 568).

Donald Trump used producerism in order to promote his anti-tax ethos, to assign blame, and to make his narrative salient amongst workers who may already have felt ill-served by the government. Of course, he did not use it in its original form, but he constructed a causal narrative why well-paid workers' jobs have vanished. This is a particularly useful strategy because the producerist narrative is based on an established cleavage-structure in the United States: in its history there were constant conflicts between self-perceived productive Americans – workers, peasants, and small entrepreneurs – and politicians, government bureaucrats, academics, and media icons. The producers were patriots but also staunch critics of the government, especially with regard to some social, cultural, and economic changes that seemed to be desired by the elites (Guardino et al. 540, Langman 491). The producers saw two groups living at their expense: not only did civil servants live off their taxes, they also passed them on to 'unworthy' poor people (Berlet 2012a: 568). Generally, producerism can be used to exploit social problems for corporate gains, especially if they are in line with populist prejudices (Langman 491). Trump also used social problems but only in terms of the ever more declining wages and the negative trends in absolute income mobility over the past decades.

In speeches of the candidate Trump the producerist sentiment was one of the most often occurring themes: He used it in nearly 92 percent of his speeches.

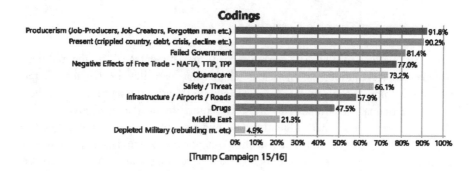

Figure 2: Coding of Donald Trump's campaign speeches

The quantitative side of the application of the narrative is quite telling, however, the qualitative side is even more interesting, particularly concerning questions of how Trump has interwoven producerism with social problems, his overall strategy, and the role of past and future government – especially a Trump-led administration.

With its causal structure, the producerist narrative directs anger about certain problems towards the government. That is why, in the end, producerism promotes the subversion of governmental structures and reinforces anti-statism (Berlet 2012a: 569). Donald Trump basically depicted the government as being the enemy of both workers and business owners because in the narrative, the political elite had caused the decline of certain American industry sectors. In this regard, he used the producerist narrative in his campaign in order to show that the economic decline in the United States is causally connected to certain policies – and in order to support the claim that their repercussions were at least knowingly tolerated. Because this narrative alleges a secret plot, it figures as part of a conspiracy theory in which jobs are willingly sacrificed. Therefore, an important point of this modern form of producerism is the denomination of job-killers vs. job-creators. The first part of why the government is a job-killer is due to taxation and regulation.

Taxes and Regulations

> We're going to have the biggest tax cut since Ronald Reagan and maybe even bigger. We're going to eliminate every unnecessary job-killing regulation.
> (Trump 2016e)

Donald Trump uses the Republican playbook of low taxation and deregulation, but he positions these conservative principles at the center of his focal theme: the demise of well-paid-jobs for unskilled workers. In his rhetoric, Trump uses narratives of decline extensively. He depicts a causal connection between a diminished industry sector and the interference of the government and assigns the responsibility for the suffering of the victim group – the workers – to the administration. According to Trump, the (Democratic) government 'kills jobs' because it taxes and regulates businesses: "[o]ur taxes are so high, our taxes are so high that businesses are forced to leave. [...]. Our businesses are being forced out, we can't let it happen" (Trump 2016d). In the causal structure of Trump's narrative, businesses must lay off workers as a result of high taxation. Therefore, the government is seen to neither act in the interests nor in the will of the people. It wastes the 'hard-earned tax money' for failed policies at best and for their own gain at worst. Because of that, businesses and business-people are suffering, and they cannot afford to pay the wages they used to – let alone higher wages – and the taxes to the government. Amongst disgruntled voters, this claim aims to fuel distrust, not only of the federal government but also of the Democrats.

As a first step, Trump promised a significant corporate tax reduction of 20 percentage points in order to stimulate the struggling economic sectors in the United States and bring back well-paid industry jobs:

> Our good jobs have really left us. [...] The business rate will be lowered from 35% to 15% and the trillions of dollars of American corporate money overseas can now be brought back at a 10% rate. It's stuck. We can't bring it back – $2.5 trillion to $5 trillion. (Trump 2016g)

In Trump's producerist argument, lower taxes mean that more money will be left to hire people in the United States and the offshore cash of the companies will be brought back into the country. It would also result in large capital expenditures.

> We're going to bring Apple and many other companies, they're going to be back in the United States. Our jobs, we're going with much lower business taxes. We're bringing the tax rate from 35 percent to 15 percent and we are going to be booming again. [...] As part of our plan to bring back our jobs, we're going to lower our business tax from 35 percent to 15 percent. Right now we're the highest in the world, we're going to be one of the lowest. (Trump 2016d)

In this perspective, tax cuts for businesspeople serve the workers well as a tax break would not only result in the creation of jobs but also bring prosperity for all: the wealth would trickle-down to the employees in form of bonuses and wage increases. This approach of utilitarian considerations re-frames the understanding of taxation. With this interpretation, the mindset of the business elite and their pledge for lowering taxes was morally redefined: it is not the entrepreneurs who prefer tax cuts who are to be criticized for not being willing to pay their fair share, but the Democrats because they harm the economy, if they insist on higher taxes (Peck 530, 532). On the basis of this theory of supply-side economics, Trump suggested that lower taxes would result in a boost in jobs:

> Reagan's tax cuts in the eighties, and Kennedy's tax cuts in the sixties, brought us tremendous growth. My economic reforms – on taxes, trade, regulation and American energy – will produce at least 25 million new jobs in a decade. It's the most pro-growth economic plan in American history. (Trump 2016c)

Tax reform would also benefit the middle class directly, so that more money would be left in the hands of those who are struggling.

> The largest tax reductions are for the middle class, who have been forgotten. It's called the forgotten man and woman. They have been forgotten. The middle class with family of two children will get basically approximately a 35% tax cut and that's what they can use and that money will go back into the economy. The current number of brackets will be reduced from seven to three, and tax forms will likewise be greatly simplified. (Trump 2016h)

The notion of the 'forgotten man and woman' is also connected to the producerist narrative: the 'forgotten people' obviously are those who suffer because of the high taxation and regulations but the phrase 'The Forgotten Man' stems from an 1893 essay by William Graham Sumner. Hailed in today's libertarian movement, Sumner also saw producerist causalities working against diligent workers:

> The Forgotten Man is delving away in patient industry, supporting his family, paying his taxes, casting his vote, supporting the church and the school, reading

his newspaper, and cheering for the politician of his admiration, but he is the only one for whom there is no provision in the great scramble and the big divide. (Sumner 491)

This narrative of producerism and the forgotten people fits well with the stricken workers and their families. It corresponds with a seemingly looming threat of even higher taxation if Hillary Clinton were to be elected.

The idea of supply-oriented economics also rests on the assumption that regulatory restrictions prevent economic recovery. In his campaign, Trump promised to put people, especially miners and steelworkers, back to work:

> That means getting rid of job-killing EPA regulations that are unnecessary. So many unnecessary. We're going to put the miners right here in Colorado back to work. We're going to put them back to work. [...]. Get ready to go to work. You want to go back to work? You're going to go back to work. Your jobs will come back under a Trump administration. Your incomes will go up under a Trump administration. Your taxes will go way, way down under a Trump administration. Your companies won't be leaving Colorado under a Trump administration. (Trump 2016h)

In the narrative, regulations are understood as being job-killing-policies; they prevent growth, and they force factories to reduce their capacities – therefore regulations put hard workers out of work. By relaxing or eliminating regulations, Trump promises to bring back the old jobs that fell victim to the supposedly unnecessary restrictions imposed by other administrations, especially those led by Democrats. He labeled them 'job-killers' not only because of regulation and taxation but also to indicate the pernicious effects of free trade agreements for the US economy: politicians supposedly shipped well-paid jobs abroad.

Free Trade

> I'm going to fight for every worker who deserves a raise, and for every community whose jobs and dreams have been ripped out and shipped to other countries.
> (Trump 2016c)

Since producerism divides society into two segments, the productive people and the 'parasites,' the narrative can be understood in terms of a populist dichotomy: the 'we and they'-perspective comprises the producers on the one hand and the parasites on the other. But the dichotomy is also perceived as the division of the people vs. the establishment/government (Peck 528). Therein lies the structural connection to common populist strategies. In Trump's producerist narrative this 'we and they'-anti-establishment-perspective is causally and explicitly linked to some form of conspiracy. He implied that the free trade agreements negotiated by former administrations are not only detrimental to the economy but also to the workers' wages. He used this notion especially by claiming that the Democrats had sent the well-paid jobs abroad for their own gain and therefore made the case that the government is corrupt:

> We're going to take on the special interests, the corrupt media – and it is corrupt – and the career politicians that have stolen your jobs, your wealth and stolen our middle class. They've stolen our middle class. We're going to make Pennsylvania rich again by bringing back our jobs. We'll bring back our jobs. (Trump 2016k)

Trump made use of his producerist-job-narrative in regions where the economic decline hit people especially hard. At a rally in Columbus, OH he stated: "These are the people who emptied the jobs out of Ohio, Pennsylvania, Michigan, and North Carolina and shipped them to other countries" (Trump 2016f).

In order to dramatize the economic problems with the biggest effect possible, Trump connected the loss of well-paid jobs to free trade and corruption. He stated that the government is led by its own special interests, suggesting that this was the cause why working people from these regions were suffering. This way, he could evoke the deepest contempt for the politicians who seemed to act irresponsibly. A Trump administration would act very differently:

> We are fighting for every community whose jobs and dreams have been ripped out and shipped to other countries. [...] We are fighting for every American who believes government should serve the people – not the donors, and not the special interests. (Trump 2016l)

Trump framed the free trade agreements as being the sole reason why certain jobs have vanished, why factories have disappeared from the United States, and why wages in some sectors of the economy have declined significantly during the past couple of decades. According to Trump, the biggest threat to workers are the free trade deals the Democrats are supposedly famous for. In his narrative, the jobs got 'shipped abroad' because of these contracts:

> The state of Maine has lost nearly 1 in 3 manufacturing jobs since NAFTA, signed by Bill Clinton and supported by Hillary Clinton. (Trump 2016c)

> We are living through the greatest job theft in the history of the world. More jobs have been stolen from our country, so stupidly we let them go. We let our companies go so foolishly. We don't know what we're doing. A Trump administration is going to renegotiate NAFTA, stand up to the foreign cheating, and stop the jobs from leaving our country, and have jobs come back in the other direction. (Trump 2016e)

> Her [Hillary Clinton] trade deal with South Korea, you know all about that one, she was pushing it so hard. Instead of making 100,000, it killed 100,000 American jobs. (Trump 2016i)

Trump's grand strategy was to declare 'America first,' and one part of that master plan was employment. The jobs would come back to the United States of America and would be given primarily to Americans:

> Many mothers across this country are worried their kids won't find jobs, and they are right to be worried. One of the biggest threats is outsourcing – jobs for college-educated kids are being sent to other countries. At the same time, companies are importing low-wage workers on H-1B visas to take jobs from young college-trained Americans. We will protect these jobs for Americans. (Trump 2016f)

However, the election campaign was not merely on jobs since unemployment is not the major factor of voter's dissatisfaction. Trump's election was about wages.

Trump addressed the problem that wages have decreased drastically in some regions and that what is commonly referred to as the American Dream was out of reach for the average person.

> You know, I tell this to people. We have people in this room right now that made more money 18 years ago than they're making now. They work a lot harder right now than they did 18 years ago. Their job was better 18 years ago and they're older. And the only thing I say is I'm older also, and I've never worked this hard either, folks, I will tell you. That's for sure. (Trump 2016b)

> The political establishment has brought about the destruction of our factories, and our jobs, as they flee to Mexico, China, and other countries all around the world. Our just-announced job numbers are anemic. Our gross domestic product, or GDP, is barely above 1 percent. And going down. Workers in the United States are making less than they were almost 20 years ago, and yet they are working harder. (Trump 2016o)

In Trump's narrative, the repercussions of the administration's purposeful actions have unintended consequences at best and intended ones at worst. This has all the ingredients of a conspiracy narrative where influential politicians conclude trade deals to serve their own ends. In this narrative, the American workers not only bear the brunt of the negative economic consequences of these deals, they also become the political victims of the government. Trump, on the other hand, was able to use one of the core elements of producerism and take up the role as the hero of the narrative, embodying the 'job-creator' in his narrative.

Job Creator

> We're going to create jobs.
> We're going to create jobs like you've never seen.
> (Trump 2016a)

Finally, Trump's narrative evolves in favor of his own policies. He casts himself as the workers' hero who can bring back both their old jobs and higher wages. He becomes the 'job-creator' in the narrative:

> A Trump administration will bring prosperity to all of our people. My economic agenda can be summed up in three such beautiful words: jobs, jobs, jobs! […] We're going to create jobs. […] I've created thousands and thousands of jobs. That's what I do. I create jobs. (Trump 2016k)

At the point at which Trump portrays himself as a 'job-creator' his producerism joins forces with his anti-free-trade-sentiment because he wants to bring back jobs by eliminating the cause of their demise, which, in his understanding, are the free trade deals: "[w]e're going to bring back our jobs, we're going to renegotiate our disastrous trade deals" (Trump 2016j). This is already Trump's proclamation of his intention to set off a new wave of protectionism:

> It's time we bring our country back. It's time we act like intelligent people. It's time that we don't let Mexico and all of these other countries take our jobs and that's what they are doing. You look at here, the miners. Look at the way they're been treated. We are going to protect our miners. We are going to protect our steel workers. We are going to protect our factories and our manufacturing. (Trump 2016k)

Trump's standing as a successful businessman who employs thousands of people probably added weight to his claim that he will bring jobs back to America. He also made use of that in his campaign:

> I'm proud of the tens of thousands of jobs that I've created, and I'm proud that I provide equal play and equal pay for equal work. And I have to do that, I have to do that. I've promoted women to the highest positions in my companies over the years, and they have done an incredible job. (Trump 2016b)

Trump's future task is mainly to bring his business-attitude into the White House and start creating jobs:

> I've spent a life in business creating tens of thousands of jobs. I built a great, great company, but I've spent a whole life I've employed tens of thousands of Americans but when I saw what was happening to our country, I just felt I had to act; I had to act and I acted I acted. (Trump 2016n)

At the same time, the status as a 'job-creator' puts the Republican candidate into one camp with the workers who have lost their old jobs or do not get paid as they used to: the businessman Trump harks back to a long tradition of producerist anti-government rhetoric. Producerism overcomes the old cleavage of capital-labor (employers vs. employees) and leads to a general alliance of working-people and entrepreneurs in order to unite them against the government. Finally, Trump's promise of what his policies will achieve is simple: "[w]ages will rise, jobs will return, and factories will come rushing onto our shore" (Trump 2016d). With the use of producerism this was not merely a promise, it became a causally related, meaningful discourse.

Producerism – a Viable Campaign Tool for a Stricken Society

With the producerist narrative of decline Trump established a causal connection and a viable explanation why the problems sketched above arose. The structural, material, and characterological coherence in this narrative are therefore fulfilled, and the narrative probability is quite evident. Furthermore, with producerism Trump has another argument in his favor: the producerist narrative is still well-known in the United States and therefore offers a resonant narration. According to Benford it has been widely identified as being part of the political culture (Benford 414f.). It is also rooted in what are considered core American values, such as independence, self-reliance, and individualism, which manifest themselves in a vision of hard work and limited government. Likewise, it echoes the dominant strands of the Protestant work ethic, which embraces the idea that hard-working citizens are likely to enjoy the fruits of their work (Boykoff et al. 341). This metaphor of the fruits of labor, anchored in the myth of the Puritans, can also be found in producerism. In the anti-tax frame, the productive people have earned their own wealth and should therefore be allowed to keep the entire yield (Peck 532). This also helps to create resonance because the Puritan work ethic also accrues a kind of cultural/symbolic capital in the United States (Paul 163). In turn, it is closely linked to the narrative of the American Dream. It implies a reasonable chance of mobility, a home, and a better life for the offspring (Langman 482). This is not only a cultural driving factor, it is also what is missing most in a lot of those regions where voters put their faith in Donald Trump: the belief in the American Dream. Narrative fidelity is therefore another factor this narrative fulfills completely.

Donald J. Trump tapped a vein of cultural indignation with a strategy that has certainly helped him win the presidency. He wooed Midwestern working-class whites who see themselves ill-served by the establishment, the elites, and the country's towering institutions with a compelling causal narrative. It is also remarkable how Trump campaigned specifically in those states that were crucial for deciding the election such as Ohio, Michigan, and Pennsylvania. Therefore, there are a lot of strategic patterns in this election campaign that suggest a carefully engineered blueprint. It was designed on a socio-cultural disconnect that has resurfaced with a groundswell of discontent among the 'disenfranchised' – voters who believe mainstream Democrats and Republicans fail to represent their interests. Trump's use of producerism and this stratagem's appeal to a crucial voting bloc probably helped Trump to pave the way to Pennsylvania Ave.

Works Cited

Arnold, Markus. "Über dieses Buch." *Erzählungen im Öffentlichen: Über die Wirkung narrativer Diskurse*. Ed. Markus Arnold, Gert Dressel, and Willy Viehöver. Wiesbaden: Springer VS, 2012. 7-13.

Benford, Robert D. "An Insider's Critique of the Social Movement Framing Perspective." *Sociological Inquiry* 67.4 (1997): 409-30.

Berlet, Chip. "Collectivists, Communists, Labor Bosses, and Treason: The Tea Parties as Right-Wing Populist Counter-Subversion Panic." *Critical Sociology* 38.4 (2012a): 565-87.

---. "Reframing Populist Resentments in the Tea Party Movement." *Steep: The precipitous rise of the Tea Party*. Ed. Christine Trost and Lawrence Rosenthal. Berkeley: University of California Press, 2012b. 47-66.

Boykoff, Jules, and Eulalie Laschever. "The Tea Party Movement, Framing, and the US Media." *Social Movement Studies* 10.4 (2011): 341-66.

Fisher, Walter R. *Human Communication as Narration: Toward a Philosophy of Reason, Value, and Action*. Columbia: University of South Carolina Press, 1987.

---. "The Narrative Paradigm: An Elaboration." *Communication Monographs* 52 (1985): 347-67.

---. "Narration as a Human Communication Paradigm: The Case of Public Moral Argument." *Communication Monographs* 51 (1984): 1-22.

Gadinger, Frank, Sebastian Jarzebski, and Taylan Yildiz. "Politische Narrative: Konturen einer politikwissenschaftlichen Erzähltheorie." *Politische Narrative: Konzepte – Analysen – Forschungspraxis*. Ed. Frank Gadinger, Sebastian Jarzebski, and Taylan Yildiz. Wiesbaden: VS-Springer, 2014. 3-38.

Guardino, Matt, and Dean Snyder "The Tea Party and the Crisis of Neoliberalism: Mainstreaming New Right Populism in the Corporate News Media." *New Political Science* 34.4 (2012): 527-48.

Hajer, Maarten. "Discourse Coalitions and the Institutionalisation of Practice: The Case of Acid Rain in Great Britain." *The Argumentative Turn in Policy Analysis and Planning*. Ed. Frank Fischer and John Forester. Durham/London: Duke University Press, 1993. 43-67.

Langman, Lauren. "Cycles of Contention: The Rise and Fall of the Tea Party." *Critical Sociology* 38.4 (2012): 469-94.

Peck, Reece "'You Say Rich, I Say Job Creator': How Fox News Framed the Great Recession through the Moral Discourse of Producerism." *Media, Culture & Society* 36.4 (2014): 526-35.

McClure, Kevin. "Resurrecting the Narrative Paradigm: Identification and the Case of Young Earth Creationism." *Rhetoric Society Quarterly* 39.2 (2009): 189-211.

Mols, Frank, and Jolanda Jetten. "No Guts, No Glory: How Framing the Collective Past Paves the Way for Anti-Immigrant Sentiments." *International Journal of Intercultural Relations*, 43 PA (2014): 74-86.

Paul, Heike. *The Myths That Made America: An Introduction to American Studies*. Bielefeld: Transcript, 2014.

Schneider, William. "American Religion and Political Polarities." *The American Sociologist* 34.1 (2003): 81-4.

Stone, Deborah. *Policy Paradox: The Art of Political Decision Making*. New York: W.W. Norton & Company, 2012.

---. "Causal Stories and the Formation of Policy Agendas." *Political Science Quarterly* 104.2 (1989): 281-300.

Sumner, William Graham. *The Forgotten Man and Other Essays*. New Haven: Yale University Press, 1919.

Trump, Donald J. News Conference in Palm Beach, FL. 1 March 2016. Transcript. 2016a. <https://www.c-span.org/video/?405774-1/donald-trump-super-tuesday-news-conference> Last accessed on 18 March 2018.

---. Rally in Ambridge, PA. 10 October 2016. Transcript. 2016b. <https://www.c-span.org/video/?416683-1/donald-trump-campaigns-ambridge-pennsylvania>. Last accessed on 18 March 2018.

---. Rally in Bangor, ME. 15 October 2016. Remarks as prepared. 2016c. <https://www.donaldjtrump.com/press-releases/trump-slams-hillary-for-open-

trade-and-open-borders-pledges-jobs-jobs-jobs>. Last accessed on 13 December 2016.

---. Rally in Cincinnati, OH. 13 October 2016. Transcript. 2016d. <https://www.c-span.org/video/?416881-1/donald-trump-campaigns-cincinnati-ohio>. Last accessed 18 March 2018.

---. Rally in Colorado Springs, CO. 18 October 2016. Transcript. 2016e. <https://www.c-span.org/video/?417109-1/donald-trump-calls-constitutional-amendment-impose-congressional-term-limits>. Last accessed on 18 March 2018.

---. Rally in Columbus, OH. 13 October 2016. Remarks as prepared. 2016f. <https://www.donaldjtrump.com/press-releases/donald-j.-trump-will-work-every-day-to-make-america-great-again-for-millenn>. Last accessed on 13 December 2016.

---. Rally in Gettysburg, PA. 22 October 2016. Transcript. 2016g. <https://www.c-span.org/video/?417328-1/donald-trump-unveils-100-day-action-plan-gettysburg-address>. Last accessed on 18 March 2018.

---. Rally in Grand Junction, CO. 18 October 2016. Transcript. 2016h. <https://www.c-span.org/video/?417108-1/donald-trump-campaigns-grand-junction-colorado>. Last accessed on 18 March 2018.

---. Rally in Grand Rapids, MI. 31 October 2016. Transcript. 2016i. <https://www.c-span.org/video/?417728-1/donald-trump-campaigns-grand-rapids-michigan>. Last accessed on 18 March 2018.

---. Rally in Lakeland, FL. 12 October 2016. Transcript. 2016j. <https://www.c-span.org/video/?416827-1/donald-trump-campaigns-lakeland-florida>. Last accessed on 18 March 2018.

---. Rally in Manheim, PA. 1 October 2016. Transcript. 2016k. <https://www.c-span.org/video/?416260-1/donald-trump-campaigns-manheim-pennsylvania>. Last accessed on 18 March 2018.

---. Rally in Minneapolis, MN. 6 November 2016. Remarks as prepared. 2016l. <https://www.donaldjtrump.com/press-releases/in-minnesota-trump-offers-voters-chance-to-take-government-back-from-the-co>. Last accessed on 13 December 2016.

---. Rally in Panama City, FL. 11 October 2016. Transcript. 2016m. <https://www.c-span.org/video/?416754-1/donald-trump-campaigns-panama-city-florida>. Last accessed on 18 March 2018.

---. Rally in Sioux City, IA. 6 November 2016. Transcript. 2016n. <https://www.c-span.org/video/?418180-1/donald-trump-holds-rally-sioux-city-iowa>. Last accessed on 18 March 2018.

---. Rally in West Palm Beach, FL. 13 October 2016. Transcript. 2016o. <https://www.c-span.org/video/?416882-1/donald-trump-calls-allegations-absolutely-false>. Last accessed on 18 March 2018.

Van Gorp, Baldwin. "The Constructionist Approach to Framing: Bringing Culture Back In." *Journal of Communication* 57.1 (2007): 60-78.

Wilentz, Sean. "America's Lost Egalitarian Tradition." *Daedalus* 131.1 *On Inequality* (Winter, 2002): 66-80.

Williams, Rhys H. "The Cultural Contexts of Collective Action: Constraints, Opportunities, and the Symbolic Life of Social Movements." *The Blackwell Companion to Social Movements*. Ed. David A. Snow, Sarah A. Soule, and Hanspeter Kriesi. Oxford: Blackwell, 2004. 91-115.

Authoritarian Populism, White Supremacy, and *Volkskörper*-Sentimentalism

Heike Paul

"Nationalists are supremely sentimental. Kitsch is the natural aesthetic of an ethnic 'cleanser.' […] The latent purpose of such sentimentality is to imply that one is in the grip of a love greater than reason, stronger than the will, a love akin to fate and destiny. Such a love assists the belief that it is fate, however tragic, that obliges you to kill." – Michael Ignatieff, *Blood and Belonging*

Introduction

With the return of authoritarian populism in Western democracies, largely taboo articulations of racist, xenophobic, and Islamophobic attitudes have massively resurged in public discourse and have already shifted the norms of political articulation. In fact, we may well consider white supremacist views to be one of the centerpieces of present-day right-wing populisms.[1] In the United States, the latter range from campaign rhetoric on border regimes and border control (as in "build the wall" or in the so-called "Muslim ban") to the indiscriminate demonization of refugees and non-white subjects (as "rapists," "drug dealers," and "murderers"; see Scott). Populism being a "thin ideology" (Mudde) and "a style of rhetoric reflecting first-order principles" (Norris et al.), populist movements thrive parasitically on pre-existing ideological formations. Right-wing populism always constructs an outgroup whose members are being pathologized or demonized and turned into scapegoats for whatever harm may have allegedly befallen 'the people.' Right-wing populism, as John B. Judis reminds us, differs from left-wing populism in that it is triadic rather than binary (us vs. them): "Rightwing populists champion the people against an elite that they accuse of coddling with a third group, which can consist, for instance, of immigrants, Islamists, or African American militants […]. Rightwing populism is triadic: It looks upward, but also down upon an out group" (15). In constructing such a triangulated constellation, authoritarian right-wing populism merges and instrumentalizes the ideologies of nativism, ethnic nationalism, biological racism, and Anti-Islamism.[2] In populist rhetoric, these newly prominent forms of racist and

---

[1] Ruth Wodak refers to this as "the normalization of exclusion" (177). See also Abrajano and Hajnal on "white backlash."
[2] For an overview of right-wing populism in Europe, see Priester 2018 and Decker in this volume.

xenophobic attack are strategically popularized by the invocation of a white *Volkskörper*, a metaphor that, as in previous instances in the twentieth century, clearly serves an ethno-nationalist agenda. This *Volkskörper* projects and mystifies the body politic as an organicist and essentialist entity and 'the people' as a somehow unified organism – rather than the sum of individuals or the individual votes of a *Staatsvolk*-electorate. In that sense, it may strike us as an anti-democratic model of a homogenous collectivity as it draws on earlier models that undergird the modern nation-state as conceived in the nineteenth century and that have also promoted the sacralization of the body politic and its purported organic unity. The *Volkskörper* as a residual organicist trope, then, lends itself to an intense emotionalization and sentimentalization in support of a political agenda that includes racist/racial exclusion and the promotion of ethno-nationalist boundary maintenance, once again, and thus intends to sway 'the people' in its favor. The monolithic *Volkskörper*, it is suggested in populist utterances, is under siege and is threatened to become violated by inimical forces. These forces may at times be conceived as abstract, in a sense, but they need to be incarnated in 'the other,' that is in individuals and specific groups, mostly non-white men, in order to produce the intended affect and its effect.

In what follows, I am using the concept of a '*Volkskörper*-sentimentalism' to address this phenomenon in populist rhetoric on both sides of the Atlantic and to examine the kind of affective power it commands.[3] *Volkskörper*-sentimentalism, as defined here, interpellates political subjects affectively as part of an imagined organic whole that is defined by a national bond and an ethnic homogeneity which both are simply taken for granted; beyond that, however, it also evokes a sense of entitlement and 'rightful' privilege due to 'whiteness' as the one prioritized dimension of affiliation, commonality, and shared belonging. This notion of whiteness as white privilege, however, can also easily surpass the borders of the nation-state and operate successfully in transnational spheres. If "sentimentalism envisions the self-in-relation" (Dobson 267), the relation/affiliation that *Volkskörper*-sentimentalism produces is not to be described in terms of subject-to-subject (such as nuclear family) relations but rather it suggests a belonging to something 'larger' and more powerful, something that transcends individual identities and may even be seen as a sacred entity. *Volkskörper*-sentimentalism, in fact, is part of the histories and ongoing evocations of a 'white Atlantic'-imaginary as it has been created by the agents of slavery, settler colonialism, and apartheid and has been successfully used in colonial discourse. As purist, exclusivist, state-

---

[3] Throughout this essay, I am using the German term "Volkskörper" rather than the English translation "body politic" due to the differences in nuance and common usage: The German term reminds us that this specific brand of ethnic nationalism can be traced to nineteenth century German romanticism, and that it has been (mis)appropriated by national socialist propaganda in the twentieth century. The present 'comeback' of the term resonates with the latter.

centered, and home-grown as they may present themselves, seemingly national archives of an exclusively national body politic share a transatlantic repertoire (to use a term that has risen to prominence through Diana Taylor's work), and they are part of transnational networks in which such nationalist movements cooperate, somewhat paradoxically, in the name of isolationism and nationalism with clear imperial underpinnings. Thus, the 'white Atlantic'-imaginary, first of all, draws attention to this paradox of national agendas that actually are transatlantic and transnational in scope. The present return of authoritarian populism on both sides of the Atlantic attests to that. It is the property and privilege of whiteness (along with the "meta-ignorance" it cultivates[4]) that forms the common ground of a shared logic of consolidation by exclusion. In that sense "Buy American," "America First," and "Pure Americanism" (and I am quoting here Trump as well as *The Constitution and Laws of the Knights of the Ku Klux Klan* from 1921, it does indeed sound partially alike) is not categorically different from similar slogans that have been coined in a mid-twentieth century German context. In fact, "America first" conjures up the cultural memory of the appalling German rhetoric of exclusivity, for one thing, that was fabricated under the arc of a different yet structurally similar exceptionalism and from whom awkward offshoots are being resurrected momentarily.[5] Second, I want to show that the proliferation of white supremacist notions rests less on pseudoscientific systematization and pseudo-rationalistic arguments than primarily on "structures of feeling" (Williams) and a sentimental politics that invests in the exceptionally 'singular' and 'precious' *Volkskörper* rather than in the survival and well-being of people. In doing so it wraps us up with much theatricality in "affective economies" (Ahmed 2004) that masquerade as empathy, often in vague resemblance with but ultimately overriding a logic of familial kinship. The (biological) *Volkskörper* is seen as superior to the (biological) family. Thus, while it usually goes hand in hand with the reinforcement of family values, it can at times also override the very attachments that it emulates and ask us to disengage from or to transcend familial attachments in the name of a naturalized collective body that, time and again, calls for sacrifice. Benedict Anderson has observed that the "horizontal comradeship" inculcated by nationalism veils the actual anonymity of the national subjects toward each other and enables them to believe that they share something fundamental. Anderson argues that the power of nationalism is to make national subjects forget their diversity and their differences in the name of a shared (and, I would add, 'felt') sense of community that is contingent – in the best sense of the

---

[4] In the field of critical whiteness studies, "meta-ignorance" is a term used by Medina and picked up by Applebaum (14).
[5] This analogy has been pointed out repeatedly. In a most persuasive manner, Michael Moore in *Fahrenheit 11/9* (2018) draws a comparison between the rise of Hitler in the Weimar Republic and the rise of Trump in the United States.

word. The construction of a putative homogenous national 'body,' however, presupposes essentialist and exceptionalist terms; it is this abstract body that is imagined as given and 'organic.' This body is the central concern of white/racist Atlantic ideology as it pits an ethnic against a demotic model of the nation. As a fierce, at times unconditional protectiveness toward this body is inculcated as well, feelings of "resentment and revenge" figure as "prime emotions" directed against the so-called "intruders," "parasites," and "carriers of disease" (Reid Ross 7) that allegedly threaten the organic integrity of the national body from within and without – and this phrasing, of course, echoes fascist ideology. Third (and deeply intertwined with the second point), a discourse of care, of preserving and perfecting this *Volkskörper* appears prominently and calls for maintaining homogeneity and purity, including the need for routine/ritualistic purification. Against this background, the sentimentalized *Volkskörper* is the subject of a discourse of suffering and victimization, and crisis scenarios are evoked again and again. As Andreas Musolff points out, the *Volkskörper*, when evoked in recent times, seems to always be in a state of bad health and to invite "comment on its pathological conditions and the chances of recovery and therapy" (2016: 62). The suggested cure for the *Volkskörper* is to curb racial mixing and obvious diversification, then and now, and according to that logic, all forms of miscegenation are seen as a kind of violation and violent trespassing of boundaries, i.e. as rape. At the same time, *Volkskörper*-sentimentalism teaches its subjects and objects how to "feel right" and how to conform with the logic of the sacred bond the *Volk* engenders at the expense of all those who are excluded and will never belong.[6] It guards the racialized subtext of authoritarian populism and it fosters white supremacist notions that are foundational for white populist state fantasies as a "dominant desire" out of which national identity can be imagined and "antagonisms" can be organized (Pease 1). Fourth, gender politics play a prominent role in these scenarios. The female body often is the site where the imagined violation of the *Volkskörper* is bound to occur. Aligned with a classical sentimental repertoire, *Volkskörper*-sentimentalism is asking us to emphatically suffer with the longstanding suffering heroine who has to be seen as an allegory of the nation rather than an individual in her own right and to try our best to prevent her moral and physical downfall. Sara Farris has coined the term "femonationalism" to describe and analyze a powerful ideological formation, namely the recent right-wing appropriation and exploitation of feminism and feminist rhetoric. Even as this rhetoric can already be identified in US justifications of the so-called war on terror in Afghanistan after 9/11 (Mackie; Rashid), it has just become a more broadly conceived argument by right-wing groups against admitting refugees into the United

---

[6] To "feel right" is taken from Harriet Beecher-Stowe's well-known afterword to her sentimental novel *Uncle Tom's Cabin* in order to indicate the normative basis evoked in this kind of ideological framing.

States and European countries. Femonationalism is defined by Sara Farris as the rhetoric and strategy through which right-wing nationalists, neoliberals, and some feminists and women's equality institutions in a strange kind of alliance invoke women's rights to stigmatize Muslim men and advance their own political objectives. Farris sees an important, yet often overlooked, political-economic dimension to account for this seemingly counter-intuitive intersection. According to her, femonationalism endorses anti-Islamic and xenophobic policies, it operates with a dubious rhetoric of emancipatory promises for non-western women, and it enlists feminism in the project of rescuing and preserving the integrity of the *Volkskörper*. The term "Alt-Feminism" is being used for right-wing women who are complicit in this scheme (see Dzodan).

In what follows, I want to briefly provide a broader, even if somewhat eclectic contextualization of the history of the *Volkskörper* and the kind of ideological usages that are to be found and the repercussions it has had in the United States and Germany (section two) before turning to two contemporary case studies. In section three, my first case study will address Donald Trump's invocation of *Volkskörper*-sentimentalism in the context of his campaign and his first two years in office. Trump may not have an ideologically coherent worldview – let alone program – that can be systematically analyzed. Yet, he has campaigned and risen to power in close proximity to people who have tried to push him into the direction of right wing-doctrines. His social Darwinist attitude and his espousing of "nativist constitutional beliefs" (Goldstein 529) alongside an emphasis on his own "good genes" places him in league with radical right-wing nativists and xenophobes (such as his earlier supporter and campaign manager Stephen Bannon). Three manifestations reiterate that Trump has used *Volkskörper*-sentimentalism: his early campaign against Obama as a spokesman for the birthers-movement which denied Obama's American citizenship and accused him of Un-Americanness and of harming America; his so-called anti-Muslim ban; and his border enforcement against illegal immigration that also involved family separation orders. Whereas all three interventions bear similar characteristics, my analysis will focus on the last one as it shows best how the *Volkskörper*-sentimentalism apparently overrides family ties/familial bonds, i.e. sacrificing the latter for the former. In section four, I turn to my second case study and to Europe's populist movements in the wake of the so-called refugee crisis. Authoritarian populism instills its white supremacist agenda in allegedly grassroots movements that pose as bottom-up initiatives. Specifically women are being recruited for the common cause (the sexism of the authoritarian male populists does not seem to have averred that), since their victim status allegorically stands in for the victimization of the *Volkskörper*. One of the more prominent manifestations of femonationalism in Germany that has gained currency in right-wing domains as the "real #MeToo" is the "#150db" by the self-declared "daughters of Europe." In a series of interventions and performances (such as the intervention at the #MeToo panel discussion at the Berlinale 2018 and the performance "Dead Girls Don't Lie") participants of that group have underscored their fear of being attacked by non-white men and their endeavor to fight and fend for themselves as the state blinded by its multicultural ideology supposedly fails to protect them. In the German context, such articulations hinge on the incidents during the 2015-*Silvesternacht* (New Year's Eve) in Cologne during which mass sexual assaults were registered against women by allegedly mostly non-German men leading to a highly emotional and controversial public debate as well as to new legislative measures. The essay will conclude by pointing out the similarities between the two case studies and by identifying *Volkskörper*-sentimentalism as a powerful affective basis for populist programs that entail and embrace nativist and racist ideologies.

Melodramas of the Beset *Volkskörper*

The term *Volkskörper* has been in use since the late eighteenth century (Musolff 2010; see Wodak 153) and literally 'embodies' the attempt and the desire to transfer the authority of the king and the king's body (or, following Kantorowicz, the king's two bodies) to the entity of the people or the nation (see Koschorke et al. 259; Lüdemann) in order to create a new imaginary of sovereignty in and by the body-state metaphor – the metaphorical discourse of the body-state *per se* is, of course, much older.[7] The body-metaphor as a crucial part of a "pre-political imaginary" (Koschorke et al. 258) appears as an exclusivist and residual figuration (in the sense that Raymond Williams uses the term "residual"; Williams 122) throughout the history of the modern nation-state, and its "latent totalitarian seductiveness" (ibid.,

---

[7] For a history of an organological conceptualization of the state and a metaphorical organicist discourse of the body politic that goes back to the Middle Ages (John of Salisbury), to Antiquity (Areopagiticus, Plato, Xenophon, Cicero, Livy), and the Bible (Paulus), see: Struve 1978; Hale. At various times, and again in the Middle Ages, following Roman traditions, "small efforts were made in using the *Organismusvergleich* as a basis for a theory of secular rule" (Struve 1984: 304, 305). Hale distinguishes a first kind of analogy that focuses on body parts "in certain structural and functional relationships to each other" (for instance in "the fable of the belly") as well as in a hierarchical order from a second kind of analogy that focuses on the humors and potential imbalances and pathologies of the body politic (15). The body politic-metaphor started as simply a signifier for unity and harmony in the Greek polis and became reconfigured in many ways through the centuries always to reflect an "anthropomorphic view of the universe" (47). Even if it is not explicitly addressed or called upon, the body is very much part of a "Hintergrundmetaphorik" (Blumenberg; see Lüdemann 38-9) of conceptions of the social and the state. For Lüdemann, the body is one of two "Ur-models" of the social/political (the second one being the contractual model). With reference to Kantorowicz, she acknowledges the "two bodies of society" and the *Volkskörper* as a variation of the body metaphor that emerges in the nineteenth century and that merges the political and the biological body in the process of/for the sake of nation-building (203). See also Musolff 2016: 57-60.

my translation) has been made manifest in ideological re-appropriations of various kinds. In the first half of the twentieth century it became increasingly politicized as an organicist metaphor of conservation and post-World War I regeneration. Throughout the Weimar Republic we encounter the term in various (pseudo)scientific discourses on the health of the nation and on the social pathologies it must fend from within and from without. The *Volkskörper* figures prominently, for instance, in discussions about the recovery of the national economy and the closing of social chasms (Halling et al.), about birth control and abortion (Patzel-Mattern) as well as about post-World War I anxieties regarding the state and the precarious future of the nation more broadly (Föllmer). It reveals the gendered and racialized dimension of the political imaginary and, as Föllmer points out, the discourse about a *Volkskörper* that is unwell and lacking gradually displaces an imaginary of the state with that of the *Volk*. Medical metaphors are used to amplify a specific post-war discourse about injury and pain to one much more sweeping and all-encompassing, suspending what Luhmann calls the modern functional differentiation of society (Luhmann) and declaring the *Wohl des Volkskörpers* (the well-being of the body politic) the one overarching argument in any political discussion. The beset German *Volkskörper* figures as the object of prime affective investment needing to heal, to be nurtured, to be protected, and to become strong (again). "Modern totalitarian movements, whether of the right or the left, have been peculiary [sic] – and revealingly – inclined to use disease imagery" (Sontag 81). Most notoriously, Hitler picked up the term and repeatedly used the phrase of the "gesunde Volkskörper" in *Mein Kampf* and on other occasions for insinuating and even propagating eugenics and euthanasia – the murder of what he considered "unfit lives" and "parasites" on the *Volkskörper*.[8] Under national socialist rule, the *Volkskörper* came to be identified with hyper-nationalism, biological engineering, and mass murder. Next to the persona of the *Führer* himself, it was the ultimate object of sacralization and of 'care' in national socialist ideology. In fascist rhetoric/ideology, the *Volkskörper* needed constant vigilance and protection from chimerical internal and external threats (see Bergdolt 143-4).

In the United States, the idea of a *Volkskörper* by any other name is connected to discourses of nativism and scientific racism that found widespread acceptance at the turn of the nineteenth to the twentieth century on both sides of the Atlantic. Roughly one hundred years ago, there were rampant discussions in the United States among nativists and others about the perils confronting Americans in the face of mass immigration and racial integration by mixing. One text exemplarily points to the trajectory of that presumed threat and to plans of how to contain it. Madison Grant's *The Passing of a Great Race* has become a blueprint for white supremacist border control efforts leading up to the 1924 Immigration Act (a praiseworthy legal measure

---

[8] Hitler refers to the Jew as "Völkerparasit." See Bein 134 and Neumann.

as we have been reassured recently by Jeff Sessions as well as Jared Kushner; see Serwer; Shear; Yee). Grant's book was hugely successful in its own days in the United States as well as abroad: Adolf Hitler called it his "bible" and sent an enthusiastic letter to the author – and borrowed some of his vocabulary.[9] To all available evidence, Madison Grant's book is enjoying quite a long life: like no other it spans the centuries of the 'white Atlantic.' In 2011, it was picked up by Norwegian Neo-Nazi mass murderer and terrorist Anders Breivik in his manifesto titled "2083: A European Declaration of Independence" and a year earlier alluded to by Thilo Sarrazin in his notorious, eugenicist bestseller *Deutschland schafft sich ab* (*Germany Abolishes Itself*, 2010) (Mezzadra 248). The debate around Sarrazin's controversial book on German demographics, a book hung up on "cultural identity" and "national character" and on spreading Islamophobia (the *Frankfurter Allgemeine Zeitung* called it an "anti-Muslim dossier based on genetics" [Geyer; see also Follath]), Frank Decker has argued, "played an instrumental role in paving the way for the entry of right-wing populism into the discursive space" in Germany (Decker 201). In many ways, thus, Madison Grant's horrendous argument about race is still with us today – or with us again. Grant ends his book: "We Americans must realize that the altruistic ideals which have controlled our social development during the past century and the maudlin sentimentalism that has made America 'an asylum for the oppressed,' are sweeping the nation toward a racial abyss" (263). Even as Grant refutes the supposedly teary sentimentalism of the immigration advocates, he himself cultivates a *Volkskörper*-sentimentalism of his own by way of fetishizing whiteness in the United States and by way of celebrating the white/Nordic race. Today's right-wing responses toward multiculturalism are often couched in similar wording. Whereas Grant in his days critically eyed immigrants coming from abroad, from Southern and Eastern Europe, as threatening the racial composition and the future of the American nation in a way that seems to be rehashed momentarily, at the same time violent activism in the United States formed on the issue of racial purity in the domestic realm: The (re)publication of *The Constitution of the Knights of the Ku Klux Klan* from 1921 that marked the 'revival' of that organization on the heels of Thomas Dixon's novels and D.W. Griffith's film *Birth of a Nation* (1915), which popularized that obsession with white supremacy in the cultural imaginary by way of narratives of war and romance. Here, we find a politics of purity geared toward a domestic regime couched into a fantastic language of medieval knighthood, crusades, and honor codes attesting to the fact that "fascism is also mythopoetic insofar as its ideological system does not only seek to create new myths but also to create a kind of mythical reality, or an everyday life that stems from myth rather than fact" (Reid Ross 6). Both, Grant and the KKK constitution are ardently devoted to and

---

[9] This has been pointed out repeatedly, recently again by Ibram Kendi in his "Preface for Readers Outside of the USA" in *Stamped from the Beginning*.

concerned with caring for the integrity of the temporarily distressed white – or whitewashed, for that matter – *Volkskörper*. The ideology of the KKK sought to contain the foreign element *within* and to consolidate strict racial segregation between white and black by force. In Griffith's notorious film that celebrates the founding of the Ku Klux Klan and its newly foundational rescue of white America after the Civil War, we find an unrivalled and at the same time quite stereotypical instance of *Volkskörper*-sentimentalism: in the film's dramatic climax, little Flora, a white girl, rejects the advances of her African American suitor Gus. It is suggested that she prefers death to interracial intimacy as she jumps from a steep cliff and kills herself. In the logic of the film, her heroic sacrifice or rather sacrificial suicide hence prevents the disgracing of her womanhood and allegorically her whole race, thus calling for empathy with the character and at the same time for self-pity among the white audience. "[M]elodramatic discourse aims to solicit affective states of astonishment, sobs and pathos from the scenes of persecution it shows" (Anker 222). Around the same time, John Harry Haiselden's work epitomizes yet another instance of *Volkskörper*-sentimentalism put into operation: Haiselden, a physician by training, refused treatment to newborn infants who were suffering from obvious "defects," as he saw it. John Bollinger, son of Anna Bollinger, was his most famous victim. Whereas the doctor was pleading concern for the baby with the parents ("suffering poor individual"), he argued in a public statement echoed by Anna Bollinger that the baby would likely have become a "an imbecile and possibly criminal" (Pernick 55). As he publicly announced his non-treatment (this was not the first case of the kind), he became somewhat of a medical celebrity. And Haiselden became the hero of his own film on the Bollinger case of eugenic infanticide: *The Black Stork* (1917), which was later reissued under the title *Are You Fit to Marry?* (1927), a melodrama of the beset *Volkskörper* – and about the person who 'fixes it' or 'heals it' to use that jargon. It clearly prefigures Nazi propaganda films such as *Erbkrank* (1936) and *Alles Leben ist Kampf* (1937). Haiselden's legacy may be among one of the most extreme early twentieth century items of a white supremacist archive.[10] Willingness to sacrifice is the leitmotif of *Volkskörper*-sentimentalism: in a most melodramatic manner, Haiselden pleads with Anna Bollinger to sacrifice her child – for the sake of the health of the American *Volkskörper*. And she complies – the *Volkskörper*-affect takes precedence over a mother's love for her newborn baby – this is Haiselden's ultimate triumph.

The logic of *Volkskörper*-sentimentalism operates on the basis of an ethnic nationalism that can sacralize and sentimentalize the body politics in organicist terms at the intersection of a political and a cultural imaginary. It should be noted that this

---

[10] For a detailed account of Haiselden's career and work, see Pernick. For contextualization of the eugenics and sterilization debate in discourses of the American family, see Heinemann (2018: 138-47).

organicist *Volkskörper*-rhetoric is somewhat at odds with a constitutional or civic nationalism of the kind that the United States officially embraces – in contradistinction to an ethnically based version. Michael Ignatieff has summarized this in his "blood versus belonging"-paradigm and distinguishes "civic nationalism" from "ethnic nationalism." The former "maintains that the nation should be composed of all those – regardless of race, color, creed, gender, language, or ethnicity – who subscribe to the nation's political creed" (Ignatieff 6). By contrast, other nations, among them Germany, rest on the notion of an "ethnic nationalism" which has lent itself particularly well to constructions of racist/racial supremacy.

Less specifically attached to questions of national identity, notions of exceptionalism, often related to an idea of 'past greatness,' may be examined as a shared mood among former European colonial powers and empires of settler colonialism which may seem particularly prone to the kind of retrotopian right-wing populism that currently attracts many followers. Retrotopia is a concept suggested by the late Zygmunt Bauman to address a *zeitgeist* of a seemingly paradoxically 'utopian nostalgia' that is embodied, for instance, in slogans such as "Make America Great Again." In fact, "[a] nativist nationalistic agenda has become hegemonic in the rhetoric and manifestos of right-wing populist parties, articulating a desire to establish a homogenous white, Christian population in the borders of the traditional nation state, all speaking the same language – the mother tongue" (Wodak 184). For the United States, a settler colony and empire in its own right, Jared Goldstein has recently revisited the history of nationalism and nativism:

> Constitutional nationalism provides a comforting, even inspiring ideal of national identity. It is said to avoid the irrational hatred and bigotry associated with more primitive forms of ethnonationalism, identified by President Bush as nations 'united by blood or birth or soil.' Instead of violent, sectarian, tribal, and other forms of nationalism, constitutional nationalism teaches that being American means being committed to universal ideals like individual liberty and human equality. (Goldstein 498)

Of course, such a description is obviously committed to the creed of American exceptionalism. In that (ideological) sense, *Volkskörper*-discourse may be considered an aberration from US constitutional traditions in itself. However, nativist prejudices have recurrently loomed large in US history and political discourse – from the Know-Nothing-Party in the nineteenth century that John Higham has analyzed in detail to more recent attempts by Pat Buchanan or Donald Trump. Lauren Berlant suggests viewing the "fantasy of a national democracy" (1997: 291) with caution and contends that the "abstract principles of democratic nationality have always been hypocritical" (1997: 291). Clearly, the persistence of nativist beliefs can be traced throughout US history and constitutional and political debates, past and present, and they keep returning, for instance, as reactions to multiculturalist policies: "white nationalists [...] believe the Immigration Act of 1965 marked the beginning of a 'white genocide,' a deliberate plot by leftists to destroy white rule" (Goldstein 556). On the heels of this history, whose outlines I have traced here only for the past 100 years, Goldstein notes that "the [present] President's policies follow a long history of American nativism" (556).

The kind of nativist politics that can be seen in the current presidency in tandem with a definition of Americanness along increasingly essentialist and narrowly ethnocentric lines began as early as 2008, with the 'birthers movement' and the denial of Barack Obama's Americanness (who was 'from elsewhere' and 'Un-American'); it was an accusation that prompted a whole set of citizenship conspiracy theories, theories that have lastingly eroded, or at least damaged, the classic US-immigrant narrative; and it has reached its preliminary endpoint in Trump's announcement to tamper with and ultimately abolish birthright citizenship, the *ius soli*, guaranteed by the fourteenth amendment.[11] Along the way, these politics have included sympathizing with right-wing politicians and activists, trivializing and normalizing white supremacist positions, and giving white supremacist and nativist groups a new respectability along with a new victim status (Abramowitz 123, 140) and implicitly tolerating racist violence. Whereas 'white racial resentment' is articulated as a reaction to a perceived victimization and experience of suffering, *Volkskörper*-sentimentalism is protective of a core white racial identity as the bedrock of being American. Resentment and sentimentality are two sides of the same coin, so to speak. At the same time, the formula of the melodrama is used for bemoaning a loss of white privilege in sacrificial logics, while reiterating a sense of entitlement and claiming a heroic resistance, on many levels. Hence, whereas in general terms, "[m]elodramatic genre conventions are found in political rhetoric, governing processes, citizenship practices, and formations of national identity. Melodrama shapes the legitimation strategies of national politics, and the very operations of state power" (Anker 2).

Donald Trump: "Families Belong Together" vs. the American *Volkskörper*

Donald Trump is not well-versed in civil sentimentalism and the corresponding civil religious pathos formulae that his predecessor applied so virtuously.[12] Kenneth T.

---

[11] The fourteenth amendment guarantees birthright citizenship: "All persons born or naturalized in the United States, and subject to the jurisdiction thereof, are citizens of the United States."

[12] In my larger project, I am pitting the tradition of a prominent "civil sentimentalism" against that of a "Volkskörper-sentimentalism" (see Paul 2018b).

Walsh, Bob Woodward, and others have noted that Trump prefers disruption to harmony and is having quite some difficulty performing a conciliatory and harmonizing presidential habitus.[13] It is not the case, however, that Trump has given up on or abstains from political sentimentalism altogether, rather he performs exactly the kind of *Volkskörper*-sentimentalism that I have introduced earlier and that seems to be built on a specific conception of 'the people' and the body politic. This sentimentalism espouses a *Volkisch* nationalism that propagates rigid mechanisms of inclusion and exclusion (along ethnic/racist demarcations) and that is prepared to sacrifice individuals, families, ethnic groups, and grown social ties for the 'conservation' of the imagined 'healthy body of the nation' or to affirm, by force, the chimera of a genetically founded racially unified society. Trump's sentimental rhetoric does not shy away from eugenic snatches or commentary either. With Trump, we can observe the populist triad in a rhetoric, which casts the middle-class or rather the "average Americans" (Middle America) as somehow squeezed between and threatened by the elite establishment and those the elite is allegedly in league with: foreigners, refugees, non-white groups of any kind. Squeezed from above and below, so to say, the 'middle' defends itself (with the help of an authoritarian leader) by claiming to be the *Volkskörper per se*. Right-wing populism "presents itself as serving the interests of an imagined homogenous people *inside* a nation state" (Wodak 47).

Especially in the context of the plan to expand the wall at the US-Mexican border the argument runs in the characteristic style of conservation and protection of the healthy American nation's body, for example when illegal immigrants are dubbed criminals or notorious rapists by the president. In this crude dichotomous logic, the integrity of the American nation's body is given priority over the respect for the fate and the right to participation of fellow human beings, the women, men, and children from Guatemala, Nicaragua, El Salvador, Honduras, and other countries. Trump's political parlance echoes the language of American nativism, which had its heyday approximately 100 years ago and which materialized itself in the form of all kinds of pseudoscientific racist modellings, apocalyptic visions, eugenic response/coping scenarios, and political agendas/grammars of exclusion. The nativism, which some imagined to have become a marginal phenomenon in American society and presidential politics, has once again, presidentially embellished with Trump's sentimentalist statements about the nation's body, moved centerstage in the form of Trump's presidentially veiled *Volkskörper*-sentimentalism and has become acceptable: "With the election of Donald Trump, nativism has moved from the margins back to the White House, and the government once again has adopted policies to exclude some people, defined by religion and national origin, out of suspicion that they are hostile to the Constitution" (Goldstein 493). Further

---

[13] Gounari refers to him as "the American agitator."

confirmation for this can also be found in reports that Trump has openly contemplated to change the current system of nationality and abolish the *ius solis* – by decree (see Hirschfeld Davis).

The tightening of border control since 2017 and the further escalation at the border in 2018 went along with a newly introduced practice, namely to separate arrested illegal immigrant families at the Mexican-US border. The border regime and ICE (immigration and customs enforcement)-politics were put in place long before Trump was elected. What is new is the *Volkskörper*-logic that is intoned by the current president suggesting restauration as well as purification. Again, it is individuals (in this case: children, foreign, non-American children) whose well-being is put at risk and who are subjected to suffering for the sake of the American *Volkskörper*.

Many thousand children were interned separately from their parents – regardless of their age. Images of those interned children – torn from the arms of their parents, without proper care, and emotional protection – caused substantial concern across the political spectrum in the United States as well as abroad. Reports about the security personnel who complained about the noise/soundscape of crying children longing for their parents and images of apathic and crying little children in cage-like housing were disturbing also for Republican mothers and fathers, the more so as the Republican Party has always stylized itself as the guardian of family values (Allen). The cognitive dissonance was hard to bear and led to unusually critical words about President Trump even from within its own party and in particular from women as the debate became increasingly emotional.

In this rather heated debate hardly an image drew as much criticism and outrage as the photograph of the President's daughter Ivanka Trump with her little son in blissful happiness. Posted on May 27, 2018, during a time when the family separation of refugee families at the border was in full swing and dramatic images of that were circulating, it is this image that threw into sharp relief the "precarious lives" (Judith Butler) of migrant families in contrast to the practice of unhampered motherly love as a privilege of the white woman – conjuring up the setting of the nineteenth century abolitionist melodrama targeting family separation under the conditions of slavery. The manifold connotations and associations with past injustices (family separation under slavery and in the prison industrial complex) were addressed in the press and circulated under the hashtag #wherearethechildren. Most vocally, the movement #familiesbelongtogether formed to indict the practices and regulations of the US Immigration and Custom Enforcement (ICE) authorized by the President himself. The movement used the echoes of the past and also employed sentimental strategies in order to appeal to the empathy of Americans with the ill-treated, thus countering *Volkskörper*-sentimentalism with civil sentimentalism, as it were (see Paul 2018a).

This mobilization qua the sentimental proved successful: outrage began to dominate public discourse and to de-legitimate nativist positions. Under huge public pressure (by women and mothers in particular) family separation at the border was ended. Since Trump took office as a president this was an unprecedented moment of relenting, not the least as it seemed to occur also under the pressure of his wife and daughter. This is how Bob Woodward describes it in his book *Fear: Trump in the White House*.[14] Trump backtracked his decision and stopped family separation on June 20, 2018 with an executive order, also forestalling a temporary legal injunction against this measure. Of course, the moral doubts and scruples, he claimed in the end/*ex post*, are presented as his alone: "We are going to keep the families together. I didn't like the sight, or the feeling of families being separated." (Donald Trump). He even talks about "feeling" here, while in the very next sentence he reiterates his "zero tolerance"-policy. Civil sentimentalism has triumphed above *Volkskörper*-sentimentalism in this particular instance without there being a 'happy ending' regardless.[15]

This symbolic victory of the civil sentimentalists against the *Volkskörper*-sentimentalists has not stopped the logic that prioritizes the protection of an "American *Volkskörper*" from concocted immigrant violence over the wellbeing of immigrant families. Just days before the 2018 midterm elections, viewers saw a veritable "discourse explosion" (Michel Foucault) around the so-called "migrant caravan" (that amazingly died down immediately after the election). One campaign ad in particular engaged in a drastic demonization of the people in the "migrant caravan" and sought to produce unequivocal affective responses. The "stop the caravan"-ad appeared to be too transgressive and crass even for Fox News, and it was taken off the program of this and other channels. Yet another law-and-order announcement, it was full of xenophobic resentments intended to produce fear and anxieties among "the American people" regarding the "caravan" and disdain for a Democratic leadership "weak on crime." In this clip, an authoritative voice warns us of the 7,000- people-"migrant caravan," and the need for militarizing US borders and protecting the American people. President Trump and his allies will keep you safe from those mobile others, South Americans on the move. The clip randomly connects images of the migrants to a convicted drug dealer and murderer, Luis Bracamontes, who killed two policemen. He is portrayed as the pars pro toto in no uncertain terms. We are led to believe, in the end, that the migrant caravan is a caravan of killers. The 'alignment' of refugee migrants with a cop killer is a rather

---

[14] To revisit my earlier reference to the American sentimental archive, Woodward's reconstruction of the situation can be read side by side with chapter nine from *Uncle Tom's Cabin*. Here, Senator John Bird is beseeched by his wife to help the fugitive slave Eliza regardless of legal stipulations regarding fugitive slaves.

[15] Blasberg et al. discuss the lasting effects of the separation.

pernicious but highly efficient move. So is the analogy of (im)migration and invasion – Trump's favorite. As Lakoff and Johnson wrote in *Metaphors We Live By*, many years ago, a classic that has been re-discovered of late in the analysis of political language and "framing" (in the work by Lakoff and Wehling):

> Metaphors may create realities for us [...] A metaphor may thus be a guide for future action. Such actions will, of course, fit the metaphor. This will, in turn, reinforce the power of the metaphor to make experience coherent. In this sense metaphors can be self-fulfilling prophecies. (156)

When CNN-White House Correspondent Jim Acosta addressed the questions to Trump on November 7, 2018: "why do you characterize it as such [an invasion – even when these people are hundreds and hundreds of miles away from the US border]?" and "do you think that you have demonized immigrants?," the president quickly lost his temper (he offered three harsh responses: indicating a "difference of opinion," suggested to "let me run the country," and accusing Acosta: "you are a rude, terrible person") and Acosta temporarily lost his White House-press pass. Metaphors like the "invasion" of the "body" conjure up a specific kind of violence, both physical and sexual. It is the literalization of this metaphoricity that will concern me in my second case study.

Yet, as a final comment on the migrants subjected to various forms of othering by the Trump administration, a shift in perspective may be helpful: In the interviews with and in the published soundbites of migrants in the so-called caravan in December 2018, one recurring theme was striking: the hegemonic script of American mobility. Refugees from Honduras, Nicaragua, Guatemala, El Salvador reiterate that they come to the United States for the "American Dream" – usually meaning safety, being able to provide for their families, and prosperity through hard work.[16] Apparently, they use the symbolic capital of the immigrant narrative to make their own journey as refugees and migrants intelligible for American (and global) audiences. One is hard pressed not to call that an irony of sorts: The hegemonic script of American mobility – that of the immigrant experience, of the upward mobility narrative, and of the American Dream – is re-energized, once again, from the margins or from beyond the borders, to be precise. In that sense, it may be used as an argument against the ethnocentric policy of the current presidency. Sarah Churchwell has recently argued that "American Dream" and "America First" (pitted against each other in the scenario I have described) have a long and complicated history *together*. Prompted by candidate Trump's line that "sadly, the American Dream is dead" and by his use of the "America First"-slogan, Churchwell went into

---

[16] See Maqbool and Lakhani.

the archive. In her 2018-book, *Behold, America*, she reveals how the "American Dream" and "America First" were always connected, and contested:

> There has always been a tension, in America, […] between liberal democracy and authoritarianism […] that debate played out between ideas represented by the phrase 'American dream' and those represented by 'America first' […] What both expressions shared were their attempts to identify a national value system, and they emerged at the same moment in America's history – as it came into its own as a world power at the beginning of the twentieth century and began debating earnest the role it would play in the world. (8, 41)

Femonationalism at Work: "Daughters of Europe," "#MeToo" Xenophobia, and the *Volkskörper*

While some second wave feminists have long decried the waning of feminist consciousness, feminism has recently become a hotbed, once again, of cultural production, scholarship, and activism, and we have seen many new variations emerge over the last year. Throughout the past years, discussions have been rampant around feminism(s) that include various facets of hashtag-feminism – most prominently the "MeToo"-movement, but also other initiatives.[17] In Sara Ahmed's words, we may want to "follow around" (2010: 14) feminism's presence und ubiquity (both symptomatic and thematic) in order to see where this takes us. In doing so, my second case study addresses several European and/or transnational (re)appropriations of the so-called "MeToo"-debate by women on the far right of the political spectrum. And even though we can witness a kind of international echo and transnational dissemination of this debate, the appropriations are culture- and context-specific and are always embedded in more complex local political formations. Nevertheless, they all share the *Volkskörper*-logic.

When we look at Europe and examine the reception of and the participation in the "MeToo"-debate, several things may be striking. Since the beginning of the campaign, apparently every western society has discovered its own league of Harvey Weinsteins: VIPs in the media business, in politics, or in the university. In the German context, a few scandals have been discussed in talk shows and comparable forums. However, it has also been noted that the "MeToo"-debate as a whole has had surprisingly little echo particularly in Germany and that there has not been a substantial feminist momentum comparable to that in the United States and elsewhere in Europe and the Americas. There was a rhetoric of cautioning against

---

[17] See <https://www.huffingtonpost.com/entry/21-hashtags-that-changed-the-way-we-talk-about-feminism_us_56ec0978e4b084c6722000d1>.

the dynamics of a witch-hunt of the kind we supposedly saw in America, and criticism regarding the "re-victimization" of women to be heard. But what exactly do we find, when we examine "MeToo"-appropriations in Germany and in adjacent countries?

A number of femonationalist organizations (Farris) have recently appropriated the "MeToo"-movement in order to spread and foster a gross white supremacist ideology that is described as women-'friendly.' In twitter-feeds, performances, films, photography, and public statements, the group I am discussing who call themselves "daughters of Europe" have reached out to enlist the feminist rhetoric of "MeToo" in right-wing propaganda and expressed a retrotopian longing for a time before the "failure" of borders and of patriarchy. The failure of patriarchy to guarantee women's sexual integrity is portrayed as at least as scandalous as the supposed crimes themselves. Under "#120dB" a self-declared feminist group of women (many of them German) are using the "MeToo"-movement to draw attention to what they consider an eminent threat to 'native' women across Europe and, more abstract, to white European womanhood as such. Their name refers to the volume (120 decibel) of a common pocket alarm that allegedly has become 'the standard equipment of women's handbags across Europe.'

Their most notable clip has been disseminated via the internet, on various social media platforms, and on their homepage (conveniently with English subtitles) and has widely resonated.[18] It orchestrates the juxtaposition of an imagined collectivity of past and potential victims (white women across Europe) with a collectivity of past and potential perpetrators (Muslim men from outside of Europe) in the tradition of dichotomous orientalist misrepresentations and stereotypes of the black rapist. Thus, simple strategies of sentimental identification juggle with "I/we" – "them/you" in order to effectively engage and to scare and unsettle a female audience. It is German-speaking women (with deliberately diverse dialects and accents to make the group seem more diverse, "exemplary," and "representative") who project their fantasy of a socially closed 'larger Europe,' whose women they purportedly speak for. Their common purpose aligns these women in their (linguistic and other) differences with a white supremacist logic. The protagonists "Mia, Maria, Ebba" figure as allegories of European womanhood; they speak out in the name of feminism while their names hint at the political background involved. "Mia" is a shorter and hipper version of Maria or Miriam, both are biblical names that have become currently very popular (again) mostly due to popular culture-usage. "Maria" unequivocally represents the Western Christian tradition alluding to quite a specific model of femininity. "Ebba" is currently among the top-ten of Swedish female first names and is considered to be an old Germanic name, the female counterpart of Eberhard, implying strength and resolution – and whiteness.

---

[18] See <http://www.120db.info/>. Last accessed on 15 June 2019.

The statements of the Mias, Marias, and Ebbas repeat or rather mimic a semantics of feminist resistance, they self-represent as a chorus of "outcriers" and as "the real MeToo" protesting violence against women. They reiterate the ubiquity of a threat of sexual violence by the racial other alone and how they go unguarded: according to their narrative of victimry, white women are "sacrificed" as both, the integrity of their bodies and of the national borders are threatened – and compromised. This again evokes the concept of *Volkskörper*-sentimentalism that I have addressed earlier. The symbolism and the language of this clip tap into a history and archive that has coupled German defeat with the humiliating presence of 'dangerous' black people/black bodies in Germany: after World War I black soldiers of the French army (soldiers from French colonies in Africa) were part of the occupying forces of the German Rhineland. This was considered by white Germans as the ultimately most painful part of their defeat (a veritable "Schmach" – a shame, disgrace, humiliation), and it disproportionately fueled fantasies of black male victorious power over white helpless female bodies that belabored the perceived loss of status and control on the part of white German men – in what could be called the German anxieties of black misrule in the cultural imaginary roughly around the time when *Birth of a Nation* (1915) was a spectacular success in the United States. This historical period obviously throws a long uncanny shadow on both sides of the Atlantic.

The all-female speakers in the clip invite women to social media platforms in order to share their own experiences of harassment as white women at the hands of non-white/non-Western men ("Muslim men"), to create a gendered, interpersonal solidarity, to raise their "voices" in public against "foreign domination, harassment, and violence." The latter is the kind of political vision that projects a dangerously regressive trajectory. *Volkskörper*-sentimentalism is, we may assume, always retrotopian (in Bauman's sense) since it fabricates a past emptied of all complexities, a past that never existed in the first place. The "#120dB"-campaign evokes the progressive language of the genre of the political/feminist manifesto with a retrotopian racist agenda that calls for consciousness-raising, claims the public sphere, and that produces female public voices which call for a reconstitution of patriarchy. Some of the women in and behind this rather low-tech, amateurish and thus seemingly 'authentic' film have been connected to the Austrian Martin Sellner (a representative of the Identitarian Movement (IB) whose Facebook account is frequently closed down due to his right-wing postings) and to the Alt-Right movement in the United States. At the same time, the clip interpellates male viewers to become active in a kind of rescue narrative of their distressed fellow countrywomen, who are now forced to take matters into their own hands – and are indirectly summoned to take knightly action against the villains, so to speak. The women are, as befits a sentimental plot, both victimized and heroic. The indictment of patriarchy's failure to guarantee women's sexual integrity (and by extension to protect the *Volkskörper*) ties in with larger, national, and international narratives of security and securitization of post 9/11 political formations. Order needs to be restored, is the simplistic message, and this calls for new endo-colonialist efforts (see Lacy) as well as for a new political mythology (see Pease; Markwardt).

Sociologist Helma Lutz was one of the first scholars to point out that the local/German responses to the "MeToo"-movement have to be viewed in a bigger picture. The latter includes most prominently another event that connects sexism and sexist violence to men of a different cultural background: New Year's Eve 2015/2016 in Cologne. In that particular night in Cologne, more than one hundred women (some of them but not all of them German) were attacked and assaulted by various groups of men of mostly African origin (most of them were not refugees). Many women were harmed physically and sexually in the face of an allegedly overall passive and unorganized local police force that reacted with much delay. This particular night has had far-reaching consequences: it has led to legislative changes under the then justice minister, now foreign minister Heiko Maas adding to the German legal norm new kinds of offenses called "gruppenförmige sexuelle Belästigung" ("sexual harrassment in/by groups") as well as bystanding. Initiatives criticizing this move such as "#ausnahmslos" ("#withoutexception"), a feminist group against racism and against the new version of the law, have had little to no public resonance. No German *Bierfest*, no *Oktoberfest*, no excessive carnival-celebration (three events where mostly autochthonous Germans engage which each other and where instances of sexual abuse regularly occur), and, yes, no "MeToo"-movement has ever led to similar consequences or follow-up measures. Even leading German feminists, among them Alice Schwarzer, identified non-white, Muslim men as the archenemy of German womanhood – and this contextualizes the "#120dB" – clip and elicits the observation that its message may have already arrived in mainstream culture. In fact, "well-known and outspoken feminists [in Germany, Italy, the Netherlands, France, and other countries have] joined the anti-Islam choir [...] denounc[ing] Muslim communities as exceptionally sexist, contrasting them to Western countries as sites of 'superior' gender relations" (Farris). Sexism and sexual abuse are depicted as having happened *in the past* or still happening *elsewhere*, i.e. in other cultures, and are now brought 'here.' Images in the press clearly exploited this anxiety and moral panic about "sex-mobs" (see Dietze) in ways that were later partially retracted.[19] All this at the same time thrived on and added to the alarmed rhetoric of the so-called "refugee crisis" that has become the arena for addressing women's rights all across Western Europe. Farris's term of "femonationalism" aptly

---

[19] See this report on the timeline of publication and (partial) retraction: <http://www.spiegel.de/kultur/gesellschaft/focus-und-sueddeutsche-zeitung-eine-entschuldigung-eine-rechtfertigung-fuer-titel-a-1071334.html>. Last Accessed on 15 June 2019.

describes an ideology that appropriates feminist concerns for nationalistic and racist political projects and thus as a convergence point for seemingly incommensurable ideologies. Such a "toxic feminism," a term that sociologists Paula Villa and Sabine Hark use (Hark et al.), combines elements that are fundamentally at odds with each other, yet, this incompatibility is effectively glossed over. According to statistical evidence, German women suffer mostly from the abuse by German men (Lutz). This logic/claim of an exclusive endo-sexual violence reveals that "training in politicized intimacy has also served as a way of turning political boundaries into visceral, emotional, and seemingly hardwired responses of 'insiders' to 'outsiders'" (Berlant 2014: 41). *Volkskörper*-sentimentalism provides the historically grounded (even grown, so to speak) and affectively attuned state fantasy that goes along with it.

It has become common practice by right-wing groups to exploit criminal acts, in particular rape cases, for the promotion of a xenophobic agenda – cases, such as the sexually motivated murder of 14-year old Susanna Maria Feldman at the hands of Ali Bashar, a young man from Iraq, whose refugee status in Germany had been denied but who was still in residence in Germany. The "Alternative for Germany" (AfD) quickly took up this 'failure' of the state to protect German women (*Staatsversagen*) and managed to amplify public sentiments by invoking the *Volkskörper*. The party openly blamed chancellor Merkel's policy at German borders for the girl's death.[20] In the most drastic rhetoric that circulated in the media, the German chancellor herself was even likened to a prostitute or, then again, a pimp offering the German *Volkskörper* for abuse to foreigners.[21] Refugees were denigrated as foreigners who supposedly only mimicked a refugee status and instead were dubbed "rapefugees."[22] It goes without saying that pointing out the specific cultural encoding of tales of sexual abuse is not intended in any way to make light of the trauma of its victims. Quite the contrary, a critical perspective on such ideological enlistments reveals that the individual trauma of the victim is often glossed over in favor of grander ethno-nationalist schemes. The perverted nature of this kind of "MeToo"-reception and appropriation and the slow mainstreaming of its

---

[20] Alice Weidel (AfD) stated: "Susanne is yet another victim of the hypocritical and egoistic welcome-policy of chancellor Angela Merkel" (my translation): "Susanna ist ein weiteres Opfer der heuchlerischen und egoistischen Willkommenspolitik von Bundeskanzlerin Angela Merkel." (see "Warum Konnte der Täter Ausreisen").

[21] One of the more dramatic examples of such verbal transgressions is credited to Peter Boehringer (AfD) for labelling the chancellor as "Merkel whore" ("Merkelnutte") and for comparing her refugee policy to a "genocide." In the same e-mail circular, he added that it is "OUR *Volkskörper* which is violently penetrated" ("Dumm nur, dass es UNSER Volkskörper ist, der hier gewaltsam penetriert wird"). Boehringer later distanced himself from such speech acts (see Amann).

[22] Rapefugee.net is a website that claims to document crimes (particularly rape crimes) against German women. Sometimes, these claims have proven to be false (see "Faktencheck"). The word "rapefugees" has been the object of legal measures against hate speech and "incitement of the masses" under the German Penal Code (§ 130 StGB *Volksverhetzung*).

agenda-setting is a transnational phenomenon. We may, for instance, consider the output of Marcus Follin from Sweden on "The Woman Question" and the Austrian presidential elections (Follin) or the "tradwives" in the United States ("The Housewives of White Supremacy," as the *New York Times* labelled them [Kelly]). The supposed violation, penetration, and rape of the *Volkskörper* and the urgency of protecting it – along with praise for the pre-feminist, or even anti-feminist ideals of the heteronormative nuclear family – looms large in all of these contexts (see Gilloz et al.).

Conclusion

Clearly, sentimental political storytelling can cut both ways, as Rebecca Wanzo has shown: it can provide a narrative of suffering as a path to equal rights and full citizenship by creating solidarity across established boundaries, but it can also be enlisted for purposes of exclusion and a nostalgic re-instatement of traditional, hierarchical systems of order. Both examples discussed in this essay fall into the latter category. They begin with "the origin point of all melodramatic plots – the scene of victimization" (Anker 237) via notions of literal and metaphorical violence and rape; both indicate the need for protection in scenarios of duress. Trump self-fashions as the hero of his own, self-made political melodrama that fends a largely symbolical conflict at the US-Mexican border in a rhetoric that conjures up nativist debates of the nineteenth and early twentieth century. The women, who call themselves "daughters of Europe," self-fashion as potential victims of male violence (suffering) who need to be safeguarded and decide to help themselves for lack of male protection (heroism). The group contends that rape by "others" is "underreported" and hence denied in a society fixated on multiculturalism and gender. These reservations echo Karin Priester's observation that a "common sense" seemingly free from ideological bias is constructed in populist narratives as superior to any form of scholarly or scientific knowledge and empirical findings (Priester 2012). In both cases, the sentimental appeal is coupled with a sense of authoritarianism and exclusion. In a revealing statement phrased in his usual gibberish, Trump announced in May 2016: "The only important thing is the unification of the people – because the other people don't mean anything." This "unification" has an organicist subtext and can be seen as one more installment of affective *Volkskörper*-politics; it is suggestive of restoration and purification with regard to race and gender regimes, on the one hand, and the defeat of 'corrupt elites' on the other. The *Volkskörper* is very obviously a concept and a metaphor which still does political and cultural work. On both sides of the Atlantic this kind of logic goes back a long way – to the rise of nationalism and scientific racism – and it has been variously used to justify excesses of violence, ethnic cleansing, and genocide. Its prehistory is part of its contemporary semantic inscriptions. In its sentimentalized (and newly sacralized) version it has returned in the melodramatic rhetoric of right-wing populist politics seeking pity for the *Volkskörper* and its suffering from injury, pain, and destruction in order to offer an affective economy to all those who feel marginalized or cheated in one way or the other. The construction of such a kind of entity, namely "an impressively organic unity, something much greater than the sum of its parts," may be referred to as "State fetishism," as Michael Taussig has written (112). In that sense, the *Volkskörper* may be considered a somewhat regressive "fetish-objectivation" of the state (ibid.). The genderedness of the present debate only reinforces the libidinal investment (along with an emotional one) in the production and reproduction of the *Volkskörper* in right-wing populist frameworks. The discourse on populism is in need of a feminist critique.

This essay has been concerned with identifying and analyzing one important dimension in the rhetoric of right-wing populist movements: the conjunction of a white supremacist agenda and a sentimental repertoire, which I am referring to as *Volkskörper*-sentimentalism in deeply racialized and gendered scenarios. *Volkskörper*-sentimentalism figures as part of "the kind of exclusionary nationalism they [populists] profess" (Judis 157). It is a strategy with which they seek to infuse the "national nervous system" (Berlant 1997: 6; see also Taussig). The scenarios I have addressed here are by no means unique: Within Europe, successful right-wing populists for instance in Italy and Hungary act similar in tone and purpose.[23] Yet, the white supremacist *Volkskörper*-sentimentalism that I have addressed is not identical with other sentimentalist figurations in American political discourse that run on affect. What Lauren Berlant has diagnosed as the "intimate public sphere" of the Reagan era is something else and it cannot be simply subsumed under the sentimental turn diagnosed by so many critics and scholars in the period after 9/11. Elizabeth Anker refers political melodrama in a state of exception and as taking shape in "orgies of feeling" – and we may remember George Bush's famous response to crisis being "Go Home and Hug Your Children," but this was still based on an individual's interaction with and on behalf of the state. Obviously, we have moved past that, too. The melodrama of the white *Volkskörper* supposedly under siege (in the invocations of Trump and the "daughters of Europe") echoes some of the rhetoric of a Madison Grant or a Lothrop Stoddard, plus quite some totalitarian views on the European side of the Atlantic, a rhetoric, that has largely absorbed the individuality of its members and has called for a complete and total identification with and surrender to the hegemon/authoritarian leader, who affectively and effectively not only guards the vulnerable body politic but who represents it, claiming to be the sole *vox populi*. On several occasions, Donald Trump has intoned

---

[23] Victor Orbán's rhetoric about community, as Madeleine Albright has pointed out, is "defined by bloodlines, not borderlines" (Albright 172).

just that: "I am your voice." The retrotopian agenda of purification and restauration thus meets a populist style of communication and a sentimental strategy that time and again offers a profound reduction of complexity and a promising economy of affect. Yet it ultimately begs the question: *Who does actually want to feel included?*

Works Cited

Abrajano, Marisa, and Zoltan L. Hajnal. *White Backlash: Immigration, Race, and American Politics*. Princeton: Princeton University Press, 2015.

Abramowitz, Alan I. *The Great Alignment: Race, Party Transformation, and the Rise of Donald Trump*. New Haven: Yale University Press, 2018.

Ahmed, Sara. *The Promise of Happiness*. Durham: Duke University Press, 2010.

---. "Affective Economies." *Social Text* 79 Vol. 22.2 (2004): 117-39. <http://cr.middlebury.edu/amlit_civ/allen/2012%20backup/scholarship/affect%20theory/22.2ahmed.pdf>.

Albright, Madeleine. *Fascism: A Warning*. London: William Collins, 2018.

Allen, Nick. "Heartbreaking Recording of Crying Children at US Border Fuels Fury over Immigrant Separations." *The Telegraph*. 19 June 2018. <https://www.telegraph.co.uk/news/2018/06/19/heartbreaking-recording-crying-children-separated-parents-us/>. Last accessed on 15 June 2019.

Amann, Melanie. "Peter Boehringer: E-Mail bringt AfD-Mann in Erklärungsnot." *Spiegel Online* 10 February 2018. <https://www.spiegel.de/politik/deutschland/peter-boehringer-e-mail-bringt-afd-mann-in-erklaerungsnot-a-1192686.html>. Last accessed on 15 June 2019.

Anderson, Benedict. *Imagined Communities: Reflections on the Origin and Spread of Nationalism*. London: Verso, 1983.

Anker, Elisabeth R. *Orgies of Feeling: Melodrama and the Politics of Freedom*. Durham: Duke University Press, 2014.

Applebaum, Barbara. "Critical Whiteness Studies." *Oxford Research Encyclopedia of Education*. June 2016. DOI: <https://dx.doi.org/10.1093/acrefore/9780190264093.013.5>. Last accessed on 15 June 2019.

Bauman, Zygmunt. *Retrotopia*. Cambridge: Polity, 2017.

Bein, Alexander. "Der Jüdische Parasit: Bemerkungen zur Semantik der Judenfrage." *Vierteljahrshefte für Zeitgeschichte* 2 (1965): 121-49. <https://www.ifz-muenchen.de/heftarchiv/1965_2_1_bein.pdf>.

Bergdolt, Klaus. "Mikrokosmos und Makrokosmos: Der menschliche Körper als staatstheoretisches Modell." *Staat und Schönheit: Möglichkeiten und Perspektiven einer Staatskalokagathie*. Ed. Otto Depenheuer. Wiesbaden: VS Verlag, 2005. 131-44.

Berlant, Lauren. "Citizenship." *Keywords for American Cultural Studies*. Ed. Bruce Burgett and Glenn Hendler. Second edition. New York: New York University Press, 2014. 41-5.

---. *The Queen of America Goes to Washington City: Essays on Sex and Citizenship*. Durham: Duke University Press, 1997.

Blasberg, Marian, Katrin Kuntz, and Christoph Scheuermann. "56 Tage." *Der Spiegel* 36 (1 September 2018): 74-80.

Blumenberg, Hans. *Paradigmen zu einer Metaphorologie*. Frankfurt am Main: Suhrkamp, 1998.

Butler, Judith. *Precarious Life: The Power of Mourning and Violence*. London: Verso, 2004.

Churchwell, Sarah. *Behold, America: A History of America First and the American Dream*. London: Bloomsbury Publishing, 2018.

Decker, Frank. "'Alternative für Deutschland': The Belated Arrival of Rightwing Populism in the Federal Republic." *Populism, Populists, and the Crisis of Political Parties: A Comparison of Italy, Austria, and Germany 1990-2015*. Ed. Günther Pallaver, Michael Gehler, and Maurizio Cau. Bologna: Il mulino, 2018. 199-216.

Dietze, Gabriele. "Okzidentalismus, anti-muslimischer Rassismus und 'Sexual Politics'." *Genderlectures. Podcast des Zentrums für Gender Studies und feministische Zukunftsforschung Marburg*. 9 December 2010 <https://podcasts.apple.com/de/podcast/gender-lectures-gabriele-dietze-okzidentalismus-anti/id370841032?i=1000094589995>. Last accessed on 15 June 2019.

Dobson, Joanne. "Reclaimng Sentimental Literature." *American Literature: A Journal of Literary History, Criticism, and Bibliography* 69 (1997): 263-88.

Dzodan, Flavia. "The New Alt-Feminism: When White Supremacy Met Women's Empowerment." *Medium. This Political Woman* 6 January 2017 <https://medium.com/this-political-woman/the-new-alt-feminism-when-white-supremacy-met-womens-empowerment-b978b088db33>.

"Faktencheck: Stimmen die Meldungen über vergewaltigende Flüchtlinge?" *Spiegel online* 6 January 2018 <https://www.spiegel.de/spiegel/stimmen-die-meldungen-ueber-vergewaltigende-fluechtlinge-a-1186254.html>. Last accessed on 15 June 2019.

Farris, Sara R. *In the Name of Women's Rights: The Rise of Femonationalism*. Durham: Duke University Press, 2017.

Föllmer, Moritz. "Der 'kranke Volkskörper': Industrielle, hohe Beamte und der Diskurs der nationalen Regeneration in der Weimarer Republik." *Geschichte und Gesellschaft* 27.1 (2001): 41-67.

Follath, Erich. "The Sarrazin Debate: Germany Is Becoming Islamophobic." *Spiegel Online* 31 August 2010 <https://www.spiegel.de/international/germany/the-

sarrazin-debate-germany-is-becoming-islamophobic-a-714643.html>. Last accessed on 15 June 2019.
Follin, Marcus. "The Golden One: The Female Question." 5 December 2016. <https://www.youtube.com/watch?v=Oaxy9mqxO-Y>. Last accessed on 15 June 2019.
Geyer, Christian. "So wird Deutschland dumm." *Frankfurter Allgemeine Zeitung / faz.net* 25 August 2010 <https://www.faz.net/aktuell/feuilleton/buecher/rezensionen/sachbuch/thilo-sarrazin-deutschland-schafft-sich-ab-so-wird-deutschland-dumm-1999085.html>. Last accessed on 15 June 2019.
Gilloz, Oriane, Nima Hairy, and Matilda Flemming. "Getting to Know You: Mapping the Anti-Feminist Face of Right-Wing Populism in Europe." *open democracy* 8 May 2017 <https://www.opendemocracy.net/can-europe-make-it/matilda-flemming/mapping-anti-feminist-face-of-right-wing-populism-in-europe>. Last accessed on 15 June 2019.
Goldstein, Jared A. "Unfit for the Constitution: Nativism and the Constitution, from the Founding Fathers to Donald Trump." (February 24, 2017). *Roger Williams Univ. Legal Studies Paper* 174/*University of Pennsylvania Journal of Constitutional Law 20* (2018): 488-559. Available at *SSRN*: <https://ssrn.com/abstract=2923343>.
Gounari, Panayota. "Authoritarianism, Discourse and Social Media: Trump as the 'American Agitator.'" *Critical Theory and Authoritarian Populism*. Ed. Jeremiah Morelock. Vol. 9. London: University of Westminster Press, 2018. 207-28.
Grant, Madison. *The Passing of the Great Race*. New York: Charles Scribner & Sons, 1916.
Hale, David George. *The Body Politic: A Political Metaphor in Renaissance English Literature*. Den Haag/Paris: Mouton, 1971.
Halling, Thorsten, Julia Schäfer, and Jörg Vögele. "Volk, Volkskörper, Volkswirtschaft: Bevölkerungsfragen in Forschung und Lehre von Nationalökonomie und Medizin." *Das Konstrukt "Bevölkerung" vor, im und nach dem "Dritten Reich."* Ed. Rainer Mackensen and Jürgen Reulecke. Wiesbaden: Springer VS, 2005. 388-428.
Hark, Sabine, and Paula Irene Villa (eds.). *Unterscheiden und Herrschen: Ein Essay zu den ambivalenten Verflechtungen von Rassismus, Sexismus und Feminismus in der Gegenwart*. Bielefeld: Transcript, 2017.
Heinemann, Isabel. *Wert der Familie: Ehescheidung, Frauenarbeit und Reproduktion in den USA des 20. Jahrhunderts*. Berlin: DeGruyter-Oldenbourg, 2018.
Higham, John. "The American Party: 1886-1891." *Pacific Historical Review* 19.1 (Feb. 1950): 37-46.

Hirschfeld Davis, Julie. "President Wants to Use Executive Order to End Birthright Citizenship." *New York Times* 30 October 2018 <https://www.nytimes.com/2018/10/30/us/politics/trump-birthright-citizenship.html>. Last accessed on 15 June 2019.

Ignatieff, Michael. *Blood and Belonging: Journeys into the New Nationalism*. New York: Faber, Straus and Giroux, 1993.

Judis, John B. *The Populist Explosion: How the Great Recession Transformed American and European Politics*. New York: Columbia Global Reports, 2016.

Kelly, Annie. "The Housewives of White Supremacy." *The New York Times* 1 June 2018 <https://www.nytimes.com/2018/06/01/opinion/sunday/tradwives-women-alt-right.html>. Last accessed on 15 June 2019.

Kendi, Ibram. *Stamped from the Beginning: The Definitive History of Racist Ideas in America*. London: Penguin, 2016.

Koschorke, Albrecht, Susanne Lüdemann, Thomas Frank, and Ethel Matala de Mazza. *Der fiktive Staat: Konstruktionen des politischen Körpers in der Geschichte Europas*. Frankfurt am Main: Fischer, 2007.

Lacy, Mark. *Security, Technology and Global Politics* (Prio New Security Studies). London: Routledge, 2015.

Lakhani, Nina. "Despite Chaos at the Border, Migrants still Hope to Find the American Dream." *The Guardian* 22 June 2018 <https://www.theguardian.com/us-news/2018/jun/21/tijuana-us-mexico-border-migrants-american-dream>. Last accessed on 15 June 2019.

Lakoff, George, and Mark Johnson. *Metaphors We Live By*. Chicago: University of Chicago, 2003.

Lakoff, George, and Elisabeth Wehling. *Your Brain's Politics: How the Science of Mind Explains the Political Divide*. Exeter: Imprint Academic, 2016.

Lüdemann, Susanne. *Metaphern der Gesellschaft: Studien zum soziologischen und politischen Imaginären*. München: Wilhelm Fink Verlag, 2004.

Luhmann, Niklas. *Soziale Systeme: Grundriss einer allgemeinen Theorie*. Frankfurt am Main: Suhrkamp, 1984.

Lutz, Helma. "Was #MeToo und die Kölner Silvesternacht eint." *Mediendienst Integration* 14 December 2017 <https://mediendienst-integration.de/artikel/was-metoo-und-die-koelner-silvesternacht-eint.html>. Last accessed on 15 June 2019.

Mackie, Vera. "The 'Afghan Girls': Media Representations and Frames of War." *Continuum Journal of Media & Cultural Studies* 26.1 (2012): 115-31.

Maqbool, Aleem. "Trump and the Facts about the Migrant Caravan." *BBC News Latin America*. 26 November 2018. <https://www.bbc.com/news/world-latin-america-45951782>. Last accessed on 15 June 2019.

Markwardt, Nils. "Politische Mythologie: Im Geisterreich des Völkischen." *Zeit Online* 15 April 2017 <https://www.zeit.de/kultur/2017-04/politische-mythologie-

rechtspopulismus-identitaere-bewegung-heimat-volk-fakten/komplettansicht>. Last accessed on 15 June 2019.
Medina, Jose. *The Epistemology of Resistance: Gender and Racial Oppression, Epistemic Injustice, and Resistant Imaginations*. New York: Oxford University Press, 2013.
Mezzadra, Sandro. "Multicultural Spectres in the Crisis of European Citizenship." *Breaching Borders: Art, Migrants and the Metaphor of Waste*. Ed. Juliet Steyn and Nadja Stamselberg. London: Tauris (IB) & Co Ltd, 2014. 239-55.
Moore, Michael, director and scriptwriter. *Fahrenheit 11/9*, Dog Eat Dog Films/Miramax Films, 2004.
Mudde, Cas. "The Populist Zeitgeist." *Government and Opposition* 39.4 (2004): 541-63.
Musolff, Andreas. *Political Metaphor Analysis: Discourse and Analysis*. London: Bloomsbury, 2016.
---. *Metaphor, Nation and the Holocaust: The Concept of the Body Politic*. New York, NY: Routledge, 2010.
Neumann, Boaz. "The Phenomenology of the German People's Body (*Volkskörper*) and the Extermination of the Jewish Body." *New German Critique* 106 (2009): 149-81.
Norris, Pippa, and Ronald Inglehart. *Cultural Backlash: Trump, Brexit, and Authoritarian Populism*. Cambridge: Cambridge University Press, 2019.
Paul, Heike. "Public Feeling, Tacit Knowledge, and Civil Sentimentalism in Contemporary US Culture." *Projecting American Studies: Essays on Theory, Method, and Practice*. Ed. Frank Kelleter and Alexander Starre. Heidelberg: Universitätsverlag Winter, 2018a. 165-79.
---."Staatsbürgersentimentalismus, American Style." Kantorowicz-Lecture. Goethe University Frankfurt am Main. 31 October 2018b. <https://www.youtube.com/watch?v=Z6H9H7IbKHA>.
Patzel-Mattern, Katja. "'Volkskörper' und 'Leibesfrucht': Eine Diskursanalytische Untersuchung der Abtreibungsdiskussion in der Weimarer Republik." *Körper mit Geschichte. Der menschliche Körper als Ort der Selbst- und Weltdeutung*. Ed. Clemens Wischermann and Stefan Haas. Stuttgart: Franz Steiner Verlag, 2000. 191-222.
Pease, Donald. *The New American Exceptionalism*. Minneapolis: Minnesota University Press, 2009.
Pernick, Martin S. *Eugenics and the Death of "Defective" Babies in American Medicine and Motion Pictures since 1915*. New York: Oxford University Press, 1996.
Priester, Karin. "Right-wing Populism in Europe." *Populism, Populists, and the Crisis of Political Parties: A Comparison of Italy, Austria, and Germany 1990–*

2015. Ed. Günther Pallaver, Michael Gehler, and Maurizio Cau. Bologna: Il mulino, 2018. 45-61.

---. "Wesensmerkmale des Populismus." *Populismus. Aus Politik und Zeitgeschichte* 5-6, 26 December 2012 (Bundeszentrale für Politische Bildung) <http://www.bpb.de/apuz/75848/wesensmerkmale-des-populismus?p=all>. Last accessed on 15 June 2019.

Rashid, Naaz. *Veiled Threats: Representing the Muslim Woman in Public Policy Discourses*. Bristol, Chicago: Policy Press, 2016. Print.

Reid Ross, Alexander. *Against the Fascist Creep*. Chico, CA: AK Press, 2017.

Scott, Eugene. "Trump's History of Making Offensive Comments About Nonwhite Immigrants." *The Washington Post* 11 January 2018 <https://www.washingtonpost.com/news/the-fix/wp/2018/01/11/trumps-history-of-controversial-remarks-about-nonwhite-immigrants>. Last accessed on 15 June 2019.

Serwer, Adam. "Jeff Sessions's Unqualified Praise for a 1924 Immigration Law." *The Atlantic* 10 January 2017 <https://www.theatlantic.com/politics/archive/2017/01/jeff-sessions-1924-immigration/512591/>. Last accessed on 15 June 2019.

Shear, Michael D. "Trump Immigration Proposal Emphasizes Immigrants' Skills Over Family Ties." *New York Times* 15 May 2019 <https://www.nytimes.com/2019/05/15/us/politics/trump-immigration-kushner.html>. Last accessed on 15 June 2019.

Sontag, Susan. *Illness as Metaphor*. New York: Farrar, Straus and Giroux, 1978.

Stoddard, Lothrop. *The Revolt Against Civilization: The Menace of the Under Man*. New York: C. Scribner's Sons, 1922.

Struve, Tilman. "The Importance of the Organism in the Political Theory of John of Salisbury." *The World of John of Salisbury*. Ed. Michael Wilks. Oxford: Blackwell, 1984. 303-17.

---. *Die Entwicklung der Organologischen Staatsauffassung im Mittelalter*. Stuttgart: Hiersemann, 1978.

Taussig, Michael T. *The Nervous System*. New York: Routledge, 1992.

Walsh, Kenneth. *Celebrity in Chief: A History of the Presidents and the Culture of Stardom*. New York, NY: Routledge, 2015.

Wanzo, Rebecca. *The Suffering Will Not Be Televised: African American Women and Sentimental Political Storytelling*. Albany: State University of New York, 2009.

"Warum Konnte der Täter Offenbar unter Falschem Namen Ausreisen?" *Welt.de* 8 June 2018 <https://www.welt.de/politik/deutschland/article177175854/Politiker-zum-Fall-Susanna-F-Warum-konnte-der-Taeter-offenbar-unter-falschem-Namen-ausreisen.html>. Last accessed on 15 June 2019.

Williams, Raymond. *Marxism and Literature*. Oxford: Oxford University Press, 1977.

Wodak, Ruth. *The Politics of Fear: What Right-Wing Populist Discourses Mean.* Los Angeles: Sage, 2015.
Woodward, Bob. *Fear: Trump in the White House.* New York: Simon & Schuster, 2018.
Yee, Vivian. "In Trump's Immigration Remarks, Echoes of a Century-Old Racial Ranking." *New York Times* 13 January 2018. <https://www.nytimes.com/2018/01/13/us/trump-immigration-history.html>. Last accessed on 15 June 2019.

Right-Wing World-Building: Affect and Sexuality in the 'Alternative Right'

Simon Strick

Skeletal Populism

Even as we speak (about populism), there is a meme[1] going around on the internet (see fig. 1): "IS YOUR CHILD A FAR-RIGHT EXTREMIST?" it exclaims in capital letters, to continue: "Look for warning signs: Aversion to drugs, alcohol, pornography. Interest in physical fitness, mental wellbeing. Monogamy, desire to marry and procreate. Increased time spent outdoors or in nature. Appreciation of nation, history, and culture. Disdain for modernism, post-modernism." In the Alternative Right's trademark style, the meme insinuates far-right ideology as a way to 'a better life,' while at the same time reversing and denouncing liberal society's discursive conventions of 'cautioneering.' Its intentionality is duplicitous and shady: is the meme *primarily* a parodic play on the discourse of 'radicalization prevention' that has tried to contain political extremism since the 1980s? Or, are we *really* supposed to think that such attitudes and practices are 'far-right,' and (consequently) *not* pursuing them is what characterizes the 'left'?

IS YOUR CHILD A FAR-RIGHT EXTREMIST?

Look for warning signs:

- Aversion to drugs, alcohol, pornography
- Interest in physical fitness, mental wellbeing
- Growing collection of classic literature
- Monogamy, desire to marry and procreate
- Increased time spent outdoors or in nature
- Appreciation of nation, history and culture
- Disdain for modernism, post-modernism

Figure 1

---

[1] A useful definition and illustration of 'memes' can be found in Shifman.

Considering the disruptive rhetorical styles (Nagle; Strick 2018; Ganesh) and ideological variabilities of right-wing agitation, these are somewhat futile questions. They aim to grasp that distinction of *rhetoric* and *ideology* quoted by Ernesto Laclau from Kenneth Minogue: "We must distinguish carefully between the *rhetoric* used by members of a movement – which may be randomly plagiarized from anywhere […] and the *ideology* which expresses the deeper current of the movement" (Laclau 10). We might indeed agree with the 'plagiarization from anywhere' suggested by Minogue, but his binary proposition offers little clarity on the meme's structure of address: what is its ideological, deeper current – outdoorsy health and monogamy, or the denunciation of a liberal public's obsession with translating extremism into 'warning signs'? What is its rhetoric – the evocation of (implicitly white) health and wellbeing, or the derogatory mimicry of liberal concern?

Stuck with such undecidability, we are compelled to acknowledge Laclau's critique of neat distinctions between surface and depth when conceptualizing contemporary populism: "[…] rhetorical operations […] *actually constitute[d] populist subjects,* and there is no point in dismissing this as mere rhetoric. Far from being a parasite of ideology, rhetoric would actually be the *anatomy* [my italics, S.S.] of the ideological world" (Lauclau 12). Laclau chooses a bodily metaphor – "anatomy" – to illustrate how rhetoric and ideology coalesce, and how the starkening effects of divisive rhetoric are instrumental in constructing the rigid bifurcations that organize right-wing populism's ideology. My article will adopt and explore this metaphor to elucidate some unexpected functions and genres that online cultures of the far-right (I shorthand these in the following as the "Alternative Right") have adopted within the current "populist moment" (Mouffe 11).

Laclau's anatomical metaphor – associating 'structure,' 'mechanism,' 'frame' – has considerable resonance in his own text, e.g. when he explains populism as the "simplification" of the political, and the production of a "stark dichotomy whose two poles are necessarily imprecise" (Laclau 18). Scholars of populism, too many to name, have long remarked on the reductive oppositions informing its ideological mappings, each presenting 'skeletal' versions of the social and political fields: 'the people' vs. 'the elites,' autochthones vs. migrants, patriots vs. globalists, and so forth. Laclau's metaphor retains a double meaning in this regard, in that not only is rhetoric the 'anatomy' (the stabilizing structure) of populist ideology, but this ideology itself enacts the 'anatomization' of social complexities – their reduction to simple, antagonistic schematics, churning out 'bare bones' versions of social realities.

Populism, according to Laclau, therefore requires an investigation into "[…] how social agents 'totalize' the ensemble of their political experience" (4), that is, how people learn to use such 'skeletal models' for orientation in their political choices, in their always complex lives, and for ways of navigating these complexities. For it is really a pertinent question, how people make use of such simplistic models – 'us' vs. 'them' – to navigate increasingly confusing realities and contradictory circumstances, which are (not lastly) produced by populist performances and politics themselves. Laclau's *On Populist Reason* of course offered some contemplation of this question, mainly taking the detour of Lacan-inspired theories of libidinal attachment: "[…] there is no populism without affective investment in a partial object" (116). However, and again many scholars have intervened against this shortcoming,[2] the term 'affect' remains somewhat undertheorized in Laclau's thinking of how emotion, affective states, and "affective economies" (Ahmed 2004) make attachments to populism's rigid modellings possible.

One helpful concretization comes from Fintan O'Toole and his recent book on *Brexit and the Politics of Pain*, which conceptualizes an enlivening calculus of (economic, symbolic) injury and counter-injury as the basis of populist sensibilities, terming the dynamic concisely as *sado-populism:* "[the populist voter] can believe that he or she has chosen who administers their pain, and can fantasise that this leader will hurt enemies still more" (O'Toole). This sadomasochistic relation between populism and its subjects requires some form of dramatics of and desire for injury, and already presents a step forward from the various – mainly negative – emotive reductions that commentators have deployed to describe populist attachments, i.e. "politics of hate," (Hockenos) "monarchy of fear," (Nussbaum) "the fearmongers," (Wagner) and so forth. In contradistinction to 'fear' and 'hate,'[3] which in some sense only offer negative orientations, 'pain' as a relational relay (Strick 2014) can give rise to 'actual' bodies, distilling experiences of embodiment and manifestations of desire. And, surprisingly, a form of bargaining for hope amid the pain, as Lauren Berlant reminds in her pointed sketch of Trump's voters: "This rebooted electorate […] thinks homeopathically that breaking the liberal difference/tolerance machine will *stanch* loss, not engender in its name surprising devastations" (Berlant 2017). Berlant speaks of an "enfleshment" (of whiteness) going on, acting itself out against perceived losses and "aggrieved entitlements" (Kimmel chapter 1), and thus prompts us to look for how Laclau's skeletal 'anatomies' of populism become fattened and meaty. So what is right-wing populism's fleshy rhetoric?

Bodybuilding on Social Media

Returning to our duplicitous meme, the bodily programs and health improvements suggested to characterize the "far-right extremist" are readily apparent. However, they seem less explicative of the sadomasochistic logistics of Trump and Brexit voters, and rather evoke a 'wholesome' imaginary for right-wing extremism: the far-

---

[2] Most recently: Martha Nussbaum, Arlie Russell Hochschild, Justin Patch.
[3] On the problematics of equating right-wing positions exclusively with 'hate,' see Duncan.

right body is averse to pornography, physically fit, and mentally sound. It procreates and spends time in nature. Its "appreciation of nation, history, and culture" (aka 'race') and the concurrent "disdain for modernism, post-modernism" (aka 'leftism') are invoked like/in? physical actions. Ironic or not, the suggestion of a *right-wing body* – healthy, reproducing – is concrete, and recalls Kathleen Stewart's description of how bodies are formed in affective lifeworlds and sensuous encounters. Apropos of how self-improvement programs and industries impact on how bodies form, Stewart writes: "[The body] loves and dreads the encounters that make it. It latches onto a borrowed intimacy or a plan of some sort. Layers of invented life form around the body's dreamy surges like tendons or fat" (114). The meme presents such a 'plan of some sort,' 'an invented life,' indeed articulating far-right extremism as a form of self-help and self-improvement.

That such 'enfleshments' of ideological oppositions are found primarily online is not coincidental, and I propose that digital media ecologies are instrumental in bestowing granularity and meatiness to right-wing paranoias. Frequently however, the digital realm and its embedded social media machines have been simplified to their function of pernicious 'radicalization' of unsuspecting audiences, and of "recruiting disaffected citizens" (Gerbaudo 4). Bharath Ganesh phrases the populist work of right-wing spaces on social media as such: "Digital hate culture goes beyond offense; it employs dangerous discursive and cultural practices on the Internet to radicalize the public sphere and build support for radical right populist parties" (32).

However, what does this "radicalization" entail with regard to affective attachments, and what does it mean to "support" populist parties and their ideas in the online world? And further, how does the evocation of 'health' and 'the outdoors' fit with Ganesh's denunciation of 'dangerous practices'? Not to downplay the extremism expunged by most brands of 'digital hate culture,' my article will suggest that the Alternative Right currently excels at devising alternative modes of discursive radicalization that imply different affects: the ordinary, harmlessness, and self-improvement. These are mobilized in the manifold genres available in social media spaces: personal videos and vlogs on Youtube, confessional debates on discussion forum *reddit.com*, opinion articles on websites. And they circulate primarily, as this article will argue, around 'ordinary affects' manifested in 'publically intimate' negotiations of romantic relationships, sexuality, and media consumption within a late capitalist market framework.

But first, let us look at a somewhat canonical text for the extreme right's presence on the video-sharing platform Youtube, a propaganda video titled "Who are we?". Uploaded by the infamous *National Policy Institute*, a far-right think tank founded by prominent 'white nationalist' Richard Spencer, the four-minute-long video shows Spencer sporting what has become the characteristic style of the Nazi Hipster (undercut, parted hair, jacket, and white shirt) interspersed with cutaways to generic images representing 'America': a multi-ethnic group of people, nature, cowboys, a shopping center, etc. In a half-whisper, Spencer announces his vision of a reinvigorated 'white race'[4] – conceived by Spencer as 'European identity' – as a necessary response to the decadence and ideological emptiness of the late-capitalist West:

> We're often told that being an American or a Briton or German or any European nationality is about being dedicated to a collection of abstractions and buzzwords. Democracy, freedom and tolerance, multiculturalism. But a nation based on freedom is just another place to go shopping. Who are we? We aren't just white. White is a checkbox on the census form. We are part of the people's history, spirit, and civilization of Europe. […] So long as we avoid and deny our identities at a time when every other people [images of protesting Jews, Muslims, etc.] is asserting its own we will have no chance to resist our dispossession, no chance to make our future, no chance to find another horizon. So who are we? I guess the real question is: are we ready to become who we are? (NPI/RADIX)

The video then cuts to a white-lettered title card proclaiming a slogan of empowerment: "Become who you are. Rise." Spencer's video is an example of the highly charged, quasi-apocalyptic 'white pride'-discourse of the US-American *Alt-Right* (see Hawley), which over the past ten years pivoted away from the traditional model of racism – 'Othering' and marginalizing non-whites – to identitarian thinking.[5] 'White' or 'European,' to ethnonationalists, are first and foremost markers of one's own marginalization and articulations of the impending demise of Western societies through shifts in 'ethnic' demographic ratios. Spencer's identitarian model sees no contradictions or power imbalances between the US and Europe but instead invents a seamless 'racial' continuity of a white people from Europe to the US that is competing against the aspirations of other 'peoples.'[6] While

---

[4] In this article, I put the term 'race' in quotation marks to denote the resurgence of older discourses on white, nationalist identity. In Critical Race Studies, the term 'race' is put in quotation marks to highlight the constructedness of 'racial' categories, whereas here it denotes the strategic evocation of these categories in the production of 'white identity,' invoking not so much political identifications – as for example 'Black' does – but rather a fictional genealogy of descent, culture, history, in short, of 'the people.' 'Race' in this sense is no less contingent but is based on a different discursive agenda.

[5] In this way, the American Alternative Right became compatible with European extremist groups such as the Identitarian Movement (IB), who similarly invoke not primarily unmarked majorities and an ethnicized abject, but instead subscribe to a view of themselves as the 'threatened ethnic majority.'

[6] This refers to a strategic discursive reformulation of white supremacy into an ostensibly egalitarian model of competition that the Alternative Right likes to refer to as 'race realism.' One definition can be found on the Neo-Nazi webpage rightrealist.com. For an explanation of the term, see also Heikkilä. The Alternative Right's 'race realism' must not be confused with

much could be said about this idiocy of US-American 'European Identitarians,'[7] I will focus here on the resonances of Spencer's 'White Power' slogan 'Become who you are' with the clichés of self-help literature.

Most products of the self-help and self-improvement industries from cosmetic surgery, dietary advice, and bodybuilding to the recent decluttering-craze (Marie Kondo, *The Life-Changing Magic of Tidying Up*) are advertised as enabling customers to attain self-actualization – *How to Become Your True Self*.[8] They offer the self, simply, "a plan of some sort." Framed within a self-help or self-improvement discourse, Spencer's 'racial consciousness' is turned, firstly, into a product in the market of identities, and, secondly, links to a commodification of racial affect. The 'racially awakened' individual – in Spencer's earnest articulation of our ironic meme – lives a better life, is more authentic, and can better resist the ubiquitous commodification of the everyday world – paradoxically, by subscribing to the market model of affects and identities that he himself denounces in his video as 'decadent.'

This paradox touches on the potentially problematic relation of social media and populism argued by Paolo Gerbaudo, who states that "social media has usually been seen as expressions of hyperindividualism, and thus much more in line with neoliberalism and its cult of individual autonomy and spontaneity, than with the communitarian spirit of populism" (4). For Spencer, this obvious contradiction between individualist 'self-optimization' and the collectivizing racial logic of ethnonationalism does not seem to present a paradox. This prompts us to ask, how such performative contradictions – denouncing identity politics through the claiming of identity, criticizing capitalism through a market-based model of 'race' – actually provide plausible scripts to convince (mostly) white, male, and heterosexual individuals of their oppression in majority white societies and of ethnonationalism as a way of individual re-empowerment. Reiterating that the Alternative Right's intervention into the political field offers (re-)legitimizations of racism, sexism, nationalism, and imperialism – i.e. a 'politics of hate and division' – is not too helpful to analyze this pertinent problem. Rather, I argue, more attention needs to be paid to the *affective value* of right-wing extremism in overall populist sentiment, how it provides inhabitable worlds, and its relentless work to generate positive and

---

the concept of 'racial realism,' a term that was introduced by law scholar and pioneer of critical race theory Derrick Bell.

[7] This phantasmatic, transatlantic 'white continuum' first and foremost is based on the new right's notion that Europe and the United States have both become victims of the same decadent model of 'multiculturalism.' This imagined 'racial continuity' between Europe and the US thus is derived from the perceived marginalization of whites and on this basis projects a common 'European' culture/'race' into the past, often back to the 'Romans,' who Spencer is also fond of invoking.

[8] To give just one example, see DePaulo.

empowering affects and scripts. We need to conceptualize the switch from (populist) 'white power' to (individual) 'white empowerment,' as it were.

Affect Theory and Metapolitics

Kathleen Stewart's above-cited *Ordinary Affects* (2006) is a helpful ethnography of affects to further this line of inquiry, and will be used here to add some granularity to Laclau's vague use of the term. Stewart's book describes and, as it were, pre-theoretically unfolds everyday situations and constellations in minute descriptive detail. In moments like those described in Stewart's book, it is not so much 'negative affect' that is experienced – anger, hate, fear – but rather a nebulous confluence of intensities, desires, fleeting impressions, details, and atmospheres that subjects attempt to process into a meaningful everyday life whose emotional 'experience' may or may not become intelligible. Stewart's preliminaries to a theory of ordinary affects have been taken up by authors adjacent to Queer Theory, such as Deborah Gould (2010), Lauren Berlant (2008), and Ann Cvetkovich (2012). These authors share Stewart's premise that affects occur prior to, 'alongside,' or 'next to' (Gould) the formation of the political and of ideology. The situatedness of subjects within ideological-emotional constructs – their subjectification, that is – proceeds from the ordinary navigation of the disparate. Stewart phrases it like this:

> Ideologies happen. Power snaps into place. Structures grow entrenched. Identities take place. Ways of knowing become habitual at the drop of a hat. But it's ordinary affects that give things the quality of a *some*thing to inhabit and animate. Politics starts in the animated inhabitation of things, not way downstream in the various dreamboats and horror shows that get moving. (15-6)

A central question of Stewart's research thus is "what counts as an event, a movement, an impact, a reason to react" (ibid.) – i.e., how, when and under what circumstances do affects and atmospheres congeal into a manifestation of an ideological stance, an action, into systemic violence, a system, or intelligible signification.

This theoretical outline of the preliminary stages of 'political feelings' delineates precisely those pressure points of the ordinary to which the new right, following Alain de Benoist, apply their weapon of choice: 'metapolitics.' The Gramscian term 'metapolitics' is generally associated with the so-called 'cultural revolution from the right' and denotes an alternative strategy to the march through the institutions and the winning of majorities in parliamentary democracies as pursued by right-wing populists. The aim of metapolitics is, as Karl Heinz Weißmann, prominent ideologue of the German new right, writes, to "renew the collective consciousness" and to occupy "fields in pre-political space" (quoted in Speit 2017; my translation).

Mario Müller, activist in the German Identitarian Movement (IB), explains the concept as follows:

> Metapolitics is [...] the 'software' of power. Whereas parties vie with each other for political office, identitarian activists have realized that any political turn must be preceded by a cultural turn. The tides have begun to turn already: The terms, images, and narratives of the left are increasingly becoming the subject of ridicule and contempt. [...] On the one hand, it is the task of identitarian metapolitics to hasten the demise of these code words [...], and to create counter-narratives of our own. (185; my translation)

The new right is fond of framing metapolitics in military language, for example Thor von Waldstein's image of achieving "air supremacy over the minds" (Waldstein 2015; my translation) [9] by influencing and pre-structuring people's everyday experiences. Ideological orthodoxy, radicalization, and hierarchy are less important in metapolitical strategizing than the moulding of media consumption habits, patterns of perception, and cultural discourse. Müller's remarks already encapsulate the manipulation of ordinary affects, when he refers to terms such as 'integration' becoming risible: right-wing metapolitics aims not only to make far-right terms such as 'ethnopluralism' socially acceptable, if not hegemonic, but also work to make democratic terms such as 'pluralism' suspect and affect-provoking.

Affect theory as pursued by Kathleen Stewart and others illuminates the level of ordinary life/experience into which the contemporary Alternative Right insinuates its metapolitical programs. Stewart's reading of *The Turner Diaries* (1978), an extreme-right utopian novel about a 'race war,'[10] emphasizes that the text describes ordinary, affective and experiential scenes that go beyond the book's function as propaganda for white supremacy:

> [W]hat is most surprising about [*The Turner Diaries*] is its focus on domestic scenes and the ordinary details of everyday life. The tips it offers are not just about how to organize armies and make bombs but also how to set up cozy shelters and keep house while living underground. [...] It's a recipe book for domestic competence. A little world comes into view. It is a world based on a military model of community and skill, but it is one that is filled, too, with the textures and sensory details needed to imagine a dream world. This lived,

---

[9] See also Thor von Waldstein. *Metapolitik. Theorie – Lage – Aktion*. Antaios 2016.
[10] *The Turner Diaries* were written by William Luther Pierce, founder of the American Neo-Nazi organization National Alliance, under the pseudonym Andrew Macdonald.

affective constellation of practices and sensibilities make the book not just an ideological diatribe (which it certainly is) but also a scene of life filled with worries, fetishes, compulsions, and hoped-for satisfactions. It is possible to imagine how, for those readers who find it compelling but are not about to build bombs, it's a kind of self-help book. (Stewart 57-8)

This new, in *The Turner Diaries* exclusively male racist thus is not solely imagined according to the *Herrenmensch*, or populism's racial communities; his striving for empowerment and will to shape the world according to his worldview also include the domestic and the bodily, and the attached emotional and ordinary dimensions of existence.

Right-Wing Relationship-Counselling

The Alternative Right, by self-description, is organized into a metapolitical and a political wing (see Sellner). It is not surprising that the populist parties representing the Alternative Right – e.g. the German AFD (*Alternative for Germany*), Trumpist Republicans, the French *Rassemblement National* (formerly *Front National*), etc. – can only peripherally help create the everyday worlds of 'right-wing affect.' Despite attempts such as those by Marx Jongen, chief ideologue of the AFD, to publicly conjure the 'thymos of the people,' the arenas of parliamentary democracy for the most part are unsuited to carry performances of ordinary, everyday racial self-improvement – their field of signification is largely disconnected from the everyday lives of 'ordinary' individuals. The right-wing publishing house Antaios, home of numerous ideologues of the Alternative Right in Germany, on the other hand, has probed into the self-help market with proto-fascist pamphlets such as Jack Donovan's *The Way of Men*, which offers advice on the formation of able-bodied and homosocial masculinities and the so-called "re-polarization of the sexes." For the metapolitical implementation of right-wing sensibilities and their translation into everyday affective and consumptive patterns, the internet is essential, especially the numerous vloggers (see Lewis) of the Alternative Right on YouTube.

These 'alternative influencers' frequently upload their political commentary within an ordinary, everyday framework, 'spontaneously' expressing feelings and reactions to political and cultural events, and generally presenting their 'lived' political selves. In doing so, they condense disparate material – experiences and media texts, moods and self-presentation, as well as their work as 'content producers' earning money through vlogging – into "an event, a movement, an impact, a reason to react" (Stewart 16). The interaction and perceived intimate connection between vloggers and audiences generates an amorphous 'community' that, in its construction of a shared horizon of experience, can be very potent on the affective level.

Following the generic rules of the micro-celebrity format (see Burgess et al.), content is characterized by a sense of confidentiality and intimacy: The ostensible daily sharing of their lives on-screen with audiences grants authenticity to the vloggers' content; political orientation is offered in the sense of actually 'being oriented' (Sara Ahmed; see Schmitz et al.): the ordinariness of vlogs imbues political attitudes with "the quality of a *some*thing to inhabit and animate" (Stewart 15; see also Strick 2015). Being (on the) right equals being connected to things, structures, and feelings: the vloggers often film their content in their private homes, personal belongings are used as part of the presentation, monologs function as 'spontaneous expressions,' as ordinary and affect-based speaking to a community. In this setting, the content creators of the Alternative Right fuse the ordinary with ideological messaging, and vice versa, communicating an entire right-wing lifestyle.

Thirty-year-old Austrian Martin Sellner, a figurehead of the extreme right Identitarian Movement (IBÖ) (see Speit 2018), has been central in ideologizing the everyday in this way in the German language area since ca. 2015, by almost daily postings on his YouTube channel *Martin Sellner GI*. The poster boy of the young right has since 2017 also capitalized on his relationship with 27-year-old Brittany Pettibone, who is an activist in American ethnonationalist circles.[11] Both present themselves as the darling couple of the young identitarians in joint vlogs, instagram pictures, and activities. This change of genre into the realm of celebrity gossip has been taken up by right-wing publications such as *Arcadi Magazine*, here commenting on Sellner's infamous seafaring intervention of 2016, *Defend Europe*:

> Since Defend Europe, mystery has surrounded Martin Sellner (IBÖ). He changed his relationship status [on facebook, S.S.] during the operation in the Mediterranean, after all. The internet community was eager to find out who his partner was. The two hottest contenders of course were the beauties Lauren Southern and Brittany Pettibone, two successful activists from America. ("Martin Sellner"; my translation)

Sellner and Pettibone organize their joint video messages to their fan community as a serialized home story, connected by 'plotlines' such as Pettibone's increasing German language skills or Sellner's continuous legal problems, which are interspersed with singular events such as a family visit over Christmas. They present themselves throughout as living a partnership in which the private and the public, feelings and ideology, all coalesce into one organic whole.

---

[11] The personal relationship between Sellner and Pettibone thus also connected two networks, as both had already been figureheads of their respective national movements.

Feeling the Replacement

A dialog between Sellner and Pettibone posted on her YouTube channel on February 2, 2019 may serve as an example of the Alternative Right's equally intimate and banal bodily and affective practices (see fig. 2).

Figure 2: Martin Sellner and Brittany Pettibone
(https://www.youtube.com/watch?v=DAIucmbEz1E)

The video's title – "FOBO: The Plague That Kills Relationships" (Pettibone 2019) – refers to the so-called FOBO phenomenon ('Fear of a Better Option'), which Sellner proceeds to explain in broken English: "[…] it's called FOBO […] and it's kind of a phobia that you can also call a mental pest that affects most of the young people in the West, not only liberals, but also a lot of conservatives." He continues: "[…] postmodernism has taken away love and happiness and replaced it with *Pornhub* and *Tinder* and it's about time to take it back." Phenomena such as online dating, consumption habits, and feminism are coalesced by Sellner and Pettibone into the argument that traditional relationships between men and women have become more difficult and less stable because individuals are constantly on the lookout for an economically or physically more attractive partner.

This claim is shared by both Sellner and Pettibone, who through affectionate glances demonstrate that they themselves are not afflicted by FOBO: the couple presents itself as the antithesis to the ostensible 'civilizational disease.' Pettibone congratulates Sellner on his coinage of the term 'mental pest' to describe how digital romantic markets infect ways of thinking, as well as intimate relationships: "I wonder if this is why people become so vitriolic online yeah," she says smilingly before Sellner rants onward:

> I think a very important point you also have to make in this video, you don't have a wife, you don't have a family, and only a family, a traditional family is where life is created traditionally, but also like empirically. So this lost family and traditional relationships means also a loss in birth rate and of course it is connected to the demographic demise and what annoys me a little bit is a lot of the people in the right-wing have a total capitalistic liberalistic modernistic materialistic approach to relationships to talk about sexual market values [...] they are completely infected with this pest, full of fear of a better option. (Sellner in Pettibone 2019)

Sellner jumps smoothly from impressionistic observations about psychological effects of dating on Tinder to the demographic situation of majority white societies and an internal critique of right-wing movements. The central claim of the new right – that whites are becoming a minority through the so-called 'great replacement'[12] – is casually mentioned and framed as a direct consequence of dating apps, online pornography, and the 'postmodern' economization of sexual relationships. Again, there is a performative contradiction: one factor driving this development is the self-promotion of celebrity couples as standards of cohabitation, of which Sellner and Pettibone are a minor example.

The emotional linkage of relationship difficulties to the 'great replacement' does not constitute the video's propagandistic climax but takes place roughly in the middle of the fourteen-minute dialog. Whereas far-right agitation videos usually visualize their 'replacement' theories with crowds of dark-skinned people at border fences (e.g. Southern), here the 'great replacement' is presented rather as an intimate aside by a concerned partner, to which Pettibone nods and smiles, giving the impression of a woman quietly and genuinely adoring her pontificating man. Racist ideology and concern for white reproduction rates are combined with a flirtatious relationship dynamic that evokes traditional gender roles: whereas Sellner's New Balance T-Shirt is casually masculine, Pettibone's brown tunic represents a virtuous

---

[12] The term "great replacement" was coined by the right-wing author Renaud Camus in his book *Le Grand Remplacement* (2011) and has since then been adopted by most extreme-right identitarian organisations; the webpage of the Identitäre Bewegung has an entire entry dedicated to the term, and Antaios published Camus' book in German in 2016. The term is less popular in the US, where its function is often performed by the older terms "white genocide" or "race suicide," which have been taken from eugenicist literature such as Madison Grant's *The Passing of the Great Race* (1916) and have been integral to Neo-Nazi discourse in the United States for a long time. The Christchurch mosque shooter titled his 'manifesto' also "The Great Replacement." See also Strick (2019).

1950s femininity. The same is true of the cover art of Pettibone's book *What Makes Us Girls* that is advertised at the end of the video, where Pettibone presents herself as author and entrepreneur in the self-help market of 'traditional femininity.' Here, too, right-wing ideology is packaged as a self-improvement program, as the tagline of Pettibone's women's advice book suggests: "We cannot give what we do not have. So, if we do not love ourselves [...] how then can we love others?"

The re-traditionalization of gender roles has been extensively discussed in the context of right-wing populism;[13] the affective modelling of the right-wing's gender revisionism and its appeal to disparate biographies, however, has so far been undertheorized: "Politics starts in the animated inhabitation of things. There's a politics to being/feeling connected (or not), to energies spent worrying or scheming (or not), to affective contagion, and to all the forms of attunement and attachment" (Stewart 15). The transnational couple Pettibone and Sellner perform their emotional attachment to each other and to their audience, show concern for the problems of the digital age, empathize with their audience, and demonstrate their ordinary, affective attunement to the ethnonationalist movement. Their performance creates an optimistic atmosphere in which the political-sexual answer to 'demographic demise' has already been found: a libidinal relationship between Austrian and US-American 'Europeans' as articulated by Richard Spencer. The transnationally ethnonational couple presents the good-humored, flirtatious answer to 'first world problems.' Setting straight those minds that have been infected by online culture, this activist couple advertises ethno-sexual traditionalism as a self-help program against postmodern control mechanisms, or in Cheney-Lippold's words, 'soft biopower.'

The Alternative Right offers traditionalism and ethnonationalism as an aid against digitalized and commodified sexualities and the confusion of the national character and will. Sellner and Pettibone return to 'love and happiness,' and perform 'ethnic bonding' in a way that recalls the genre of the contemporary 'slow movement': they patiently listen to each other, smile at each other, take the time to speak to their friends, and worry about the survival of 'European People.' Through the affective inclusion of racist talking points into their performance of light-hearted intimacy – common concerns for the nation, movement, and contemporary culture beyond resentment and racism against migrants, agitation against elites, or hate messages – Pettibone and Sellner turn their relationship into an easy-to-digest 'better living through ethnonationalism.' Sara Ahmed (2016) writes:

> [Such narratives] show us [...] the production of the ordinary. [...] The ordinary becomes that which is already under threat by the imagined others whose proximity becomes a crime against person as well as place. The ordinary subject

---

[13] See the contributions in the special issue "Angriff auf die Demokratie," *femina politica* 1 (2018).

is reproduced as the injured party: the one that is 'hurt' or even damaged by the 'invasion' of others.

Sellner and Pettibone represent the transformation from hate to 'love' movements that Ahmed describes in her important text 'Fascism as Love,' in which she expounds on the key figuration through which right-wing extremism reinvented itself as a movement united by 'love' (for the 'race,' people, nation, culture, tradition, and one another). Referring to Judith Butler, Ahmed notes that such groups portray their 'love' as a 'collective vulnerability' in order to claim feelings of marginalization. Activism, denigration of others, and self-defense against the system are all justified through this feeling of violation. Markedly, the performance of Pettibone and Sellner as relationship partners and political activists does not rely on demonizing others. They are not primarily fighting against 'brown hordes,' but against the 'infection' and 'invasion' of their affective economies through digital media and the colonization of their minds through market logics. Their fight and optimism are explicitly organized and performed as ordinary – they are concerned with the everyday thinking and feeling of relationship and political work.

No-Fap and Right-Wing Anti-Pornography

By thus targeting late capitalist media economies – to which Sellner and Pettibone as influencers belong themselves – the Alternative Right has found a suitable bogeyman, which seems to carry much broader appeal than racist resentment. And the critique of media corporations and the environments they provide can further be easily warped into optimistic self-improvement narratives. The central issue of the Alternative Right's attack on media economies is, apart from the omnipresent discussion around 'free speech' and 'deplatforming,' the influence of media on performances of gender and sexuality. Within the Alternative Right, it is mainly influencers in the so-called 'manosphere' (see Ging) who attempt to shape the masculinities of their adolescent target audiences by giving metapolitical and affective interpretations of the contemporary world. The manosphere, as Shawn Van Valkenburgh writes, presents itself as a "loosely connected group of anti-feminist Internet communities comprised of phenomena as diverse as #gamergate, the alt-right, men's rights activism, and pickup artist forums" (1). Within this loose network of websites, internet fora, and YouTube channels, the (mostly male) participants attempt to find 'sexual self-realization' strategies for becoming more successful in precisely that commodified market of sexualities that was denounced by Sellner: the manosphere is exemplary of what he criticized as a "total capitalistic liberalistic modernistic materialistic approach to relationships" (see above). The masculinities wing of the Alternative Right in this regard seems to be at odds with 'traditional couple politics' as espoused by Sellner and Pettibone, as it is concerned with (re-) empowering ostensibly marginalized men in what they call "female-dominated societies" (e.g. Wickelus). The website *returnofkings.com* for example sees its task in helping users improve their 'mating ratios,' which have allegedly been in decline because of technological change, the immigration of unwed non-white men, and feminism:

> Due to changes in mating behavior and pair bonding brought on by technology, shifting demographics, migration to cities from rural towns, universal suffrage, promotion of sexually promiscuous behaviors, and destruction of traditional sex roles, most men do not have the ability or knowledge to successfully reproduce with a modern woman on a comparable attractiveness and socioeconomic level (Roosh V),

writes manosphere author Roosh V under the heading "What is Neomasculinity?". The strategies offered to improve men's chances in the sexual market always rely on the reduction of women and women's sexual agency to pseudo-evolutionary patterns that men have to learn to manipulate (e.g. a kind of Machiavellian reproductive egotism that is only interested in the 'best genes,' which of course inevitably are signified by male strength and success). Another oft-used concept is 'female hypergamy,' i.e. women's ostensible preference for economically higher positioned men, which is similar to the aforementioned FOBO but ascribed exclusively to women. Self-help tips offered in the manosphere suggest that men become egotistical themselves and (re-)discover male independence from couple- and relationship-oriented affective patterns, as they, it is argued, have been sexually and economically 'exploited' by women (see Van Valkenburgh 10-12).

The necessary process of unlearning is called 'redpilling' in the jargon of the manosphere, a reference to the 1999 film *The Matrix*. *The Red Pill Handbook*, an anonymous collection of manosphere-articles, explains the 'Red Pill'as follows:

> It's a reference to *The Matrix*, in which Morpheus offers Neo a choice of one of two pills... a blue pill, which will make him forget and allow him to contentedly go back to a life of brainwashed mediocrity, or a red pill, which will wake him up to an unpleasant truth but grant him great power. (*The Red Pill Handbook* 73)

'Taking the red pill' accordingly refers to a process of awakening and disillusionment, through which *man* can opt out of the delusion of contemporary 'female-dominated' and anti-male societies.

It should be noted that unlearning this 'false consciousness' is supposed to be achieved not solely by optimizing one's 'mating' behavior – called 'game' (see Goldwag) – but also through recalibrating one's everyday patterns of 'doing masculinity.' In an entry of *The Red Pill Handbook* titled "A 7-Step Guide To Swallowing The Pill," author *no_face* recommends following seven steps to achieve 'remasculinization,' ranging from simple bodily exercises ("before you start lifting [weights], you need to make sure your posture is OK"), to mental exercises ("You need to develop alpha characteristics in your frame such as stoicism, abundance mentality and high value"), to strict rules of conduct in relationships:

> You need to dominate your woman physically (lift, MOFO, lift!) mentally (you are smarter than a woman, right?), emotionally (be stoic, bro), and sexually (escalate). You also need to dominate the relationship (no supplication, no compliments unless its for something she did to please you) and sex acts (read Daniel Rose's Sex God method). (*The Red Pill Handbook* 142ff)

The manosphere's subfora often refer to current self-help books in the area of so-called alpha masculinity,[14] which for the most part advocate models of masculinity based on antifeminism (see Dignam et al.).

Besides such 7-step programs focusing on reclaiming masculinity as dominance over women, physical strength, and self-confidence, the influence of media is a central issue in the manosphere's self-help discourse. As the primary target group of this network consists of white, single, adolescent internet users, it is unsurprising that the psychological effects of online media, especially pornography, are frequent concerns: "Quit playing video games [...] in your mom's basement while jerking off to porn every day, and start working out, eating right, excelling professionally, and learning skills," *Red Pill Handbook* author *Archwinger* (272) scolds the RedPill community, addressing the nexus of media consumption and bodily exercise as a key area of remasculinization.

Pornography and masturbation occupy a special place in the misogynistic worldview of the Alternative Right,[15] as in their view, the primary function of pornography consists in making 'cuckoldry' socially acceptable. 'Cuckoldry' or 'cucking' refers to a pornographic genre in which a man watches his female partner having sex with another man. Consuming pornography supposedly normalizes this sexual configuration, i.e. consumers are said to become habituated to sexual gratification through watching other men have sex with attractive women. In manosphere terms, this supposedly leads to a loss of self-confidence and turns men into 'betas,' lost in a vicious cycle of self-doubt, failure with women, pornography, masturbation, and so on. As a reaction to this 'deferred' sex addiction, internet users

---

[14] A German example would be Kollegah. *Das ist Alpha! Die 10 Boss-Gebote*. PLACE: Riva, 2018.

[15] This also marks one of the numerous shared interests of the Alternative Right with Christian fundamentalists; see Sauter.

have formed abstinence communities that seek to attain self-empowerment through avoiding pornography and masturbation (see Taylor et al.). On fora such as *reddit.com/r/NoFap*, which since 2011 has amassed ca. 425,000 members, so-called 'monthly challenges' are collectively endured and articulated in the language of contemporary detox discourse. 'No-fapping' (i.e., abstaining from masturbation) is understood as a detoxing of desire and a form of consumptive 'hygiene' preventing addiction. The forum describes its goals as follows:

> We host rebooting challenges in which participants ('Fapstronauts') abstain from pornography and masturbation for a period of time. Whether your goal is casual participation in a monthly challenge as a test of self-control, or whether excessive masturbation or pornography has become a problem in your life and you want to quit for a longer period of time, you will find a supportive community and plenty of resources here. (cited in reddit.com/r/NoFap)

R/NoFap thus appears to be a 'critical consumer movement' similar to popular self-help programs such as 'Digital Detox,' but instead of focusing on 'slower,' more consciously experienced living, it holds out the prospect of an empowering experience of sexual self-control liberated from corporate pornography's enticements. This detoxification of the masculine eros, which (considering the working conditions in the pornography industry) should be applauded, however, enters strange coalitions with the racist worldviews of the Alternative Right. User *MrFredstt* for example tells his story of suffering as a 'beta' and his final liberation through abstinence like this: "In a way, watching porn is cucking yourself. As for my story, sadly, I got hooked on porn at a young age (13) and for the last year have worked on quitting it. So far I'm pretty good, though I fail from time to time."

Whereas 'before-after' narratives such as *MrFredstt*'s could considerably help change contemporary images of masculinity and consumption habits, the context of his comment is crucial: this posting reacted approvingly to a YouTube video by Swedish ethnonationalist and bodybuilder *The Golden One* (Marcus Follin), titled "Why I Hate Porn and Why You Should Stop Watching It." Follin, whose channel has close to 100,000 subscribers, is an active member of the European Neo-Nazi scene and belongs to the pop-culture wing of the Alternative Right. On his channel, in addition to racist theories of 'Nordic superiority,' he offers dietary supplements for bodybuilders and self-help tips on relationships, bodily exercise, and media consumption.

Follin uploaded a series of vlogs on the subject of pornography, denouncing it as a 'cultural weapon': "[…] porn is a weapon which exploits primarily white women and destroys their lives, and destroys the masculine virility of Western men […] it hurts you over a long period of time and it causes relations between men and women to become worse […]" (Follin 2016). Whereas Follin himself largely avoids explicit references to right-wing conspiracy theories, and instead focuses on physical and mental self-improvement (albeit for white men) (see Strick forthcoming), the comments on his videos often pick up on the racist and ethnonationalist context. Three examples might illustrate how Follin's exercise and media consumption advice is translated into nationalist empowerment discourse in the comment sections. User *Henry115* writes:

> Thank you Marcus, you've really helped me remove porn from my life. I'm finally starting to enjoy intimacy with my fair maiden. My confidence has skyrocketed and i've truly taken the path to the glorious pill. I'm working out reading more and fighting for Europe. Planning on living a porn free life with 6 kids [.]

User *Jupiter Rising*: "Porn is a weapon against Western civilization. They know there is a very low birth rate among Europeans and porn is promoting Degeneracy, and so is a weapon against the Family Values of [sic] which Western Civilization is based"; user *Gustav Elofsson* seconds: "[abstinence] is not a battle you against you, it's a battle you against Jew!"

The last comment refers to ideas on the far-right that Western culture industries are dominated by Jews trying to undermine white dominance by disseminating pornography and 'anti-white' Hollywood films.[16] Calling pornography 'anti-white' propaganda touches upon another racist subtext relating to 'cuckolding.' The online-networks of the Alternative Right coined the term 'cuckservative,' referring to conservative politicians not espousing ethnonationalism, and thus not helping the fight against 'the great replacement' and the alleged mass rapings of white women by non-white men (Dietze 2016). The extreme-right website *rightrealist.com* explains the ideological significance of 'cuck' as follows:

> The term 'cuck' from an alt-right perspective began as a very simple analogy: Allowing foreigners to invade, exploit, or attack your nation or people is compared with cuckoldry. In other words, a cuck is a man who allows his wife (nation) to sleep with another man (foreign people), and who invests time and resources into raising a child that is not his own. The term can be used more generally either as a noun to describe a man who has emasculated himself, or as

---

[16] On the notorious message board *8ch.net*, which likewise has a *nofap*-subboard, the antisemitic premise of the right-wing anti-porn movement is discussed more explicitly. Anonymous there posted the question "ARE THE JEWS BEHIND PORN OR NOT? THIS IS IMPORTANT," and receives the anonymous answer: "Yes. Do a google search for names of directors, producers and male stars. Also note how many of the male stars have jewish features and how disgustingly ugly most of them are, they look like jew rats." <https://8ch.net/nofap/index.html>. Last accessed on 30 April 2019.

a verb for weak and submissive behavior. ("The Alt-Right FAQ", rightrealist.com)

In the Alternative Right's imaginary, the 'great replacement' is again and again depicted through 'cuckold'-images showing dark-skinned men raping white women, with white men as the observing bystanders. Escaping this scenario und its implied 'degeneracy' (see above) – i.e. becoming 'uncucked' or 'red-pilled' in the jargon of the Alternative Right – thus also means fighting against the normalization of pornography, becoming abstinent, and regaining 'white control' and virility. Thus, the Neo-Nazi website *The Daily Stormer* can link Follin's 'NoFap' videos without having to explicate the context of a racist culture war, as it is already implied in the call to join the 'movement' by becoming abstinent: "If you are watching pornography, you are destroying your life and you probably are not even aware of it. We need strong young men. We do not need wankers." (Anglin 2017)

Apocalyptic (Consumer) Whiteness

In conclusion, I would like to emphasize two aspects regarding the interconnection between anti-pornography discourse, self-help, relationship advice, and neo-fascism. These discourses aim specifically at 'usability' in everyday life, both as a form of political agitation and for their consumers' lifeworlds. In the above analyzed connections between sexual politics and self-help, racism and sexism become disarticulated,[17] i.e. present implicit components of the discourse instead of being advanced as their expressive core. The affective revaluation of media-consumption and sexual habits within extreme right and racist ideologies can thus be experienced as a positive return to one's true personality, desires, gender role, or bonding behaviors. Right-wing social media discourse's focus on the domestic and the private, the intimate and the intersubjective allows audiences (at least at first) to disregard any ideological underpinnings. For example, anti-pornography stances on the far-right can also be seen as a reaction to the pornographic coding of sexuality as violence against women, a point of concern also voiced by some second-wave feminists such as Andrea Dworkin. Anti-pornography and NoFap present themselves as a search for non-toxic and progressive gender roles, even as they partake in gendered and racialized narratives that are no less violent, to say the least. Similarly, Sellner and Pettibone's description of the commodification of sexuality online can be read as accurate and pertinent to the problems of their Tinder-exposed audiences. Audiences of these postmodern fascisms need concern themselves with the implied racist-segregationist worldviews only secondarily, or may come to

---

[17] 'Disarticulation' is a term coined by queer theorist Beatrice Michaelis, see Michaelis.

tacitly accept its tenets without consciously 'supporting' them. This demonstrates how the Alternative Right has recalibrated its political approach, primarily focusing on connectivity and affective affiliation rather than ideological coherence and radicalization. Gabriele Dietze describes this strategy of right-wing metapolitics concisely as building "affective bridges," (Dietze 2019 forthcoming; my translation) a term that captures the potential of this approach to make extreme-right ideologemes appear as 'constructive' and peaceable to the public, rather than as 'disruptive agitation' (see Strick 2018).

Here I once more have to point to the foundational ideologeme of the 'great replacement' (see also Ganesh) and the pornotropic[18] constellation it evokes. In Renaud Camus' *grande remplacement* the so-called 'rape epidemic' plays a decisive role, which (similar to miscegenation discourse in the US-American context) alleges that non-whites pose a demographic threat to majority-white societies through sexual violence as well as higher birth rates. The practices in the areas of relationship-formation, media consumption, and sexual behaviour discussed above thus cannot be said to merely constitute the ordinary counterparts to right-wing and ethnonationalist proposals, such as segregation and the 'remigration' of non-whites. These discourses as a whole rather indicate that 'white supremacy' constitutes a sexual fantasy, and that the contemporary surge of the extreme right should be understood as also entailing a 'sexual revolution.' The re-empowerment (or re-racialization) of white male sexuality here is key, which, faced with the threat of the 'great replacement' or 'white genocide,' is ascribed the role of 'race saviour.'

Sheronda Brown in this context describes a sexually charged 'apocalyptic whiteness' that is imagined within a pornotropic scenario of sexually threatened purity and demographic demise:

> Fear of the corruption of 'white purity'– whether by non-white immigrants and citizens gaining institutional power over white nationalists or by the Black phallus gaining sexual power over white cuckolds and miscegenating with white women – is also a fear of sexual and social humiliation. Both of these fears are tied up with the fetishization of power and power play. And these fears often result in apocalyptic whiteness, a violent response to the white genocide fable. (Brown)[19]

The self-help discourses discussed in this article evoke this 'apocalypse' only in passing – in the form of casual references to 'demographic demise,' comments on the 'Jewish-dominated' pornography industry, or the bad effects of gaming on one's posture, media addiction, or lack of self-confidence in the 'arena of heterosexuality'.

---

[18] On Alexander Weheliye's concept of "pornotroping," see also Menzel.
[19] See also Keilty.

These casual observations of demise and deficiency and their possible remedies broadly distribute the sexual phantasm of 'white genocide' onto micro-phenomena and integrate audiences/users into the Alternative Right's 'worldbuilding': even the smallest act, change of mind, or desire for improvement can link itself to racist conspiracies without necessitating implicit ideologies to become explicit. Users are embedded in a kind of 'affective bargaining' – a negotiation and generation of reclaimed sovereignty whose prior loss hardly needs explication. Feelings of self-improvement and empowerment 'tune in' into apocalyptic and sexual phantasms in which the 'white' subject needs to prevail against non-white hypersexuality and 'Jewish / female mind control.'

Furthermore, the NoFap-movement and their extreme-right proponents articulate hostility toward migrants, antifeminism, gender traditionalism, and racism not explicitly, but rather as subcutaneous stabilizers within a discourse on affective-material improvements of personality and everyday life. They thus manifest not primarily as an 'ideological position' or 'political awakening,' but as ordinary, experiential affective patterns of feeling better, being more active, etc. Again, Kathleen Stewart catches how affects model the body and integrate it into social or ideological signification, instilling a sensation of 'surging':

> The body surges. Out of necessity, or for the love of movement. Lifestyles and industries pulse around it, groping for what to make of the way it throws itself at objects of round perfection. [...] Layers of invented life form around the body's dreamy surges like tendons or fat. (Stewart 113-4)

Right-wing bodily practices of self-mastery, sexual sovereignty, and media consumption pre-structure the layers of 'invented life' that form around this experiential body. Red-Pill discourse constructs layers of positively connoted self-becoming and self-actualization that link up with quotidian uses of media and the body, conveying the sense of having 'a plan of some sort,' and orient bodily affect.

The undercurrent of hatred within these forms of racist self-help is re-oriented toward negative aspects of one's *self*-image: 'white genocide' and the 'culture war' take place, as it were, on the level of individual bodies, their fitness and virility, posture and feeling. In an article in the *Daily Stormer*, intolerance of racialized others accordingly is translated into intolerance against flaws in one's own body:

> [K]eep your goals realistic, but do something. Do not tolerate being fat. Do not tolerate having no muscle mass. Do not tolerate bad posture. Seek to look like the average man looked 100 years ago, and you'll do fine. You can check the *Daily Stormer Health section* for more informations. (Anglin 2019)

The postmodern return of fascism as self-help in this sense is connected to a kind of 'apocalyptic consumerism': Neoracism and ethnonationalism have become – in the words of Richard Spencer cited above – "a place to go shopping"; a consumable, daily obtainable experience of gratification servicing one's need for coherence, energy, and feeling alive. The Christchurch shooter, who in March 2019 killed more than fifty mosque attendants and severely injured fifty more, opened his manifesto 'The Great Replacement' (see Moses) with the slogan: "It's the Birthrates. It's the birthrates. It's the birthrates." Later, he describes the 'race war' in a language that merges neoliberal catchphrases, advertising sloganeering, motivational speaking, and Neo-Nazi propaganda: "You will risk, struggle, strive, drive, stumble, fall, crawl, charge and perspire, all in the name of victory. Because you cannot accept anything less."

The manifesto is, contrary to what several media commentators have suggested, not an insiderist articulation of hate speech encrypted in references to online-culture, but a very clear and transparently worded how-to-document: it translates the antagonistic anatomies of populism into personal messages; refashions hate speech as motivational language; and distills an utterly private and simultaneously apocalyptic view of the world from statistics, feelings, and quotidian observations. All speech acts, networked discourses, and informational politics of the Alternative Right – from casual dating advice to manifestos for racial violence and murder – engage in this kind of worldbuilding that fatten the skeletal models of populism, and flesh them out into lifeworlds that reorganize violence and hate into something inhabitable in the ordinary; an environment that is hospitable for some *because* it implies the deaths of others. In such environments, radicalization and prepping for (discursive and material) violence seem like self-care; and ideology itself, populist or neofascist, seems to merely "happen" as part of the bargain for a better life.

Works Cited

Ahmed, Sara. "Fascism as Love." Blog *feministkilljoys.com* 9 November 2016 <https://feministkilljoys.com/2016/11/09/fascism-as-love/>. Last accessed on 30 April 2019.

---. "Affective economies." *Social Text* 22.2 (2004): 117-139.

Anglin, Andrew. "Self-Help Sunday: Do Not Compare Yourself to Steroid Twink Hollywood Actors." *Daily Stormer* 28 April 2019 <https://dailystormer.name/self-help-sunday-do-not-compare-yourself-to-steroid-freak-hollywood-actors/>. Last accessed on 30 April 2019.

---. "The Golden One on the Pornography Issue." *Daily Stormer* 25 April 2017 <https://dailystormer.name/the-golden-one-on-the-pornography-issue/>. Last accessed on 30 April 2019.

Archwinger. "The Most Unattractive Trait of All: Trying to Attract a Woman." *The Red Pill Handbook* <http://redpillhandbook.com/The%20Red%20Pill%20Handbook%202nd%20Ed.pdf>. 270-2.

Bell, Derrick. "Racial Realism." *Connecticut Law Review* 24 (1991): 363-78.

Benoist, Alain de. *Kulturrevolution von Rechts. Gramsci und die Nouvelle Droite.* 1985. Dresden: Jungeuropa Verlag, 2017.

Berlant, Lauren. "Big man." *Social Text Online* 19 (2017). <https://socialtextjournal.org/big-man/>.

---. *The Female Complaint: The Unfinished Business of Sentimentality in American Culture*. Durham: Duke University Press, 2008.

Brown, Sherronda. "Erotic Race Play Reveals How White Supremacy Is a Perversion of Unmatched Proportions." *Black Youth Project* 2 October 2017. <https://blackyouthproject.com/white-supremacy-perversion-unmatched/>. Last accessed on 30 April 2019.

Burgess, Jean and Joshua Green. *YouTube: Online Video and Participatory Culture*. Second edition. Cambridge: Polity Press, 2018.

Camus, Renaud. *Revolte gegen den Großen Austausch*. Schnellroda/Steigra: Antaios, 2016.

Cheney-Lippold, John. "A New Algorithmic Identity: Soft Biopolitics and the Modulation of Control." *Theory, Culture & Society* 28.6 (2011): 164-181.

Cvetkovich, Ann. *Depression: A Public Feeling*. Durharm: Duke University Press, 2012.

DePaulo, Bella. "How to Become Your True Self – What Social Science Tells Us About Living Authentically." *psychologytoday.com* 18 November 2014 <https://www.psychologytoday.com/us/blog/living-single/201411/how-become-your-true-self>. Last accessed on 30 April 2019.

Dietze, Gabriele. *Sexueller Exzeptionalismus*. Bielefeld: transcript, 2019 forthcoming.

---. "Das Ereignis Köln." *Femina Politica* 1 (2016): 93-102.

Dignam, Pierce Alexander, and Deana A. Rohlinger. "Misogynistic Men Online: How the Red Pill Helped Elect Trump." *Signs: Journal of Women in Culture and Society* 44.3 (2019): 589-612.

Donovan, Jack. *Der Weg der Männer*. Schnellroda/Steigra: Antaios, 2012.

Duncan, Pansy Kathleen. "The Uses of Hate. On Hate as a Political Category." *M/C Journal* 20.1 (2017): no pag.

Follin, Marcus (*The Golden One*). "Why I Hate Porn and Why You Should Stop Watching It." *Youtube.com* 14 June 2017 <https://www.youtube.com/watch?v=guck9gUOIls&frags=pl%2Cwn>. Last accessed on 30 April 2019.

---. "My Best Advice for Quitting Porn for Nerds. Also a Message from Teddy." *Youtube.com* 10 October 2016 <https://www.youtube.com/watch?v=bmePrgRdRlQ>. Last accessed on 30 April 2019.

Ganesh, Bharath. "The Ungovernability of Digital Hate Culture." *Journal of International Affairs* 71.2 (2018): 30-49.

Gerbaudo, Paolo. "Social Media and Populism: An Elective Affinity?" *Media, Culture & Society* 40.5 (2018): 1-9.

Ging, Debbie "Alphas, Betas, and Incels: Theorizing the Masculinities of the Manosphere." *Men and Masculinities* (2017): 1-20. <https://doi.org/10.1177/1097184X17706401>.

Goldwag, Arthur. "Leader's Suicide Brings Attention to Men's Rights Movement." *Southern Poverty Law Center* 1 (2012). <https://www.splcenter.org/fighting-hate/intelligence-report/2012/leader's-suicide-brings-attention-men's-rights-movement>.

Gould. Deborah. "On Affect and Protest." *Political Emotions: New Agendas in Communication*. Ed. Janet Staiger, Ann Cvetkovich, Ann Reynolds. New York: Routledge, 2010. 32-58.

Grant, Madison. *The Passing of the Great Race*. New York: Charles Scribner's Sons, 1916.

Hawley, George. *Making Sense of the Alt-right*. New York: Columbia University Press, 2017.

Heikkilä, Niko. "Online Antagonism of the Alt-Right in the 2016 Election." *European Journal of American Studies* 12.2 (2017): 12-2.

Hochschild, Arlie Russell: *Strangers in Their Own Land: Anger and Mourning on the American Right*. New York: The New Press, 2016.

Hockenos, Paul. *Free to Hate: The Rise of the Right in Post-Communist Eastern Europe*. New York: Routledge, 2013.

Keilty, Patrick. "Pornography's White Infrastructure." *Catalyst: Feminism, Theory, Technoscience* 4.1 (2018): 1-9.

Kimmel, Michael. *Angry White Men: American Masculinity at the End of an Era*. London: Hachette UK, 2017.

Laclau, Ernesto. *On Populist Reason*. London: Verso, 2005.

Lewis, Rebecca. "Alternative Influence Network, Data & Society Report 2018". 18 September 2018 <https://datasociety.net/output/alternative-influence/>.

"Martin Sellner und Brittany Pettibone sind ein Paar!" *Arcadi Magazin* 27 September 2017 <https://arcadimagazin.de/martin-sellner-und-brittany-pettibone-sind-ein-paar/>. Last accessed on 30 April 2019.

Menzel, Annie. "And the Flesh Shall Set You Free: Weheliye's Habeas Viscus." *Theory & Event* 19.1 (2016).

Michaelis, Beatrice. *(Dis-)Artikulationen von Begehren: Schweigeeffekte in Wissenschaftlichen und Literarischen Texten*. Berlin: De Gruyter, 2011.

Moses, Dirk. "'White Genocide' and the Ethics of Public Analysis." *Journal of Genocide Research* (2019): 1-13.

Mouffe, Chantal: *For a Left Populism*. New York/London: Verso, 2018.

Müller, Mario. *Kontrakultur*. Schnellroda/Steigra: Antaios, 2017.

Nagle, Angela. *Kill All Normies: Online Culture Wars from 4Chan and Tumblr to Trump and the Alt-Right*. Alresford: Zero Books, 2017.

NPI/RADIX. "Who Are We?" *Youtube.com* 12 December 2015 <https://youtu.be/3rnRPhEwELo>. Last accessed on 30 April 2019.

Nussbaum, Martha. *The Monarchy of Fear: A Philosopher Looks at our Political Crisis*. New York: Simon and Schuster, 2018.

O'Toole, Fintan. *Heroic Failure: Brexit and the Politics of Pain*. London: Apollo, 2018.

Patch, Justin. *Discordant Democracy: Noise, Affect, Populism, and the Presidential Campaign*. London: Routledge, 2019.

Pettibone, Britanny. "FOBO: The Plague That Kills Relationships." *Youtube.com* 19 February 2019 <https://www.youtube.com/watch?v=DAIucmbEz1E&frags=pl%2Cwn.> Last accessed on 30 April 2019.

---. *What Makes Us Girls: And Why It's All Worth It*. No Place Given: Reason Books, 2018.

reddit.com/r/NoFap. Last accessed 30 April 2019.

Roosh V. "What Is Neomasculinity?" *rooshv.com* 6 May 2015 <https://www.rooshv.com/what-is-neomasculinity>. Last accessed on 30 April 2019.

Sauter, Monika. *Devoted! Frauen in der evangelikalen Populärkultur der USA*. Bielefeld: transcript, 2017.

Schmitz, Sigrid, and Sara Ahmed. "Affect/Emotion: Orientation Matters. A Conversation between Sigrid Schmitz and Sara Ahmed." *FZG – Freiburger Zeitschrift für GeschlechterStudien* 20.2 (2014): 97-108.

Sellner, Martin. "Politische Paradoxien." *Sezession* 79 (2017): 22-5.

Shifman, Limor. "An anatomy of a YouTube meme." *New media & society* 14.2 (2012): 187-203.

Southern, Lauren. "The Great Replacement." *Youtube.com* 3 July 2017 <https://www.youtube.com/watch?v=OTDmsmN43NA>. Last accessed on 30 April 2019.

Speit Andreas (ed.). *Das Netzwerk der Identitären: Ideologie und Aktionen der Neuen Rechten*. Berlin: Ch. Links, 2018.

---."Neurechter Denker Karlheinz Weißmann: Der Oberintellektuelle." *taz – die Tageszeitung* 21 April 2017 <http://www.taz.de/!5399096/>. Last accessed on 30 April 2019.

Stewart, Kathleen. *Ordinary Affects*. Durham: Duke University Press, 2007.

Strick, Simon. "The Alternative Right, Masculinities, and Quotidian Affect", in: *Rightwing Populism and Gender*, Gabriele Dietze and Julia Roth (eds.), Bielefeld: transcript, 2019. Forthcoming.

---. "A Genealogy of the Very Idea of White Genocide." *Aussterben*. Zentrum für Literaturforschung, Berlin. 26 April 2019. Lecture.

---. "Alt-Right-Affekt: Provokationen und Transgressionen." *Zeitschrift für Medienwissenschaften* 19 (2018).

---. "How do you live? From Construction to Habitation." Blog *critical habitations*, 2015. <https://criticalhabitations.wordpress.com/debate/debate-1-habit-and-habitation/how-do-you-live-from-construction-to-habitation/>. Last accessed on 30 April 2019.

---. *American Dolorologies: Pain, Sentimentality, Biopolitics*. Albany: SUNY Press, 2014.

Taylor, Kris, and Sue Jackson. "'I Want that Power Back': Discourses of Masculinity within an Online Pornography Abstinence Forum." *Sexualities* 21.4 (2018): 621-39.

"The Alt-Right FAQ." *rightrealist.com* <http://rightrealist.com/#q16>. Last accessed on 30 April 2019.

The Red Pill Handbook. Second edition, online, 2015 <https://www.reddit.com/r/AlreadyRed/comments/39cufk/the_red_pill_handbook/>.

Van Valkenburgh, Shawn P. "Digesting the Red Pill: Masculinity and Neoliberalism in the Manosphere." *Men and Masculinities* (2018): 1-20.

Wagner, Thomas. *Die Angstmacher: 1968 und die neuen Rechten*. Berlin: Aufbau 2017.

Waldstein, Thor von. *Metapolitik: Theorie – Lage – Aktion*. Schnellroda/Steigra: Antaios, 2016.

---."Metapolitik und Parteipolitik – Festvortrag Thor v. Waldsteins." *IfS webpage* 28 July 2015 <https://staatspolitik.de/metapolitik-und-parteipolitik-festvortrag-thor-v-waldsteins/>. Last accessed on 30 April 2019.

Wickelus, Charles. "American Masculinity is Based on Female Approval." *returnofkings.com* 14 July 2013 <http://www.returnofkings.com/13859/american-masculinity-is-based-on-female-approval>. Last accessed on 30 April 2019.

Wilde, Gabriele, and Birgit Meyer (eds.) "Angriff auf die Demokratie." Special issue *femina politica* 27.1 (2018).

Feminism for the 99%: Towards a Populist Feminism?[1]

Akwugo Emejulu

Can Feminism for the 99% Succeed as a New Kind of Populism?

As they seek to find a place in and/or confront the contemporary populist zeitgeist, feminists supporting intersectional justice-claims face very real, destabilizing and contradictory challenges. Intersectional feminists recognize race, class, gender, sexuality, disability, and legal status as interlocking systems of oppression, and pay attention to the ways in which these particular intersections generate agency and solidarity for different kinds of women. Populism, on the other hand, is a political strategy that seeks to articulate popular grievances in a way that can unify a 'sovereign people' against corrupt and self-serving political, economic, and cultural elites. It is less interested in recognizing difference within its construction of the people.

The new wave of populist politics that is sweeping across both Europe and the United States – from Britain's vote to leave the European Union, to Donald Trump's successful US presidential campaign, to Viktor Orban's brutal and illiberal democratic practices in Hungary – is currently destabilizing 'politics as usual' and ushering in a new political order, and this has had disastrous consequences for the most marginalized, particularly women of color.

Recently, however, a new movement has emerged, Feminism for the 99%, which seeks to co-opt the languages and practices of populist politics. In this short article, I briefly look at the ways in which this new mobilization attempts to connect feminism and populism, in its attempt to build transnational solidarity for racial and gender justice.

As I have previously argued, populism is poison for feminist politics (Emejulu). In both theory and practice it is anathema to the aims and goals of a feminism that seeks redistributive and intersectional justice. Its discursive construction of a homogenized and reified 'people,' its promotion of a crude majoritarianism, and its (mostly) uncritical support for popular belief systems means that it is incredibly difficult to build feminist politics and a feminist collective identity with and through

---

[1] This article is a reprint and was originally published by Akwugo Emejulu. "Feminism for the 99%: towards a populist feminism?" in *Soundings: A journal of politics and culture* 66 (2017): 63-7.

traditional populist practices. For example, in our project on minority women's activism in anti-austerity movements in Britain and France (which often also operated as populist spaces), Leah Bassel and I found that minority women activists were excluded from these protest spaces when they sought to advance anti-austerity critiques that took seriously the racialized and gendered effects of the cuts and privatizations of the welfare states in each country (Emejulu et al; Bassel et al.). There could be no space for analyses and actions that centered race and gender since these supposedly 'controversial issues' could potentially fracture the unified 'people' (for a detailed discussion of these dynamics see Emejulu). Bice Maiguashca, Jonathan Dean and Dan Keith found similar issues at play in Occupy in Britain, where feminist and anti-racist politics were relegated to a supporting role in affirming an affective disposition for interpersonal relations in protest spaces but did not seem to inform either protest strategy or the political education of activists.

The hostility of populism to intersectional ideas and practices (or to merely single-strand issues of racial or gender justice) is unsurprising given that there is an unacknowledged ethno-nationalism embedded in many populist movements, whether or not they are consciously based on xenophobic sentiments. 'The people' in populist politics are constituted as stewards of the nation, defending themselves and their institutions from destructive and treasonous elite power. The familiar political slogans of 'Taking Back Control,' 'I Want My Country Back,' and 'Make America Great Again' position the people as true patriots seeking to restore past national glories and build a brighter future for 'us.' The populist project cannot accommodate subversive intersectional positions that undermine these national mythologies and spotlight the imperial, white supremacist, capitalist, and patriarchal foundations of the nation.

A feminist politics that ignores white supremacy and imperialism can, however, quite easily be put to work for populist ends. A feminism that simply seeks equality between women and men, and not the transformation of the social and economic order, can be encompassed within a populist politics. For example, in the name of 'liberty' and the 'will of the people,' we have seen white feminists in France supporting the hijab and the (now overturned) burkini ban; white feminists in Germany supporting the surveillance and over-policing of migrants and refugees after the Cologne railway station attacks in 2016; and white feminists in Britain supporting Theresa May even as she continues her crackdown on migrants through her 'hostile environment' policy.

Feminism for the 99% (F99), however, seeks to creatively challenge the apparent impossibility of intertwining feminism with populism – by subverting the constituent elements of populism. Mobilized to action in response to the election of Trump and the worldwide Women's March in January 2017, and drawing inspiration from an already existing decolonial feminist politics in the Global South, F99's aim is to cultivate this 'new wave of militant feminist struggle' (Davis et al.). F99 rejects 'lean-in feminism' – the individualistic, corporate-inspired version of feminism that seeks women's inclusion in institutions rather than the transformation of these institutions – and campaigns against 'the casualization of labor, wage inequality [...] homophobia, transphobia and xenophobic immigration policies.' It seeks to build 'a new internationalist feminist movement with an expanded agenda – at once anti-racist, anti-imperialist, anti-heterosexist, and anti-neoliberal.' The goal is 'a grassroots, anti-capitalist feminism.'

The agenda of F99 is striking in that it seeks to occupy populism by turning some of its key tenets on their head. It seizes on the idea of majoritarianism and expands it into transnational solidarity. F99's majoritarianism, rather than referring to the numerical white majority and its supposedly homogenous interests in the Global North, interpellates all women in the Global South and North in order to build collective consciousness, identity, and action. By paying attention to women who are disproportionately concentrated in poverty and low-paid work, F99 seeks to build a majority of the dispossessed. By starting from the experiences of the most marginalized – women of color, migrant women and women in precarious work, who must negotiate predatory capitalism, sexism, and racism – F99 undermines populism's latent ethno-nationalism. From these shared experiences of intersectional inequality and discrimination, it grounds its politics in transnational movements that are attempting to challenge structural domination: anti-imperialism, anti-capitalism, anti-racism, and anti-transphobia.

F99 also attempts to co-opt the language of Occupy. As Keeanga-Yamatta Taylor argues: "The problems experienced by women [...] are rooted in an economic system that privileges the 1% over the 99%." The reasons behind women's relative poverty are not simply economic questions, however: "they are related to an economic arrangement that relies on the free labour of women to [...] reproduce itself as a political system."

Through this intervention, F99 attempts to challenge de-raced and de-gendered understandings of how capitalism operates and makes foundational an analysis and politics rooted in countering the dynamics of racial capitalism and exploitative reproductive labor. A key practice of realizing these ideals was F99's organizing of the Women's Strike to mark International Women's Day in 2017, and to ground this populist feminist action in the history of materialist struggles for gender justice.

There is some debate, however, as to whether F99 is actually populist. In my view it is, because it fundamentally reshapes the idea of 'the people' and popular grievance. Using a capacious and differentiated idea of 'the people' which transcends national borders, F99 attempts to unify and call to action an anti-capitalist, anti-racist, and anti-imperialist feminist movement for justice against elites. As June Jordan (quoted in Palmer 6) reminds us:

We are the people [...] As Black women, we are most of the people, any people you care to talk about. And therefore, nothing that is good for the people is good unless it is good for me, as I determine myself.

So, although I remain aware of the dangers of populist politics, I recognize that F99 offers a novel response that harnesses the potential of popular grievance and cultivates a renewed solidarity politics for feminist activism across the globe.

Works Cited

Bassel, Leah, and Emejulu, Akwugo *Minority Women and Austerity: Survival and Resistance in France and Britain.* Bristol: Policy Press, 2017.

Canovan, Margaret. "Trust the People! Populism and the Two Faces of Democracy." *Political Studies* 47.1 (1999): 2-16.

Davis, Angela, Barbara Ransby, Cinzia Arruzza, Keeanga-Yamahtta Taylor, Linda Martín Alcoff, Nancy Fraser, Rasmea Yousef Odeh, and Tithi Bhattacharya. "Beyond Lean-In: For a Feminism of the 99% and a Militant International Strike on March 8." *Viewpoint Magazine* 3 February 2017 <https://www.viewpointmag.com/2017/02/03/beyond-lean-in-for-a-feminism-of-the-99-and-a-militant-international-strike-on-march-8/>.

Delphy, Christine. *Separate and Dominate: Feminism and Racism After the War on Terror.* London: Verso Books, 2015.

Emejulu, Akwugo, and Leah Bassel. "Minority Women, Activism and Austerity." *Race & Class* 57.2 (2015): 86-95.

Emejulu, Akwugo. "Can 'the People' Be Feminists? Analysing the Fate of Feminist Justice Claims in Populist Grassroots Movements in the United States." *Interface*: *Special Issue on Feminism, Women's Movements and Women in Movements* 3.2 (2011): 123-51.

Hill Collins, Patricia. *Black Feminist Thought: Knowledge, Consciousness and the Politics of Empowerment.* New York: Routledge, 2000.

Jordan, June. "Where is the Love?" *Some of Us Did Not Die: New and selected Essays of June Jordan.* New York: Basic/Civitas Press, 2002.

Kazin, Michael. *The Populist Persuasion: An American History.* Ithaca: Cornell University Press, 1998.

Maiguashca, Bice, Jonathan Dean, and Dan Keith. "Pulling together in a crisis? Anarchism, Feminism and the Limits of Left-Wing Convergence in Austerity Britain." *Capital and Class* 40.1 (2016): 37-57.

Moore, Jina. "Why the New Year's Attacks on Women in Germany Weren't Even a Crime" *Buzz Feed News* 26 March 2016 <https://www.buzzfeed.com/jinamoore/cologne-attacks-on-women?utm_term=.qkRa17Mkm#.wc1q7Y8LR>.

Mudde, Cas. "The Populist Zeitgeist." *Government and Opposition* 39.4 (2004): 542-63.

Palmer, Lisa A. "'In Britain too, it's as if we don't exist': Black 'British' Feminism's Decolonial Imperatives." Unpublished conference keynote paper for the British Sociological Association, Social Theory Stream Plenary, 6 April 2017, Manchester.

Taylor, Keeanga-Yamattha. (2017) "A Feminism for the 99 Percent: Keeanga-Yamahtta Taylor on the March 8 Women's Strike." Interviewed by Sarah Jaffe. *Truth Out* 28 February 2017 <http://www.truth-out.org/opinion/item/39639-a-feminism-for-the-99-percent-keeanga-yamahtta-taylor-on-the-march-8-women-s-strike>.

Redefining "We, the People": Black Lives Matter and the Democratization of Political Culture

Nicole Anna Schneider

Introduction: Democratic Images and the Protests for Black Lives

In the recent protests for black lives and their digital, photographic, and journalistic afterlives, numerous images emerged, depicting individual protesters standing in front of long lines of heavily armed police officers. Their imagery connects specific local actions to larger frameworks of community building, spatial and theoretical positioning, as well as to the overall legitimacy and agency of the Black Lives Matter (BLM) movement.[1] This photographic imagery visualizes the movement's struggles as well as its demand to unsettle the understanding of the constitutional 'We, the People.'[2] In considering the popular sovereignty approach to contemporary democracy, I examine how the visual representation of the movement attempts to change the constitution of 'the people' in an all-inclusive way. The movement's online presence on *blacklivesmatter.com* directly voices this demand by proclaiming that once black lives truly matter, every life is valued. It is the sovereignty of this 'the people' and their "right to appear" (Butler 11) that is present on the streets and presented in the images. This sovereignty is employed in the general demands of the BLM movement involving the understanding of a 'the people' that more truthfully represents US society.

This essay is going to look at the community building actions of the BLM organization displayed and negotiated in press photographs affiliated with the movement. Through these images, both grassroots actions and concepts of popular sovereignty are accentuated as important elements of participatory democratic cultures. This reading of the protests and the resulting images is further based on Grattan's concept of 'aspirational democratic populism,' which, as she writes in her

---

[1] Important to note is that I am not referring to one specific organization but to a network of several groups and chapters that organize around the premise to improve the lived reality of black lives in the United States and to end police brutality especially against black people.

[2] The term 'unsettle' and its underlying project of re-evaluating existing structures, rely on Sylvia Wynter's and Katherine McKittrick's discussion of "being human as a praxis." For them, antiprecarity work is not a question of overthrowing and destructing existing orders of knowledge but of reworking, undoing, and unsettling them from within (Wynter et al. 2).

book *Populism's Power*, combines the desire for a share in power with pluralistic and egalitarian local actions (40). Her approach focuses on the ideologically unattached democratic principles and potential underlying the concept of populism. Her "ambitions in democratizing populism," she notes, "stretch to the horizons that are not yet imaginable: democracy beyond capitalism, whiteness, nationalism, and other models of domination and dehumanization" (Grattan 48). This understanding and my reading in relation to BLM are largely based on the concepts of 'popular agency,' as proposed by scholars such as Ernesto Laclau, Benjamin Arditi, and Francisco Panizza. What becomes central in this account of the idea of 'the people' is the constant negotiation between collective identities and experiments in community building and the local practices improving everyday lives (Grattan 40; Laclau 203). That is to say, 'the people,' as the decisive element in democratic cultures, is constituted through direct actions within society on the one hand, and overarching ideals and beliefs concerning aspirations for a different future, as well as the make-up of this very community, on the other. For the BLM movement, this involves ideals of "freedom and justice for Black people and, by extension, all people" (*Celebrating Four Years*); including, among other things, the presence on the streets, healing justice or community leader workshops, and gestures like shared food or subway fares.

Patrisse Khan-Cullors, one of the founders of the movement, and her co-author and journalist asha bandele note in their memoir *When They Call You a Terrorist* that the movement's struggle is to get the nation to "see, say and understand that Black Lives Matter" (205). That is to say, their goal is to "change the culture" (204) in order to create a world in which black lives are valued. This, however, does not reflect a wish for the mere inclusion of black people into this already existing transcendent entity (see Vorländer 16, 18), but calls for a thorough restructuring and unsettling of the national community, its culture, and society.[3] Stressed in the movement's principles is the fight against the structural inequality and criminalization of black lives, which has been present in the 'war on drugs' or in the ostensible role of violence in street-culture in urban neighborhoods (Anderson 285).

Protest photographs seemingly juxtapose the force of the police with the strength and endurance of activists and victims. They visually connect the institutions of the state and society to their role in a system that renders black lives precarious and invisible (*Celebrating Four Years*). Conversely, the individual protester in such

---

[3] The long existing notion of the refusal to be included into the white-centered structures of society was among others brought up by Rinaldo Walcott (University of Toronto) in his presentation "The Long Emancipation: Antiblackness, Settlement, and the Problem of the Nation" at the international conference *A Mobile World Literature and the Return of Place* at the University of Eichstätt-Ingolstadt in December 2016.

photographs stands for a community that forms itself out of the claims of its individual members, their actions, and gestures.[4] As a community that tries to locally improve the living conditions of those marginalized in society, the BLM movement sets out to end state-sanctioned and institutionalized violence against black lives nationwide. Such a community focused on its inclusivity is founded, among other aspects, in its opposition to 'the other,' seen here, significantly, as the system of institutionalized and racialized inequality in the United States. To some extent, this mirrors the ideologically unattached version of the contested concept of populism: In its very basic terms, populism is constituted in a community that sees itself as 'the people' and positions itself against elites and political structures (Laclau 203). Essentially, these parameters entail questions of popular agency of such a community whose disruptive voice forms the fundamental impetus for politics, democracy, and social change (Arditi 93).

Visual Activism, 'The Voice of the People,' and Popular Sovereignty

The images of the street protests show individual demonstrators and their political, visual actions. These acts fall into the general category of visual activism, as it is theorized, for instance, in a recent themed issue of the *Journal of Visual Culture* edited by Julia Bryan-Wilson, Jennifer González, and Dominic Willsdon. Through the visualization of demands, alternatives, and problems present in today's society, demonstrators reclaim the public sphere, presenting their dissent in gestures or signs. Using the realm of the visual, as the editors of the journal write, "in the service of wider political efforts" (Bryan-Wilson et al. 6), visual activists artistically recalibrate aesthetic value to generate creative political capital (Moten 2007: 104). Many of these actions, such as handwritten signs, hands held up in surrender, or nooses worn around the neck, give direct comments on society and offer visual invitations to join larger conversations and the protests (Demos 89; Chatelain 6). For Nicholas Mirzoeff, as he describes in his book *How to See the World*, "visual culture activism [involves] creating, performing, and disseminating memes in urban public space and across social media networks to involve, extend, and create a political subject" (279).

This is especially relevant to the BLM movement and its visual protest and activism. The movement originated in a social media response to the acquittal of the neighborhood watchman who shot Trayvon Martin in Sanford, FL, in 2013. In a virtual call-and-response exchange, Khan-Cullors and Alicia Garza phrased the hashtag #blacklivesmatter to counter the continuous devaluation of black lives

---

[4] This already mirrors Ernesto Laclau's theorization of the community of 'the people' and his concept of the 'empty signifier,' which I will refer to later in this paper.

(Khan-Cullors et al. 180). This dehumanization is most prevalently visible in deaths of unarmed black people in police custody, in the disproportional incarceration rates of African-Americans, which Michelle Alexander refers to as *The New Jim Crow* (11), and in the criminalization of black lives as a part of "institutional racism," which Keeanga-Yamahtta Taylor traces in her book *From #BlackLivesMatter to Black Liberation* (8). The BLM movement has since developed, acting out of the shared sentiment of outrage and the will to fight off the helplessness felt at the acquittal. It has set out to battle systemic racial violence within the United States and fights racism as what Ruth Gilmore calls "the state-sanctioned or extralegal production and exploitation of group-differentiated vulnerability to premature death" (25). Overall, the movement is grounded in the radical black tradition and more specifically Afro-pessimism, which recognizes that the negated status of black life, which Christina Sharpe refers to as an ontological negation of blackness (14), is deeply engrained in the structures and hierarchies of contemporary Western societies and their orders of knowledge (see Wynter et al. 29; Moten 2003: 7).

Due to its radical demands for broader changes within society and its rejection to play by the rules and advice of earlier movements, the movement has frequently been criticized for an ostensible lack of organization, harmful protest tactics, or a seemingly singular focus on black communities. Barbara Reynolds, an activist in the 1960s Civil Rights Movement for instance, writes in an article for *The Washington Post* that she can only reluctantly support a movement which courageously fights for its causes but fundamentally differs in its approach from her own activism. In her portrayal of the BLM movement, Nicole Hirschfelder similarly points to these conflicting policies between both movements (246). Additionally, focusing on what she sees as structural problems within the BLM movement, she remarks that there is a difference between the theoretical basis of the movement as calling for all black lives to matter and the practical application of these ideals on the streets (254). In my analysis of protest photographs and of the concepts of community building, I will mostly focus on the theoretical framework set by the BLM movement and the visual presentation of these ideals in affiliated press photographs.

Fighting the normalization of violence against African Americans, the BLM movement visually presents new perspectives, alternative conceptions and ways of life, and pays attention to those marginalized in society. According to Chantal Mouffe, it is exactly the artistic form of protest which aims "at giving a voice to all those who are silenced within the framework of the existing hegemony" (Mouffe 2007). Both topics and individuals, which are not considered in general discussions, are brought to the fore through aesthetic interventions on the streets and are disseminated through images.

The rhetorical phrase of giving voice to someone, as Mouffe uses it here, presents the concept of popular sovereignty as it is ascribed specifically to the 'voice of the people.' It is this "disruptive 'noise,'" as Benjamin Arditi notes (93). This voice interrupts political proceedings and structures. As the mouthpiece of a community of 'the people,' it functions, as Arditi states, as "an internal element of the democratic system which also reveals the limits of the system and prevents its closure in the pure and simple normality of institutional procedures" (88). If, as is criticized by the BLM movement, the institutionalization of black criminalization and state sanctioned violence against black citizens are not seen as problematic by large parts of the nation, the movement presents an intervention and the call to action from within the community that performatively institutes itself as part of 'the people' (Butler 7).

It is an interesting interrelation, in which the police and the state act as representatives of its citizens, reflecting the power of the transcendental 'the people,' while in part seemingly leading institutionalized lives of their own, in which, for example, the police-industrial-complex defines the equipment for police riot gear (Shine). Apparently independently, these institutions act at times against what seems to be the democratic will. Addressing this correlation, Coates notes in his article on 'Blue Lives' in *The Atlantic* in 2014, that the criminal-justice policy has over time been determined by the very demands of the American people. "The abuses that have followed from these policies," he writes, "[…] are, at the very least, byproducts of democratic will" (Coates). Pointing to the troubled notion of this 'the people' and its popular sovereignty, his remarks reflect the wish and the struggle to reimagine the community defined as 'the people' and its values in a more inclusive way. It does not seem to be enough to rally against the police. Rather, protests, actions, and discussions address American culture and society as a whole, reaffirming its fundamental principles by reconfiguring the nation's values, the constitution of its body politic, as well as the demands carried out in 'the people's' name. Tellingly, Coates notes that these policies were "not imposed on Americans by a repressive minority." This implies that the movement's challenge is to unsettle the deep-set principles underlying American society, for example, the racist ideas grounded in American history (Kendi 7). Referring to Coates' article, Grattan similarly points out that "[i]f the norm of popular sovereignty legitimates state violence against marginalized actors, it is difficult to imagine solutions that do not entail oppositional contests over the boundaries of the people" (Grattan 27). The very composition of the politically central entity of 'the people' needs to be rethought on behalf of those marginalized in today's society.

Scott Olson's photograph taken in Ferguson on August 15, 2014, visualizes these interrelations between this sovereign community, the police, and the protesters (fig. 1). The image shows a scene from the protest after Michael Brown's death in August 2014. A young protester stands on a street and blocks the traffic. Wearing a baseball cap and holding a soft drink in his hands, he is confronting the camera.[5] This nightly scene is ablaze with light coming from different sources, such as the traffic lights and the headlights of oncoming cars. With both his hands, the protester depicted tucks at the shoulders of his black t-shirt, as if to emphasize the words printed in white font on its front:

> Stop Killing Us
> (My Skin Color is Not a Crime/No Flex Zone)[6]

Figure 1: Demonstrators gather along West Florissant Avenue to protest the shooting of Michael Brown on August 15, 2014 in Ferguson, Missouri. (Photo by Scott Olson/Getty Images).

In a sense, the image's emphasis on the 'us' on the t-shirt shows the focus on a community of black lives. But this 'us' does not only refer to African-Americans. By extension the word's referent includes society as a whole. Through the criminalization of black lives and counterinsurgency practices such as the 'war on drugs,' the police are attacking parts of the very 'people' from whom they received

---

[5] In reading the photographs, I use Ariella Azoulay's general concept of the "event of photography," which sees photography as a political event that is enacted in the continuous encounter in and with the image over time (26). This way, the discussion about the image is not fixed on the position of a photographer (118-9), nor can it be closed in one singular reading (219).

[6] The format of presenting the text on signs and t-shirts in the images in an unconventional form, treating them like quotes, comes from Michael Taussig's essay "I'm So Angry I Made a Sign" in *Occupy: Three Inquiries in Disobedience*.

their authority. Conversely, this message addresses not only the police and the structures of state sanctioned violence but also parts of the community whose sovereignty authorizes the officials and institutions of the state to act. What is addressed is not the individual police officer or a generalized community of officers but the need for a fundamental rethinking of society and its values. This call for action includes the demand to challenge 'food deserts' (those inner-city areas with lacking access to groceries), denied access to health care, and other fundamental resources that would benefit society. The dedication "No Flex Zone" refers to the debut single of the American hip-hop duo Rae Sremmurd, published on August 11, 2014. For the artists, a 'no flex zone' is "a place where everybody is just being themselves" (Acevedo), an approach adapted by protesters as it reflects the movement's demand for an inclusive society.

The role of the ostensibly unified popular community as "political actor," as Francisco Panizza asserts (3), is central to these considerations. Underlying this notion is an understanding of politics that is based on antagonism and agonism as the foundation of political debate. In her book *On the Political*, Chantal Mouffe discusses the status of politics in today's post-political societies. These societies are, as she explains, no longer grounded in political debate and the negotiation of opposing values but focus on agreement and the "negation of antagonism" (2). She notes that when conflict is displaced into consent and compromise, the very composition of democracy as debate is in danger (29). Both politics and democracy need vivid discussions and contrasting opinions in order to function. This stands in opposition to practices and ideals of liberal pluralism, which Mouffe sees in contemporary culture and governments. The ideal of the "harmonious and non-conflictual ensemble" of the typical liberal understanding of pluralism, she writes, "must negate the political in its antagonistic dimension" (10). Lacking the confrontations that bring upon the practices and philosophies of the political, these ideals of pluralism constitute a halt to political developments, and the gaps thus emerging through the lack of critical opposition run the risk of being filled by anti-democratic inclinations.

The task, Mouffe writes in the article "The 'End of Politics' and the Challenge of Right-wing Populism," is to find a way in which such political debates are held and peoples' desires and passions are mobilized without risking to give room to right-wing populist politics. If possible alternatives to the neoliberal world-order are negated within politics, Mouffe notes in *On the Political*, right-wing populism seemingly offers such alternatives in "collective identifications with a high affective content like 'the people,'" who are ostensibly given back their sovereignty (2005a: 70). Mouffe further reminds us in "The 'End of Politics'" that it is not the reference to 'the people,' which is problematic, but the lack of popular agency in today's democracies (Mouffe 2005b: 69). Since the definition of 'the people' always necessarily remains open and heterogeneous, the danger lies specifically in the way the concept is filled and appropriated by right-wing actors. This happens, for instance, when the popular will and agency which reassert "the democratic side of liberal democracy, and [...] reactivat[es] the notion of popular sovereignty" are ignored (2005b: 69). If 'the people' is not constituted by ideals of democratic participation, popular sovereignty, and the address of politics from within, the articulation of this very community can become a danger to democracy itself. The BLM movement reinstates this very application of popular agency and democratic principles in its attempts to create a more inclusive and tolerant society.

Mouffe declares that in democratic politics, passions towards democratic designs need to be mobilized with "a real purchase on people's desires and fantasies" (2005a: 6). Democracy needs to take the wishes of its citizens seriously, addressing them within democratic systems and with a view to shared values regarding democracy, sovereignty, and justice (2005a: 14). Mouffe proposes the concept of agonism, which she defines as follows:

> While antagonism is a we/they relation in which the two sides are enemies who do not share any common ground, agonism is a we/they relation where the conflicting parties, although acknowledging that there is no rational solution to their conflict, nevertheless recognize the legitimacy of their opponents. (Mouffe 2005a: 20)

In their conflict, these 'adversaries,' as Mouffe calls them, share the common symbolic space of democracy and acknowledge mutual rules and values, while acknowledging disagreements with opponents (2005a: 20). When the BLM movement writes on its website that its members have set out to change "the terms of debate on Blackness" and have "won critical legislation to benefit Black lives," it affirms its status as adversary within a symbolic democratic space (blacklivesmatter.com). Its focus on local actions and caring communities (blacklivesmatter.com) allows for further democratic change from within. For the movement, this does not entail the overthrowing of entire governmental structures but individual attempts to reveal and fight "the dangerous impacts of anti-Blackness" in today's societies (blacklivesmatter.com). BLM activists have, for instance, interrupted the Democratic presidential candidate Bernie Sanders during a speech in Seattle in 2015, to demand the inclusion of criminal justice reform and racial equality in his campaign (Basu; Lind). While his campaign was focusing on issues of economic populism, the activists remarked, racial inequality was merely treated as "a symptom of economic inequality," writes Dara Lind for Vox.com. The protesters' criticism asked the populist campaign to address the demands of what protester Marissa Johnson called the "biggest grassroots movement in this country right now," disrupting Sanders's campaign speech (Johnson in Basu). Local community and grassroots work form the basis of the movement's organizing, while fostering the greater, universal goal of "a world free of anti-blackness" (blacklivesmatter.com). Like other manifestations of popular will, which Arditi writes about, the movement for black lives represents "the return of the founding negativity of the political" (93), addressing and fighting ills in contemporary society.

The understanding of 'the people' as sovereign and as a re-imaginable entity is based on politics that seek to create equal opportunities for all people. In this relation, Robert Post has argued in 1998 that "popular sovereignty [is] the subordination of the state to the popular will" (437). Being elected by a community of 'the people,' state officials and governments should work in the interest of 'the people.' Barack Obama held a similar view, when he proposed on June 29, 2016 during the North American Leaders' Summit in Ottawa, Canada, that his actions were supposed to be beneficial for the community. For him, tailoring political actions towards popular sovereignty and 'the people's' well-being is an act of populism. Conversely he notes, rhetoric labeled as populist used in the 2016 presidential campaign showed no connection to popular sovereignty and thus, for Obama, to populism. For him this rhetoric can be more truthfully named "nativis[t] or xenophobi[c]" (Obama, transcript mine). Making controversial statements in order to win votes and please the masses, to Obama, is not empowering 'the people' in the way populism should pay heed to popular sovereignty. Rather, in his understanding, the government as elected officials should assume actions and decisions to secure jobs and health care, to provide aid for workers, and support education for socially marginalized children (Obama, transcript mine).

Questions of being in the service of 'the people,' of acting on behalf of a popular will, and the consideration who constitutes this sovereign come up in a photograph taken on September 20, 2016, by Adam Rhew in Charlotte, NC, where the National Guard was deployed to curb protests (fig. 2). Demonstrations took place after Keith Lamont Scott was fatally shot by a police officer that same day. The dark scene in the photograph, set on a street, is shrouded in fog, most likely tear gas, which is eerily illuminated by the headlights of an oncoming bus in the center of the image. In the front, lighted from the back by the same source of light, are the silhouettes of soldiers in riot gear, threateningly positioning themselves in a line to push back protesters. As if commenting on the guards and the paradoxical notion of their involvement and the source of their authority, the bus's electronic display shows the message:

Not In Service

Read in support of the protests, the bus's sign stands in for the movement's call to end police violence. The scene, as if taken in a war zone and not an urban center in America, suggests in the most drastic reading a war waged on the backs of the nation's citizens. The bus almost disappearing in the fog, the machine-like appearance of the guards with their helmets and clubs, and the anonymity brought upon through the image's paper-cut composition, render the scene threatening.

Figure 2: Police gather around protestors following the fatal police shooting of a black man, with a dozen officers and several demonstrators injured in the violence on September 20, 2016 in Charlotte, North Carolina. (ADAM RHEW/AFP/Getty Images).

Whether or not the guards, the police, and by extension the politicians, act according to a people's will, remains open, as does the question who belongs to this 'the people.' The photograph suggests that those on whose mandate the guards supposedly act belong as much to the community of 'the people' as those who stand and assemble to protest against police violence. It poses the question if politics, governmental structures, and regulations are truly working in the service of society and its citizens, and conversely if, to return to Coates' notion, the guards are not authorized by exactly the same American society to act with full force. That is, this image, too prompts us to challenge the cultural and social values to make the promises of the Constitution available to all American citizens – to unsettle the idea of the 'power of the people' in contemporary democracy.

The BLM organization's goal is, to quote Shanelle Matthews and Miski Noor from the Black Lives Matter Global Network,

> to earn the trust of future generations to defend economic, social and political *power for all people*. We are confident that we have the commitment, the *people power*, and the vision to organize our world into a safe place for Black people –

one that leads with inclusivity and a commitment to justice, not intimidation and fear. (Matthews et al. 50, emphasis mine)

It is the power for all people that is addressed, making this community more inclusive, especially for those marginalized in today's society. The popular sovereignty, here referred to as the 'people power,' adds political weight and democratic determination to the movement. The employment of popular sovereignty and the movement's inclusivity is based on the assumption that in order to foster an inclusive and empathetic community within society, it is necessary to change the lived realities of black people (Matthews et al. 51). Entailed therein is both community work (Matthews et al. 51) and the claim to speak for the community of 'the people' and to act on their behalf, as Grattan notes, eschewing "the limits that constitutions, representative democracy places on popular sovereignty" (24). Therefore, movements like the BLM movement "are often said to enact the people's power beyond politics" (ibid.). This is usually linked with various direct forms of participation such as protests, community organizing, or legislative and electoral strategies (ibid.). This political grassroots power of 'the people' is fostered and enacted in the BLM protests, as local projects are organized, engagement with political institutions is sought, and protests are choreographed.

Especially in the United States, these ideals link up with the founding principles of the nation. Echoing Frederick Douglass's speech on the relevance of the Fourth of July for the slave, BLM activist John Sloan writes in his article "Black, on the Fourth of July" on the social journalism platform *Medium* about his heartfelt wish to be part and be proud of the nation and its ideals. Yet, he says he cannot fully embrace the national holiday, as it is steeped in the nation's troubled origins and its ongoing entanglement with slavery. "I want to celebrate my nation," he writes, and "to cheer for fireworks and awe at parades marched to the music of John Philip Sousa." This, however, does not quite seem right to him, as 'the birth of the nation' on land that once belonged to Native Americans and its economic development at the expense of his ancestors betray those very ideals.

It is a society he notes, that is still caught in the system instituted at its very beginning, which, as Sloan writes, "is not broken; it's working exactly how it was intended." Needed therefore is not a process of fixing this very system but its overturning and unsettling within the framework of the nation and its democratic principles. If the pledge of allegiance to the Stars and Stripes is overshadowed by the open display of the 'Stars and Bars' on the flag of the Confederacy and its ideology, as Sloan writes, then the nation is still caught in what Bryan Stevenson calls the legacy of slavery. According to Stevenson, the nation is gridlocked in the thought of the old South as if it had ideologically won the Civil War. The 'Stars and Bars' are present throughout the nation, and so are monuments to the Confederate generals, while the victims of slavery and Jim Crow remain invisible and forgotten. Poetically, Sloan sums up this conundrum:

> I carry with me the pain of my ancestors, and the contradiction of my citizenship; the pride of my Fathers and resilience of my Mothers; the strength of my nation and the power of its freedoms. (Sloan)

It is in this contradiction – oscillating between the idolized ideals of freedom and equality embedded in the nation's origins and the dehumanization of black lives that, as Sloan says, occurs systematically and on a daily basis – that the claims of the BLM movement are grounded. While wanting to be a proud member of 'the people' of the US-American nation, Sloan is daunted by the continuing anti-black violence he sees bound up in the structures of the states and the nation.

'The People' as an 'Empty Signifier' and the Social Imaginary of the Movement

An important observation about the political sovereignty and the concept of 'the people' is the general vagueness of this very term. The community that addresses and is addressed as 'the people' is conceptually open, as its composition cannot be unequivocally defined. If the sovereignty of the community defined as 'the people' lies in its power to decode and determine its own fate, as Robert Post remarks, "it thus requires a social structure that continuously preserves the potential for remaking individual and collective identity" (439). The principal ability for the remaking of identity becomes important in the formation of this community. Central for the realization of popular politics is a rhetoric of peopling, as Grattan notes, "that could leave 'the people' an open call to be imagined and reworked by disparate and emerging actors" (62). The general concept of 'the people' remains open to be heterogeneously filled. Grattan further writes "the inherent instability of the people enables, indeed demands, persistent efforts to narrate and enact more rebellious visions of populism [...] as part of radical democratic struggles to reconstitute the terms of collective identification and democratic politics" (Grattan 11). This is populism understood as radical democratic participation, enactment of popular sovereignty, and direct political engagement in a theoretical composition of the term that is compatible with contemporary democratic grassroots movements such as Occupy, UndocuQueer, as in Grattan's analysis, or the BLM movement. The rebellious aspirations of sovereignty inherent in the term need to be filled by actors supporting democratic cultures rather than by its opponents (Grattan 20). Grattan reads Ernesto Laclau's notion of popular sovereignty in populism as the element, which "can rupture hegemonic orders and open spaces to reconstitute the rules of the game" (Grattan 15). Before rules are reconstituted, however, the basic terms of this understanding of 'the people' ought to be delineated.

Laclau describes 'the people' as an 'empty signifier' that can never truly achieve the full representation of the community it stands for (71). Its "embodied totality" is an "impossible object" he writes, which, in a catachrestical paradox, can never be homogeneously unified and heterogeneously constituted at the same time (71). This definition opens the possibility of seeing 'the people' as a conceptually open and constantly shifting political construct, which is continually renegotiated. Laclau thus states "[t]he empty signifier arises from the need to name an object which is both impossible and necessary" (Laclau 72). In order to call for and implement popular sovereignty, a communal 'general will' of a harmonized community of 'a people' needs to be acknowledged, while such a community and its common will can necessarily only ever be partial and internally diverse. "By identifying 'the people' and its 'enemy' as unstable categories," Grattan observes, "Laclau leaves them open to internal contestation and redefinition" (32). She further elaborates that "in Laclau's theory, populist discourse is able to reconstitute symbolic political community along lines that allow for deeper internal agonism and greater recognition of the impermanent edges of every expression of collective identity" (Grattan 32).

If the BLM movement sets out to reconstitute the politically valid concept of 'the people,' they do so along the lines of this empty signifier. The movement fosters 'rebellious aspirations' towards the future in actions which are to a large extent carried out locally, demand a universal approach to popular sovereignty, and offer a direct say in local communities. For Grattan, who coined the term, these rebellious aspirations are endeavors and ambitions that address "sources of power that undermine people's capacities or exclude them from membership in the body politic or relegate them to chronic states of precarity" (41). These aspirations form a central prerequisite for (radical) democratic participation and institute new visions of alternative politics through grassroots actions (41). They cultivate engagements, and practices towards a common community, and by extension, the body politic. In the foreword to Khan-Cullors' memoir, Angela Davis writes, "[w]e learn not only about the quotidian nature of state violence but also about how art and activism can transform such tragic confrontations into catalysts for greater collective consciousness and more effective resistance" (Davis xii). These seem to be the aspirations and communities striving for a better future as well as political participation.

The requests of a community of 'the people' oscillate between particular demands of individuals who feel unacknowledged by those in power, and the general demands these specific requests come to signify in a "total chain of equivalential demands" (Laclau 95). Thus, Laclau further points towards the "dichotomic division between unfulfilled social demands, on the one hand, and an unresponsive power, on the other" (86). Both are present in the construction of a collective that appeals to the concept of the people (86). Once unfulfilled desires add up and converge, a common association is formed through discursive manifestations of discontent with those in power. "Chains of equivalence," Grattan writes, "have their source in the shared experience of lack, rather than in any positive substance or aspiration" (30). This way, as she remarks, these individual requests form a larger set of social claims (30). In her concept of radical aspirations, she deviates from Laclau's general definition, as she sees positive prospects and commonalities emerging from these discontents that unite actors in grassroots democratic actions, promote political participation, and move them toward enacted citizenship in everyday politics (41).

Following Laclau, demands are at the same time highly specific as well as arbitrary. While a request remains particular, it comes to stand for a wider universality (95), he writes, which is discursively constructed (85-6) through the "crystallization" of individual demands (93). In the protests on the streets and the images, these processes of group formation and oscillation between the universal and the particular become visible in signs and actions. When accountability for the murder of a black person is demanded, this encompasses more universal demands such as equality and ending state sanctioned violence against black people. An image taken in 2014 by Michael B. Thomas during the protests in Ferguson seems to particularly offer its own take on these considerations. Tinted in the yellow light of a street lamp at night, softened through an indiscernible shadow, a paper sign with slightly burned edges lies on the tarmac of what seems to be a street. The sign fills the entire image and is itself covered in words written with a felt marker:

> This is NOT about the 'alleged' stealing of cigars.
> This about the loss of LIFE in a system that habitually
> Criminalizes and KILLS black PEOPLE

This sign sums up a significant objection of the protests, as it juxtaposes the phrases used to paint the victim of police violence in a negative light with the call to action against the structures of anti-black violence.

In at least three respects, the sign demands accountability for the premature loss of black life. As a basis, the word 'alleged' in quotes fundamentally questions the legitimacy of accusations of theft as the justification for the fatal shots. It points to the criminalization of black lives and the politics of respectability, which Khan-Cullors sums up in her memoir as always having to be better and stronger than others: "I feel like I have to be the particular kind of strong Black people are always asked to be. The impossible strong. The strong where there's no space to think about your own vulnerability" (178). Looking at individual and universal demands, the sign broadens the scale of the movement's requests. The protests present a direct response to Michael Brown's death at the hands of the police. The first part alludes to the individual demands in relation to the adequate legal persecution of Michael Brown's death.

In a larger picture, the sign condemns the systems of slow and social death[7] of black people in today's society, which cannot be reduced to one particular aspect. The protests of the BLM movement are not, essentially, about the singular deaths of individual persons, nor about ostensible justifications of the actions against them. They question the wider precarity of black lives in the United States. Lives, as Khan-Cullors notes, "unable to escape the constant monitoring by police" (Khan-Cullors et al. 185). The names, places, and last words presented on signs are the reference points, substituting their individual signification for the universal challenges of the movement. That is, a universality in Laclau's terms, reflected in the 'empty signifier' of the community of 'the people,' which, as he observes, "can never fully control which demands they embody and represent" (108). The call for 'justice' and 'freedom' used in the protests are also significantly 'empty' but not meaningless.

Other images from Ferguson in 2014 reference community building practices beyond the 'empty signifier.' A photograph by J.B. Forbes for the St. Louis-Post Dispatch, for instance, directly remarks on the common markers and delineations of communities (fig. 3).

Figure 3: A protester shouts as she moved down W. Florissant Avenue away from the line of riot police in Ferguson on August 13, 2014 in Ferguson, Missouri. (Photo by Forbes, J.B.; Courtesy of the photographer).

---

[7] The terms refer, respectively, to Orlando Patterson's notion of 'social death' (1985) and Lauren Berlant's reading of 'slow death' (2007).

The scene is set in an intersection, showing an armed national guard atop a military tank in the background. In front of the tank, soldiers have positioned themselves in a line. Some seem to hold guns and all wear helmets and Kevlar vests. In the foreground a woman in a white t-shirt confronts the camera, turning her back towards the soldiers. She, like the man in the black T-shirt in Olson's image, appears to be saying something while her face bears a painful expression. With the left hand of her extended arm she points towards the scene behind her. She holds a cell phone in her left hand while the other clenches a white paper sign that reads the carefully drawn words:

> EXCUSE ME...
> WE NEED ANSWERS
> FOR Michael Brown Jr.
> (StL; #RIPMikeBrown; @alidelan)

This protest sign directly articulates notions of identity, individualism, and community. "Excuse Me... We need Answers" posits the individual – 'Me' – within a community of protesters, that is, within the 'people' of the movement. This 'We' directly states its immediate demands – 'Answers For Mike Brown' – along with the general demands of this 'people' – justice. It connects the mourning for Mike Brown with a universal call for accountability. This image confirms Laclau's notion of the empty signifier in community building. The protester's hand, pointing at the group of soldiers in the background, positions both the protester and the community of the movement she embodies in opposition to 'the other' or the 'them,' as the institutionalized system.

With a focus on her gesture towards the soldiers, the photograph poses the question of the adequacy of the measures used to confront the protests in Ferguson. The tank and the soldiers seem to belong to war zones, not urban centers in the United States. According to a CNN report by Barbara Starr and Wesley Bruer, the national guards used designations such as 'enemy forces' and 'adversaries' to describe the protesters on the streets (Starr et al.). Her motion also addresses the conundrum of contemporary US politics and police actions, as the protester is gesturing towards those who are officially sworn in to protect her as part of the people.[8] The cellphone in her hand points to another aspect of the movement, which is networking via social and alternative media as well as blogging platforms, symbolized by the smartphone and its camera. Along with the phone in her hand, the twitter handle on the sign contains an invitation to engage virtually in discussions about the protests and the underlying problems. Thus, she positions herself within a

---

[8] Another image by Seth Wenig from the protests in New York shows a protester holding a sign stating "Afraid of those who swore to protect me."

network of media engagement that uses the Internet and social media to protest systemic racism.

Linked to cultural discourse and community building are images, stories, and legends. To change these is part of the movement's work. For instance, when the hashtag #IfTheyGunnedMeDown [which picture would the media choose?] battles biased portrayals of black persons in media reports and accompanying photographs. By starting this social media campaign, Tyler Atkins sought to criticize the media's use of an image that shows Michael Brown as a teen who provokingly looks into the camera, posing presumably to be perceived as tough (Wray). While this image does not say anything about the victim, it was frequently used to portray him in a stereotypical way as violent (Berger). According to Patricia Hill Collins, such photographs fall into the category of 'controlling images' (69), which naturalize and perpetuate racial violence and oppression through formulaic depictions and narrations (73). To address such violent depictions is an essential part of the BLM movement, as these images and their perception form deceptive ideological foundations that lead to real life consequences for black people. Processes like these are best summed up in Charles Taylor's concept of the "social imaginary," which conceptualizes the formation of social communities through imagined relations between individuals (23).

According to Taylor, a society is formed by individuals imagining their own social existence, relations to others, and expectations. This generally happens on the basis of images and normative notions that underlie the common understanding of the community (23). Society depends on a 'repertory' of collective actions, as Taylor notes, that ranges from elections to casual, uninvolved conversations (25). It also includes protests with their tactile, hand-made signs, artworks, and experiments, as Grattan notes, "rooted in local communities and traditions [...] oriented toward the constructive work of transforming democratic cultures" (33). Common practices and perspectives, if changed carefully and persistently, begin "to [re]define the contours of [the people's] world and can eventually come to count as the taken-for-granted shape of things, too obvious to mention" (Taylor 29). Under the precept of the 'social imaginary,' societies and communities are fluid and constantly negotiated in relation to common understandings and perceptions. They also rely on empty signifiers and deliberative demands. The imaginary character of the social further depends on its construction based on narrative and performative notions of community, society, and normalcy.

These social imaginaries permeate every aspect of our everyday lives. Any action undertaken by an individual is influenced by their grasp of the wider field (Taylor 27). In relation to popular sovereignty and the BLM movement, this becomes especially interesting, as a sense of legitimacy is developed through the notion and narration of consent (Taylor 4). An institution's actions are seen as legitimate when they are by and large in line with the demands of a 'general public' and its demands

(Taylor 4). Simultaneously, a counter movement's actions and protests are rendered legitimate by the narrated history and the alternative imaginary of the right of 'the people' to speak up (Taylor 27). This happens for example, as Grattan notes, in the American populist imaginary (12) but also in the rebellious aspirations she attributes to contemporary social movements. Crucial is the connection to 'images, stories, and legends,' as it is through these that 'the people' are engaged. A new narration of possible futures of collective, political subjects is thus created, including the representation of a community of a common 'us' (Grattan 12; Taylor 175). The photographs of BLM protests feed into the social imaginary of the movement as well.

American author Teju Cole's distinction of superhero photographs becomes noteworthy in this regard. When confronted with images of civilian individuals opposing officials in "storm-trooper get-up," as he suggests, we are reminded of iconic scenes from popular culture. He draws a connection between such images and the popular culture figure of the comic book superhero, which as he notes, with discursive clarity and definite answers to unanswerable questions, "fill[s] a psychological need in a world of drift and inchoate war." It is the individual here as well who stands up against unjust or corrupted systems of power and overpowering threats to human life. The images reflect the communal wish for moral justice, which the hero embodies, as well as the 'cultural force' of this figure able to influence the social imaginary of a given community. "The 'superhero' photographs of protesters, with their classic form and triumphal tone," Cole writes, "are engaged in a labor of redress. They bring a counterweight to the archive. Against death and helplessness, they project power and agency." On the one hand, the cultural, reparative force of the superhero and the images are inscribed with the social imaginary of a given culture. On the other hand, they themselves become fragments of this imaginary and are thus able to influence the ideals of culture and society, the notions of what constitutes the people, and the community of the movement.

In Lieu of a Conclusion: Grassroots Actions and Translocal Networks

The similarities of protest, community building, and enacted popular sovereignty are captured within the negotiation between individual demands and local practices, on the one hand, and larger frameworks on the other. In relation to rebellious aspirations, Grattan proposes the concept of 'the translocal' in order to elaborate on these processes. This concept, too, is based on the realization that political engagement needs to be situated in two distinct loci. That is, in the direct grassroots actions within local communities and the virtual, broader space of communal and national discourse (Grattan 65):

> Translocalism emphasizes the transformative potential of everyday practice to cultivate people's tastes and capacities to power; at the same time, the concept recognizes that everyday practice often generates myopic forms of power if it fails to bring people into relationship across social distances and hierarchies. (Grattan 69)

Thus, translocalism contains the realization that grassroots activism demands broader points of reference and overarching frames in order to reach the aspirational moment necessary for social change. This dualism pertains to the BLM movement with its decentralized structure and its guiding principles as well.

During an interview with Christina Heatherton, Patrisse Khan-Cullors outlines the movement's architecture as "an organizing that is rooted in healing justice and in principles of abolition. It's an organizing that rejects respectability politics and reinforces the fight for all Black lives" (38). Referencing the movement's grounds in healing and reparative justice, theory, and practice, Khan-Cullors emphasizes the individual actions and local organization of 38 individual chapters in the United States and the guiding principles of the organization. The popular agency of the movement is fostered among other aspects in this combination of engagement in the local lived experience of black communities and the wide-reaching demands and principles for a generalized idea of improvement. Khan-Cullors further specifies in her memoir how individual BLM chapters "begin a list of local demands and add to the evolving national demands, which begin, not surprisingly, with slashing police budgets and investing in what actually keeps communities safe: jobs, good schools, green spaces" (203). The call for action of the BLM movement contains both individual particular demands and broader, universal scopes, such as the national and international acknowledgement of black lives and the practice of "justice, liberation and peace in [...] engagements with others" (Khan-Cullors et al. 203). These broader goals need to be addressed on a local grassroots level. The movement's importance lies in the translocal scope of the local, everyday actions, discussions, and interventions.

As the cell phone in Forbes's image has already implied, virtual and social networks have become central in the creation of the translocal scope of the movement, which points to the networked character of the organization and its affiliates. In relation to different protest movements, Manuel Castells has coined the term "networked social movement," which, according to him, functions in the hybrid space and alternative public sphere between social networks online and occupied urban spaces (10). Local experiences are virally shared across large distances. They enter a national discursive space about the value of black lives, offer examples of local healing justice, and grassroots practices, and both share and manifest the principles of the movement. The possibility of interactive communication reinforces the non-hierarchical organization of the movement and its participatory character

(Castells 15). The way Grattan identifies the movement's gravity as local actions and translocal experiments, Castells sees the utopian promise of networked social movements in the interaction of local and virtual communities (228). The network is an open system that, in its negotiation between local-particular and translocal-general demands, forms both a community of 'the people' and the movement, making the systemic character of the predicament of black lives visible, while also presenting grassroots actions and change.

The translocal character of both the precarity faced by black lives and the democratic engagement which counters it, is visualized in the online project and police violence report of the research collaboration 'Mapping Police Violence.' This organization counted 1,147 deaths through police violence in 2017, collecting its information from comprehensive crowdsourced databases and extended research in "social media, obituaries, criminal records databases, police reports and other sources" (mappingpoliceviolence.org). In a digital map of the United States, a red flag marks each of these incidents involving the police. Thus, it offers both visualization and localization of incidents and their responses. Through this meditation of individual incidents connected to a general problem, the database references the translocality of the movement. This is echoed in the organization's mission "to provide greater transparency and accountability for police departments as part of the ongoing campaign to end police violence in our communities" (mappingpoliceviolence.org). Transparency and accountability, as universal demands of the BLM movement, require direct involvement – here in the form of crowdsourced databases reliant, in part, on community information on police violence. The points on the map, however, also mark the locales that become important in the struggles of the movement. Each flag stands for a name, as well as a community impacted by police violence, and thus becomes a place of local involvement. This translocalism, according to Grattan, connects the particular, local actions with each other and to a broader demand of large-scale participation in democracy (69). Formed by individual incidents, demands, and experiments, the movement is embedded in various local sites. Yet, an overarching frame mirroring the demands of accountability, justice, and equality resurfaces and influences direct actions within local communities.

Moreover, local sites of engagement gain symbolic significance, as can be observed in a photograph by Scott Olson, taken in Ferguson in August 2014. Olson's photograph shows what seems to be the underside of the roof of a gas station and dispersed groups of people walking towards it (fig. 4). A large metal column dominates the right half of the image. Recent protests around the world have been mapped onto the surface of the column. Each of these is referenced by both a space and a time; each presents a community of 'the people' feeling disrespected; and in each, this community has reclaimed their voice to protest local issues and the larger claim of popular sovereignty, and equality:

Spain '36 | Watts '65 | Paris '68 | Italy '77 | Brixton '81
L.A. '92 | Cincy '01 | Cairo '11 | Ferguson '14

Figure 4: A reference to protests around the world throughout recent history is written on a sign as demonstrators protest the killing of teenager Michael Brown on August 17, 2014 in Ferguson, Missouri. (Photo by Scott Olson/Getty Images).

The names of these places and the respective dates have become icons for instances of popular uprisings. They represent the disruptive voice of 'the people' and of social movements that demands larger changes in society and national culture.

The concepts of popular sovereignty present in this image, coupled with grassroots actions, community improvement, and street protests of the BLM movement speak in relation to the construction and redefinition of 'the people.' What these images show is the movement's formation and its fostering of a communal demand for the recognition of the value of black lives. This functions within the framework of democracy, popular agency, and the assertion of the will of a 'people.' Seen as monumentalized moments, fixed or frozen onto the screen, the photographs signify the particular, direct demands and actions of local participants and communities, while also feeding into the social imaginary of the movement. Their constant negotiation between particular and universal demands, individuals and their (imagined) communities, local actions and translocal messages, tangible materiality and online networks, leaves the movement and its 'people' in a paradoxical yet productive state of political participation. With these actions, activists engage in an attempt at consciousness-raising that tries to unsettle the community of 'the people' of the United States in order to redefine it in a more inclusive way.

Works Cited

Acevedo, Kai. "Rae Sremmurd Speak On 'No Flex Zone,' Mike Will Made It, and Brotherly Love." *Life + Times*. 30 July 2014 <http://lifeandtimes.com/rae-sremmurd-speak-on-no-flex-zone-mike-will-made-it-brotherly-love>. Last accessed on 9 June 2019.

Alexander, Michelle. *The New Jim Crow: Mass Incarceration in the Age of Colorblindness*. New York: The New Press, 2012.

Anderson, Elijah. *Code of the Streets: Decency, Violence, and the Moral Life of the Inner City*. New York: Norton & Company, 2000.

Arditi, Benjamin. "Populism as an Internal Periphery of Democratic Politics." *Populism and the Mirror of Democracy*. Ed. Francisco Panizza. London: Verso, 2005. 72-98.

Azoulay, Ariella. *Civil Imagination: A Political Ontology of Photography*. London: Verso, 2015.

Basu, Tanya. "Black Lives Matter Activists Disrupt Bernie Sanders Speech." *Times* 9 August 2015 <http://time.com/3989917/black-lives-matter-protest-bernie-sanders-seattle/>. Last accessed on 9 June 2019.

Berger, Maurice. "In Ferguson, Photographs as Powerful Agents." *New York Times Online* 20 August 2014 <https://lens.blogs.nytimes.com/2014/08/20/in-ferguson-photographs-as-powerful-agents/>. Last accessed on 9 June 2019.

Berlant, Lauren. "Slow Death: (Sovereignty, Obesity, Lateral Agency)." *Critical Inquiry* 33.4 (2007): 754-780.

Blacklivesmatter.com. *#blacklivesmatter Organization*. Webpage. N.d. <blacklivesmatter.com/>. Last accessed on 9 June 2019.

Bryan-Wilson, Julia, Jennifer González, and Dominic Willsdon. "Editor's Introduction: Themed Issue on Visual Activism." *Journal of Visual Culture* 15.1 (2016): 5-23.

Butler, Judith. *Notes Towards a Performative Theory of Assembly*. Cambridge: Harvard University Press, 2015.

Castells, Manuel. *Networks of Outrage and Hope: Social Movements in the Internet Age*. Cambridge: Polity, 2015.

Chatelain, Marcia. "Making a Movement." *American Review* 37.3 (2016): 6.

Coates, Ta-Nehisi. "Blue Lives Matter." *The Atlantic* 22 December 2014 <www.theatlantic.com/politics/archive/2014/12/blue-lives-matter-nypd-shooting/383977/>. Last accessed on 9 June 2019.

Cole, Teju. "The Superhero Photographs of the Black Lives Matter Movement." *The New York Times Magazine* 26 July 2016 <nytimes.com/2016/07/31/magazine/the-superhero-photographs-of-the-black-lives-matter-movement.html>. Last accessed on 9 June 2019.

Collins, Patricia Hill. *Black Feminist Thought: Knowledge, Consciousness, and the Politics of Empowerment*. London: Routledge, 2000.

Cullors, Patrisse, and Cristina Heatherton. "#BlackLivesMatter and Global Visions of Abolition: An Interview with Patrisse Cullors." *Policing the Planet: Why the Policing Crisis Led to Black Lives Matter*. Ed. Jordan T. Camp and Christina Heatherton. London: Verso, 2016. 35-40.

Davis, Angela. "Foreword." *When They Call You a Terrorist: A Black Lives Matter Memoir*. Patrisse Khan-Cullors and asha bandele. Edinburgh: Canongate, 2018. xi-xiv.

Demos, T.J. "Between Rebel Creativity and Reification: For and Against Visual Activism." *Journal of Visual Culture* 15.1 (2016): 85-102.

Douglass, Frederick. "What to the Slave Is the Fourth of July?" 5 July 1852. *Teaching Tolerance* <www.tolerance.org/classroom-resources/texts/what-to-the-slave-is-the-fourth-of-july>. Last accessed on 9 June 2019.

Forbes, J.B. "A Protester Shouts as She Moved Down W. Florissant Avenue Away from the Line of Riot Police in Ferguson." *St.Louis Post-Dispatch* 13 August 2014 <www.nydailynews.com/news/violence-ferguson-missouri-michael-brown-shooting-gallery-1.1903203?pmSlide=1.1903193>.

Gilmore, Ruth. *Golden Gulag: Prisons, Surplus, Crisis, and Opposition in Globalizing California*. Berkeley, CA: University of California Press, 2006.

Grattan, Laura. *Populism's Power: Radical Grassroots Democracy in America*. Oxford: Oxford University Press, 2016.

Hirschfelder, Nicole. "#BlackLivesMatter: Protest und Widerstand heute." *Von Selma bis Ferguson: Rasse und Rassismus in den USA*. Ed. Michael Butter, Astrid Franke, and Horst Tonn. Bielefeld: transcript, 2016. 231-60.

Kendi, Ibram X. *Stamped from the Beginning: The Definitive History of Racist Ideas in America*. London: Bodley Head, 2017.

Khan-Cullors, Patrisse, and asha bandele. *When They Call You a Terrorist: A Black Lives Matter Memoir*. Edinburgh: Canongate, 2018.

Laclau, Ernesto. *On Populist Reason*. London: Verso, 2007.

Lind, Dara. "Black Lives Matter vs. Bernie Sanders, explained." *Vox.com* 11 August 2016 <www.vox.com/2015/8/11/9127653/bernie-sanders-black-lives-matter>. Last accessed on 9 June 2019.

Mapping Police Violence. Webpage, 24 June 2017 <mappingpoliceviolence.org/>. Last accessed on 9 June 2019.

Matthews, Shanelle, and Miski Noor (eds.). *Celebrating Four Years of Organizing to Protect Black Lives*. Black Lives Matter Organization. N.d. <drive.google.com/file/d/0B0pJEXffvS0uOHdJREJnZ2JJYTA/view>. Last accessed on 9 June 2019.

Mirzoeff, Nicholas. *How to See the World: An Introduction to Images, From Self-Portraits to Selfies, Maps to Movies, and More*. New York: Basic Books, 2016.

Moten, Fred. "Gestural Critique of Judgment." *The Power and Politics of the Aesthetic in American Culture*. Ed. Klaus Benesch and Ulla Haselstein. Heidelberg: Winter, 2007. 91-111.

---. *In the Break: The Aesthetics of the Black Radical Tradition*. Minneapolis: University of Minnesota Press, 2003.

Mouffe, Chantal. "Artistic Activism and Agonistic Spaces." *Art and Research* 1.2 (2007): n.p.

---. *On the Political*. London: Rouledge, 2005a.

---. "The 'End of Politics' and the Challenge of Right-wing Populism." Panizza. 2005b. 50-71.

Noor, Miski, and Shanelle Matthews. "Where We Are Headed." *Celebrating Four Years of Organizing to Protect Black Lives*. Black Lives Matter Organization. Ed. Shanelle Matthews and Miski Noor. N.d. <drive.google.com/file/d/0B0pJEXffvS0uOHdJREJnZ2JJYTA/view>. Last accessed on 9 June 2019.

Obama, Barack. "Barack Obama Warns Against the Rise of Populism During A Speech in Montreal." *Time* 7 June 2017 <www.youtube.com/watch?v=ZJWji1faMc8>. Last accessed on 9 June 2019.

Olson, Scott. "A Reference to Protests Around the World Throughout Recent History Is Written on a Sign." *Getty* 17 August 2014 <darkroom-cdn.s3.amazonaws.com/2014/08/AFP_Getty-453769576-760x506.jpg>. Last accessed on 9 June 2019.

---. "'Stop Shooting Us' T-shirt" *Getty*. 15 August 2014 <darkroom-cdn.s3.amazonaws.com/2014/08/AFPGetty-453673816-760x506.jpg>. Last accessed on 9 June 2019.

Panizza, Francisco. "Introduction." *Populism and the Mirror of Democracy*. Ed. Francisco Panizza. London: Verso, 2005. 1-31.

Patterson, Orlando. *Slavery and Social Death: A Comparative Study*. Cambridge: Harvard University Press, 1985.

Post, Robert. "Democracy, Popular Sovereignty, and Judicial Review." *California Law Review* 86.3. (1998): 429-43.

Reynolds, Barbara. "I Was a Civil Rights Activist in the 1960s. But It's Hard for Me to Get Behind Black Lives Matter." *The Washington Post* 24 August 2015. <www.washingtonpost.com/posteverything/wp/2015/08/24/i-was-a-civil-rights-activist-in-the-1960s-but-its-hard-for-me-to-get-behind-black-lives-matter/?noredirect=on&utm_term=.fc7c4557c19b>. Last accessed on 9 June 2019.

Rhew, Adam. "Police officers wearing riot gear block a road during the protests." *Reuters* 20 September 2016 <s1.ibtimes.com/sites/www.ibtimes.com/files/styles/lg/public/2016/09/23/charlotte-2.jpg>. Last accessed on 9 June 2019.

Sharpe, Christina. *In the Wake: On Blackness and Being*. Durham: Duke, 2016.

Shine, Jacqui. "Inside the Police-Industrial-Complex." *Pacific Standard* 12 January 2016 <psmag.com/news/inside-the-police-industrial-complex>. Last accessed on 9 June 2019.

Sloan, John Philip. "Black, on the Fourth of July." *Medium* 5 July 2017. <medium.com/@BlackLivesMatterNetwork/black-on-the-fourth-of-july-d768a953c7dc>. Last accessed on 9 June 2019.

Starr, Barbara, and Wesley Bruer. "Missouri National Guard's Term for Ferguson Protesters: 'Enemy Forces.'" *CNN* 17 April 2015 <edition.cnn.com/2015/04/17/politics/missouri-national-guard-ferguson-protesters/index.html>. Last accessed on 9 June 2019.

Stevenson, Bryan. "Slavery and its Legacies." Episode 2, from *The Gilder Lehrman Center for the Study of Slavery, Resistance, and Abolition*, Yale University. 6 February 2017 <glc.yale.edu/SlaveryanditsLegacies/episodes/BryanStevenson>. Last accessed on 9 June 2019.

Taussig, Michael. "I'm So Angry I Made a Sign" *Occupy: Three Inquiries in Disobedience*. Ed. W.J.T. Mitchell, Bernhard E Harcourt, and Michael Taussig. Chicago: Chicago University Press, 2013. 3-43.

Taylor, Charles. *Modern Social Imaginaries*. Durham: Duke University Press, 2004.

Taylor, Keeanga-Yamahtta. *From #BlackLivesMatter to Black Liberation*. Chicago: Haymarket Books, 2016.

Thomas, Michael B. "A Sign Left Behind by a Protester after a Protest on West Florissant Road in Ferguson, Missouri." *AFP* 18 August 2014 <darkroom-cdn.s3.amazonaws.com/2014/08/AFP_Getty-532530753-760x505.jpg>. Last accessed on 9 June 2019.

U.S. Constitution. Preamble. <www.usconstitution.net/xconst_preamble.html>.

Vorländer, Hans. "Demokratie und Transzendenz: Politische Ordnungen zwischen Autonomiebehauptung und Unverfügbarkeitspraktiken." *Demokratie und Transzendenz*. Bielefeld: Transcript, 2013.

Walcott, Rinaldo. "The Long Emancipation: Antiblackness, Settlement, and the Problem of the *Nation*." *A Mobile World Literature and the Return of Place*, University of Eichstätt-Ingolstadt, 9-10 December 2016.

Wenig, Seth. "Protesters March through the Streets in Response to the Grand Jury's Decision in the Eric Garner Case in Times Square in New York. [Afraid of Those Who Swore to Protect Me]." *AP*. N.d. <www.peoplesworld.org/wp-content/uploads/2016/08/afraidofthose510x300.jpg>. Last accessed on 9 June 2019.

Wray, Dianna. "HSPVA Student's #IfTheyGunnedMeDown Tweet Draws National Attention." *Houston Press Online* 14 August 2014 <www.houstonpress.com/news/hspva-students-iftheygunnedmedown-tweet-draws-national-attention-6747807>.

Wynter, Sylvia, and Katherine McKittrick. "Unparalleled Catastrophe for our Species." *Sylvia Wynter: On Being Human as Praxis.* Ed. Katherine McKittrick. Durham: Duke University Press, 2015, 9-89.

Missing the People: Populist Aesthetics and Unpopular Resistance

Sascha Pöhlmann

Populism and Popular Culture: Three Ways of Missing the People

My paper will explore a potential correlation between populism and popular culture from the perspective of literary and cultural studies, and I will offer two basic arguments in doing so. First, I will argue that popular culture engages in the imagination of 'the people' through a populist aesthetics that shares central aspects of the "thin-centered ideology" (Mudde 68) of political populism. Second, I will argue that popular culture also contains elements of resistance to such populism, which I will describe in terms of an *un*popular culture that seeks to counter or remove itself from an imagination of 'the people.'

This dialectic of populist aesthetics and unpopular resistance is an integral part of popular culture at large, and the oscillation between these two poles is captured concisely by the phrase in the first part of my title, "missing the people." This phrase refers to a passage in Gilles Deleuze's book *Cinema 2: The Time-Image*, in which he states that "if there were a modern political cinema, it would be on this basis: the people no longer exist, or not yet…*the people are missing*" (216). It also refers to Michael Hardt and Antonio Negri's incomplete quotation of said statement in *Empire* (2000), in which they use only its second half as a chapter epigraph. I want to begin this essay by discerning three meanings of that phrase to indicate the three steps my argument will take. First, I am interested in cultural artifacts that are 'missing the people' in the sense of sentimentally longing for them in their absence, not necessarily because the people had existed and are now gone, but perhaps because there is a need to construct them in the first place. Second, I am interested in artifacts that are staging this absence in some way or another without any desire for presence; in other words, in anything that does not presume the a priori existence of 'the people' but rather indicates the contingent and accidental aspects of the concept. Third, I am interested in artifacts that are 'missing the people' in the sense of failing to meet or have an impact on them; this might be a deliberate miss that makes a point of not having aimed at the people in the first place, or it might be an inadvertent miss that happened even though the aim was careful and the intention clear. This is the conceptual framework in which the dialectic of populism and the unpopular within popular culture play out, and it offers one possible way of theorizing it, among others.

Let me make explicit what is only implicit above: my essay is based on the premise that "'the people' do not exist in any finite sense" (McGuigan 15), but that 'the people' is always a construct that is secondary to other imaginations of community, most notably those of nationality or statehood, and particularly in their combination with the nation-state. The comeback of populism is therefore synonymous with a comeback of nationalism. The notion of 'the people' as a collective of individuals sufficiently unified by certain common aspects is created as an imagined community in order to imagine other communities, and while it is posited in the process as something prior, essential, or given, it is constructed nevertheless. This is how Hardt and Negri theorize 'the people' in *Empire* in the chapter introduced by the epigraph from Deleuze: "Although 'the people' is posed as the originary basis of the nation, the modern conception of the people is in fact a product of the nation-state, and survives only within its specific ideological context" (102). In short, 'the people' is a "constituted synthesis" (103). Presented as something natural and always already unified, the "identity of the people was constructed on an imaginary plane that hid and/or eliminated differences" (103), which involved "the eclipse of internal differences through the representation of the whole population by a hegemonic group, race, or class" (104). Thus "the concepts of nation, people, and race are never very far apart," and neither of these terms is any more fundamental or natural than the other, but instead they all co-constitute each other in a symbiotic and ultimately hegemonic relation that "provides a single will and action" (103) despite the numerous differences that resist such singularity.

The concept of 'the people,' then, serves a political purpose by posing "an identity that homogenizes and purifies the image of the population while blocking the constructive interactions of differences within the multitude" (113). Populism fundamentally relies on such an imagination of identity, homogenization, and indeed purification, and it must gloss over, ignore, or actively fight the differences that oppose it. One defining feature of the usefully fuzzy concept of populism is that it will never say: "it's complicated." As a consequence, one might rephrase Ernest Gellner's famous statement that it is "nationalism which engenders nations, and not the other way round" (55) by saying that it is populism which engenders the people, and not the other way round. Or, as Ernesto Laclau has it in Althusserian terms of interpellation: "the 'people,' as operating in populist discourses, is never a primary datum but a construct – populist discourse does not simply *express* some kind of original popular identity; it actually *constitutes* the latter" (2005: 163).[1] This

---

[1] Laclau's theories of populism are as influential and important as they are problematic; while there is much to criticize, it is especially the posited *desirability* of populism and of a popular identity that I take issue with, which finds expression in the title of one of his essays that is really a prolonged engagement with Slavoj Žižek, "Why Constructing a People is the Main Task of Radical Politics" (2006), although I am unable to find an answer to this question in the essay itself beyond the mere claim that, "[i]n a heterogeneous world, there is no possibility of

constitutive aspect of populism is what I am particularly interested in here, as it is what connects populism to popular culture, which similarly constructs 'the people' as a community rather than being an expression of what an already existing, unified people are doing, thinking, and enjoying. (Note that neither populism nor popular culture would constitute Laclau's "popular identity" conclusively or completely even if they succeeded in one of their manifold and contradictory acts of constitution; in fact, it might be best to understand these processes as constitutive *attempts* that seek to install a hegemonic notion of 'the people.') Even as one explores such similarities between populism and popular culture, one must be careful in distinguishing the two, and it would be much too simple a statement to say that all popular culture is populist.[2] In fact, one of the most striking and important qualities of popular culture is that it may embrace but just as well resist the simplifications of populism and complicate the very notion of the popular and the people, if not outright reject it. This is the subversive element of unpopular culture within popular culture that Martin Lüthe and I have identified in our theorization of the concept, an irreducible, productive element of instability and heterogeneity:

> if popular culture – just as much as high culture – is being used to create the people in the first place, not as a culture for the people but a culture constructing the people as a people by giving them a history and an identity, then unpopular culture is the disruptive element in this construction, resisting its homogenizations and omissions, opposing the complete smoothing of a striated cultural space. (Lüthe and Pöhlmann 27)

---

meaningful political action except if sectorial identity is conceived as a nucleus and starting point in the constitution of a wider popular will" (189). Even more problematically, Laclau connects populism too closely with the political itself so as to make it impossible to conceive of politics without a notion of the people, whereas it seems to me one of the most crucial challenges today to imagine community and politics *beyond* the irreversibly tainted fantasy of unity that is 'the people' (and Laclau fails to recover the concept from its history just by calling it an "empty signifier" (2006: 170)). I recommend Karin Priester's book *Mystik und Politik* for a sophisticated critique of Laclau's concept of populism; Priester's works are among the most lucid and insightful on the topic of populism in general.

[2] This is why I am skeptical of Jim McGuigan's all too general claim in *Cultural Populism* that "[a]ny form of culture that appeals to ordinary people could reasonably, in my view, be called 'populist culture' with no necessarily evaluative judgment implied, although this is rarely so in prevailing cultural discourses" (2). Yet McGuigan is really concerned with cultural populism in the sense of "*the intellectual assumption, made by some students of popular culture, that the symbolic experiences and practices of ordinary people are more important analytically and politically than Culture with a capital C*" (4), and thus with a critique of cultural studies rather than of the cultural production it takes as its object, and he makes a very valuable and valid point about how the academic study of popular culture has participated in the construction of 'the people' (see chapter 1, 9-44).

This dialectic is built into the conceptual ambiguity of the term *popular culture* itself, which does not easily translate into other languages without losing its nuances. A good starting place for a concise consideration of these meanings is Raymond Williams's *Keywords: A Vocabulary of Culture and Society* (1976), in which he offers the following definition:

> **Popular culture** was not identified by *the people* but by others, and it still carries two older senses: inferior kinds of work [...]; and work deliberately setting out to win favour [...]; as well as the more modern sense of well-liked by many people, with which of course, in many cases, the earlier senses overlap. The sense of popular culture as the culture actually made by people for themselves is different from all these. (233)

The importance of Williams's first point can hardly be overstated: popular culture is always constructed (rather than identified, which implies an existence prior to description) from the outside, not only by those who study it as such academically, but also as a political element that provides an apparent bedrock foundation for the imagination of community, so that "the discovery of popular culture was also an expressly political move, related to ideas of nationhood" (McGuigan 10). (One of the most well-known European examples is the collection of 'folk tales' by Jacob and Wilhelm Grimm that would form the basis of a certain imagination of Germanness.) Williams identifies the basis of this construction of 'the people' in and through popular culture in Herder's notion of *Kultur des Volkes*, and while this meaning has certainly become somewhat marginalized in favor of the more dominant meaning of "well-liked by many people" (233), it nevertheless retains its presence and relevance. John Fiske makes a point of defining popular culture in distinction from that sense when he first states that "'the popular' serves the interests of 'the people'" and then adds that he is using that term not as "a class or social category, but rather a shifting set of social interests and positions that are defined by their relation to the dominant society" (322). He summarizes this perspective by saying that "'[t]he people,' then, are better recognized by what they *do* than by who they *are*" (323). Yet the processual quality Fiske ascribes to popular culture still retains the element of homogenization that characterizes 'the people' in the singular as a group and that combines and unifies the multiple "social interests and positions" (Fiske 322) it contains (in the double sense of the term), so that ultimately, in Hardt and Negri's words, "the multiplicity and singularity of the multitude are negated in the straitjacket of the identity and homogeneity of the people" (107).

Needless to say, some parts of popular culture resist and challenge this homogenization while others embrace it, as popular culture "contains elements of disrespect, and even opposition to structures of authority, but it also contains 'explanations' [...] for the maintenance of respect for those structures of authority"

(Ross 3). Williams highlights the potentially populist aspect of popular culture by referring to a sense of "work deliberately setting out to win favour" (233), which may also be taken as a concise definition of populism in politics – and perhaps one might describe both as an aesthetics and politics of the "lowest common denominator" (McGuigan 1). Yet one should be careful not to judge this with the clichéd arrogance of the highbrow critic valuing only art that is autonomous of or even openly hostile to its reception, according to the normative standards of Culture that have been set in and by Modernism at the latest. Cher Krause Knight provides a crucial counterpoint to such negative readings by defining the "palpable populist sentiments" of public art as *the extension of emotional and intellectual, as well as physical, accessibility to the audience*" (x); this general definition of a populist aesthetics is useful in making accessibility its central aspect, and in understanding accessibility not just in terms of sophistication.

Krause Knight situates the public art she discusses within its political contexts, and yet it is necessary to include the political notion of populism even in the definition of the term, as her understanding of it points toward the *construction* of an audience (and various normative assumptions about them) rather than assuming that it exists as a given. Therefore, in describing a populist aesthetics that constructs 'the people' and deliberately sets out to win their favor through accessibility and other means, I will use a working definition of populism that is also based on the concise outline Cas Mudde offers in *On Extremism and Democracy in Europe*:

> [P]opulism is best defined as a thin-centered ideology that considers society to be ultimately separated into two homogeneous and antagonistic groups, 'the pure people' and 'the corrupt elite', and which argues that politics should be an expression of the *volonté general* (general will) of the people. […] Its essential features are: morality and monism.
> The key point is that populism sees both groups as essentially homogeneous, i.e. without fundamental internal divisions, and considers the essence of the division between the two groups to be moral. Consequently, its main opposites are elitism and pluralism. (68)

Mudde adds that populism "rarely exists in a pure form, in the sense that most populist actors combine it with another ideology," the "so-called host ideology, which tends to be very stable" (68).[3] While these host ideologies may vary, it is

---

[3] A perfect illustration of this malleability is how 'the people' can be enlisted for very different purposes; compare the liberatory, empowering slogan "Wir sind das Volk" [we are the people] as it was used in demonstrations in East Germany in 1989 against an oppressive government to the discriminatory, essentialist slogan "Wir sind das Volk" as it was and is used in demonstrations in Germany under the banner of 'Pegida.'

especially that thin-centered ideology I am interested in here, and especially the ideological notion of purity (or at least unity) of 'the people,' how it is imagined, and what normative and simplifying assumptions as to its homogeneity and properties one might derive from this construction. The simultaneous construction of a 'corrupt elite' in a clear-cut binary opposition is certainly one of the most effective strategies of a populist aesthetics, but it may not always occur explicitly or prominently, and thus will ultimately remain somewhat secondary in my analysis.

Before I begin this analysis, however, it is necessary to comment on my focus on popular culture here in terms of its binary opposite, high culture (a binary that is worth challenging on many levels but which also cannot be denied as part of its historical and contemporary discursive functions). I am not concentrating on popular culture here because this is where populism can be found while high culture is exempt from it. Instead, I am marginalizing high culture because it is always already constructing peoplehood *as* high culture, in the sense that cultural artifacts are canonized in connection with a particular imagined community so that high culture *is* national culture. Such an inscription occurs with regard to popular culture as well when it is understood as *Volkskultur*, but not necessarily when it is understood in reference to works that are "well-liked by many people" or "deliberately setting out to win favour" (Williams 233). The ambiguity of the English term allows for a crucial conceptual split that makes popular culture a site of populist constructions of 'the people' as well as unpopular resistance to it, and this dialectic is at least less pronounced, if not entirely absent from high culture due to the strong symbolic purpose it serves in imagining community.

Missing the People: Desire

Fittingly, the writer I want to analyze first as an example of a populist aesthetics cannot easily be placed in either popular or high culture, as his texts ended up thoroughly canonized as the latter but actually aimed at the former: Walt Whitman. Of course, applying the binary of high and popular culture to Whitman and the mid-nineteenth century is anachronistic, if not ahistorical, and yet it is as fruitful as reading his work anachronistically in terms of the concept of homosexuality. While some Romantic writers such as Henry David Thoreau have openly embraced unpopularity as an artistic liberation from the demands of an (imaginary or real) audience, others have complained about theirs and denounced the popularity of others. This is Hawthorne's famous sexist complaint when he writes in a letter to his editor William D. Ticknor on January 19, 1855: "America is now wholly given over to a damned mob of scribbling women, and I should have no chance of success while the public taste is occupied with their trash – and should be ashamed of myself if I did succeed" (quoted in Frederick 231). Hawthorne manages to simultaneously crave popularity and reject it; even if he did obtain it, it would be the wrong kind, as he would need the right kind of "public taste" to meet the standard of his works. In contrast, Emily Dickinson was a woman neither scribbling nor part of any mob but remained rather indifferent to the popularity Hawthorne despised and desired, and she "limited her self-promotional activities to a series of private letters" (Blake 52) while proclaiming in her poetry: "How dreary – to be – Somebody! / How public – like a Frog – / To tell one's name – the livelong June – / To an admiring Bog!" (133). Walt Whitman, however, differs from all these exemplary Romantic writers in that he sought popularity without qualification, and would not have shared Hawthorne's (alleged) shame in succeeding. Perhaps no other writer in the nineteenth century deliberately set out to win the favor of his audience like Whitman, and he did so by espousing a populist aesthetics that co-constructs the American people *as that audience*, and his audience as the American people.

It would take at least a monograph to consider Whitman's populism over the course of his career as a writer: his beginnings as a journalist and novelist; the permutations of *Leaves of Grass* and Whitman's persona; his move from nationalism to globalism in search of an audience; his texts on the Civil War and his self-construction as the 'wound-dresser' of America; his jeremiad *Democratic Vistas* and its argument that literature thus far lacks a "reverent appreciation of the People" (1996: 968); and generally Whitman's ever-inventive tactics of seeking critical, commercial, and popular popularity. Since I can only address part of that vast subject here, I will limit my analysis to what is no more than an exemplary and fruitful detail in the bigger picture: the frontispiece and preface to the 1855 edition of *Leaves of Grass*, and the changes Whitman made to the book itself for the 1856 edition.

The first edition famously opens with an image of its author which, although nameless, serves to provide "a physical corollary to his words, a manifestation of his poetic persona" (Genoways 89). This persona is Walt Whitman, and he is "one of the roughs" (*Leaves of Grass* 50),[4] "dressed as a day laborer in workingman's trousers" (Erkkila 3). Visually presenting himself not as "a poet but a common workman" (Pannapacker 7) despite the fact that he was rather "not actually a member of the 'working class' but an artisan possessed of a skilled trade and a measure of independence" (Lawson xvi) may be understood as Whitman's first populist stratagem in *Leaves of Grass*: this is a man of the people eschewing the elitism of poetic tradition and convention, speaking to the common people as one of them, and not from the position of a literary establishment distinct from them. As Whitman wrote in a review of his own book, he is a poet "who has deliberately and insultingly ignored all the other, the cultivated classes as they are called" (1984: I.333). The reason why he "has not dressed up to meet his reader" (Asselineau 48) is that they

---

[4] The 1855 edition of *Leaves of Grass*, as reprinted in *Poetry and Prose*, will be cited as *LoG* in subsequent references.

are both part of the people, meeting on equal terms in a setting private enough to allow for such intimacy. The frontispiece implies visually what Whitman wrote in the unpublished poem "To the Prevailing Bards": "But I alone advance among the people en-masse, coarse and strong" and "I alone of all bards, am suffused as with the common people" (1984: I.410). Notably, Whitman constructs his readership along with his persona: if this is a man of the people, then the people are imagined in such a way as to be able to accept this man as one of their own, to identify with him in one way or another. The frontispiece may be read as an act of visual interpellation that invites readers to imagine themselves a certain way as much as it invites them to imagine the author's persona. (Whitman will address and interpellate a very different readership with the 1860 engraving that depicts him as a Bohemian poet rather than the working-class man of the people, and will later return to a more populist self-construction in the personas of the 'wound-dresser' and 'good gray poet.')

The frontispiece is not the only part of *Leaves of Grass* in which Whitman is "deliberately setting out to win favour" (Williams 233) with the people by presenting himself as one of them (and thereby constructing 'the people' in a certain way). Especially the preface, which is the poetic and political manifesto of a one-man avant-garde, is worth analyzing in this regard. One of its central motifs, and the basis of the populist aesthetics it outlines, is the notion that "a bard is to be commensurate with a people" (*LoG* 7), and this symbiotic co-construction of poet and people creates both in the process. By writing about the American people as if it existed, and as if they existed in such a way as to be commensurate with a future poetry that may well be the one his audience are about to read, Whitman can ensure that he is speaking from the people to the people, and yet there is a fundamental double act of construction at the heart of this correspondence: the

> America that ostensibly required his poems is largely his own construction, a time and place that just happened to demand the sort of poems that he, alone among the poets of his nation, wanted to write. To ascribe *Leaves of Grass* to the America that they themselves evoke is merely to utter a tautology. (Spengemann 60-1)

In order to insist even further on this constructed commensurability, Whitman famously describes the American people in poetic terms right from the start of the preface: "The Americans of all nations at any time upon the earth have probably the fullest poetical nature. The United States themselves are essentially the greatest poem" (*LoG* 5). Whitman then goes on to emphasize the primacy of the 'common people' over their representatives, mildly indicating the rift between people and elite that defines populism:

Other states indicate themselves in their deputies . . . . but the genius of the United States is not best or most in its executives or legislatures, nor in its ambassadors or authors or colleges or churches or parlors, nor even in its newspapers or inventors . . . but always most in the common people. Their manners speech dress friendships – the freshness and candor of their physiognomy – the picturesque looseness of their carriage . . . their deathless attachment to freedom – their aversion to anything indecorous or soft or mean – the practical acknowledgment of the citizens of one state by the citizens of all other states – the fierceness of their roused resentment – their curiosity and welcome of novelty – their self-esteem and wonderful sympathy – their susceptibility to a slight – the air they have of persons who never knew how it felt to stand in the presence of superiors – the fluency of their speech – their delight in music, the sure symptom of manly tenderness and native elegance of soul . . . their good temper and open-handedness – the terrible significance of their elections – the President's taking off his hat to them not they to him – these too are unrhymed poetry. It awaits the gigantic and generous treatment worthy of it. (*LoG* 5-6)

One might describe this lengthy passage rather casually by saying that Whitman is missing the American people and therefore has decided to invent them. This is not just about creating the perfect audience for his poetry, it is more importantly about imagining community, about defining in an appropriately vague yet also distinct (and distinctly positive and romanticized) way the nature of the American people. Jason Frank poignantly describes this dialectic of Whitman's populist poetics in terms of an aesthetic democratic education:

For Whitman the popular commitment to democracy requires an aesthetic evaluation, and he aims to enact the required reconfiguration of popular sensibility through the poetic depiction of the people as a sublimely poetic, world-making power. Whitman's invocation of the people's constituent power is in this sense sublimely autopoetic rather than autonomic; the people are at once the inexhaustible inspiration and the effect of poetic mediation. (182-3)

Whitman is therefore populist in creating 'the people' and insisting that he is commensurable with them, and one way of doing so is highlighting the accessibility of his poetry: according to the preface, the "art of art, the glory of expression and the sunshine of the light of letters is simplicity" (*LoG* 13). The poet swears: "I will have nothing hang in the way, not the richest curtains. What I tell I tell for precisely what it is" (*LoG* 14). This populist appeal to simple truths spoken simply and with "perfect candor" (*LoG* 16) is even consequently elevated to a standard of democratic poetics: "The messages of great poets to each man and woman are, Come to us on equal terms, Only then can you understand us, We are no better than you, What we enclose you enclose, What we enjoy you may enjoy" (*LoG* 14). It is worth emphasizing that Whitman's explicit inclusion of women into an imagination of the people is far from the contemporary norm but perhaps the most progressive element of his populism as it latches onto a less thin ideology of equality and democracy. In doing so, Whitman employs the strategy of juxtaposing the morally pure people with a corrupt elite; the most notable instance of this in the preface is when Whitman imagines the death of liberty, which will only occur

> when the swarms of cringers, suckers, doughfaces, lice of politics, planners of sly involutions for their own preferment to city offices or state legislatures or the judiciary or congress or the presidency, obtain a response of love and natural deference from the people whether they get the offices or no. . . . when it is better to be a bound booby and rogue in office at a high salary than the poorest free mechanic or farmer with his hat unmoved from his head and firm eyes and a candid and generous heart [...]. (*LoG* 18)

Distinguishing the "lice of politics" from the people constructs the latter as honest and generous, and the former as corrupt and parasitic, and the preface continues its anti-elitist argument that had included the poet speaking to the people from the people.

The preface may thus conform to many of the aspects Cas Mudde lists in his definition of populism, and indeed to a sufficient number of them that it may be called populist; however, there is one decisive aspect of populism it struggles to avoid, namely the notion that the people are "essentially homogeneous, i.e. without fundamental internal divisions" (Mudde 68). Whitman embraces pluralism and in fact bases his whole aesthetic on its cultivation within a common framework: he needs to posit the *unity* of Americanness in constructing the people, but he insists on *heterogeneity*. As he famously puts it in "Song of Myself":

> Do I contradict myself?
> Very well then . . . . I contradict myself;
> I am large . . . . I contain multitudes. (*LoG* 87)

Whitman imposes a certain unity on that multitude by his use of the self as a focal point, and yet he does not impose homogeneity along with it. Whitman imagines the multitude as a people in the preface, and he strongly constructs the people as a group with certain properties, and yet he stops short at essentializing or fixing its qualities, but rather insists on its pluralistic openness in terms of community and also time: the "people invoked by Whitman do not aim at the realization of a common essence or at the construction of such an essence, but are only realized through their continual political reinvention out of a collective reservoir of sublime potentiality" (Frank

206). This potentiality means that for Whitman, in Jacques Rancière's phrase, "the people are always more and less than the people" (qtd. in Frank 183), and this incongruence and instability is what elevates his construction of the people from populism into a more complex aesthetics of future-oriented political and aesthetic cultivation. This does not make him less populist in his attempt to devise a poetry that is "uniform with my country" (*LoG* 25), and he closes by insisting that the "proof of a poet is that his country absorbs him as affectionately as he has absorbed it" (*LoG* 26); yet this mutual absorption of poet and people does not mean that it provides either with fixed properties or mistakes unity for homogeneity.

Whatever absorption might have meant exactly to Whitman, it clearly did not occur after the publication of the first edition of *Leaves of Grass*, and he received neither popular nor critical acclaim (nor attained commercial success) with his self-published book. This failure resulted in yet another populist move on Whitman's part, only that this time it pertained to the book itself and not its contents. Deliberately setting out to win favor, desperate for popularity and recognition, Whitman decided to create a book that would be more accessible and more attractive to a large readership. First of all, he reduced the book in size: "His dream now was to have working people carry his poetry with them and read it during breaks: 'to put a book in your pocket and off to the seashore or the forest—that is an ideal pleasure.' So he created a book that he hoped would 'go into any reasonable pocket,' something the first edition clearly would not do" (Folsom and Price 57).[5] The second edition would not fit most pockets either, but the populist intention was clear: making the book smaller was supposed to make it more accessible as an artifact, to make it as quotidian an object as the pocket it would go in. Secondly, Whitman decided to employ a marketing stunt America had never seen before, as the second edition "brazenly features Emerson's name and endorsement on the spine of the book, thus inventing the cover blurb that we have since become so accustomed to" (Folsom) – without asking Emerson for permission, of course. Using Emerson's name and fame to advertise *Leaves of Grass* was an attempt to draw on his immense popularity at the time, and yet the second edition, much like the first, was missing the people in the sense of failing to reach the target audience and become as popular as possible, and it failed to be absorbed by the very people Whitman constructed for that very purpose.

---

[5] Ed Folsom's essay "Whitman Making Books/Books Making Whitman" provides the best available overview of Whitman's publication practices with regard to the book objects themselves.

Missing the People: Absence

I presented Whitman's constructive aesthetic populism in terms of a desire for 'the people' in their absence, missing them in the sense that they are not there but should be, which is especially relevant in terms of nation-building. In the next step of my argument, I want to analyze an aesthetics of unpopular culture in which the people are missing, in which their absence is not the cause of a desire for their presence, but which rather serves to present the people as contingent and transitory for the purpose of undermining their constructions as essential, persistent, and most of all 'natural.' While there are plenty of cultural artifacts that are devoid of both people and 'the people,' I am especially interested here in works that explicitly stage this absence as such. At this point, my line of argument will somewhat shift gears to recognize more fully the aspect of mediality that the preceding section on Whitman concluded with. Therefore, my choice of material will be more diverse, not least in order to reflect at least to a certain extent the large variety of media that constitute contemporary popular culture. Instead of focusing closely on a single author in a literary analysis, I will rather discuss a broader selection of textual, visual, and interactive media in order to explore the different and indeed media-specific ways in which they convey a sense of missing the people without implying a desire for their presence.

For continuity's sake, though, my first example will be a literary one, and a particularly pertinent example as well: Thomas Pynchon's 1997 novel *Mason & Dixon*, whose narratives straddle pre- and post-revolutionary America and which basically shows "something styling itself 'America,' coming into being" (Pynchon 405). Yet as the novel depicts an America without Americans, it does not follow the teleological and celebratory nationalist narrative of nation-building that necessarily and conclusively culminates in the only way one can imagine community; instead, the novel presents an open space of potential in which a multitude is gradually being formed into the fickle and changeable construct of 'the people' through acts of symbolic and material demarcation (such as the Mason-Dixon line) but not without resistance to the power behind such acts. The novel juxtaposes processes of nation-building with non-national, transnational, and global phenomena, and it celebrates the spatial loopholes that resist the territorialization in the name of peoplehood and identity, for example

> the notorious Wedge, – resulting from the failure of the Tangent Point to be exactly at this corner of Maryland, but rather some five miles south, creating a semi-cusp or Thorn of that Length, and doubtful ownership,– not so much claim'd by any one Province, as priz'd for its Ambiguity,– occupied by all whose Wish, hardly uncommon in this Era of fluid Identity, is not to reside anywhere. (Pynchon 469)

Mason & Dixon is certainly not the only example of the unpopular in American literature, of a deliberate refusal to accept 'the people' as a given and instead show their construction beyond any sense of naturalness but instead for various purposes served in a complex network of power relations. In the following, however, I want to move away from such textual examples and consider two other forms of cultural expression that have their own unique ways of missing the people and which are worthy of a closer look in their medial particularities.

The first of these examples is Richard McGuire's comic *Here*, as it was published in book-length form in 2014, although its first version of only six pages and 36 panels was published in *Raw* magazine as early as 1989. The blurb describes the comic as "the story of a corner of a room and of the events that have occurred in that space over the course of hundreds of thousands of years." Yet that summary is misleading in that the corner and the room are only present in that space for a small fraction of that time period, from 1907 to 2111, when we see water burst through the window, and an underwater scene from 2113 shows that the entire room has vanished (along with the house, presumably). The comic is therefore the story of a place rather than of a corner or a room, and the domestic setting – while undoubtedly important – is less central to the visual narrative than placeness itself, and the juxtaposition of times in that place. What makes the comic so relevant to my project as an example of unpopular resistance to a populist aesthetics is that it deliberately stages people as missing, in the more general sense of an absence of people/humans and in a more concrete sense of an absence of 'the people' as a particular community of humans. The comic is quite universal in its representation of the unfathomable depths of time – it starts with the year 3,000,500,000 BCE – but is very particular in its sense of place. Generic as the room or the setting of the house may be, it can nevertheless be located rather precisely, and it conveys a specificity that serves as a counterpoint to its abstract movement through deep time. The corner is in the United States of America but the place is not, or only for a little while. The inhabitants of the house speak English, and before it is built we witness Benjamin Franklin arriving on site, visiting his son in the adjacent colonial home and promising his grandson that he will not get into a fight about politics with his father (and promptly does, of course, just a page later). This cameo and the fight identify the place as American at the historical moment of the creation of the United States, a setting similar to Pynchon's *Mason & Dixon*, and they at least hint at the creation of the American people and the formation of a US-American nationality in subsequent years, even though such notions of community and identity are not commented on further. What is crucial here is that American people and *the* American people are embedded in such a long temporal context that they are all revealed as historically contingent instead of universal, just like the Native Americans that are shown to live in that place in the early seventeenth century. Showing a historical time before the existence of a people is a powerful symbolic move of undermining any claims to universality or essential properties that define a community, as it reveals as imagined and constructed what claims to be natural; it is just as powerful to show a future time *after* the existence of a people to indicate that this form of community is not eternal and immutable but rather subject to change to the point of dissolution. This is the most relevant aspect of the unpopular aesthetic of *Here*: It shows people and even hints at the construction of *a* people through certain references to national identity, but it then takes the reader into a future that is missing the people, when there are neither humans nor human communities. The very page that shows us the fight between Benjamin Franklin and his son includes a panel from the year 10,175 that depicts a four-legged creature of what appears like a vague amalgamate of species, roaming the place at a time when human politics have ceased to matter there. This sense of missing people is especially evoked on a double page that juxtaposes the corner on the left in 1935, where a voice asks "Hello?" through the window, with a scene on the right from the year 22,175, in which plants and animals have reclaimed that domestic space and utterly eradicated any trace of human culture in it. That natural scene is then further juxtaposed with a panel showing a phone call in 2006 going to the answering machine ("Hi, we're not home. Please leave a message after the beep."), as if to further highlight the absence of people in the future, a species that will not even take your message any more but is simply gone. In thus representing the people as missing, *Here* comments on the contingency of individual and social human existence, and it thus counters any populist constructions of communal identity as natural, essential, universal, and timeless.

Changing media once again, video games offer similarly valuable material for a consideration of unpopular resistance to populism in popular culture. For example, the game *Everything* (2017) parallels the texts quoted above in that it is entirely missing any people, and that this absence is explicitly staged and highlighted as such by the inclusion of human artifacts in the game that seem like remnants of a humanity that has vanished, and by the even more abstract fact that one can indeed play *everything* in the game, as the title promises – *everything but humans*. The most fascinating examples to me, however, are those games that are explicitly about human civilization and politics, the games that could easily have a populist notion of 'the people' at their conceptual center *but do not*. This absence is most palpable in the *Civilization* series, which at first glance espouses precisely the populist notion of a homogeneous community of people as the most fundamental political actor: the player starts the game by choosing a civilization – each with slightly different properties, bonuses, or units – and then guiding it through history to victory, which can be achieved in various ways (winning the space race, war, etc.). In *Civilization*, human history is the history of different peoples, and while they interact in various ways, they never merge or lose their traits. Yet this populist pipe dream of 'ethnopluralism' is actually deconstructed by the game itself, and the unpopular strategy it employs in doing so is to stage the people as missing. While the people *appear* to be the basic unit of geopolitical action in the game, they are actually entirely absent from the game itself, and the real actor is their leader, the player, who remains outside of the in-game time. The only people of consequence in the game are very few individuals – specialists, advisors – but never *the* people as a group, not even as the most abstract of homogeneous masses and never as a multitude of individuals that only barely coheres into the fiction of the people (as for example in the *Tropico* or *Democracy* franchises, in which each member of the people is actually simulated in their differences to such an extent that this may be understood as resistance to the populist myth of popular homogeneity). The people in *Civilization* are simply of no consequence; the happiness of 'citizens' in the cities is an important aspect of the gameplay, but this is about as much as the people matter in the game, and they certainly do not matter *as a people*. Thus the game subverts its own populist aesthetic by first implying that the people are homogeneous and timeless and then to render them utterly meaningless in its gameplay, as if they were missing from the game; the implication, then, is that geopolitical action is not popular action, and politics is actually independent of such categories of identity. After all, *it does not matter* which civilization the player picks, as they are, fundamentally, all the same, except for a few bonuses and maluses here and there that provide variety but not imbalance, so that the game can be won or lost with any civilization in any constellation.

Missing the People: Targeting

The examples above have shown how certain cultural artifacts may stage the absence of the people as an unpopular strategy of resistance against populism within popular culture: *entvölkerte Kunst*. My final part will move away from this level of content and discuss artifacts that are themselves used and designed as part of such an unpopular strategy and which oppose the notion of a unified group of 'the people' as the target group of popular culture and, by extension, as an imagined community. In other words, these works are missing the people in the sense of targeting, aiming elsewhere to avoid the large group of consumers that is often implied by popular culture, deliberately setting out *not* to win favor but to offer a critique of popularity in both the sense of 'well-liked' and 'imagining the people.' Missing the people in this sense is always related to the culture industry that either produces much of contemporary popular culture or at least serves as the unavoidable negative standard outside of which other works deliberately place themselves to oppose its mechanisms of commodification and homogenization – in the knowledge that any, really *any* artifact may be commodified and brought in from the furthest margins into the center of mass culture. Edginess may be the perfect unique selling point. Yet even though works that deliberately miss the people may be brought back on target somehow, their symbolic resistance to an *a priori* assumption of the existence of the sufficiently defined 'people' (as a homogeneous group and an audience) remains important nevertheless.

A particularly poignant and well-publicized act of resistance to the cultural market in recent years was the release of the Wu-Tang Clan album *Once Upon A Time In Shaolin* in 2015, although 'release' is perhaps not the right term, as there is only a single copy (or rather 'original'?) in existence, which was auctioned rather than sold conventionally, with the proviso that it may not be made commercially available for 88 years. One may consider this merely a publicity stunt, but even then it was one that sought attention while at the same time deliberately *not* winning the favor of a mass audience but rather making the work inaccessible to any audience but the person who bought it. While Wu-Tang Clan were not the first musicians to do that – there is also only a single copy/original of Jean-Michel Jarre's album *Musique pour Supermarché* (1983) – their strategy of unpopularity is particularly noteworthy as it occurred within the framework of one of the most popular contemporary music genres, HipHop. Furthermore, it fundamentally opposes the thoroughly digital distribution mechanisms in that genre by producing not a simulacrum, a copy without an original, but a work that restores the aura of art Walter Benjamin saw compromised – for better or worse – in the age of mechanical, not to mention digital, reproduction. Wu-Tang Clan produced not just an album but an *object*, which has a unique, material existence and also contains data that may be copied and distributed without destroying the original. Thus, the album *may* become popular and accessible, but only if the owner of that unique object decides to share it (while still retaining the object itself). A review of the album in *Rolling Stone* claims after a listening session that, "[s]imply put, if the full, 128-minute *Once Upon A Time In Shaolin* [...] is as solid as the 13 minutes heard on Monday night, it could be the group's most popular album since 1997" (Weingarten), yet this popularity depends on accessibility, and this is precisely the quality of the album that has been withdrawn from it by making scarce what is usually abundantly available. That in itself would make the album an artifact of unpopular culture that is missing the people because it deliberately rejects the mass market of popular culture and seeks a market elsewhere (while the music remains firmly rooted in popular culture). Yet there is even more to its unpopularity than that, as the album was sold for two million dollars to Martin Shkreli, perhaps one of the most unpopular persons in the US after having obtained the manufacturing license for an antiparasitic drug and raising its price from 13.5$ to 750$ a pill. Shkreli said he would make the album available if Donald Trump won the 2016 presidential election.[6] True to the spirit of campaign promises, he has only shared the intro and a single song by 2017, but what he did do

---

[6] See Hauser for a brief overview of the whole case.

is use the album in a populist political context as a kind of pop-cultural leverage – drawing on the very mass popularity that the album itself questions and resists.

In this case, unpopularity is central to the conception and creation of the album, and it may be seen as both an affirmation of cultural commodification and a rejection of the mass market for such commodities on the part of the artists. Yet unpopularity may also be used against popular culture by the very consumers themselves, as they resist not only the demands and offers made to them on that market but also refuse to be standardized as a homogeneous group. In other words, sometimes people may refuse to be 'the people' as they refuse to be the passive recipients of popular culture, and they may claim their own unpopular culture in opposition and resistance to the one that constructs them as a unified set of consumers who all like, need, and want the same. The best example of such unpopular resistance within popular culture I know of is the act of commercial disobedience committed by British consumers in 2009, when the mainstream culture industry did its best to turn "The Climb," the debut single of X-Factor winner Joe McElderry, into the number one Christmas hit of the year, a symbolic position occupied by the song the British people like best. Yet the massive ad campaign not only missed its target but actually brought about a counterreaction to that very attempt to standardize popular taste. Instead of merely refusing to buy what they are being sold, consumers remained within the framework of the culture industry to reject its own homogenizing tendencies with a clear statement, and by a rather uncoordinated yet popular effort they took a very different song to the top of the singles charts in the UK that year: "Killing in the Name of" by Rage Against the Machine, released in 1992, with its iconic chorus of "Fuck you I won't do what you tell me." Of course, this is far from beating the culture industry with its own weapons, but it is nevertheless a statement against the tendency to manufacture aesthetic consent for commercial gain. Furthermore, it is an assertion within mass culture itself that it is not merely "imposed upon a passive populace like so much standardized fodder" (Ross 4), but rather that popular culture itself is a multiplicity that may oppose such simplifying assumptions about the populace that allegedly constitutes it.

My final example of a work of unpopular culture that is missing the people also works against populism by positioning itself against another cultural artifact in a revisionist act. Douglas Gordon's film *5 Year Drive-By* from 1995 stretches John Ford's 1956 classic Western *The Searchers* to the length of the film's narrative, so that the screening of the movie takes five years. The original film is not revised in itself but only manipulated temporally, and this radical slowing down makes the film unwatchable *as* a film for two reasons: first, it stops being a film and becomes "a series of stills. Each frame of the film is held for about sixteen minutes, and thus each second of film time takes about a working day to project" (Monk 81). Second, it will not be watched by anyone in its entirety. As a result, *5 Year Drive-By* turns an iconic popular movie into an artifact of unpopular culture by using the medium itself against the conventions of its reception, making the film nigh impossible to consume and thus utterly inaccessible. Yet missing the people in the sense of any target audience also entails missing the people in terms of a resistance to populist constructions of the people: in making *The Searchers* inaccessible, it opposes its symbolic content that might be used to construct a notion of the American people in reference to masculinity, the West, space, imperialism, and so forth. Going against the grain of the classic, pre-revisionist Western and its symbolic and ideological outlook that comprises an imagination of national community, *5 Year Drive-By* deprives *The Searchers* of its populism and renders it unavailable for a construction of the people.

Conclusion

Missing the people, then, is a complex affair, and the ambiguous connection between populism and popular culture may be described in terms of its three-fold movement between desire, absence, and targeting. This conflict may even be considered one of the defining features of a popular culture that resists attempts at homogenization and negotiates between various strands of popularity and unpopularity while being haunted by fantasies of unity and homogenization, for better or worse. An imagination of the people, a populist desire, may be an irreducible element of popular culture that can only be managed and controlled but not subdued or even expulsed; at the same time, the unpopular resistance to such populism seems to me just as irreducible an element of popular culture. Scholars of popular culture participate in the maintenance of this dialectic as much as the individuals and groups that constitute, define, and affect popular culture in other ways, and how we position ourselves towards and within this dialectic is fundamentally political. One way of such a critical positioning is implied, I believe, by my final example of unpopular culture that seems perhaps an unlikely candidate, John Steinbeck's *Travels with Charlie: In Search of America* (1962), in which the author-narrator relates the following brief dialogue: "'There used to be a thing or a commodity we put great store by. It was called the People. Find out where the People have gone. [...]' I remember retorting, 'Maybe the People are always those who used to live the generation before last'" (153). This retort fundamentally challenges 'the people' as an ideological concept by describing it as an inherently nostalgic element of imagining community. It also implies that, when confronted with the cultural situation in which the people are missing, we are not supposed to find out where they have gone; instead, we are supposed to find out how we may imagine community differently and in more complex and less reductive ways, in popular culture and wherever else we may.

Works Cited

Asselineau, Roger. *The Evolution of Walt Whitman*. 1960. Iowa City: University of Iowa Press, 1999.
Blake, David Haven. *Walt Whitman and the Culture of American Celebrity*. New Haven: Yale University Press, 2006.
Civilization 5. Firaxis Games/2K Games. 2010.
Deleuze, Gilles. *Cinema 2: The Time-Image*. Minneapolis: University of Minnesota Press, 1997.
Dickinson, Emily. *The Complete Poems*. Ed. Thomas H. Johnson. London: Faber and Faber, 1975.
Erkkila, Betsy. *Whitman: The Political Poet*. Oxford: Oxford University Press, 1989.
Everything. David O'Reilly. Double Fine Productions. 2017.
Fiske, John. "Popular Culture." *Critical Terms for Literary Study*. Ed. Frank Lentricchia and Thomas McLaughlin. Second edition. Chicago: The University of Chicago Press, 1995. 321-35.
Folsom, Ed. "Whitman Making Books/Books Making Whitman: A Catalog and Commentary." The Walt Whitman Archive, 2005. <http://whitmanarchive.org/criticism/current/anc.00150.html>. Last accessed on 28 May 2019.
Folsom, Ed, and Kenneth M. Price, eds. *Re-Scripting Walt Whitman: An Introduction to His Life and Work*. Malden, MA: Blackwell Publishing, 2005.
Frank, Jason. *Constituent Moments: Enacting the People in Postrevolutionary America*. Durham: Duke University Press, 2010.
Frederick, John T. "Hawthorne's 'Scribbling Women.'" *The New England Quarterly* 48.2 (June 1975): 231-40.
Gellner, Ernest. *Nations and Nationalism*. Oxford: Blackwell, 1983.
Genoways, Ted. "'One Goodshaped and Wellhung man': Accentuated Sexuality and the Uncertain Authorship of the Frontispiece to the 1855 Edition of *Leaves of Grass*." *Leaves of Grass: The Sesquicentennial Essays*. Ed. Susan Belasco, Ed Folsom, and Kenneth M. Price. Lincoln: University of Nebraska Press, 2007. 87-123.
Hardt, Michael, and Antonio Negri. *Empire*. Cambridge, MA: Harvard University Press, 2000.
Hauser, Christine. "Martin Shkreli Releases Parts of Wu-Tang Clan Album After Trump Victory." *The New York Times* 11 November 2016 <https://www.nytimes.com/2016/11/11/arts/music/martin-shkreli-releases-parts-of-wu-tang-clan-album-after-trump-victory.html?_r=0>. Last accessed on 28 May 2019.
Hobbes, Thomas. *De Cive*. 1642. New York: Appleton Century-Crofts, 1949.
Howarth, David, ed. *Ernesto Laclau: Post-Marxism, Populism and Critique*. Oxon: Routledge, 2015.

Krause Knight, Cher. *Public Art: Theory, Practice and Populism*. Malden, MA: John Wiley & Sons, 2011.

Laclau, Ernesto. "Why Constructing a People is the Main Task of Radical Politics." 2006. Howarth 165-95.

---. "Populism: What's in a Name?" 2005. Howarth 152-64.

Lawson, Andrew. Walt Whitman and the Class Struggle. Iowa City: University of Iowa Press, 2006.

Lüthe, Martin, and Sascha Pöhlmann. "Introduction: What is Unpopular Culture?" *Unpopular Culture*. Ed. Martin Lüthe and Sascha Pöhlmann. Amsterdam: Amsterdam University Press, 2016. 7-29.

McGuigan, Jim. *Cultural Populism*. London: Routledge, 1992.

McGuire, Richard. *Here*. New York: Pantheon Books, 2014.

Monk, Philip. *Double-Cross: The Hollywood Films of Douglas Gordon*. The Power Plant, and Art Gallery of York University, 2003.

Mudde, Cas. *On Extremism and Democracy in Europe*. Oxon: Routledge, 2016.

Pannapacker, William. *Revised Lives: Walt Whitman and Nineteenth-Century Authorship*. New York: Routledge, 2004.

Priester, Karin. *Mystik und Politik: Ernesto Laclau, Chantal Mouffe und die radikale Demokratie*. Würzburg: Königshausen & Neumann, 2014.

Pynchon, Thomas. *Mason & Dixon*. New York: Henry Holt and Company, 1997.

Ross, Andrew. *No Respect: Intellectuals & Popular Culture*. Oxon: Routledge, 1989.

Spengemann, William C. *Three American Poets: Walt Whitman, Emily Dickinson, and Herman Melville*. Notre Dame, IN: University of Notre Dame Press, 2010.

Steinbeck, John. *Travels with Charley: In Search of America*. 1962. London: Arrow Books, 1997.

Tropico 4. Haemimont Games/ Kalypso Media. 2011. Video game.

Weingarten, Christopher R. "Inside Wu-Tang Clan's 'First, Last, Only' Listening Session for New LP." *Rolling Stone* 3 March 2015 <http://www.rollingstone.com/music/news/inside-wu-tang-clans-first-last-only-listening-session-for-new-lp-20150303>. Last accessed on 28 May 2019.

Whitman, Walt. *Poetry and Prose*. Ed. Justin Kaplan. New York: The Library of America, 1996.

---. *Notebooks and Unpublished Prose Manuscripts*. Ed. Edward F. Grier. 6 vols. New York: New York University Press, 1984.

Williams, Raymond. *Keywords: A Vocabulary of Culture and Society*. 1983. Second edition. London: Fourth Estate, 2014.

Pop(e)ulism: Populist Miracles and Neoliberal Theologies

Donatella Izzo

This essay is part of an unfolding project, prompted by the "questions worth asking" debated at the Futures of American Studies Institute at Dartmouth College over the last few years, and concerning narratives of governmentality at times of crisis. The broader project addresses various aspects of the ongoing dismantling of Max Weber's once normative ideal of social and political modernity: secularism and the 'disenchantment of the world'; capitalist rationalization; and the modern state as based on the monopoly of the legitimate use of violence and regulated through bureaucracy, specialization, and expertise, regarded as the administrative equivalent of the 'technical' superiority of the capitalist mode of production: in other words, as the most efficient, standardized, calculable, and cost-effective form of social organization (Weber 973-5). The ongoing collapse of each of these Weberian tenets is visible around us in many different ways, from the growing instabilities and crises of global capitalism in the economy, to the spread of populism and the resurgence of fascism and Nazism in politics; from the rejection of science and expertise, to post-truth culture and the rise of new regimes of belief, which affect the political no less than the religious and the philosophical sphere. My project focuses on a number of recent verbal and visual narratives, variously mirroring or responding to the political and cultural moment, which I read as a twenty-first century equivalent of the Medieval 'ship of fools': quasi-allegorical engagements with the question of leadership as the epitome of – or, possibly, as a substitute for – politics under the conditions of neoliberalism. This essay will examine one of these exemplary parables of contemporary government: Italian film director Paolo Sorrentino's drama series *The Young Pope* (2016).

In order to create a meaningful context for *The Young Pope*, however, let me offer a short digression about the growing narrative relevance of theology and belief as a frame for representing, and therefore understanding, the contemporary moment. Over the last few years, a whole range of TV series have displayed a growing tendency to stage overt discussions of questions of faith, religion, and theology. A particularly striking example is provided by the fourteenth season (aired in 2018) of *Grey's Anatomy*, one of the most popular shows on US television. April Kepner, the voice of Christian belief in the series, has been undergoing a crisis of faith as a result of her failure to avert the death of her former fiancé's wife in childbirth and of an innocent black teenager shot by the police while he was climbing into his own home through a window. After several weekly episodes of uncharacteristically cynical and unruly behavior, with lots of drinking and casual sex, in episode seventeen, "One Day like This," her faith is finally restored by her encounter with a rabbi, who is dying in excruciating pain due to an extremely rare reaction to an antibiotic, and who sensing her own pain, induces her to reveal her doubts and scolds her for the lack of faith manifested in her childish expectation that God will reward the righteous and that life should be fair. The sequence, which goes on for several minutes, is a true moment of interconfessional theodicy, epitomizing the debate in the Book of Job, with the rabbi, incidentally, dying from skin sores, which is one of Job's afflictions in the Bible. Nor is that all: in episode twenty-three of the same season, "Cold as Ice," April is the protagonist of an almost literal return from the dead – death of hypothermia as a result of a car accident – that is represented as a triumph less of medical science than of faith: her co-workers, feeling helpless to save her, collectively pray for her in the O.R. and her former husband, Jackson Avery, who had always described himself as a non-believer, prays to God promising to believe if April won't be taken away – and at that moment, she wakes.

In a medical series, you do not usually expect to find religious belief mobilized as a major storyline, and theological discussions and miraculous resurrections operating as the literal *deus ex machina* that produces its happy denouement. Shonda Rhimes's *Grey's Anatomy* has always distinguished itself for being sensitive to current social and political issues. So, when I find the character of a white Christian woman from Ohio having a religious crisis and a theological discussion alongside with, and in fact as a direct response to, a reference to #BlackLivesMatter, I cannot help suspecting that religion may have become as politically symptomatic as the allusions to #MeToo and to the expulsion of the Dreamers, which were also explicitly thematized in the same season. Another example: In May 2018, the Italian branch of the satellite broadcasting company Sky started airing a new original series written by novelist Niccolò Ammaniti, titled *Il Miracolo* [The Miracle] and revolving around a statue of the Virgin Mary crying tears of real human blood, found by the police in the secret lair of a boss of organized crime, and kept a secret because the miracle, if revealed, might affect the impending elections. Among the characters are a skeptical but thorough police investigator; a biologist involved in the scientific analysis of the Virgin's blood, who secretly steals some drops of the sample in the hope that they may heal her dying mother; a Catholic priest who has lost his faith and recovers it by being exposed to the statue; and the dysfunctional family of a fictional Italian Prime Minister, whose cynicism is shattered by an accident threatening the life of his child, to the point that he offers frantic prayers to the miraculous statue in a desperate attempt to save the little boy's life. The events take place on the eve of a fictional – but not utterly implausible – referendum that might decide Italy's withdrawal from the European Union. In the end, the Prime Minister's son dies in spite of his father's prayers, but on the wave of the voters' sympathy for his loss, the Prime Minister wins the elections and Italy stays in the EU. The show's narrative perspective is detached throughout, and consequently there is no saying whether this particular outcome should be read ironically, as reflecting the voters' emotionality and their susceptibility to the sentimental power wielded by the tragic death of a child, or else as an authentic miracle averting political disaster. Other subplots end on an equally ambivalent note. The biologist, after her vain attempt to save her mother, has a self-styled pioneer of medicine implant in her uterus a clone obtained from the miraculous blood, in an absolute belief that she will thus become the new Mary, giving birth to a new messiah: faith or grief-induced delusion? Meanwhile, abstracted from its hypersurveilled shelter by the police officer, and secretly replaced by an identical plastic statue bought at a church souvenir shop, the crying Virgin will remain safely hidden from sight in the police officer's freezer, where her blood tears, now frozen, can no longer flow. Is that the sign of a reluctant conversion on the officer's part, or the result of an arbitrary rational decision to suppress a potentially subversive agent for the sake of public order and the political status quo?

These incursions of faith and transcendence into otherwise 'realistic' narratives of the ordinary mundane world are perplexing. What is it about miracles that so appeals to the imagination of twenty-first century script writers and TV audiences? And why are they so recurrently mingled with political concerns? Are these fictional miracles a metaphor for, or a symptom of, the acknowledged demise of Max Weber's secular, rationalist, and disenchanted modernity? Is this collective celebration of the suspension of disbelief a response to the uncontrollable irrationality and scary unpredictability of ordinary life under the conditions of neoliberal capitalism? Or is it rather its product and extension – an implicit invitation to yield trustfully to the ultimate wisdom of an invisible but omnipotent power (be it the hand of the market or the hand of God)?

If, in this always-already post-secular age, a sense of miracle is part of the new equipment required for both spectatorship and citizenship, I would suggest that this interweaving of the miraculous and the political has little or no connection with the time-honored concept of 'civil religion' as originally theorized by Robert Bellah. If anything, it is rather symptomatic of its opposite: the perceived lack of any inherent transcendent dimension capable of grounding the political domain in a rational moral consensus, and the need to replace it by a literal leap of faith. I would also argue that on the one hand, this particular kind of convergence between politics and belief is closely linked to the spread of populism in both the United States and Europe, and on the other hand, the convergence is nowhere more evident than in the growing relevance of one of the essential features of populism itself, charismatic leadership. In the rest of this essay, I will explore the ways in which I see this nexus represented in Paolo Sorrentino's *The Young Pope*. My reading will be partly based on a recent comprehensive discussion of populism by Spanish political philosopher José Luis Villacañas Berlanga, who, while building on Ernesto Laclau's classic theorization, is more distinctly concerned with European politics and has a more sustained attention to the question of leadership. The critique of charismatic leadership, though, has a longer history, and before proceeding to examine Sorrentino's narrative, I wish to briefly invoke two earlier authorities.

Between the 1940s and the 1960s, Italian anthropologist, historian of religions, and philosopher Ernesto De Martino devoted numerous studies to the question of belief, an intellectual concern that was prompted, as he himself declared, by the experience of witnessing Adolf Hitler "shamanizing" – De Martino's term – "in Germany and Europe," like an "atrocious European shaman trying to bury humankind in a fire coffin" (de Martino 2002: 85; translation mine).[1] In the collective political manifestations that De Martino designates as modern forms of shamanism, the appeal to mythical, folkloric, and ritual symbols and practices operates, he argues, as the mediator of irrational and nostalgic attitudes that take root at moments of failure in participatory democracy, when citizens perceive their lack of control over the political sphere and no longer experience themselves as active protagonists of social life (see de Martino 2002: 167-90, especially 173-4). In this view, the emergence of "shamans" – that is, charismatic leaders – is the symptom of a crisis not just in political representation, but more radically, in systems of social belief, prompting individuals to seek a sense of transcendence capable of being deployed as both "a principle of intelligibility of human, historical, and cultural reality and [...] a regulatory ideal" (de Martino 1977: 431; translation mine). Antonio Gramsci (who was able to access Weber's thinking on charisma only through the mediation of Weber's pro-Fascist pupil Robert Michels)[2] had similarly understood and critiqued the charismatic form of leadership as the symptom of a crisis in social authority, that is, a failure of hegemony: a political impasse created as a result of the modern party's failure to produce a coherent worldview geared to the interests and needs of a historically progressive class:

> so-called "charisma," in Michels' sense, always coincides in the modern world with a primitive stage of mass parties, the stage at which doctrine appears to the masses as something vague and incoherent, something that needs an infallible Pope to interpret it and adapt it to the circumstances. (Gramsci 320)

Let me dwell on this image of the Pope, which has inspired my reading, providing a key link between Gramsci's conceptualization of charismatic leadership and

---

[1] Close to the Socialist and Communist party, strongly influenced by Antonio Gramsci's thought, and best known for his studies on the social functions of magic and on mourning rituals in the South of Italy, De Martino, like Max Weber, was keenly interested in the connections between early religious thinking and ritual, and modern social and political forms.

[2] Gramsci devoted paragraph 75 of his Notebook 2 (1929-33) to extensive critical comments on Michels's 1928 essay "Les partis politiques et la contrainte sociale" (see Gramsci 1992: 318ff).

Sorrentino's narrative rendering of a contemporary version of the same phenomenon. Atheist and communist Gramsci is certainly using the Pope as a metaphor suggested by the Catholic environment of Italy to convey the notion of a subjection to unenlightened and unquestioned authority. But the Pope is also, as Gramsci is well aware, a head of state, and as such, an embodiment of political power, and thus the aptest image for the dangerous overlapping of political conviction and religious belief that Gramsci is trying to diagnose through his critique of Michels's celebration of Benito Mussolini as a charismatic leader.

Another implication of Gramsci's use of the Pope as a trope is the association it evokes between populism and Catholicism. This link has been repeatedly theorized, most notably by Margaret Canovan and, more recently, by Loris Zanatta. According to this genealogy, which relies on a theory of unfinished but ongoing secularization, populism is the political form of backward rural areas, falling back on a retrotopian revival of a traditional universe of sacred values whenever they are faced with a crisis of modernization – in this case, the pressure of global financial capitalism. For Zanotta, this nostalgic appeal is grounded in the Roman Catholic notion of the mystical body of Christ, that is, the mystical union of all Christians in the true Church, which is an extension of Christ's body. The community invoked and elicited by populism would therefore be an organic and ancestral one, originally existing as a body of believers, whose deep mystical unity populism revives and retools to political purposes. In chapter three of his book, José Luis Villacañas Berlanga critiques this genealogy on both historical and philosophical grounds, pointing out that many historical forms of populism, including the American "We, the People," could never be accounted for in Catholic terms, and that conceptually, a more relevant way of deploying Catholicism in connection with populism would be by foregrounding its important conceptual intersections with Carl Schmitt's political theology, as displayed, for instance, in Chantal Mouffe's lifelong interest in Schmitt's political philosophy and its impact on her collaboration with the most influential modern theorist of populism, Ernesto Laclau. In accordance with Laclau, Villacañas maintains instead the constructed and discursive quality of the populist bloc. But if populism is not a spontaneous residual phenomenon but rather a thoroughly modern and constructed one, the Catholic flavor of its reliance on charismatic leadership needs to be understood as strictly an element of its present- and future-oriented political strategy.

And indeed, who or what could be more literally charismatic than a Pope? And more future-oriented than a *young* Pope? In inventing his young Pope, I believe Paolo Sorrentino to have created one of the most powerful narratives of, and artistic reflections on, politics and leadership in recent years.

The series, in ten episodes of about one hour each, was filmed in English, premiered at the Venice film festival in September 2016, and was run by Sky Atlantic in Italy starting on October 21, 2016 and by HBO in the United States in

January 2017, shortly after the inauguration of Donald Trump as the new president. The coincidence was such that American reviewers almost unanimously commented on the parallels between the new fictional American Pope and the new actual American president: the series, one reviewer wrote, is about "how high the stakes become when an insecure narcissist gains absolute power" (Framke). Sorrentino was able to plausibly deny any such link, given the fact that he had been working on the show since 2015. When interviewed – especially in Italy, where the Vatican and the Pope continue to be highly sensitive topics – he always rejected any suggestion that the show might be a Vatican version of *House of Cards* or have a specific political import, choosing instead to emphasize the theme of solitude, the essential loneliness of those who are in power and more generally, of every human soul faced with the ultimate questions (for an English-language interview along those lines see Bentley). I think it may fairly be stated that in this respect, Sorrentino's claims were somewhat disingenuous: best known in the United States for his Oscar prize winning *The Great Beauty*, Sorrentino has always been an inherently political author, whose inventive style and visual magnificence have been again and again put in the service of an exploration of the psychic life of power within and around the powerful. In 2008 he directed *Il Divo*, a biopic on Giulio Andreotti, for decades Italy's most powerful and controversial, as well as secretive Italian politician. In 2018 he released *Loro* (they, or them, or their, as well as a near homophone for "l'oro," the gold), a 204-minute movie in two parts, focusing on three critical years in the personal and political life of former Italian prime minister and political leader Silvio Berlusconi, on some of the sexual scandals surrounding him, and on the desire for money, sex, and power endlessly circulating around him.

Though set in the Vatican and featuring an imaginary Pope rather than an actual political figure, *The Young Pope* is even more saturated with politics than the director's more overtly politically themed films. It is no easy task to summarize the complicated plot of *The Young Pope*, and the task is made even more difficult by the fact that the story is partly narrated through flash backs, surrealistic dream sequences, painterly tableaus, and sudden, startling images. In its main outline, the story revolves around Lenny Belardo (played by Jude Law), the 47-year old Pope from New York that the College of Cardinals have elected as a result of a compromise between the progressive and the conservative wings, masterminded by the wily Secretary of State, liberal cardinal Voiello (played by Silvio Orlando), who had mistakenly expected him to be a docile puppet in his hands. Young, athletically built, exceptionally handsome, unpredictable, ironical to the point of sarcasm, and politically astute, Pope Pius XIII – a chosen name that affiliates him with the most conservative popes of the twentieth century[3] – shocks everyone by rejecting all advice, any attempt to direct him, and any form of publicity: having announced that he will never appear in public, he delivers his first papal address at night, appearing only as a dark silhouette against the lit window of the Apostolic palace; subsequently, he will regularly turn his shoulders to the crowd during benediction, and refuse to circulate any picture of himself, whether to the press or as part of Vatican merchandizing. Fully availing himself of his sovereign powers, he uses them in a reactionary way to reverse the modernizing trend of the Church, enjoining believers to forget about free will and embrace fear and suffering as the only path to God. He rejects liberal openings to individual freedoms and emancipations, threatens to excommunicate women for having an abortion, reinforces the vow of celibacy, condemns homosexuality, and prohibits gay men from being admitted to the seminary (thus inducing a rejected young man to commit suicide, a circumstance that will also indirectly lead to the death of his best friend, Cardinal Dussollier). As a result of his decisions, he alienates Catholics around the world, causing general worry for the future of the church and inducing Cardinal Voiello to unsuccessfully try to involve him in a sexual scandal in an attempt to blackmail him into relinquishing the papal office. A ruthless politician, the Pope does not hesitate to break the seal of confession in order to acquire full knowledge of the cardinal's secrets, and to use blackmail in his turn, in order to wield absolute power in the Roman Curia, to influence Italian politics, and to circumvent Cardinal Voiello's attempts to recover political control over the Church. In the course of the episodes, we learn about the deep personal lack that seems to be the root of both his actions and his personality: as a child, he was raised by a nun, Sister Mary (Diane Keaton), having been abandoned by his hippie parents, whom he is still seeking and hoping to reunite with. Finally, unable to reconnect with his parents, discouraged by the seeming failure of his plan for the church, tormented by guilt and surrounded by death – the death of his best friend, Cardinal Dussollier, of his mentor, Cardinal Spencer, and even of the kangaroo that he had received as a gift and set free in the Vatican gardens, and that uncannily obeyed his order to jump – the Pope decides to change his ways. He travels to an African country where he delivers a speech against injustice, and he punishes powerful New York archbishop Kurtwell, guilty of sexually abusing children. Kurtwell's attempt to avert punishment by blackmailing the Pope backfires: the love letters written by young Lenny to his only girlfriend the summer before he entered the seminary, which Kurtwell has leaked to *The New Yorker*, far from damaging Pius XIII make him immensely popular: "the world has stood still to talk about love," says a voice on the radio at the beginning of episode

---

[3] "They all went white when they heard the name I had chosen, I revelled in their fear. They were beginning to realize who I am. That is the enormous error they committed. They chose a Pope they didn't know and today they began to understand" (E 3).

ten. Now loved and admired by the faithful, the Pope, in another attempt to find his parents, chooses Venice, the city they meant to visit when they abandoned him, for his first public appearance. After addressing the public from Saint Mark's Basilica with an inspiring and emotional homily about the smile of God, Lenny sees in the crowd a couple that might be his parents, who look at him and once again turn away from him. At that moment he is seized by a heart attack and collapses, fainting or possibly dead, as the camera moves up into the space, showing the earth getting smaller and smaller.

It is impossible within the scope of this essay to do justice to the richness of texture of the show, and to the countless details that compose its complex, contradictory, and puzzling narrative of power and faith – or rather, of the politics of faith. Thus, well aware that what will be left out is infinitely more than what will be actually addressed, I will focus only on a few keywords that I consider especially relevant to a political reading of the narrative. The first one is absence, and its more prominent instance is, rather surprisingly, the absence of God.

In the story, the existence of God is again and again questioned by none other than the Pope himself. As early as the first episode he declares to his shocked confessor that he does not believe in God: "God, my conscience does not accuse me because you don't believe that I'm capable of repenting, and therefore I do not believe in you. I don't believe you're capable of saving me from myself. […] I'm saying that I don't believe in God." Though on that occasion Pius XIII immediately retracts, saying that he was joking, statements to that effect recur again and again: as a charge from which he does not defend himself;[4] as a challenge addressed to the faithful ("Are you capable of proving that God does not exist?" [E 2]); as the reassurance that comes with final knowledge – "God, the absence of God, only is reassuring and definitive" (E 5); or else as self-affirmation: "I forgot to thank God because I didn't think God had illumined me either. I love myself more than my neighbor, more than God, I believe only in myself. I am the lord omnipotent. Lenny, you have illumined yourself, fuck!" (E 3) – the latter immediately followed, in the next scene, by a passionate prayer to God for forgiveness, which, however, only reinforces the sense of God's absence: "I keep praying for you to make something happen. So why this awful, crawling feeling that nothing ever does. Dictate to me, Lord, yes dictate to me. I've always been good at taking notes, you know that" (E 3). At other moments, the absence of God is rendered in notes of postmodern absurdist playfulness: "[God] is angry, and so in protest he has moved to a new place. He's gone in the outskirts of town, filthy studio apartment upstairs of a tire repair job. At night God suffers from the heat, getting no sleep because he has come to the conclusion that there's nothing he can do about human beings" (E 4).

---

[4] "You don't believe in God, Holy Father, you don't believe in God" (E 7); "You don't believe in God" (E 8).

During his first solitary prayer in episode 1, Lenny repeatedly invokes "God's infinite silence," while ironically, the radio set behind him emits the kind of electrical noise that suggests bad transmission. And indeed, the well-known theological motif of *Deus Absconditus* is played out in many ways and registers, becoming a pervasive, though puzzlingly ambivalent model. The Pope's own refusal to show his image ("I do not have an image, my good lady, because I am no one. Do you understand? No one. Only Christ exists, only Christ [...] They will not see me because I don't exist" [E 2]) and his expressed wish to be "an invisible Pope" (E 2) are alternately described as a marketing strategy – as suggested by the Pope's allusion to the way invisibility has enhanced the reputation of Salinger, Kubrick, and Banksy,[5] and his claim that in order for the small Vatican state to survive, "its leader has to make himself as unreachable as a rockstar" (E 2) – or as a theological statement about the mystery of God: "absence is presence. These are the fundamentals of mystery, the mystery that will be at the center of my papacy. Mystery is a serious matter, it's not some marketing strategy" (E 3). But the motif of absence is also obviously and prominently linked to the absence of the Pope's own parents, to whose abandonment of Lenny as a child his mentor, Cardinal Spencer, openly ascribes his present stern and punitive attitude towards the whole of Christianity ("God help us. You want to make the world pay for the wrong they did you" [E 2]), defining him "a vindictive little boy" (E 3). And while Lenny rejects this reading as "dime-store psychoanalysis" (E 3), Spencer's interpretation is in fact partly confirmed both by Belardo's persistent search for his parents and by his dreams, as well as by his own words at other moments ("I search everywhere, I pray, but I don't see God because I don't see my father, I don't see my mother" [E2]). Incidentally, most of the main characters share the same condition of being orphans (Sister Mary, Cardinal Duvallier) or betrayed and abused children (both Cardinal Gutierrez and archbishop Kurtwell).

Reading all these variations on absence in terms of characterization, in line with the author's insistence on the existential question of loneliness, or even as iterations of the familiar Lacanian notion of desire structured around absence, would indeed smack a little of the "dime-store psychoanalysis." What if we read them, instead, as political metaphors? What does it mean to have a story about a Pope that might be an atheist, and how does that possibility, or doubt, inflect the nature of his power, and our understanding of it?

José Luis Villacañas Berlanga writes that populism "understands that every society is based on an absent ground – the lack of ground illustrated in Heidegger's philosophy – and that when this feeling of operating on a void emerges, a dangerous

---

[5] "None of them let themselves be seen, none of them let themselves be photographed" (E 2).

excess is also manifested" (Villacañas Berlanga 16).[6] Both historically and philosophically, the starting point of populism is the rejection of Marxism and of the Marxist ontology of social classes as created by the social divide between production and appropriation of surplus value. While adopting the liberal notion of demand, Villacañas argues, populism recognizes that "there is no ontological equivalent capable of operating as a fundamental comprehensive demand," in the way that class and production do in Marxism: "populism leaves the social locus of this demand empty, and uses this void as the presupposition of its post-marxist politics," (Villacañas Berlanga 37) by creating the "equivalential chain" discussed by Laclau (74 ff.): in other words, a chain of empty equivalences for disparate unfulfilled demands, whose circulation operates in similar ways to the operation of financial capitalism. Therefore, Villacañas adds, "[f]rom the philosophical point of view, populism is post-metaphysical" (Villacañas Berlanga 33).

It may seem counter-intuitive to link this understanding of populism as a post-metaphysical theory of politics and society with a narrative revolving around Catholicism, the Pope, and God – all entities that have a certain vested interest in the metaphysical. And yet, if there is a metaphysics in this story it can be only a metaphysics of power, as that is the one entity whose existence is never questioned but rather perpetually reinscribed: it is repeatedly discussed by the Pope himself, by Cardinal Voiello,[7] and finally by all the assembled popes of the past that Lenny dreams of in the final episode: "'I beg of you, confide in me the wisest thing you have ever learned.' 'In the end more than in God it is necessary to believe in yourself, Lenny.' 'Oh. Have you got something a little better? That's a banal platitude.' '[…] After all, look at us. We are power, and power is a banal platitude'"). And while a couple of figures of prime ministers appear in the story (including one transparently based on then Italian Prime Minister Matteo Renzi), the real discussion of the definitions, methods, and ends of political power is really unfolded, both implicitly and explicitly, through the opposition between Cardinal Voiello and Pius XIII.

Let me provisionally define this as the binary of policy or "the police" and politics or the political, in Jacques Rancière's sense of the management of the status quo through naming, ordering, and partitioning, on the one hand, and the radical refiguration of the very political space, on the other. There is little doubt that Voiello stands for the former option: astute, savvy, and practical, well connected both inside and outside of the Vatican, repeatedly touched but never permanently defiled by financial and political scandals, and universally regarded as the most powerful man

---

[6] Page references are to the Italian edition, *Populismo* (Milan: Mimesis, 2018). All English translations are mine.

[7] "Federi', tu lo sai perché tutte le anime candide di questo mondo tuonano contro il potere? Molto banalmente perché non sanno cos'è. … Il potere è conoscenza" ["Federico, do you know why all the naive souls are always inveighing against power? Quite simply because they don't know what it is. […] Power is knowledge"] (E 1, in Italian in the original).

in the Vatican, he stands (at least initially) for a *realpolitik* that is thoroughly secular in its means and ends and does not refrain from adopting immoral or illegal measures in the interest of the state's stability: "The Vatican is a state. There is politics, finances, there are very delicate balances, and great dangers if those balances are upset. [...] We are an anomalous state and diplomacy is all we have" (E 2). And yet, he is also, in his way, a principled and charitable man: just as we expect to catch him having sex with a prostitute we learn, instead, that he takes care of a physically and mentally disabled boy hosted in his rich state apartment, lovingly feeding him and talking to him at the end of each day: "aiutami tu a espiare tutto il male che dovrò fare per salvare la Chiesa" [help me to expiate all the evil things I'll have to do in order to save the Church], he whispers to him, crying, after having heard the Pope's intimidating harangue in episode 2.

As for the Pope, he declares his vision in one of the dialogues with his confessor: "'Your holiness, what do you intend to do?' 'Revolution, Tommaso. I intend to start a revolution'" (E 4). It is initially unclear what the character and direction of this revolution will be: not only is Pius XIII an expert dissimulator ("ever since I was little I've learned to confound people's ideas of what's going on in my head" [E 1]), but he is also repeatedly declared and shown to be mutable and contradictory in his feelings and intentions: "'Who are you Lenny?' 'I'm a contradiction. Like God, one in three and three in one. Like Mary, virgin and mother. Like man, good and evil'" (E 1). This is nowhere more evident than in his twofold first address as a Pope. In the first one, which we later realize to have taken place only in his dreams, he smilingly shows his face to the acclaiming crowds, greeting them with a jocular "Ciao, Rome!," brings out the sun on a dark and rainy day, and addresses the faithful with a reassuring "What have we forgotten? What have we forgotten? We have forgotten you! [...] God does not leave anyone behind. I serve God, I serve you!" He then proceeds to declare that "to be in harmony with God we have to be in harmony with life" and invites the faithful to play, love, enjoy, masturbate, use contraceptives, have sex, have gay marriages, have divorces, have abortions, and be happy – "and there is only one road to be happy, and that road is called freedom" (E 1). The Pope's actual address, which takes place at the end of the second episode, is a perfectly symmetrical inverted mirror of the first: showing himself only as a dark shadow at night, amid lightning and rain, Pius XIII enjoins the faithful, in a thundering and irate voice, to seek God in suffering:

What have we forgotten? What have we forgotten? We have forgotten God! You, you have forgotten God! I am closer to God than I am to you [...] because everyone is alone before God. I have nothing to say to those who have the slightest doubt about God. All I can do is remind them that I scorn them and that they are wretcheds. I don't have to prove that God exists. It is up to you to prove that he doesn't. Are you capable of proving that God does not exist? If you are unable to prove it that means God does exist. God exists, but he isn't interested in us until we become interested in him. In him exclusively. Do you understand what I'm saying? Exclusively, twenty-four hours a day. [...] There is no room for free will, no room for liberty, no room for emancipation. Free yourself from God, some people say, liberate yourself from God. But the pain of liberation is unbearable, sharp enough to kill. Without God you are as good as dead. Dead, abandoned strays, wandering streets. [...] You want to look me in my face? Go see God first! [...] When you've found God perhaps you will see me as well. (E 2)

Followed by a sudden turning away from the window as a laser light tries to reach up to the Pope's face – "What you're doing is more than a simple lack of respect. I don't know if you deserve me" – this intimidating speech leaves the crowds speechless and dumbfounded as a bolt of lightning strikes the stormy night sky. If this is a revolution, it is an unmistakably conservative one, in sharp contrast with the hedonistic license that seemed to emerge from Belardo's unconscious in the previous dream sequence.

And yet, while certainly easy to trace to the character's ambivalent response to his parents' hedonistic hippie lifestyle, both the Pope's contradictions and his overcoming of those contradictions, I would contend, demand to be addressed not just in a psychological key but first and foremost as politically symptomatic. The casting of polarly opposite contents in an identical rhetorical form amounts to an unsettling interchangeability of love and fear, the smile and the frown. Such a style of address, which capitalizes not on rational argument but rather on the direct interpellation of the masses and the production of a strong emotional response, is a recognizable feature of the "affective politics" of the so called political revolution of populism.[8] And while the Pope's deliberate rejection of popularity seems to deny a basic tenet of populism – the need to appeal to the masses – Pius XIII himself immediately presents his choice to distance himself from the faithful, as has been seen, not as the "media suicide" that the Vatican marketing specialist thinks it to be but rather as a sophisticated new strategy of apophatic communication expressly designed to command interest in an overcrowded media world: "We should generate hyperbole, but this time in reverse" (E 2).

It is this primary focus on the modes and strategies of communication, coupled with the actual interchangeability of the content of the message, I would argue, that makes the young Pope such an effective embodiment of the style and operation of populist charismatic leadership, and enables – in ways that are far more significant than the character's individual psychological contradictions – his disconcerting metamorphosis from permissive paladin of license and individual freedom to

---

[8] This term is proposed by both Sara Ahmed (64) and Brian Massumi (56, 65ff).

inflexible authority, and then again, from inflexible authority to bearer of unconditional love. Indeed, his final address in Venice depends for its effect not just on the Pope's finally revealed, sweet, and tearfully smiling face, but on its careful rhetorical construction, entirely aimed at a rejection of rational discourse and of the binary partitioning of the real inherent in the logic of non-contradiction. The Pope's speech, in fact, is entirely based on the incantatory recitation of a list of fundamental, naïvely formulated questions that Pius presents as posed to the blessed Juana by the children around her – "are we dead or are we alive? [...] Are we healthy or are we sick? Are we good or are we bad? [...] Are we young or are we old? Are we clean or are we dirty? Are we fools or are we smart? Are we true or are we false? Are we rich or are we poor? [...] Are we men or are we women?" – whose dichotomous arrangement is finally rejected ("It doesn't matter, replied the blessed Juana") and overcome by the final reassurance: "God smiles. And only then did everyone understand. Now I beg all of you: smile, smile, smile" (E 10). The Pope's final message is not a dialectical resolution but a mystical *coincidentia oppositorum*: God's smile subsumes and transcends all earthly differences and distinctions. From a mundane perspective, though, this message is as empty as a commercial, or rather, as empty as the "empty signifier" of Laclau's theory: what it names is not a transcendent totality but an equivalence. Its constitutive role in bringing forth what Laclau terms "the absent fullness of society" (Laclau 229) relies exactly on its capacity to achieve symbolic unification by annihilating distinctions through the creation of an affective bond with and among the mass of the faithful. The emotional response displayed by the speaker and elicited in the viewers creates a shared affective dimension in which the different demands of individuals are subsumed into a singular faith.

The young Pope's interchangeable production of inclusion or exclusion, reassurance or dread, then, is less a tactical need than a constitutive condition of his political logic. In this sense he is really a *young* pope, whose style of religious and political communication marks a perceptible difference from the past. Again, the representative divergence here is with Cardinal Voiello, whose more liberal political attitude is nevertheless expressed through a thoroughly traditional style aimed at achieving agreement, rational conviction, and consensus: "balance" is, in fact, a crucial word in Cardinal Voiello's political lexicon, which he repeatedly attempts to persuade the Pope to embrace. Unsurprisingly, he fails. The new Pope diminishes the role of Voiello and the Roman Curia, and breaks with the pursuit of balance, mediation, and consensus: "Haven't you found out that your methods only worked with the old popes, who were afraid of losing consensus? They don't work with me. I am a young pope. I put no stock in consensus" (E 5). Such an attitude is in fact typical of populist politics, which always defines itself as a radical break with the past and a revolutionary rejection of existing elites, bureaucracies, and institutional administrators, and in fact, Pius XIII embraces the methods and objectives that are typical of the populist turn: the mobilization of mutable, tactical, and interchangeable demands through the affective appeal to emotions, aimed at the ex novo construction of a community that will not be based on rational interests, national or class belonging, or pre-existing ideological and religious allegiances, but on absolute commitment to an indefinite but unquestionable end, as he states in his address to the cardinals:

> I want fanatics for God, because fanaticism is love. [...] I have no idea what to do with the friendship of the whole wide world. What I want is absolute love and total devotion to God. To that means, a church only for the few. [...] you cannot measure love with numbers, you can only measure it with intensity, in terms of blind loyalty to the imperative – fix that word firmly in your souls, imperative. From this day forth that's what the Pope wants, that's what the Church wants, that's what God wants. [...] there is nothing outside your obedience to Pius XIII, nothing except hell. [...] This Pope does not negotiate on anything with anyone and this Pope cannot be blackmailed. From this day forth the word compromise has been banished from the vocabulary. I just deleted it. (E 5)

"Fanaticism" and "blind loyalty" versus "hell": this is not eschatology but politics. Despite the Pope's stated indifference to making friends for the church, what is unmistakably taking place here is the primordial division that creates the political field, according to Carl Schmitt's famous claim that "The specific political distinction to which political actions and motives can be reduced is that between friend and enemy" (Schmitt 26) – a distinction that in the political logic of populism is not grounded on any pre-existing national or class category but always produced anew by requesting a fideistic, pre-emptive allegiance, in order to create the conditions for the taking and keeping of power. It is here that charismatic leadership meets sovereignty. "The Pope is an absolute sovereign," Pius XIII declares in episode 3.

I believe that the real genius of Sorrentino's apparently bizarre decision to choose a pope as the vehicle for his interrogation of the political in our day is the unique possibility such a figure offers to stage a charismatic leader who is simultaneously and inherently a sovereign figure, and whose association with questions of faith and belief is a natural premise rather than an artificial construction. This presupposition enables the author, through the convergence of politics and belief, to stage the political convergence of charismatic leadership – which is an inevitable need of populist politics and is politically legitimated by popular vote (or, in this case, by the cardinals' vote) – and absolute sovereignty, which by being associated with charismatic leadership is revealed as its ultimate goal.

In this view, the charisma of Sorrentino's Pope is a striking combination of literal charisma in the theological sense – the gift of grace emanating from God (though, as we have seen, the existence of God here is not taken for granted) – and charisma in Max Weber's political sense, describing the emergence of the exceptional leader at times of crisis, based on the affective bond created with a community of supporters. Max Weber's charismatic leader draws his authority and legitimation from his apparently transcendental gifts, and deploys them in order to sustain the establishment or re-establishment of the state (Weber 241). The charismatic leader of populism, according to Villacañas, operates in the opposite fashion: he performs a suturing function, symbolically transforming the people into a totality at an affective level, by giving visible personal embodiment and affective force to the empty chain of equivalences that subsume the disparity of social demands, which he is able to articulate exactly by virtue of his emptiness and which must remain unfulfilled in order for populism to stay alive. Unlike Weber's charismatic leadership (and unlike Gramsci's theory of hegemony or Niccolò Machiavelli's Prince), the populist leadership is not teleological, it is not aimed at the reconstruction of the state according to new principles and interests, but rather at perpetuating the institutional crisis. The charismatic leader of populism, therefore, operates as pure representation, as, in Villacañas's terms, "a condensation of dreams, the locus of a tension"; his name "covers the void" of political direction: "what it names is an active people set against an enemy" (Villacañas Berlanga 56).[9] His charisma is not the revolutionary and creative one of Weber's leader, but – again in Villacañas's terms – an "iconographic charisma" (Villacañas Berlanga 55).[10] It seems to me that this is exactly what the young Pope stands for: while the word charisma recurs more than once in the dialogues, and despite his investiture, the charisma of Pius XIII seems to be founded not so much on the intangible Holy Spirit (whose operation in his election is as repeatedly denied as it is affirmed) but rather on his self-aware deployment of his extraordinary good looks ("I might be more handsome than Jesus, keep that to yourself" [E 3]),[11] on his markedly embodied – and frequently half naked – presence, as well as on his unexpected communication strategies, his carefully cultivated unpredictability, and his capacity to charm, to unsettle, to threaten, to coax, and to lure. His charisma, in other words, regardless of its divine origin or lack thereof, is a matter of performance and effect, recalling nothing so much as Machiavelli's prescriptions for lie, deception, and the unsettling multiplication of masks, in chapter 18 of his *The Prince*.

---

[9] For Laclau, the creation of a dichotomous, antagonistic camp through the exclusion and demonization of a section of the population is the first step of the creation of "the people."

[10] In his interview with Joel McKim, "Microperception and Micropolitics," Massumi reformulates "affective politics" as "aesthetic politics" and defends both from the widespread charge of being inherently fascistic (Massumi 65 ff).

[11] In one of the show's typical ironical counterpoints, the sequence of Belardo's dressing in his full regalia for his first address to the cardinals in episode 5 has LMFAO's "Sexy and I Know It" as its soundtrack.

One of the reasons why Max Weber is ultimately skeptical of charismatic leaders is that they seem to him little suited to stabilize the state, in that it is difficult for them to keep their popular support under routine political conditions: they would have, he writes, "to work miracles" (Weber 1114-5). And of course, though I have tactically abstained from mentioning this up to now, performing miracles is exactly what the young Pope does.

In the course of the show, we listen to the Pope relate to his confessor his intense prayer to God for his own election ("and now I'm the Pope [...]. Sister Mary would call it a miracle, others would call it the answer to a prayer, I don't know what to call it" [E 3]). We see him intensely pray to the Virgin Mary to give a child to a sterile woman, who then becomes pregnant. We see him pray to God at night, kneeling in the parking area of a gas station on his way back from his travel to Africa, asking him to do something about Sister Antonia, who abuses her power as the leader of a chain of schools in Africa to exact sexual favors, and the alternate montage suggests that the sudden stroke killing the nun in Africa just as the Pope is praying is an actual result of his prayer. Towards the end of the story, Lenny confirms to his dying mentor that as a teenager he actually healed through his prayer the dying mother of one of his friends – the reason, we now learn, for Sister Mary's unshakeable conviction that he is a saint. These miracles of life and death, covering the whole range from biopolitics to the exercise of sovereignty as the extrajudicial power to take someone's life, need not of course be seen as 'real' miracles: the woman's pregnancy and the nun's sudden death might be coincidences, and the healing of the friend's mother might be just a story told to comfort a dying man. The Pope himself declares his skepticism when a Cardinal reports the blessed Juana's miraculous healings in Guatemala (though it is to the blessed Juana that he will repeatedly refer in his last inspiring address), and defines "calumny" (E 9) the rumors depicting him as a saint. Furthermore, while lending an evocative mystical aura to the Pope's miraculous performances, the show unsettlingly juxtaposes them with other, much less mystical forms of belief: Neapolitan Cardinal Voiello's devotion to Diego Maradona and the Naples soccer team, whose games he follows on TV with a rosary in his hands; and the subplot concerning Tonino Pettola, a rural prophet who gains followers in the countryside south of Rome by claiming that the Virgin Mary has appeared to him in the shape of a sheep, and that this sheep can perform miraculous healings.

What the show seems to suggest is that miracles are in the eye of the beholder, and there is nothing too absurd that somebody will not believe it. The question is not one of evidentiary truth, criteria of validation, or thresholds of plausibility: it is strictly a question of affect, and of the affective production of belief. Through its crafty narrative construction and arresting aesthetic quality, the show stages structures of belief that it simultaneously undermines by its unsettlingly alternating registers: tragedy, comedy, sentimental melodrama, breathtaking beauty, and hilarious farce. The show's unsettling irony is epitomized in its opening credits, in which the Pope walks along a gallery of paintings, followed by a meteor which produces material effects within the paintings, and finally strikes down an older pope, in a live performance of Maurizio Cattelan's controversial installation *The Ninth Hour*. Having completed his walk along the gallery, and immediately before the meteor is seen to strike the old Pope, the young Pope winks at us, looking straight into the camera with an indecipherable smile. Is he interpellating us as skeptical subjects or seducing us into his world? Making fun of us or seeking our complicity? Who knows. What the show does is usher us into the regime of post-truth, not only by representing its operation in and through the story, but by creating for us the same experience as viewers. Through its dazzling visual opulence and puzzling plot, *The Young Pope* lures us into a position in which we can experience—and perhaps learn to resist—our own demise as secular rational citizens.

Works Cited

Ahmed, Sara. *The Cultural Politics of Emotion*. 2nd ed. Edinburgh: Edinburgh University Press, 2014.

Bellah, Robert N. "Civil Religion in America," *Daedalus* 96:1 *Religion in America* (1967): 1-21.

Bentley, Jean. "'The Young Pope' Creator on Parallels to Donald Trump – and All Those Memes." *The Hollywood Reporter* 16 January 2017 <https://www.hollywoodreporter.com/live-feed/young-pope-creator-parallels-donald-trump-all-memes-964459>. Last accessed on 9 June 2019.

Canovan, Margaret. *Populism*. New York: Harcourt Brace Jovanovich, 1981.

De Martino, Ernesto. "Promesse e Minacce dell'Etnologia," *Furore Simbolo Valore*. Milan: Feltrinelli, 2002, pp. 84-118.

---. *La Fine del Mondo. Contributo all'Analisi delle Apocalissi Cultural*. Ed. Clara Gallini. Turin: Einaudi, 1977.

Framke, Caroline. "HBO's *The Young Pope* stars Jude Law as a smirky pontiff. It's sly, sinister, and a whole lot of fun." *Vox* 16 January 2017 <https://www.vox.com/culture/2017/1/16/14274000/young-pope-premiere-recap-review-hbo-jude-law>. Last accessed on 9 June 2019.

Gramsci, Antonio. *Prison Notebooks*, vol. 1, Ed. and transl. Joseph A. Buttigieg. New York: Columbia University Press, 1992.

Laclau, Ernesto. *On Populist Reason*. London: Verso, 2005.

Massumi, Brian. *Politics of Affect*. Cambridge: Polity Press, 2015.

Rancière, Jacques. *Disagreement: Politics and Philosophy*. Minneapolis: University of Minnesota Press, 1998.

Schmitt, Carl. *The Concept of the Political*. Expanded ed., transl. and with an introduction by George Schwab. Chicago: University of Chicago Press, 2007.

Villacañas Berlanga, José Luis. *Populismo*. Milan: Mimesis, 2018 (Italian translation). First published as *Populismo*. Madrid: La Huerta Grande, 2015.

Weber, Max. *Economy and Society: An Outline of Interpretive Sociology*. Ed. Guenther Roth, Claus Wittich, trans. H. H. Gerth, C. Wright Mills. Berkeley: University of California Press, 1978.

Zanatta, Loris. *Il Populismo*. Rome: Carocci, 2013.

What Can We Learn from Latin America to Understand Trump's Populism?

Carlos de la Torre

Even though it is uncertain what impact Donald Trump's populism will have on American democracy, it is worth learning from Latin America where populists have been in power since the 1930s/40s to the present. Even though Latin American populists like Juan Perón and Hugo Chávez included the poor and the non-white in their political community, they moved democracy towards a gray zone between dictatorship and democracy. Are the foundations of American democracy and the institutions of civil society strong enough to resist Trump's right wing populism?

My argument is divided into four sections. The first defines populism. The second section compares populist ruptures in the Americas, discussing Latin American leftwing populists like Hugo Chávez in Venezuela, Evo Morales in Bolivia, and Rafael Correa in Ecuador, who ruptured the neoliberal order and the rule of traditional political parties, with Trump, who is breaking down the neoliberal multicultural consensus of the elites of the Republican and Democratic parties. Third, the paper explores how 'the people' is performed to create solidarity among followers while hailing a politician as their savior. The last section uses the experiences of Latin American populists in power to speculate about the future of American democracy under Trump.

What is Populism?

I understand populism as political discourses and strategies that aim to rupture institutional systems by polarizing society into two antagonistic camps. In this regard, I differentiate social movements that use a populist rhetoric of the people against the establishment from populism. Without the presence of a leader, as Nadia Urbinati wrote, "a popular movement that uses a populist rhetoric (i.e., polarization and anti-representative discourse) is not yet populism" (129). Populist leaders claim that they represent and even embody the interests, will, and aspirations of a homogeneous people. All of those who challenge their claim to be the incarnation of the people are branded as enemies of the people, the leader, and the nation. Populists do not face political adversaries; they confront enemies at the symbolic level. As Juan Perón put it, when political adversaries become "enemies of the nation" they are no longer "gentlemen that one should fight fairly but snakes that one can kill in any way" (quoted in Finchelstein 86).

Populist parties seeking power need to be distinguished from populists in power. Whereas populists challenge the system or the establishment by promising to give power to the people, once in power they show their true anti-pluralist and antidemocratic colors. Once in office, populists concentrate power in the hands of the executive, disregard the division of power and the rule of law, and attack dissident voices in civil society and the public sphere. When populists assume power under conditions of crises of political representation and with weak democratic institutions, they move democracy toward authoritarianism. In more institutionalized political systems, they disfigure democracy by reducing its complexity to a Manichaean struggle between the leader as the embodiment of the people and their enemies.

Rightwing and leftwing variants of populism are not the same. To a large extent, the difference lies in how they imagine and construct the people. This category can be conceived with religious, ethnic, or political criteria, and as a diverse population or as a homogeneous actor. Constructs of the people as a community of believers, even when these communities are imagined as egalitarian, inherently exclude nonbelievers. Vedi R. Hadiz shows how the *ummah* of Islamic populism is made up of internally diverse social interests, homogenized as those pious members of the community who possess virtue through juxtaposition against immoral elites and their foreign non-Islamic allies. Similarly, the three Israeli populist parties – the ultra-orthodox Mizrahi party 'Shas,' Israel Our Home and the Likud party – are inclusionary of the community of believers while excluding nonbelievers (Filc). Likewise, in Western Europe and the United States, Christianity, Judeo-Christianity, or Christian-Secularism are politicized as an identity against Islam. Some European populist parties proclaim to be defenders of Western civilization, secularism, and individual freedom by casting Islam as the antithetical and inassimilable ultimate Other. Olivier Roy wrote that religion in Europe and the United States is a marker of cultural identity that enables populist parties to distinguish the 'good us' from the 'bad them,' understood in essentialist and ahistorical terms: "Christian identity for populists is strongly linked to a romanticized idea about how things were" (Roy 197). This promotes a kind of reconquering of a public space as Christian, and even of the human body by opposing circumcision and halal food.

Some populist movements in Europe and the United States, as well as Jair Bolsonaro in Brazil and Narendra Modi in India, use ethnicity to exclude minority populations. The people as constructed by Donald Trump, for example, confront ethnic and cultural enemies such as Muslims, Mexicans, or militant black activists (de la Torre 2017a). The image of the Mexican, as most Latinos in the United States are nowadays called, is built on longstanding nationalist stereotypes that marked them as lazy, dangerous, and as the ultimate outsiders to the US nation. Regardless of whether Mexicans and other Latino populations have lived for long periods in the United States, they are regarded as recent and passing immigrants, and as freeloaders who drain white taxpayers. The notion of the Muslim terrorist is not only a xenophobic reaction to 9/11, but is also built on legacies of the image of the United States as a Christian nation. Contrary to Latinos and Muslims, who can be attacked with blatantly racist words, Trump as well as the Tea Party and other conservatives use code words of law and order to mark the unruly black militant as a criminal and as the opposite of the law-abiding and taxpaying citizen.

The Tea Party and Trumpism, for example, contrast a virtuous white, hardworking, taxpaying, and law-abiding middle class against blacks and other people of color who are beneath them, while the controlling liberal and cosmopolitan elites are above (Judis). Similarly, right-wing European populists defend the ordinary people against those below such as immigrants, refugees, and former colonial subjects, while placing the privileged 'New Class' above.

Contrary to the exclusionary and racist view of the people as white, Evo Morales and his political party MAS (Movimiento al Socialismo), as Raúl L. Madrid in *The Rise of Ethnic Politics in Latin America* shows, successfully used inclusive ethnopopulist appeals. Given the fluidity of race and ethnic relations in Bolivia, they were able to create an inclusionary ethnic party grounded in indigenous social movements that appealed to different indigenous groups while also incorporating mestizo organizations and candidates.

An alternative conceptualization of the people is primarily political and socioeconomic. Left-wing populists in Latin America and Europe construct the category of the people as the majorities in their nations who are excluded by neoliberal policies imposed by supranational organizations like the IMF or the Troika. Podemos in Spain, for example, used an antagonistic discourse that aimed to rupture Spain's institutional system. It constructed an enemy, branded as 'the caste,' which has dominated political, economic, social, and cultural life since the pacted transition to democracy in the mid-1970s. 'The caste' is in an antagonistic relationship with the people, understood as the disenfranchised victims of neoliberalism. Similarly, Alexis Tsipras, the leader of Syriza in Greece, constructed the antagonism between the people and the neoliberal establishment in political and socioeconomic terms. The French socialist Jean-Luc Mélenchon also refuses left and right distinctions, claiming that when he gets to power his party La France Insoumise will not follow class-based politics, but politics for the people.

Hugo Chávez in Venezuela framed the political arena so that he did not face political rivals, but instead an oligarchy that he defined as the political enemy of the people, "those self-serving elites who work against the homeland" (Zúquete 105). His rhetoric politicized relationships of inequality between different classes and ethnic groups. He reclaimed Venezuela's indigenous and black heritages that were downplayed by the elites. Chávez tapped into the "deep reservoir of daily humiliation and anger felt by people of the lower classes" (Fernandes 85).

As Jürgen Habermas pointed out, "'the people' does not comprise a subject with a will and consciousness. It only appears in the plural, and as a people, it is capable of neither decision nor action as a whole" (469). Following these constructs, democrats imagine the people as a plurality of actors with different views and proposals. By constructing the people as plural, democrats face democratic rivals that have legitimate institutional and normative spaces.

On the contrary, populists like Donald Trump or Hugo Chávez claim, according to Jan Werner Müller, "that they and only they represent the true people" (40). Donald Trump, for example, has a unitary view of the people. In a rally in Florida he said, "The only important thing is the unification of the people – because the other people don't mean anything" (Müller 22).

Chávez constructed the 'people' as a sacred entity with a single consciousness and a will that could be embodied in his persona, the redeemer of the people. Chávez boasted, "This is not about Hugo Chávez; this is about a 'people.' I represent, plainly, the voice and the heart of millions" (quoted in Zúquete 100). On another occasion he commanded, "I demand absolute loyalty to me. I am not an individual, I am the people" (quoted in Gómez Calcaño et al. 20). Even though Chávez's populist political and socioeconomic construction of the people was inclusionary, his view of the people-as-one was anti-pluralist, and in the end anti-democratic, because a part of the population claimed to be its whole, and Chávez attempted to become its only voice.

Contrary to autocratic constructs of the people as one, left-wing populist parties like Syriza, Podemos, and Morales's MAS, claim to have plural views of the people. Yet at times their leaders also claim to be the only voice of the people. When indigenous people from the lowlands challenged Morales's policies on mineral extraction, they were dismissed as having been manipulated by foreign NGOs and not as authentically indigenous. Morales's regime attempted to construct an indigenous identity centered on loyalty to his government, which excluded and delegitimized all those who opposed him. But because of the power of social movements in whose name he argues he is ruling, Morales has not been able to impose his vision of the people-as-one. In contemporary Bolivia, according to anthropologist Nancy Postero, there is an "ongoing struggle to define who counts as *el pueblo boliviano*, and what that means for Bolivian democracy" (422). Similar tensions between the populist leaders attempting to be the only voice of the people and the resistance of their constituencies to become embodied in the voice of the leader occurs in Syriza and Podemos. Their constituencies have not succumbed to their leaders' claim.

When ethnic or religious views of the people are combined with constructs of the people as one, populism becomes exclusionary and antidemocratic. Under these conditions, populism can be a threat to the basic values of modernity as embodied in a plural, critical, and inclusive civil society. Political and socioeconomic constructions of the people can lead to inclusionary policies. Yet when 'the people' is viewed as one, as Chávez did, his populism was inclusionary and antidemocratic because he assumed that the part of the people he embodied was the only authentic people. Pluralist views of the socioeconomic and political constituency can be inclusionary and lead to more democracy. Yet as the cases of Morales and Tsipras illustrate, these leaders tried to be the only voice of the people.

Populist Ruptures in the Americas

Populist narratives paint existing institutional arrangements as impediments for the people to express its voice and will. As a consequence, populists aim to overhaul the establishment while promising to give power back to the people. Populism is a revolt against the appropriation of the popular will by political elites and the surrendering of national sovereignty to supranational institutions. The logic of populism is based on the construction of an enemy. Moreover, it is anti-institutional and can lead to the rupture of the existing system. Yet populist challenges do not always lead to ruptures. The latter take place only when political parties and the institutional framework of democracy are in crisis. In Venezuela, Bolivia, and Ecuador, populist leaders ruptured the elite consensus that linked neoliberal policies with electoral democracies. Hugo Chávez, Evo Morales, and Rafael Correa overhauled neoliberalism, enacted new constitutions, and displaced traditional political elites.

Néstor Kirchner assumed power in 2003 in a conjuncture that could have led to a populist rupture. Political parties were in crisis, Argentina had just gone through a deep economic collapse in 2001 and 2002, and there were strong movements of resistance to neoliberalism as workers took over factories and the unemployed occupied the streets and plundered supermarkets. Despite using a populist language of refoundation, the Kirchners were not committed to a populist rupture (Peruzzotti). But most importantly, their ambivalence in following the populist script was explained by how social movements and civil society reacted against what they perceived as authoritarian policies and practices. Thousands mobilized against Cristina Kirchner's agrarian policies. Her attempts to modify the constitution to allow for her reelection were resisted by civil society and an independent constitutional court. In sum, relatively strong democratic institutions and a complex civil society were impediments to a populist rupture in Argentina.

Donald Trump captured the Republican Party in a context of relative crisis of political parties but not of a generalized collapse of all democratic institutions. He nonetheless ruptured the elite consensus that linked globalization with limited policies of multicultural recognition to women, non-whites, and the LGBTQ communities. Whereas it will be easier to get rid of political correctness to please nationalist, racist, and xenophobic constituencies, it will be more difficult to abandon globalization, specifically by an administration committed to the free market ideology and to the dismantling of the regulatory welfare state.

Venezuela, Bolivia, and Ecuador underwent major crises of political representation. Political parties were perceived as instruments of local and foreign elites that implemented neoliberal policies and thereby increased social inequality. Traditional parties in these nations appeared as "a closed, self-interested, and self-reproducing governing caste insulated from popular needs and concerns" (Roberts 149). Traditional political parties collapsed as political outsiders rose to power on platforms that promised to eliminate corrupt politicians, use constitution-making to revamp all existing institutions, experiment with participatory forms of democracy, abandon neoliberal orthodoxy, and implement policies to redistribute income.

A second factor that led to populist ruptures was previously widespread popular resistance to neoliberalism. Examples of these popular insurrections against neoliberalism were the Venezuelan *Caracazo*, a massive insurrection against a hike in the price of gasoline named after the country's capital that was brutally repressed with as many as 400 casualties in February 1989 (López Maya et al. 244). Massive movements of resistance occurred against the three presidents of Ecuador that attempted to implement neoliberal structural reforms and were prevented from finishing their terms in office between 1997 and 2005 (de la Torre 2010: 142-155). The cycle of protest and political turmoil in Bolivia resulted in the collapse of both the party system that was established in 1985 and the neoliberal economic model (Dunkerley).

A third factor that led to populist ruptures and to the rise of left-wing populism in Latin America was the perception that politicians and neoliberal elites had surrendered national sovereignty to the US government and supranational institutions like the International Monetary Fund. These left-wing leaders proposed a counterproject to US dominated neoliberal trade initiatives. The Bolivarian Alliance for the Americas (ALBA) aimed for a real Latin American and Caribbean integration based on social justice and solidarity among the peoples. Their goals were to stop US domination in the region by promoting Latin American unity and to create a multi-polar international system.

Donald Trump's electoral campaign and presidency ruptured the neoliberal multicultural consensus. He promised to revise free trade agreements and bring back manufacturing jobs while using blatantly racist language against Mexicans and Muslims that challenged views of the United States as a post-racial society. He seemed to be the inheritor of the Tea Party, the rightwing insurrection against the first non-white president and his limited policies of redistribution such as universal health care.

Neoliberal deregulation of the financial system resulted in a housing boom that crashed in 2008. Millions lost their homes and financial institutions were at risk of collapsing. Barack Obama was elected with the hope that he would help citizens over bankers, yet his policies prioritized the financial system. Nonetheless, Obama introduced a stimulus package and a bill to help homeowners. In addition to this, he launched a national health insurance plan. In reaction, conservatives created the Tea Party in 2009 to resist his policies. The Tea Party was a collection of grassroots organizations, rightwing media, especially FOX News, and elites that funded conservative candidates and ideas (Skocpol et al. 190). They opposed Obamacare and mortgage relief as an attack by liberal elites against hard working citizens to give handouts to the undeserving poor.

The Tea Party was also a conservative reaction to the first non-white president. Obama was perceived as a foreigner, "an invader pretending to be an American [...]. His academic achievements and social ties put him in league with the country's intellectual elite whose [...] cosmopolitan leanings seemed unpatriotic" (Skocpol et al. 79). Donald Trump, a Birtherist who denied Obama's Americanness, reached beyond the Tea Party's social base of white older, wealthier, and more educated conservatives, appealing also to the white working class.

Trump challenged some basic tenants of neoliberalism. He opposed NAFTA and the Trans-Pacific Partnership agreement. He linked national decline with the absence of industrial production. He told crowds: "'We don't win anymore.' 'We don't make anything.' 'We are losing so much'" (quoted in Lowndes 2016: 99). Trump singled out corporations like Ford, Apple, Nabisco, and Carrier for moving factories overseas. He promised to bring manufacturing jobs back to the United States, and once in power, entered into trade wars with China.

Trump's nationalist critique of globalization was linked to the construction of illegal immigrants as parasitical 'others.' In 2011, he wrote: "Illegal immigration is a wrecking ball aimed at U.S. taxpayers." He urged elites to fight for "We the People, not for special interests who want cheap labor and a minority blocking block" (Judis 70). In his book entitled *Great Again: How to Fix Crippled America* Trump wrote, "we are the only country in the world whose immigration system places the needs of other nations ahead of our own" (2015a: 22). He argued that foreign governments encourage illegal immigration "to get rid of their worst people without paying any price for their bad behavior" (Trump 2015b) and launched his presidential candidacy from Trump Tower in New York City asserting,

When Mexico sends its people, they're not sending their best [...] They're bringing drugs. They're bringing crime. They're rapists. And some I assume, are good people [...]. I would build a great wall, and nobody builds walls better than me, believe me, and I'll build them very inexpensively. I will build a great, great wall on our southern border. And I will have Mexico pay for that wall." (23)

He expanded his racist platform by calling Muslims terrorists and promising to monitor Muslims within the United States and to ban those who want to enter the country. His anti-immigration racist and xenophobic words were similar to the views of many Tea Party supporters. Skocpol and Williamson wrote, "concern about illegal immigration is widespread in Tea Party circles, and draconian remedies are in vogue" (57). They viewed illegal immigrants as freeloaders who are draining US taxpayers by using social services and government funds. Tea Partiers advocated "restrictions on birthright citizenship, abridgments on freedom of religion for Muslim Americans, and suspension of protections in the Bill of Rights for suspected terrorists" (Skocpol et al. 50).

Like Tea Partiers, Trump did not use openly racist terms but coded words to describe African Americans as people who are held back because of their own personal failings. Trump's expressions of hostility were against African American protest groups like Black Lives Matter. Yet instead of repudiating his white supremacy supporters connected to the KKK or the alt-right, Trump embraced them, signaling that African Americans and non-whites were "members of the out group" (Hochschild 226). Liberal multicultural elites were depicted as hypocritical and corrupt because they aimed to have cheap Mexican labor and turn Hispanics into their voting block. Trump aimed to abolish multiculturalism and political correctness, promising a new era when white heterosexual males could express freely their views and opinions. Some of his fervent white supporters were filmed yelling, "Fuck political correctness" (Berenstein et al.).

Trump's message made sense to white voters' feelings of economic anxiety and racism (Cramer 89). His support base was not only made up of the 'losers' of globalization and uneducated white males. Middle class and educated white men and women also supported him because many felt that they were not getting their fair share, and that they faced economic insecurity in their lives that had not been previously addressed. They felt that women, blacks, Hispanic, and gays were empowered by unfair policies of affirmative action and political correctness that negatively targeted white heterosexual males. Many

> also felt culturally marginalized: their views about abortion, gay marriage, gender roles, race, guns, and the Confederate flag all were held in ridicule in the national media as backward. And they felt part of a demographic decline [...]. They'd begun to feel like a besieged minority. (Hochschild 221)

Trump, in sum, was "the identity politics candidate for white men" (Hochschild 230).

Populist ruptures in Latin America led to the abandonment of neoliberal policies. Chávez, Morales, and Correa strengthened the state and used it to redistribute wealth and reduce poverty and inequality. Venezuela, Bolivia, and Ecuador reaped huge benefits from the commodity boom of the 2000s, which had pushed up oil and natural gas prices to record levels. As a result of enhanced revenues, public investment and social spending skyrocketed, and poverty rates – and to a lesser extent inequality – fell when the prices of oil and other commodities were high (de la Torre et al. 2013: 12). It remains to be seen to which extent Trump's administration will dismantle the institutions and policies of the last decades that linked open markets and globalization to the limited cultural inclusion of minorities, women, and the LGBTQ communities. He aims to get rid of a consensus regarding multiculturalism, while attempting to restore a nostalgic mythical view of America as a white, protestant, heterosexual, and male dominated nation.

Performing the People

'The people' is performed and embodied in struggles and confrontations between politicians who claim to be their leaders, and even saviors, against those constructed as their enemies. Despite an innovative use of television to create media spectacles and social media like Twitter, Trump's campaign, like that of Latin American populists, made ample use of mass rallies. Trump's rallies showed his followers, who for the most part were whites, that they were no longer a 'besieged minority.' A politician who claimed to represent their interests and identities finally addressed thousands like them. As Trump said, he was the candidate of "the forgotten men and women of this country," the white working and middle class (Shane). To those "who attended his rallies, the event itself symbolizes a rising tide" (Hochschild 226).

In Ecuador, Rafael Correa, a college professor of economics-turned-politician creatively used television, the Internet, and mass rallies. In his first bid for the presidency in 2006 his campaign appearances blended music and dance with speech making. He spoke briefly, presenting an idea, while protest music of the 1970s played and Correa and the crowd sang along to the campaign tunes and danced. When the music stopped, Correa spoke briefly again, followed by music, songs, and dance. This innovative style allowed people to participate and produced feelings that under Correa's leadership all his followers were part of a common political project, a "citizens' revolution" against neoliberal politicians (de la Torre 2010: 184).

'Love' is the link between a leader and his followers. Donald Trump said that he loved the poorly educated. Hugo Chávez always talked about how much he loved his people. In the 2009 campaign to change the constitution with a referendum to allow for his permanent re-election, the following reasons were given to vote for Chávez's proposal: "because Chávez loves us, and we have to repay his love; because Chávez loves us and will not harm us; because Chávez and us are one" (Torres 2009: 231).

Populist mass rallies are designed to gratify followers and to make them feel good. Trump often told his audience: "let's go and have fun tonight." Chávez' mass rallies were often parties where he and his followers danced and proudly occupied public spaces. Other populists used violence to generate in-group solidarity. "Violent antagonism played a particularly strong role in the case of George Wallace, the threat, anticipation and performance of which was central to his image and success" (Lowndes 2005: 148). Trump used verbal and encouraged physical racial violence to create frontiers between his followers and the 'out groups,' and to arouse passions of anger in his rallies. Sociologist Arlie Russell Hochschild reports some of Trump's words about what to do with those protesting in his rallies: "I'd like to punch him in the face." "Knock the crap out of him, would you? I promise you I will pay the legal fees" (224). In one campaign rally, Trump pointed to a critic and said, "'There is a remnant left over. Maybe get the remnant out. Get the remnant out.' The crowd, taking its cue, then tried to root out other people who might be dissenters, all the while crying 'USA.' The candidate interjected: 'Isn't this more fun than a regular boring rally?'" (quoted in Snyder 45).

Some Trump supporters felt empowered to attack non-whites. In Boston, for example, two white men beat and urinated on a homeless Latino man saying, "Trump was right; all these illegals need to be deported." Instead of denouncing them, Trump justified their attack by asserting that the "people who are following me are very passionate. They love this country, and they want this country to be great again" (quoted in Lowndes 2016: 100).

Populist gatherings also intend to make a leader into a character larger than life. Chávez was erected into a savior who even risked his own life leading a military insurrection against president Carlos Andrés Pérez in 1992. At a rally in July 1998 declaring his candidacy, the former leader of a coup d'état was transformed into the embodiment of the democratic ideal.

> Chávez donned his trademark paratrooper's red beret and pumped his fist in the air before a cheering throng of ten thousand supporters [...]. 'Go ahead call me a coup leader,' he bellowed. Then he added: 'Raise your hands if you think the coup was justified.' A sea of hands went up. (Jones 215-6)

Since the beginning of his campaign, Trump referred to his own extraordinariness. "[...] [W]e need a truly great leader now. We need a leader that wrote 'The Art of the Deal' [...]. We need somebody that can take the brand of the United States and make it great again." Billionaire Donald Trump himself, "not a perfect fit for upper class America," (Judis 71) claimed to represent the people's dream for social mobility. He flaunted his wealth, his name became a brand for skyscrapers, hotels, casinos, and other commodities, he owned the Miss Universe franchise, and was a media celebrity. People in his rallies told ethnographer Arlie Russell Hochschild that they felt amazed to "be in the presence of such a man" (226). Despite his wealth, he was one of the common people but also incredibly superior to them. He shared their taste for wrestling, but unlike most fans he was inducted to the WWE Hall of Fame in 2013 with the words "Donald Trump is a 'WrestleMania' institution" (Oster).

Populist leaders are linked to myths. Some are religiously inspired, others more secular. The persona of Hugo Chávez symbolized the myths of Bolivar, the liberator, and of Jesus Christ, the Savior. His political movement, the new constitution and Venezuela were re-baptized as 'Bolivarian.' He was erected by his followers into the carrier of Bolívar's project of national and continental liberation. He asserted to be following in the footsteps of the "true Bolívar, the Bolívar of the people, the revolutionary Bolívar" (Torres 246). He even changed the old whitish images of Bolivar's representations. Chávez's Bolivar was portrayed with a brown skin color similar to his devotees,' regardless of the fact that the liberator came from a family of slave owners. To celebrate the tenth anniversary of his presidency, Chávez visited the tomb of Bolívar and asserted, "Ten years ago, Bolívar – embodied in the will of the people – came back to life" (Lindholm et al. 24).

Chávez constantly invoked "Jesus as 'my commander in chief' and as 'the Lord of Venezuela'" (Lindholm et al. 33). Chávez compared his leadership to Jesus Christ's. In 1999 he asserted, "true love for other human beings is measured by whether you can die for others; and here we are ready to die for others" (Torres 230). His prophetic words of following Jesus' example of giving his life to liberate his people were dramatically manifested when Chávez compared his agony with cancer with the passion of Christ. During a religious service broadcast by national television during Holy Week in 2012, he prayed out loud:

> Give me life [...]. Christ give me your crown of thorns. Give it to me that I bleed. Give me your cross [...]. Give me life because I still need to do things for this people and motherland. Do not take me. Give me your cross, your thorns, your blood. I will carry them, but give me life. Christ my Lord. Amen. (Chavez; translation mine)

His followers erected Chávez into a saint-like figure with the powers to heal. Psychoanalyst and writer Ana Teresa Torres in *La Herencia de la Tribu* (229) narrates two episodes: In 1999, an elderly woman grabbed him by the arm to beg "Chávez help me my son has paralysis." A crying young man stopped him outside the door of Caracas Cathedral and told him, "Chávez help me, I have two sons that are dying of hunger and I do not want to become a delinquent, save me from this inferno."

After his death, his handpicked successor, Nicolás Maduro, consecrated Chávez into a secular saint. Mariana González Trejo's Ph.D. dissertation (138-41) explains how Maduro buried Chávez in a newly built shrine, a pantheon that "symbolizes the renaissance of the homeland and the immeasurable life of the Eternal Commandant." His coffin has the inscription "Supreme Commander of the Bolivarian Revolution."

And above his sarcophagus in the center there is a portrait of Bolívar next to one of Chávez as his 'son.'

Donald Trump triumphed in two mythical and almost religious arenas of American capitalism: the business world and mass entertainment. Billionaire Donald Trump with the TV show *The Apprentice*, which he hosted for fourteen seasons, became a media sensation, claiming "we need somebody that can take the brand of the United States and make it great again."

Like other populist politicians, Trump personalized politics. He demonized his enemies as inherently immoral and corrupt: 'Crooked Hillary' and 'Corrupt Kaine.' Hillary Clinton used a sophisticated technocratic language to make arguments about the economy or world politics, while Trump resorted to commonplaces and generalities. To 'Make America Great Again', he argued what was needed was a successful businessman and popular culture impresario who has not been corrupted by the deals of politicians and lobbyists. He stirred emotions and was able to construct politics as a wrestling match between good incarnated in his persona and the crooked establishment personified by Hilary Clinton. She was portrayed as the embodiment of all that is wrong with America, and without a proper trial Trump and his followers condemned her to prison, chanting in his rallies "Lock her up!" Many proudly wore T-shirts or carried signs that read "Hillary for Prison."

Trump claimed to be the only truth teller, "someone who could represent what Americans really think, and perhaps more importantly, feel" (Lowndes 2016: 99). A biker for Trump told journalist Ed Pilkington that Trump "speaks his own mind." A woman with the colors of the American flag in her hat said that Trump spoke from the heart, which was different from professional politicians. "He's down to our level. He speaks it like it is." British journalist Matt Taibbi reported that a young Pennsylvanian supporter of Trump told him, "[W]hen Trump talks, I actually understand what he's saying ... But like, when fricking Hillary Clinton talks, it just sounds like a bunch of bullshit" (Taibbi 2016).

Similarly to leftwing populist that confronted traditional political parties and the oligarchy, Trump claimed: "the establishment, the media, the special interest, the lobbyists, the big donors, they are all against me" (quoted in Judis 72). His final TV campaign advertisements indicted the "failed and corrupt political establishment" for giving up America's sovereignty to global and greedy elites that brought "destruction to our factories." With images of the predominantly white crowds that attended his rallies he concluded, "The only thing that can stop this corrupt machine is you. I am doing this for the people and for the movement" (*Trump for President*).

Populist leaders project a variety of masculine images to suggest that they are "uniquely suited to attacking elites, to uniting the people against outsiders, to embodying the nation" (Kampwirth 10). Some brag about their hyper-masculinities. Ecuadorian populist Abdalá Bucaram said that one of his rivals had watery sperm, and of another that he had no balls (de la Torre 2010). Similarly, Trump bragged about the size of his genitalia, and his purported masculine superiority seemed manifested in his power to grab any desirable women, pointing to middle-aged Hillary Clinton as undesirable.

Some populist leaders use their personal success in business, the media, mass culture, the military, or sports to show their extraordinariness. Like Silvio Berlusconi, Trump used his success in the business world to claim his superiority. Brazil's former President Fernando Collor de Mello used his triumphs in the world of sports. Perón and Chávez presented themselves as brilliant military men who sacrificed their military careers for their nations.

The image most populist leaders share is their claim to be the fathers of their homelands. The former Brazilian president Getúlio Vargas claimed to be "the father of the poor," while Lázaro Cárdenas was "tata Lázaro." During his campaign, Trump represented the image of a good father by surrounding himself with his children. Later, he named his eldest daughter and son-in-law political advisers with almost unrestricted access to the White House. His image as a wealthy good father symbolically promised to gather under his wise paternal tutelage all of those who uncritically accepted his wisdom. The father metaphor, as Karen Kampwirth wrote, "turns citizens into permanent children. It turns a politician into someone who understands the interests of citizens – even when they do not – and who may punish wayward children who fail to recognize their wisdom" (12). The job of a father never ends, which can be seen in populists from Perón to Chávez and Morales, who attempted to stay in power indefinitely.

Populists in Power

This section discusses how Latin American populist presidents used a playbook to concentrate power in their hands, restrict pluralism, and curb freedoms of expression and association. I then draw lessons from these Latin American experiences to speculate about the future of democracy in America under Trump.

By 1950, when the Argentine President Juan Perón had been in office for four years, he reformed the constitution to allow for his reelection. By that time, all institutions of government were in Peronist hands. Perón "had already replaced the members of the Supreme Court with staunch defenders of the regime, had gained firm control over Congress, and had tamed the labor movement" (Plotkin 98). As historian Luis Alberto Romero argues, "at every level of government, all power was concentrated in the hands of the executive – whether mayor, governor, or president – making it clear that the movement and the nation were considered one" (110).

Similarly, Chávez in Venezuela, incrementally gained nearly absolute command of all institutions of the state. He had a supermajority in the legislature, and in 2004 put the highest judicial authority, the Supreme Tribunal of Justice, in the hands of loyal judges. Hundreds of lower court judges were fired and replaced by unconditional supporters (Hawkins 11). The National Electoral Council was politicized. Although it made sure that the moment of voting was clean and free from fraud, it did not enforce rules during the electoral process routinely favoring Chávez and his candidates. In Ecuador, Rafael Correa also put loyal followers in charge of the electoral power, the judicial system, the electoral board, and all the institutions of accountability, such as the Ombudsman and the Comptroller (de la Torre et al 2016: 225).

To impose their version of reality as the only permitted truth, Perón closed oppositional newspapers. Chávez and Correa also created laws to control the content of what the privately owned media could publish or broadcast. In 2000, the Organic Law of Telecommunication allowed the Chávez government to suspend or revoke broadcasting concessions to private outlets when it was "convenient for the interest of the nation" (Corrales 39). In 2013, Correa enacted a communication law that created a government institution tasked with monitoring and regulating the content of what the media could publish. These presidents took away radio and television stations from critics. Under Chávez, the Venezuelan state became the main communicator by controlling 64 percent of television channels (Corrales 41). Correa created a state media conglomerate that included the two most-watched TV stations in Ecuador as well as several radio stations and newspapers (de la Torre et al 2016: 231).

Chávez and Correa suffocated the private media by reducing government advertisement to critical media venues and by manipulating subsidies for the price of paper (Waisbord). They used discriminatory legalism understood as the use of formal legal authority in discretionary ways to sue, harass, and intimidate journalists and private media owners (Weyland 23).

Populist administrations regulated the work of non-governmental organizations (NGOs). In Venezuela, NGOs that defended political rights or monitored the performances of public bodies were forbidden from receiving international assistance (Corrales 39). Correa enacted legislation that gave the government the authority to sanction NGOs for engaging in politics or for interfering in public policies in a way that allegedly contravened internal and external security or disturbed public peace. To set an example, the environmentalist organization Pachama Alliance was closed down for supposedly deviating from the original organization's goals and for interfering with public policy and security (de la Torre et al 2016: 229-230).

To counteract the power of worker's unions, unionized teachers, students, and indigenous groups, loyal social movements were created top down. Protest was criminalized in these nations. Union leaders and striking workers, even when they were sympathizers of Chávez, were charged with terrorism (Iranzo 28-31). In

Ecuador, hundreds of peasant and indigenous activists were accused of terrorism and sabotage.

It is worth using Latin American experiences with populists in power to speculate about the future of democracy under Trump. The constitutional frame of American democracy constrains and fragments political expression. The Constitution "separates governance between three branches of government, breaks up representation over time and space (staggered elections, overlapping electoral units), divides sovereignty between the national government and the states, and filters political expression into two parties" (Lowndes 2016: 97). Under these institutional constrains, it is difficult to find majoritarian control of government as in Latin America, and, until Trump's election, populism was confined to the margins of the political system. Perhaps populist movements are ultimately unsustainable in America's liberal democracy. "Homogeneous notions of the people and the transparency of representation between the people and its leaders in a large, diverse and modern society is no more than a fantasy of wholeness" (Lowndes 2005: 169). Trump's populism under this hypothesis would be no more than a passing nightmare, and the institutional framework of US democracy and civil society would be strong enough to process populist challenges without major destabilizing consequences (Weyland et al.).

An alternative and plausible scenario is that Trump, who comes to the presidency when the executive has more power over the legislative, when the Senate and Congress are in the hands of Republicans, and with the power to name ultra-conservatives to the Supreme Court, could attempt to follow the Latin American populist playbook of trying to control all the institutions of the state. He has already placed loyalists in key positions of power, he has threatened Republicans who did not support him wholeheartedly during the campaign, and he aims to transform the Republican Party – a party to which he does not have any long lasting loyalty – into his personal venue.

Like his Latin American populist cousins, Trump does not like the media. In his campaign rallies, he led his followers to heckle journalists who were seated in a separate section. He has threatened to use libel and to sue newspapers, examples of which include when he said, "The Rolling Stone magazine should be put out of business," and when he threatened to sue *The New York Times*. During the campaign, "journalists who opposed Mr. Trump received photos of themselves — and in some cases their children — dead, or in gas chambers. Jewish and Jewish-surnamed journalists were particular targets [...]" (Caldwell; see also de la Torre 2017b). After assuming power Trump embarked on a war against the media. Like Chávez and Correa, he has argued that the media is a political machine that aims to harm his policies on behalf of the American people. He tweeted that the *New York Times*, NBC, ABC, CBS, and CNN are the "enemy of the American people" (@realDonaldTrump, 17 Feb 2017).

Trump's policies of massive deportation, stop and frisk in poor and predominantly Black and Latino neighborhoods, surveillance of American Muslims, and rolling back gender and LGBTQ rights will lead to confrontations with civil and human rights organizations. Even if the institutional framework of democracy does not collapse under Trump, he has already damaged the democratic public sphere. Hate speech and the denigration of minorities are replacing the politics of cultural recognition and tolerance built by the struggles of feminist and anti-racist social movements since the 1960s. Trump's potential incremental attacks on civil liberties and human rights, confrontations with the media, use of the legal system to silence critics, could, as in Venezuela and Ecuador, disfigure democracy.

Conclusion

Populists challenged neoliberal orthodoxy and the rule of experts, politicizing the political economy. They construct powerful anti-establishment identities, and give their followers the feeling that their voices are no longer marginalized. Leftwing Latin American populists abandoned neoliberalism; Trump, as well, might terminate the neoliberal multicultural consensus of Republican and Democratic elites based on linking globalization with the cultural recognition of different identity groups.

This article also showed how different constructions of the people could or could not lead to autocratic forms of populism. Rightwing populism is based on portrayals of the people as ethnically 'pure,' and racist and xenophobic constructs of the out groups. They also view the people as a unitary collective threatened by non-white and/or Muslim foreign others. Rightwing populists like Trump do not promise more democracy. They are backward-looking and want to restore an imaginary glorious past.

The examples of Chávez and Correa illustrate that populist promises of redemption made in the name of a unitary people end in authoritarianism. In their respective nations, populists did not only restrict the rights and freedoms of the oligarchy, the rightwing, or the upper classes. Chávez and Correa, for example, silenced, coopted, and repressed critical social movements, NGOs, and parties of the left as well. They used discriminatory legalism to mute critics and undermined the freedoms and rights that would allow social movements to push for their demands. Populists in Latin America did not obliterate democracy. They created hybrid regimes that preserved some democratic freedoms like elections, and regulated but not totally dominated civil society and the public sphere. This hybridity meant that some institutional spaces could be used to resist the leader's attempts to create the fantasy of the people as one.

Chávez and Correa tried to construct the people as one homogenous entity whose will they claimed to embody. Morales' and his political party, the MAS, differed from these autocratic constructs by having a more pluralist view of the people. Morales, at times, tried to follow the populist playbook by attempting to be the only and truthful voice of all Bolivians. Yet, powerful social movements used the notion that they were the voice of the people to challenge Morales.

Populism is not a pathology – it is part of democracy (Arditi). Populists politicize exclusions, point to the malfunctions of democracies, and demand better forms of democratic representation and participation. The populist critique of existing democracies cannot be ignored or dismissed. It is pointless to defend existing democracies without taking into consideration the populist critique. Ernesto Laclau and his collaborators argue that given the inevitability of populist revolts against the marginalization of citizens from politics, the task of the left is to construct popular democratic subjects (Errejón et al.). Otherwise, rightwing populists would give expression to popular grievances, and working class politics would be expressed through nationalist and xenophobic languages (Errejón et al.). They maintain that with the global rise of neoliberalism, understood as a rational and scientific mode of governance, public debate on the political economy is closed and replaced by the imposition of the criteria of experts. When all parties accept neoliberalism and the rule of technocrats, citizens cannot choose between alternatives. Politics would then be reduced to an administrative enterprise. Democracy is depoliticized and citizens transformed into mere consumers.

Populism, Laclau and others argue, entails the renaissance of politics. It is a revolt against technocratic reasoning, the surrendering of national sovereignty to supranational institutions and of the popular will to neoliberal political elites. Instead of allowing the right to politicize fears of migration and multiculturalism, they argue for the necessity of leftist variants of populism. Yet, Latin America's experience with populists in power should give words of caution to praises of leftwing populism, tout court. Whereas Laclau is right in arguing that populism politicized neoliberal administrative orders, populist Schmittian views of the political are dangerous because they are anti-pluralist, and in the end antidemocratic. Populism attacks institutions that are "an indispensable bulwark against political despotism" (Wolin 251). Constitutionalism, the separation of powers, freedom of speech, assembly, and the press are necessary to the politics of participatory democracy, to strengthen the public sphere, and to allow independent social movements to push for their democratizing demands. Populists in power, even those that promised more democracy and the end of neoliberalism, targeted precisely the constitutional framework of democracy. At first, populists eroded and disfigured democracy using democratic procedures and tools like elections towards undemocratic ends. In the end, their systematic attacks on civil rights and liberties and their attempts to control and coopt civil society and the public sphere pushed democracy towards authoritarianism. Institutionalized democracies are not immune to populist autocratic challenges. Trump disfigured the democratic and tolerant public sphere, normalizing hate speech, xenophobia, and racism. It is an open question whether his incremental attacks on civil liberties and human rights, confrontations with the media, and potential use of the legal system to silence critics, especially if there is a crisis of national security provoked by a terrorist attack or war, could give Trump the excuse to crackdown on dissent to impose his autocratic nationalist policies. In this bleak scenario his populism could lead, as in Venezuela, to the slow death of democracy.

Works Cited

Arditi, Benjamín. *Politics at the Edge of Liberalism. Difference, Populism, Revolution, Agitation*. Edinburgh: Edinburgh University Press, 2007.

Berenstein, Erica, Nick Corosaniti, and Ashley Parker. "Unfiltered Voices from Donald Trump's Crowds." *The New York Times* 3 August 2016 <https://www.nytimes.com/video/us/politics/100000004533191/unfiltered-voices-from-donald-trumps-crowds>.

Caldwell, Christopher. "What the Alt-Right Really Means." 2 December 2016 <http://www.nytimes.com/2016/12/02/opinion/sunday/what-the-alt-right-really-means.html?smprod=nytcore-iphone&smid=nytcore-iphone-share&_r=0>.

Chavez, Hugo. <http://runrun.es/runrunes/40538/la-nueva-religiosidad-de-chavez-revelala-gravedad-de-su-cancer.html>.

Corrales, Javier. 2015. "Autocratic Legalism in Venezuela." *Journal of Democracy* 26.2 (2015): 37-51.

Cramer, Katherine. "Listening to Rural Populist Support for Right-Leaning Candidates in the United States." *Comparative Politics Newsletter*. Ed. Matt Golder and Sona N. Golder. 26.2 (Fall 2016): 86-91.

de la Torre, Carlos (ed.). *The Routledge Handbook of Global Populism*. New York: Routledge, 2019.

---. "Trumps Populism. Lessons from Latin America." *Postcolonial Studies* 20.2 (2017a): 187-98.

---. "Trumpism and the Future of Democracy in America." *Clingendael Spectator* 71.3 (2017b):1-9. <https://www.clingendael.org/pub/2017/3/trumpism-and-democracy/>.

--- (ed.). *The Promise and Perils of Populism*. Lexington: The University Press of Kentucky Press, 2015.

---. *Populist Seduction in Latin America*. Athens: Ohio University Press, 2010 (second edition).

de la Torre, Carlos, and Cynthia Arnson (eds.). *Populism of the Twenty First Century*. Baltimore, MD and Washington, DC: The Johns Hopkins University Press and the Woodrow Wilson Center Press, 2013.

---. "Introduction: The Evolution of Latin American Populism and the Debates over its Meaning." Carlos de la Torre and Cynthia Arnson. 1-35.

de la Torre, Carlos, and Andrés Ortiz Lemos. "Populist polarization and the slow death of democracy in Ecuador." *Democratization* 23.2 (2016): 221-41.

Donald J. Trump for President. Advertisement. "We'll take our country back': Trump's final campaign ad released." 8 November 2016 <https://www.dailymail.co.uk/video/news/video-1354417/We-ll-country-Trump-s-final-campaign-ad-released.html>.

Dunkerley, James. "Evo Morales, the 'Two Bolivias' and the Third Bolivian Revolution." *Journal of Latin American Studies* 39 (2007): 133-66.

Errejón, Iñigo, and Chantall Mouffe. Construir Pueblo. *Hegemonía y radicalización de la democracia*. Madrid: Icaria, 2015.

Fernandes, Sujatha. *Who Can Stop the Drums? Urban Social Movements in Chávez Venezuela*. Durham: Duke University Press, 2010.

Filc, Daniel. "Populism in the Middle East." Carlos de la Torre (2019). 385-402.

Finchelstein, Federico. The Ideological Origins of the Dirty War. Oxford: Oxford University Press, 2014.

Gómez Calcaño, Luis, and Nelly Arenas. "El populismo chavista: autoritarismo electoral para amigos y enemigos." *Cuadernos del CENDES* 82 (2013): 17-34.

González Trejo, Mariana. *Pueblo y Democracia en el Populismo Venezolano*. Tesis Doctoral. Departamento de Ciencias Políticas y Relaciones Internacionales, Universidad Autónoma de Madrid, 2017.

Habermas, Jürgen. *Between Facts and Norms*. Cambridge: MIT Press, 1996.

Hadiz, Vedi. "Islamic Populism and the Politicization of Neoliberal Inequalities." Carlos de la Torre (2019). 176-90.

Hawkins, Kirk. "Responding to Radical Populism: Chavism in Venezuela." *Democratization* 23.2 (2016): 242-62.

Hochschild, Arlie Russell. *Strangers in Their Own Land. A Journey to the Heart of Our Political Divide*. New York: The New Press, 2016.

Iranzo, Consuelo. "Chávez y la política laboral en Venezuela 1999-2010." *Revista Trabajo* 5.8 (2011): 5-37.

Jones, Bart. ¡Hugo!. Hanover New Hampshire: Steerforth Press, 2007.

Judis, John B. *The Populist Explosion: How the Great Recession Transformed American and European Politics*. New York: Columbia Global Reports, 2016.

Kampwirth, Karen. "Introduction." *Gender and Populism in Latin America*. Ed. Karen Kampwirth. University Park: The University of Pennsylvania Press, 2010. 1-25.

Lindholm, Charles, and Zúquete, José Pedro. *The Struggle for the World: Liberation Movements for the 21st Century*. Stanford: Stanford University Press, 2010.

López Maya, Margarita, and Alexandra Panzarelli. "Populism, Rentierism, and Socialism in the Twenty First Century." Carlos de la Torre and Cynthia Arnson 239-69.

Lowndes, Joseph. 2016. "Populism in the 2016 U.S. election." *Comparative Politics Newsletter*. Ed. Matt Golder and Sona N. Golder. 26.2 (2016): 97-101.

---. "From Founding Violence to Political Hegemony: The Conservative Populism of George Wallace." *Populism and the Mirror of Democracy*. Ed. Francisco Panizza. London: Verso, 2005. 144-72.

Madrid, Raúl. *The Rise of Ethnic Politics in Latin America*. Cambridge. Cambridge University Press, 2012.

Müller, Jan Werner. *What is Populism?* Philadelphia: University of Pennsylvania Press, 2016.

Oster, Aaron. "Donald Trump and WWE. How the Road to the White House Began with Wrestlemania" *Rolling Stone* 1 February 2016 <http://www.rollingstone.com/sports/features/donald-trump-and-wwe-how-the-road-to-the-white-house-began-at-wrestlemania-20160201>.

Peruzzotti, Enrique. "El kirchnerismo y la teoría política: la vision de Guillermo O'Donnell y Ernesto Laclau." *¿Década Ganada? Evaluando el Kirchnerismo*. Ed. Carlos Gervasoni and Enrique Peruzzotti. Buenos Aires: Debate, 2015. 389-411.

Pilkington, Ed. "Inside a Donald Trump Rally: Good People in a Feedback of Paranoia and Hate." *The Guardian* 30 October 2016 <https://www.theguardian.com/us-news/2016/oct/30/donald-trump-voters-rally-election-crowd>.

Plotkin, Mariano. *Mañana es San Perón: A Cultural History of Peron's Argentina*. Wilmington: Scholarly Resources, 2003.

Postero, Nancy. "'El Pueblo Boliviano de Composición Plural': A Look at Plurinational Bolivia." Carlos de la Torre 2015: 398-431.

Roberts, Kenneth. "Populism, Political Mobilizations, and Crises of Political Representation." Carlos de la Torre 2015: 140-159.

Romero, Luis Albero. *A History of Argentina*. University Park: Pennsylvania State University Press, 2002.

Roy, Olivier. "Beyond Populism: The Conservative Right, the Courts, the Churches, and the Concept of a Christina Europe." *Saving the People: How Populist Hijack Religion*. Ed. Nadia Marzouki, Duncan McDonnell, and Olivier Roy. Oxford: Oxford University Press, 2016. 189-203.

Shane, Scott. "Combative Populist Steve Bannon Found his Man in Donald Trump." 27 November 2016 <http://www.nytimes.com/2016/11/27/us/politics/steve-bannon-white-house.html>.

Skocpol, Theda, and Vanessa Williamson. *The Tea Party and the Remaking of Republican Conservatism*. Oxford: Oxford University Press, 2012.

Smith, David. "Populism, Nationalism, and U.S. Foreign Policy." *Comparative Politics Newsletter*. Ed. Matt Golder and Sona N. Golder. 26.2 (Fall 2016): 101-7.

Snyder, Timothy. *On Tyranny: Twenty Lessons from the Twentieth Century*. New York: Tim Duggan Books, 2017.

Taibbi, Matt. "President Trump: How America Got It So Wrong." *Rolling Stone* 10 November 2016 <https://www.rollingstone.com/politics/politics-features/president-trump-how-america-got-it-so-wrong-112032/>.

Torres, Ana Teresa. *La Herencia de la Tribu: Del Mito de la Independencia a la Revolución Bolivariana*. Caracas: Editorial ALFA, 2009.

Trump, Donald. *Great Again: How to Fix Crippled America*. New York: Threshold Editions by Simon & Schuster, 2015a.

---. "Presidential Announcement Speech." 16 June 2015b <http://time.com/3923128/donald-trump-announcement-speech/>.

Urbinati, Nadia. *Democracy Disfigured: Opinion, Truth, and the People*. Cambridge: Harvard University Press, 2014.

Waisbord, S. Vox Populista, Medios, Periodismo, Democracia. Buenos Aires: Gedisa, 2013.

Weyland, Kurt. "The Threat from the Populist Left." *Journal of Democracy* 24.3 (2013): 18-33.

Weyland, Kurt, and Raúl Madrid. "Liberal Democracy, Stronger than Populism So Far." *The American Interest* 13.4 (2018): 24-9.

Wolin, Richard. *The Frankfurt School Revisited*. New York and London: Routledge, 2006.

Zúquete, José Pedro. "The Missionary Politics of Hugo Chávez." *Latin American Politics and Society* 50.1 (2008): 91-122.

Populism in Brazil: Getúlio Vargas and Jair Bolsonaro

Ursula Prutsch

On October 28, 2018, more than thirty years after the end of the military dictatorship in Brazil, Jair Bolsonaro won the presidential election after openly campaigning on a platform advocating torture, persecution of dissidents, and the dissolution of democratic institutions. His victory can serve as a warning with regard to the rapid erosion of stable democracies – his victory, after all, was based on a combination of collective dissatisfaction with the government, religious indoctrination, misguided historical policies, and an aggressive social media campaign.

After two decades of left-wing populist regimes in Latin America, the election of a right-wing populist prompts two necessary and critical questions: Is this shift to the right in Brazil's history unusual? And, did recent developments in Brazil foment the establishment of such a regime? To answer these questions, I will describe Bolsonaro's campaign strategies as those of, allegedly, a newcomer to Brazilian politics, and the first political decisions under his presidency. First, as a preface for my discussion, I will outline my understanding of populism in an introductory chapter and then provide some reasons as to why populist policies historically unfolded in Brazil much later than in the United States.

Remarks on Populism

Populism is a multi-faceted term that has undergone numerous changes throughout its history on the American continent. In contrast to Cas Mudde and Rovira Kaltwasser, my understanding of populism is not that of a 'thin-centered ideology' but of a bundle of domination techniques that can fit into different political and economic systems, dictatorships and democracies, as well as co-exist with economic nationalism as well as neoliberalism (Prutsch 2019).

Populism often results from internal and external political situations of crisis, but it can also manifest itself in power conflicts between rival parties and contrasting world views. To be sure, populists often talk about crises – or even create crises – and exploit the shortcomings of established politicians. Populists attack liberal representative democracy, which they believe to be elitist. They want to end the claim to power of a 'bourgeois' middle class by demanding equal rights for the poorer classes and by opening up opportunities for social aspirants. It is not a coincidence that many populist leaders in Latin America have been promoters of social policies.

Populism is not bound to specific religious beliefs. It is often – but not always – anti-elitist and anti-intellectual, as I will show through my examination of Getúlio Vargas' policy in Brazil. Populism can be an authoritarian form of governance or develop from a broad civic base. It can, as in the United States, have roots in a rural movement or, as in Latin America, can unfold in an urban metropolis and seek to integrate rural life. Populist politics are developing in industrial nations and in so-called emerging countries, in centers and in peripheries. Its identity-determining role is decisive. However, very few populist regimes would describe themselves as such. Moreover, it is a relative term that bears some complexity primarily in its relationship to an adversary (see the contribution of Carlos de la Torre in this volume).

While considering this relativity, I assume a more definite concept of populism. I strictly differentiate between populist movements and their governmental claims vis-à-vis popular grassroots strategies. My concept of populism does not include situational elements such as when a politician mingles with the people, calls upon the people, or makes his phone number public – this, for me, is not yet populism. In line with Jan-Werner Müller (2016, 2017), I believe that there is no 'good' populism. Moreover, from a historical point of view, it makes little sense analytically to define a populist prototype in order to describe deviations afterwards, especially considering the long historical development of this kind of rule in different geographic and socio-political contexts. This is a quality typical of concepts that turn into sites of struggle – a tendency towards vagueness and being devoid of meaning – and this also applies to populism. This tendency has the potential to prevent us from describing it methodically and analytically.

For me, there are ten defining characteristics of populism and populist rhetoric: crisis and stasis, (re)gaining individual sovereignty, (re)gaining national sovereignty, inclusion and exclusion, the relationship between 'the people' and democracy, 'the people' versus elites and experts, populism as a counter-movement, the principle of irreconcilable worlds through demagogy and polarization, the instrumentalization of media through fake news and conspiracy theories, and, finally, the personality of populist leaders, their origins, and their charisma.

When reading about Latin America in various media and in a number of studies on populism from a global perspective (Jörke et al.), it becomes apparent that populism is seen as an unchanging phenomenon there. But there are very different manifestations of populist systems, because each Latin American nation has its own historical development and distinct ethnic and political characteristics.

The Recent Development of Populism in Latin America Compared to the United States

There are historical reasons why Latin American populists – regardless whether they are to be seen as politically left or right – are often members of the military (such as Juan Perón, Hugo Chávez, Jair Bolsonaro, Velasco Ibarra) and inclined to authoritarian and autocratic behavior. They mostly steer their politics 'from above,' while generating discourses of being representatives of 'the people.' The late appearance of populist regimes compared to the United States has also historical reasons. In contrast to the United States, where the grass root movement of the *People's Party* had consolidated in the 1890s, the first wave of populist politics in Latin America developed in the late 1930s.

When thirteen British mainland colonies broke away from Britain in a war of independence to establish the United States, they continued building on the experience of a 250-year old tradition of partial self-government (Hochgeschwender). The wars of independence in Spanish America thirty years later were also wars for domestic power. As a result, the Spanish colonial empire in America (with the exceptions of Cuba and Puerto Rico) disintegrated into nation-state republics. Their rapidly changing governments formulated idealistic constitutions, mostly based on the United States or France, which often quickly fell apart due to their lack of political experience and political will (Tobler et al.). Governments swayed between Pan-American visions, centralist versus federalist models, democratic ideals, and autocratic realities (Rinke). Brazil was unique in that it gained autonomy from Portugal without a war of independence but rather through local revolts. It was an empire until 1889 and maintained a system of slavery until 1888, which the Spanish-speaking republics gradually abolished from the middle of the nineteenth century onward.

Local military leaders – Spanish *Caudillos* or Portuguese *Coronéis* – with their networks as well as the persistence of a hierarchical church also led to a greater paternalism in Latin America and to this day continue to enforce developments and power strategies centrally 'from above.' Latin American governments are mostly presidential democracies and the most important office in the state is determined by direct elections. The immediate re-election of a president was often constitutionally prohibited to prevent the kind of personalism, inherent in *Caudillismo*, but in the twentieth century, a couple of states have overturned this rule by way of constitutional amendments. Some of these states' leaders were populists such as Juan Perón in Argentina, Hugo Chávez and Nicolás Maduro in Venezuela, and Evo Morales in Bolivia.

Whereas General George Washington disbanded the army in 1783 due to an obvious lack of money, the new nation states in Spanish America never demilitarized. The war of independence against Spain had led to the formation of numerous private armies and guerrillas (Tobler et al.). It was not uncommon for local landlords to be village leaders and leaders of their guerrillas at the same time. Feudal structures survived in the countryside. Due to the short-lived nature of many governments, the military took on political functions, and in some places the armed forces became a 'fourth power.' Thus, the army did not only assume security and border protection functions, it also saw itself as an institution of political reform and as such it even operated companies in various countries and sectors, such as real estate in the tourist sector (Tobler).

Political stability and the availability of land, which had been brutally seized from Native Americans in the course of westward expansion, led to a systematically promoted immigration policy in the United States, earlier than in Latin America. Pivotal laws such as the land ordinances of the 1780s and the Homestead Act of 1862 on the parceling and sale of cheap state land provided affordable terrains for poorer migrants in the United States, while large estates dominated in Latin America. Universal male suffrage was introduced in the United States in 1830, at a time when a technology 'revolution' created a new middle class, but the Latin American states remained elitist and upheld a suffrage that required a certain income, and specifically a particular tax. Emergency regulations maintained social and ethnic hierarchies in multi-ethnic states.

Both nation-building processes and the rise of a broad middle class began earlier in the United States. Considering the high degree of literacy, far more population groups could be reached and mobilized in the late nineteenth century in the United States than in the 'South.' In Latin America, populist movements became possible when the radio became affordable as a tool of communication and entertainment, which was not until nationalist governments accelerated industrialization and discovered urban workers as a new mass base – in particular in Brazil and Argentina. Radio, and later television, helped to steer clear of education policies geared toward achieving sound reading and writing skills.

The world economic crisis of 1929 also led to political shifts in Latin America. Bourgeois-liberal elitist regimes were replaced by politically visionary (but eventually autocratic) personalities who promised national sovereignty and individual advancement rather than international dependence. The internal and external political constellations led to systems that are referred to as 'classical populism' from a contemporary perspective. These include the regime of Getúlio Vargas in Brazil and the 1940s regime of Juan and Eva Perón in Argentina.

"The Father of the Poor": Getúlio Dornelles Vargas (1930-1945)

In 1929, the Great Depression hit Brazil hard. Brazil lost its currency reserves, exports fell by half, and an estimated two million people became unemployed. The 'coffee-with-milk policy,' a political power play by coffee barons from São Paulo and the milk producers of Minas Gerais, who had served alternately as Federal President, was radically interrupted in 1930 by the South Brazilian Getúlio Dornelles Vargas. Getúlio Vargas (1882-1954) came from a large landowning family in Rio Grande do Sul and had studied law in Porto Alegre. After several years in federal politics and as governor of his native state he campaigned in the presidential election in 1929. He did not win but did not accept his defeat against the candidate from São Paulo either. In a revolt commonly referred to as *revolução*, he came to power with the support of a group of social military reformers in October 1930 and was appointed president; he was confirmed in 1934 through an indirect election (Fausto).

Vargas was a positivist. With the leitmotiv *ordem e progresso* (order and progress), which still today is on the Brazilian flag, his strand of positivism – seen in Brazil since the 1870s – sought to make politics and society new and efficient with the help of empirical methods and scientific disciplines. The conviction that social problems would be solved by technocrats and scientists suggested that the regime would not be anti-intellectual. However, Vargas never trusted democracy. He ruled with a handful of followers and built his power not on parties but rather on an alliance of landowners, military personnel, entrepreneurs, the Catholic Church, and the gradually depoliticized industrial workers. His regime relied on right-wing intellectuals to distinguish it from the anti-clerical positivism of the turn of the century, which had blamed the Catholic Church for centuries of backwardness and slavery.

An important goal of the government was national sovereignty. The eight and a half million square kilometers of heterogeneous agricultural state was to become a modern industrial nation. The government burned tons of coffee to keep prices up. Farmers were exonerated, loan repayments to British and Americans were suspended for several years, imports of manufactured goods were restricted, and mining as well as energy and water management were all nationalized – these sectors were no longer allowed to be run by foreigners or foreign entities (Hentschke 1996, 2007; Pandolfi). A law was passed stipulating that two-thirds of all employees in a company that had more than three employees had to be Brazilian (Prutsch 2018: 313).

Brazil no longer wanted to imitate Europe but rather to accept foreign ideas – to absorb the useful and self-determined elements and to spit out the rest "in a cannibal way," as the principle itself was called *Manifesto Antropófago* (Oswald de Andrade). In this sense, the Vargas government developed a distinctive national culture, the *brasilidade*, which drew on its own creativity. The cultural policy claimed to bring previously neglected groups into the nation. The foundation for this was Gilberto Freyre's concept of 'racial democracy.' In his masterpiece *Casa-Grande e Senzala* (1933), Freyre wrote that there was no racism in Brazil because immigrants from Europe, Afro-Brazilians, and indigenous peoples lived together peacefully in a kind of cultural mélange. Particularly in light of the rise of the Third Reich, Freyre elevated the Brazilian model as a positive social alternative, negating everyday racism and discrimination.

Industrial workers acted as a pillar of power. The new social legislation introduced an eight-hour day, a minimum wage, guaranteed leave, and compulsory insurance. It was from this legislation that Vargas was given the nickname 'Father of the Workers.' Industrial workers in the booming manufacturing metropolis of São Paulo and the capital of Rio de Janeiro benefited from the social legislation; they were included in the national project. Agricultural workers and servants, however, were excluded. Thus, the legislation targeted primarily urban areas. Poverty continued to exist. In the strictly censored media landscape, however, it was forbidden to write about it (Wolfe; Pandolfi 13-37).

All those who criticized the national project, which, by 1937 was driven by a right-wing dictatorship, were blacklisted. From 1935 onwards, Vargas successively prohibited left and left-liberal parties; some party members were even imprisoned and tortured. The fascist party of the *Ação Integralista Brasileira* (AIB), founded in 1932, was also overthrown; the movement, which had a platform based on God, the fatherland, and family, had found support in circles of young Brazilians with German and Italian ancestry and was becoming a viable political competitor. From 1938 on, Vargas's countermovement ruled without parties and by decrees. (Bertonha 220-22).

Moreover, in contradiction with Vargas's platform of inclusion was his treatment of Jews. Anti-Semitism played a significant role in the right-wing Catholic milieu. It influenced the persecution of 'politically subversive Jews' and informed Brazil's immigration legislation and the refugee policy. The fact that an estimated 19,000 German-speaking exiles were admitted until 1941 has much to do with corrupt officials, individual humanism, and political pragmatism: they wanted to integrate highly qualified Europeans as helpers for domestic progress. In addition, the hatred for communists, Jews, and freemasons under Vargas shaped political culture (Lesser).

More enemy images were created during World War II, such as that of the 'unassimilable' Germans and Japanese. Although the organization of the NSDAP abroad only had an estimated 2,900 members, about 800,000 people of German descent lived in Brazil at the time. The numerous German schools were places of foreign propaganda, where a sense of German superiority was nurtured. Brazil decided to side with the United States after a power play with Germany and the United States. The partnership with the United States for industrial goods and commodity exports made geostrategic sense. In August 1942, Brazil declared war on the Axis powers; in 1944, it sent a troop contingent as part of a US unit to Italy.

After Japanese airmen attacked Pearl Harbor's US naval base on December 7, 1941, the wrath of politicians, reinforced by the censored press as well as by orchestrated public anger hit numerous Japanese communities – Brazil was home to the largest Japanese minority outside of Japan. The United States was also involved in the monitoring, prosecution, and abduction of Japanese in the inland. Since they had several military bases for the transatlantic crossing of their troops in Brazil, they exerted massive pressure on the South American state for 'security policy reasons' to intern suspicious Japanese, Germans, and Italians. By 1945, an estimated 11,000 "enemies of the nation" had been deported to more than 30 internment camps (Ferreira Perazzo; Sioli 121).

The Vargas government used World War II for its economic interests, gaining a steel mill and good credit from the United States; they also used it for building strong feelings of unity. From then on, as 'leftist subversion' was considered to have been eliminated, any external threat was now a welcome vehicle for consolidating Brazil as a strong and powerful nation.

Surveillance and the discourse of security purported to protect *o povo brasileiro* – the Brazilian people. Brazilian populism was authoritarian; controlled from the top. Vargas saw himself as a fatherly leader in a country with a high degree of illiteracy. Inspired by Portugal – but not as consistently as in Portugal – the constitution of 1937 anchored a state-owned, 'organic' order and dissolved the parliament. This system was sold to the population as especially democratic. After the US-American filmmaker Orson Welles had been a cultural ambassador to Brazil in 1942, Foreign Minister Oswaldo Aranha confidently wrote that Welles had now become acquainted with the "most democratic country in the world" (Aranha). The deployment of Brazilian troops in Italy gave additional weight to the bond between the *líder* and the people in this 'democratic' struggle against totalitarian powers.

Vargas stayed attuned to the people of Brazil. Since he did not like to travel and with Brazil being nearly the size of Europe, more efficient media and central control mechanisms were needed for disseminating a sense of the dictator's omnipresence as either Dr. Getúlio or President Vargas. Vargas was always present in newsreels, on the radio, and in newspapers. In cities, loudspeakers were attached to pillars or columns in government offices and train and bus stations to announce political messages to the people working, traveling, or waiting. The regime, thus, managed to establish a personal bond between the father of the country and its children, so to speak.

Unlike most other populists, Vargas was not an anti-intellectual; indeed, he himself was well educated. What is more, his young polyglot Minister of Education, Gustavo Capanema, was able to involve elites from the arts, culture, and science in politics, such as the sociologist Gilberto Freyre, the composer Heitor Villa-Lobos, the landscape architect Burle Marx, the politically left urbanist Oscar Niemeyer, and the writer Drummond de Andrade. Included in these elites were also some European exiles in various roles: the German journalist Richard Lewinsohn worked as an economic researcher, the Austrian writer Stefan Zweig wrote a Vargas-friendly cultural history of Brazil, the French anthropologist Claude Lévi-Strauss studied indigenous peoples, and his compatriot, the historian Fernand Braudel, taught at the

University of São Paulo. Although women's suffrage had existed in Brazil since 1932, women played no official role in politics.

The Vargas regime saw itself as a revolutionary countermovement to liberal democracy, which it deemed a threat. Despite or because of its strong economic ties to the United States, Brazil sold itself as a culturally superior power: While the US South still practiced racial segregation, Brazil stylized itself as the perfect 'harmonious racial democracy.' However, while World War II bound both countries closer together, their relations had been solid since the independence of Brazil in 1822. The anti-Americanism cultivated by left-liberal intellectuals was rarely incorporated within Brazilian foreign policy.

The Vargas-led coup of 1937 to consolidate his power before the foreseen presidential elections was justified by a communist conspiracy, which was given a Jewish name: the 'Cohen Plan.' When Vargas also banned the party of fascist integralists, his official argument was that the Brazilian fascists had been massively supported by the Third Reich. New research shows that this was not the case because the Integralists were seen as competitors by the NSDAP (Klein 72). In 1942, when Brazil declared war on the Axis powers, rumors spread that Japanese fishermen were agents of the Japanese emperor. Popular anger, stirred up by the media, was then directed against owners of Japanese and German businesses.

Getúlio Vargas was not seen as a militant leader but as a benevolently smiling patriarch in civilian clothes; he was the father of the poor (*o pai dos pobres*) and of the workers. *O Sorriso do Presidente* ('The President's Smile,' 1940), by Paulo Roberto, was the title of a children's book. His smile symbolized the special 'heart culture' of the country – it was the culture of embrace, hospitality, and generosity towards political friends and business partners, and considered an element of Brazilian mentality. However, this 'heart culture' disguised clientelism and corruption.

Unlike the Argentine populist Eva Perón, who mixed with the crowd, liked to touch and be touched by people, the intellectual positivist Vargas preferred to remain at a distance, since he was only 1.57 meters tall. The conviction that Brazil's fortune was in his hands was symbolically anchored. Vargas's birthday was a holiday on which thousands of schoolchildren sang in the Vasco da Gama Stadium. The selective image of history often linked to dictators and populists was evident in the founding of the Imperial Museum in Petrópolis which contained artifacts from the Brazilian Empire. That the Vargas period was the preliminary manifestation of a glorious historical development was a sentiment widely disseminated (Capelato).

Getúlio Vargas's authoritarian government came to an end in October 1945. He founded the *Brazilian Labor Party Partido Trabalhista Brasileira* (PTB) and came back to power in 1950 as a democratically elected president. The class identity of industrial workers had been created by Vargas in the 1930s, but it was only with the transition to democracy after 1945 that a civil society was created whose members could vote and freely mobilize. In 1953, Vargas founded the oil company Petrobrás with the slogan "*O petróleo é nosso*" ('the oil belongs to us').

In 1954, before taking his own life after allegations of corruption and rumors that he had been involved in a planned assassination attempt on an investigative journalist, Vargas left an official suicide note. The *Carta-Testamento* is a masterpiece of populist rhetoric that students are still made to memorize today. Through his self-sacrifice as a 'slave to the people,' Vargas hoped to go down in history as a martyr for the people and the fatherland. Throughout his life, Vargas had understood himself as a nationalist, not as a populist.

Starting with Francisco Weffort's analysis of 1978, domestic historiography began to deal with the regime as a populist system in the years of the military dictatorship between 1964 and 1985. Until the election of Jair Bolsonaro, Vargas was considered Brazil's most prominent populist.

The Emergence of a New Right-Wing Populism: Jair Bolsonaro

The reign of left-liberal President Luiz Inácio Lula da Silva (2003-2011) of the Worker's Party (*Partido dos Trabalhadores*, PT)[1] granted Brazil much international recognition. Lula and his successor Dilma Rousseff (2011-2016) pushed for inclusion through social transfer programs, the promotion of women, cosmopolitan and gender-sensitive cultural policy, and quota regulations for Afro-Brazilians in universities and in public service. This way, forty million people were brought into the nation, and advancement opportunities for dark-skinned Brazilians were created.

Gilberto Freyre's ideology of racial democracy, which had been shaped during the Vargas period and had been in effect for decades, was questioned and deconstructed. In the former slave-holding society that had come to be characterized by a great deal of social differences and racism, the policies of Lula and Dilma were quickly met with criticism from the white, conservative middle and upper classes. However, during economically flourishing years and also due to the consensual policies of the former union leader Lula, the criticism did not threaten their policy. Apart from that, the government continued to support major investors and paid tribute to a classic idea of progress, promoting less sustainable large-scale projects and extractivism (Drekonja et al. 2014).

After a ten-year boom, protests in 2013 against the organization of sport mega events like the FIFA World Cup in the following year signified a turning point. Protesters called for sustainable funding of educational institutions and hospitals

---

[1] The Partido dos Trabalhadores ('Worker's Party') was founded in 1980. The Partido Trabalhista Brasileiro ('Brazilian Labour Party'), founded in 1945 by Getúlio Vargas, was dissolved in 1964.

rather than sports events tainted by accusations of corruption. A considerable part of the civil society responded critically to the government's decision to host the 2016 Summer Olympics shortly after the World Cup and to the numerous corruption cases in Brazilian politics, the Labor Party included. Although the charismatic Lula had introduced anti-corruption laws, some of his party members ignored them. When Lula's successor Dilma Rousseff put high-level politicians behind bars during the onset of the economic crisis, she was deposed by a dubious impeachment trial in 2016. The media remained passive and did not support Dilma in this situation, as the PT-dominated government had failed to build an independent, critical media system. The right-wing liberal media giant Globo had always opposed the Labor Party.

Moreover, the less consensus-oriented Dilma Rousseff was not able to cushion the economic and financial crisis, which began around 2013. Prices nosedived. Indebtedness and Brazil's 30 percent reliance on primary commodities plunged the country into the worst recession since 1929. The thirty to forty million people who had been lifted out of dire poverty by the Lula government ended up in poverty once again. They could not repay the loans they had borrowed in the boom years – loans that had been granted too readily. Misery and unemployment led to new waves of violence, especially in the urban slums. In 2017 alone, nearly 64,000 people were murdered (Darlington).

When the still popular ex-president Lula da Silva announced to run for president again in 2018, he was put on trial in January 2018 by judge Sérgio Moro, who was close to the right-wing conservative PSDB party (and is currently Attorney General in the Bolsonaro government), because of corruption allegations. Despite dubious testimonies and a lack of evidence, Lula was sentenced to twelve years in prison. This act was a drastic step towards the dismantling of democratic constitutional structures. Rousseff's Vice-President Michel Temer ruled from 2016 to 2019, combining a policy of social cuts with identity politics of white elite supremacy, the years of his presidency systematically laying the foundation for the far-right ex-captain Jair Bolsonaro.

Bolsonaro pooled the deep frustration of different social classes in Brazil, not only those who were hit hardest during the crisis. Despite high tax benefits, the predominantly white (lower) middle class only had poorly equipped public institutions at its disposal. During the boom years, it suddenly faced increasing competition on the labor market by the rising lower class. The crisis in turn threatened the middle classes with social decline. The elite upper middle class felt provoked by the statutory minimum wages of the Lula period for domestic, and usually dark-skinned, workers. They were suddenly entering exclusive spaces such as shopping centers or airplanes which had traditionally been reserved for the wealthy. In remembering the past, the middle and upper classes longed for the 'good old days of natural hierarchies.'

This is why Bolsonaro did not just win in the big cities plagued by violence but also in the prosperous southern states, where urban violence is rarer. Bolsonaro skillfully sold himself as an outsider with moral integrity against the corrupt establishment in spite of his 28-year Congress membership during which he changed sides eight times. He promised to restore former order by force. In the past, he had attracted much attention for his inhumane statements against women, blacks, indigenous people, lesbians, and homosexuals, and the fact that he had defended torturers and encouraged teaching children how to handle weapons.

Bolsonaro represents the bipartisan faction of the *biblia, boi e bala* in Congress – that is, the agricultural and weapons lobby and the evangelical Pentecostal churches, which are rapidly expanding in Brazil. He plans to withdraw Brazil from the Paris Climate Agreement. He already relaxed Brazil's stringent gun laws, arguably the reason that the drug mafia supports him as well. Bolsonaro pledges to continue saving in the education and health sectors, despite the increases in child mortality and the spread of diseases such as malaria and syphilis. The 'Chicago Boy' Paulo Guedes is Bolsonaro's Minister of Economic Affairs – Guedes is part of the libertarian *Instituto Millenium*, a think tank belonging to the US Atlas Network, which now has eighty neoliberal think tanks in Latin America (Fang).

Essential to Bolsonaro's victory were the widespread evangelical churches, but conservative Catholics and the orthodox Jewish community support him as well – the latter, because like Donald Trump he promised to transfer the embassy of Brazil in Israel to Jerusalem. Bolsonaro himself was Catholic. A year before the election, he allied himself with Edir Macedo, self-appointed bishop of the *Igreja Universal do Reino de Deus* and billionaire who owns about forty TV channels and radio stations under the umbrella *Record TV*. The Pentecostal churches make use of a highly professional media structure and have long since discovered the advantages of social media and WhatsApp, which is very widespread in Brazil and throughout Latin America in general. Bolsonaro relied on social media campaigning from the outset, as the official presidential election campaign in Brazil is brief and regulated in the traditional media but not on the internet.

Bolsonaro belongs to the Social Liberal Party (PSL), until recently a small and insignificant party. During election campaigns, small parties are granted only eight seconds of party advertising on radio and television three times a week. Such a time slot is clearly too short to explain a program or present a candidate's profile. However, as with Trump's election campaign, Bolsonaro showed that dominating social media and foregoing any ethical criteria gives a candidate a good chance of winning.

Machismo and domestic violence are widespread in Brazil. Choosing a right-wing politician has also become a matter of faith, as he is seen to stand for religion, patriarchy/family, and security. Fifty million evangelical Brazilians were ordered by their churches to elect Jair *Messias* Bolsonaro before the first ballot; in a propagandistic and highly emotional battle, Lula was equated with the Anti-Christ. Linked to this statement was outlandish fake news: supposedly Lula had sacrificed 50 bulls so Satan would support his bid for election. Another rumor had it that Bolsonaro's challenger Fernando Haddad from the Labor Party (PT), a former mayor of São Paulo, planned to sign an executive order allowing men to have sex with 12 years-olds (Nemer; Brum). The knife attack on September 7, 2018 on Bolsonaro, which hurt him seriously, made him a martyr in a biblical battle.

Brazil has been a military dictatorship for twenty-one years. Compared to Chile and Argentina, 'only' 400-900 people died, which led to the belief that a comprehensive politics of commemoration is not necessary. The comparatively small efforts to deal with Brazil's past never effectively took hold in collective memory. Only when Dilma Rousseff, a former victim of torture during the military dictatorship, assumed the presidency, a truth commission was set up in 2011, and its results were published in 2014. However, the years from 1964 to 1985 were not the specific focus of the study; the research went back to 1946, which blurred the boundaries between dictatorship and democracy.

Bolsonaro and his followers used the last three years for a slanderous crusade that played up the PT as a communist threat and imagined a coming Cold War. He succeeded in overpowering the memory of Lula's successful years and acted as if the Labor Party PT was still in power after 2016. In his crusade against 'communism' he was supported by the mainstream media, corporations, and the Temer government as well. Bolsonaro was able to further widen the deep political rifts that had been running through institutions and families since 2016 – and not just rhetorically. Clashes before the election left some dead and injured. The fact that his challenger Fernando Haddad received forty-five percent of the vote in the second ballot demonstrates that nearly half of the population knew what was at stake.

Jair Messias Bolsonaro will make life more difficult for critical media and intellectuals over the next few years. Like the Tea Party movement and Steve Bannon in the United States, Bolsonaro is ready to wage a cultural war. Under Bolsonaro, schools are supposed to teach creationism instead of the theory of evolution; Paulo Freire's critical pedagogy, aimed at liberation from oppression, is to be abolished and replaced by a system that believes in and builds on authority. This new (old) pedagogy is to be implemented by the secretary of education, the Colombian-born Ricardo Vélez Rodríguez and his follower Abraham Weintraub. Having studied philosophy, Vélez Rodríguez is influenced by the thinking of Miguel Reale, a right-wing Catholic philosopher who was a sympathizer of the fascist integralists in the Vargas period and well-esteemed during the military dictatorship.

Vélez Rodríguez was forced to resign by President Bolsonaro in April 2019 and is followed by the economist Abraham Weintraub, who declared the government's intent to "decentralize investments in philosophy and sociology" within public universities and to shift financial support to areas that give "immediate returns to taxpayers, such as engineering, and medicine" (Strutz). In May, tens of thousands of students and teachers protested across Brazil against sharp cuts to education. Minister Weintraub announced that he was freezing up to 30 per cent of discretionary spending due to the precarious fiscal situation of Brazil (Kaiser).

Vélez Rodríguez, Weintraub, and the Secretary of Foreign Affairs Ernesto Araújo are political disciples of Olavo de Carvalho, a philosophical autodidact and astrologer, whom President Bolsonaro considers his political guiding spirit (Winter). The staunch anti-communist, who lives in the United States, is also a member of the ultra-conservative John Birch Society, known for its conspiracy theories about a socialist world order, dictated by rich bankers and the United Nations (Berlet et al.). The impact of dubious thinkers on President Bolsonaro and its government is a drastic example of how right-wing-populism is characterized by anti-intellectualism, irrational thinking, and the cultivation of enemy images like 'communism.' Bolsonaro's son Eduardo, a former police officer, recently joined Stephen Bannon's extremist global network *The Movement* as his Latin American representative (Anderson).

'Communism' is the universal weapon against everything that disturbs the interests of the financial sector, the agribusiness, and the industrial complex. Bicycling is considered 'communist,' just as climate change is. In this logic, environmental protection and social redistribution will have no political relevance in the next few years. Violence has increased massively since Bolsonaro's incumbency, especially in the Amazon state of Pará. IBAMA, the environmental authority, has been cut back on the charge of being ideological and capricious. The FUNAI, the traditional organization for indigenous affairs, was partially transferred to the Ministry of Agriculture which, under the leadership of Minister Tereza Cristina Dias, who wants to open indigenous land to commercial farming, promotes the mass use of environmental toxins and threatens the indigenous reservations in the Amazon region.

It is only a grain of comfort that opinion polls after Bolsonaro's first 100 days in office show that the President's approval ratings are on the decline due to incompetent ministers and internal power conflicts, even between Bolsonaro and his Vice-President General Hamilton Mourão (Gonzalez et al.). Nevertheless, the groundwork done by the government will again lead to a more violent society in an authoritarian state that strengthens its monopoly to use force but withdraws from social and educational responsibility.

Vargas, Bolsonaro, and Trump: A Summary

Getúlio Vargas's war alliance with the United States, his centralist policy and the expansion of army and police forces helped to create the basis for the military dictatorship between 1964 and 1985. While the military coup of 1964 was strongly supported by the United States, the Brazilian dictators downplayed the US influence by using national discourses of Brazilian sovereignty. Ideologically, Bolsonaro, seeks to align himself with the military dictatorship. The presence of more than 40 high-ranking military officers in the 21 departments of Bolsonaro's government illustrates that, like Vargas, he adheres to the positivist creed of order and progress taught in military academies since the late nineteenth century. However, no other Brazilian president so far has cast himself so explicitly as the junior partner of the US like Bolsonaro. If Vargas's policy was Keynesian and that of the military dictators ordoliberal, then Bolsonaro's is extremely neoliberal. Even his vice-president, Hamilton Mourão, who has indigenous Amazon origins, distances himself from the politics of privatization and the plans to open indigenous lands in the Amazon region to large-scale farming and mining.

There are various connections between Bolsonaro and Donald Trump, whose populism exists on a different plane than the more left-wing populist tradition of the *People's Party* of the late nineteenth century. For the first time, Donald Trump has given authoritarian populism, as embodied by the Southern Democrats Huey Long in Louisiana and George Wallace in Alabama, a national stage.

Although democracy in the United States has an incomparably longer tradition than in Brazil, the recent developments in both countries easily offer points of comparison. For centuries, both were slave-holding societies with a white elite and a firm belief in a 'natural ethnic order.' Both countries deal poorly with their past when it comes to slavery, and racism and discrimination have deep roots. Barack Obama and Lula da Silva recalibrated traditional politics with their personal backgrounds and their policies of empowerment towards Afro-Americans and other minorities. Both raised great expectations and could only partially deliver on them. Both underestimated the strategies of right-wing opposition and the aftermath of the global economic crisis.

Bolsonaro's orientation towards Trump's politics is obvious. Both intensify deep political and social divisions through their aggressive rhetoric of otherness. They equate socialist and social-democratic with 'communist' or 'anarchist' and use it to legitimize their backward-looking, elitist politics, even as they present themselves as the voice of 'the people.' They regard climate change as an invention of the left and the conservation of nature as an obstacle to progress. They sympathize with authoritarian and right-wing populist leaders on a global scale and want to shield their states from refugees and 'mass migrations' by evoking images of states under siege by foreign powers. Both promote militarism and armament, and both undermine the separation of powers and criminalize alternative social and gender models. Both distrust intellectual elites and elevate the ignorant. Both have an economic policy reliant on tax cuts; here, Trump is more economically protectionist than Bolsonaro, who defends a neoliberalism that is unusual even for Brazil in its radicalism. For both politicians, the driving force behind their actions lies in their systematic destruction of everything that left-liberal predecessors had established or enforced.

And both, Bolsonaro and Trump, are expressions of a globally existing right-wing populism that has comparable actors in Europe.

Works Cited

Anderson, Jon Lee. "Jair Bolsonaro's Southern Strategy." *The New Yorker* 25 May 2019 <https://www.newyorker.com/magazine/2019/04/01/jair-bolsonaros-southern-strategy>. Last accessed on 3 June 2019.

Andrade, Oswald de. *Manifesto Antropófago*. São Paulo, 1928 <https://pib.socioambiental.org/files/manifesto_antropofago.pdf> Last accessed on 15 April 2019.

Aranha, Oswaldo. Oswaldo Aranha to Orson Welles, 13 August 1942. National Archives Records Administration, Maryland, USA, Record Group 229, Coordination Committee for Brazil, Box 1261, Folder 2.7.

Berlet, Chip, and Matthew Lyons. *Right-Wing Populism in America: Too Close for Comfort*. New York, London: Guilford Press, 2000.

Bertonha, João Fábio. *Plínio Salgado: Biografia Política*. São Paulo: edusp, 2018.

Brum, Eliane. "Como Resistir em Tempos Brutos." *El País* 9 October 2018 <https://brasil.elpais.com/brasil/2018/10/08/opinion/1539019640_653931.html>. Last accessed on 10 October 2018.

Capelato, Maria Helena R. *Multidões em Cena: Propaganda Política no Varguismo e no Peronismo*. São Paulo: editora unesp, 1998.

Comissão Nacional da Verdade. <http://cnv.memoriasreveladas.gov.br>. Last accessed on 15 April 2019.

Darlington, Shasta. "A Year of Violence Sees Brazil's Murder Rate Hit Record High." *The New York Times* 10 August 2018 <www.nytimes.com/2018/08/10/world/americas/brazil-murder-rate-record.html>. Last accessed on 10 August 2018.

Drekonja, Gerhard, and Ursula Prutsch (eds.). *Brasilien 2014: Aufbruch und Aufruhr*. Wien: Lit-Verlag, 2014.

Fang, Lee. "Esfera de Influência: Como os Libertários Americanos São Reinventando a Política Latinoamericana." *The Intercept-Brasil* 17 August 2017 <https://theintercept.com/2017/08/11/esfera-de-influencia-como-os-libertarios-americanos-estao-reinventando-a-politica-latino-americana>. Last accessed on 9 September 2018.

Ferreira Perazzo, Priscilla. *Prisioneiros da Guerra*. São Paulo: Fapesp, Humanitas, imprensaoficial, 2009.

Fausto, Boris. *Getúlio Vargas*. São Paulo: Companhia das Letras, 2006.

Gonzalez, Elizabeth, and Luisa Leme. "Tracking the First 100 Days of Brazilian President Jair Bolsonaro." *Americas Society/Council of the Americas* 11 April 2019 <https://www.as-coa.org/watchlisten/latam-focus-jair-bolsonaro's-first-100-days>. Last accessed on 19 April 2019.

Hentschke, Jens (ed.). *Vargas and Brazil: New Perspectives*. Basingstoke, New York: Palgrave Macmillan, 2007.

---. *Estado Novo: Genesis und Konsolidierung der Brasilianischen Diktatur von 1937*. Saarbrücken: Verlag für Entwicklungspolitik, 1996.

Hochgeschwender, Michael. *Die Amerikanische Revolution: Geburt einer Nation, 1763-1815*. München: C.H. Beck, 2016.

Jörke, Dirk, and Veith Selk. *Theorien des Populismus*. Hamburg: Junius, 2017.

Kaiser, Anna Jean. "Brazil's Bolsonaro dismisses 'imbecile' students as he faces biggest protests yet." *The Guardian* 16 May 2019 <https://www.theguardian.com/world/2019/may/16/brazils-bolsonaro-dismisses-imbecile-students-as-he-faces-biggest-rallies-yet>. Last accessed on 3 June 2019.

Klein, Marcus. *Our Brazil Will Awake! The Acção Integralista Brasileira and the Failed Quest for a Fascist Order in the 1930*. Amsterdam: Volken Beck (= CEDLA 17), 2004.

Lesser, Jeffrey. *Welcoming the Undesirables: Brazil and the Jewish Question*. Berkeley: University of California Press, 1994.

Mudde, Cas, and Cristóbal Rovira Kaltwasser (eds.). *Populism in Europe and the Americas: Threat or Corrective for Democracy*. Cambridge: Cambridge University Press, 2012.

Müller, Jan-Werner. "Populismus gegen Demokratie?". *Populismus: Varianten von Volksherrschaft in Geschichte und Gegenwart*. Ed. Thorsten Beigel, and Georg Eckert. Münster: Aschendorff, 2017. 257-66.

---. *Was ist Populismus? Ein Essay*. Berlin: Edition Suhrkamp (3. Aufl.), 2016.

Nemer, David. "The Three Types of WhatsApp Users Getting Brazil's Jair Bolsonaro Elected." *The Guardian* 25 October 2018 <https://www.theguardian.com/world/2018/oct/25/brazil-president-jair-bolsonaro-whatsapp-fake-news>. Last accessed on 30 October 2018.

Pandolfi, Dulce (ed.). *Repensando o Estado Novo*. Rio de Janeiro: Fundação Getúlio Vargas, 1999.

Prutsch, Ursula. *Populismus in den USA und Lateinamerika*. Hamburg: VSA Verlag, 2019.

---. "Labour Policy, Germanness, and Nazi Influence in Brazil." *Nazism Across Borders: The Social Policies of the Third Reich and their Global Appeal*. Ed. Sandrine Kott, and Kiran Klaus Patel. Oxford: Oxford University Press, 2018. 309-34.

Rinke, Stefan. *Revolutionen in Lateinamerika: Wege in die Unabhängigkeit*. München: C.H. Beck, 2010.

Sioli, Harald. *Gelebtes, Geliebtes Amazonien*. Ed. Gerd Kohlhepp. München: Verlag Dr. Friedrich Pfeil, 2007.

Strutz, Julia. "Open Letter from U.S. and Global Sociologists in Support of Brazilian Sociology Departments." 2 May 2019. <https://www.academy-in-exile.eu/2019/05/02/open-letter-from-u-s-and-global-sociologists-in-support-of-brazilian-sociology-departments/>. Last accessed on 3 June 2019.

Tobler, Hans Werner. *Staatliche und Parastaatliche Gewalt in Lateinamerika*. Frankfurt a.M.: Vervuert, 1991.

Tobler, Hans Werner, and Peter Waldmann (eds.). *Lateinamerika und die USA im 'Langen V' 19. Jahrhundert: Unterschiede und Gemeinsamkeiten*. Köln, Weimar, Wien: Böhlau, 2009.

Vargas, Getúlio. *Carta-Testamento*. Rio de Janeiro, 1945. <http://www.ebooksbrasil.org/adobeebook/cartatestamento.pdf>. Last accessed on 18 April 2019.

Weffort, Francisco. *O Populismo na Política Brasileira*. Rio de Janeiro. Editora Paz e Terra, 1978.

Winter, Brian. "Jair Bolsonaro's Guru." *Americas Quaterly* 17 December 2018 <https://www.americasquarterly.org/content/jair-bolsonaros-guru>. Last accessed on 19 April 2019.

Wolfe, Joel. *Working Women, Working Men: São Paulo and the Rise of Brazil's Working Class*. Durham, NC, London: Duke University Press, 1993.

Notes on Contributors

John Aldrich is professor of political science at Duke University, Durham, NC. His research fields are American politics and behavior identities, political parties, and methodology. He is the author of *Before the Convention: Strategies and Choices in Presidential Nomination Campaigns* (1980), *Why Parties? The Origin and Transformation of Political Parties in America* (1995), and, with John D. Griffin, *Why Parties Matter: Political Competition and Democracy in the American South* (2018). He has also published a series of books on US elections.

Frank Decker is professor of political science at Rheinische Friedrich-Wilhelms-Universität Bonn. His research fields are the German party system, parliamentary reform, populism and extremism, and the European Union. He is the author of *Parteiendemokratie im Wandel* (2nd ed., 2018) as well as co-editor of *Handbuch der deutschen Parteien* (with Viola Neu; 3rd ed., 2018), and *Europas Ende, Europas Anfang. Neue Perspektiven für die Europäische Union* (with Jürgen Rüttgers, 2017).

Carlos de la Torre is professor of sociology at the University of Kentucky, Lexington. His research interests are political sociology, global populism, Latin American Studies, and racial formations. He has published *Populist Seduction in Latin America* (2nd ed., 2010) and edited *The Promises and Perils of Populism: Global Perspectives* (2015) as well as *The Ecuador Reader: History, Culture, Politics* (with Steve Striffler, 2008).

Akwugo Emejulu is professor of sociology at the University of Warwick. Her research focusses on political sociology, in particular inequalities across Europe and grassroots campaigns for women of color. Her recent publications include *Community Development as Micropolitics: Comparing Theories, Policies and Politics in America and Britain* (2015), *Minority Women and Austerity: Survival and Resistance in France and Britain (*with Leah Bassel, 2017) as well as the edition *To Exist is to Resist: Black Feminism in Europe* (with Francesca Sobande, 2019).

Jürgen Gebhardt is professor emeritus of political science at Friedrich-Alexander-University Erlangen-Nürnberg. His research fields are the history of political ideas, political theory, and comparative political science. He has published *Die Krise des Amerikanismus* (1976) and numerous essays on the work and legacy of Eric Voegelin, on liberalism, republicanism, civil religion, and constitutional hermeneutics. He is the co-editor of *Demokratie, Verfassung und Nation: Die politische Integration moderner Gesellschaften* (1994) and the editor of *Religious Cultures: Communities of Belief* (2009).

D. Sunshine Hillygus is professor of political science at Duke University, Durham, NC. She has published on American political behavior, campaigns and elections, survey methods, public opinion, and information technology and politics.

She is co-author of *The Persuadable Voter: Wedge Issues in Political Campaigns* (2008) and author of *The Hard Count: The Social and Political Challenges of the 2000 Census* (2006).

Michael Hochgeschwender is professor of North American cultural history, empirical cultural research, and cultural anthropology at the Ludwig-Maximilians-University Munich. His research interests include the history of the American Revolution and the long nineteenth century, the history of American Catholicism, the cultural history of the Cold War as well as women's and gender history in the USA. Among his publications are *Amerikanische Religion: Evangelikalismus, Pfingstlertum, Fundamentalismus* (2007), *Der Amerikanische Bürgerkrieg* (2010), and *Die Amerikanische Revolution: Geburt einer Nation, 1763 – 1815* (2016).

Donatella Izzo is professor of Anglo-American literature at the University of Naples "L'Orientale" and co-director of "The Futures of American Studies Institute" at Dartmouth College. Her research fields are the writings of Henry James, American popular culture (in particular television series), and theories of American studies. She is the author of *Portraying the Lady: Technologies of Gender in the Short Stories of Henry James* (2007) and co-editor of *Transforming Henry James* (2013).

Michael Oswald is lecturer in political science at the University of Passau. His research interests are political parties and companies (especially Germany and USA), extremism and terrorism, and framing processes. He is the author of *Die Tea Party als Obamas Widersacher und Trumps Wegbereiter: Strategischer Wandel im amerikanischen Konservatismus* (2018) and co-editor of *Die gespaltenen Staaten von Amerika: Die Wahl Donald Trumps und die Folgen für Politik und Gesellschaft* (with Winand Gellner, 2018).

Heike Paul is professor of American Studies at Friedrich-Alexander-University Erlangen-Nürnberg and director of the Bavarian American Academy. She is the author of *Kulturkontakt and Racial Presences: Afro-Amerikaner und die deutsche Amerikaliteratur, 1815-1914* (2005) and *The Myths That Made America* (2014). Among her (co-)edited volumes are *Pirates, Drifters Fugitives: Figures of Mobility in the US and Beyond* (with Alexandra Ganser and Katharina Gerund, 2012), *Amerikanische Fernsehserien der Gegenwart* (with Christoph Ernst, 2015), and *Critical Regionalism* (2016, with Klaus Lösch). Her current research focuses on civil sentimentalism as well as comparative reeducation studies.

Sascha Pöhlmann is interim professor of North-American literature and culture at the University of Konstanz. He works on contemporary fiction and poetry, queer theory, film, video games, and black metal, among other things. He is the author of the monographs *Pynchon's Postnational Imagination* (2010), *Future-Founding Poetry: Topographies of Beginnings from Whitman to the Twenty-First Century* (2015), and *Stadt und Straße: Anfangsorte in der amerikanischen Literatur* (2018). He edited and co-edited essay collections on Thomas Pynchon, Mark Z.

Danielewski, foundational places in/of modernity, electoral cultures, American music, and unpopular culture.

Ursula Prutsch is professor of history of the USA and Latin America at the Ludwig-Maximilians-Universität München. Her research fields are US history and inter-American relations from the eighteenth to the twenty-first century, European-Transatlantic relations, the history of Latin America in a global context, and the history of Spain and Portugal. She is the co-author of a cultural history of Brazil (with Enrique Rodrigues-Moura, 2nd ed. 2013) and the author of *Eva Perón. Leben und Sterben einer Legende* (2015*), Creating Good Neigbhbors? Die USA und Lateinamerika im Zweiten Weltkrieg* (2008), and *Das Geschäft mit der Hoffnung: Österreichische Auswanderung nach Brasilien 1918 - 1938* (1996).

Nicole Anna Schneider is lecturer in American studies at the Catholic University Eichstätt-Ingolstadt. Her research interests are photography, Native American studies, and postmodern and contemporary American literature. She currently works on her PhD-thesis on "Visual Protest, Virtual Participation, and Viral Images: Protest Photography in Contemporary U.S. Media."

Simon Strick is a postdoctoral researcher in American studies at the John F. Kennedy-Institute, Freie Universität Berlin. His research fields are media and film studies, feminist and queer theory, disability theory, medical history, and performance art. His publications include *American Dolorologies: Pain, Sentimentality, Biopolitics* (2014) as well as numerous essays on empathy, constructions of masculinity, plastic surgery, the history of science, and digital humanities.

Laura Vorberg is a PhD-candidate at Friedrich-Alexander-University Erlangen-Nürnberg and works on "Politische Präsenz, politische Macht: Strukturelle Kopplung massenmedialer Operationen und demokratischer Legitimierung in den US-Präsidentschaftswahlkämpfen 2008, 2012 und 2016." She has published numerous essays on social media and the political campaigns of Obama and Trump.

Hans Vorländer is professor of political theory and the history of ideas at the TU Dresden and director of the Centre for the Study of Constitutionalism and Democracy. His research fields are political theory, history of ideas, political cultures, democracy, liberalism, populism, migration, and integration. Among his recent publications is *PEGIDA: Entwicklung, Zusammensetzung und Deutung einer Empörungsbewegung* (with Steven Schäller and Maik Herold, 2016; English transl. 2018). He is the author of *Hegemonialer Liberalismus: Politisches Denken und politische Kultur in den USA 1776-1920* (1997) and of *Demokratie: Geschichte, Formen, Theorien* (2003) as well as editor and co-editor of numerous volumes, among them *Zur Ästhetik der Demokratie: Formen der politischen Selbstdarstellung* (2003).

Jack Zhou is a political scientist at Duke University, Durham, NC. His research interests are American climate change politics, public opinion, and political communication. His scholarship addresses the ways in which climate change is affected by political polarization in contemporary American politics.